APPLIED
PSYCHOLOGY

APPLIED PSYCHOLOGY
ADJUSTMENTS IN LIVING AND WORK

Second Edition

B. von Haller Gilmer
Professor of Psychology
Carnegie-Mellon University

McGraw-Hill Book Company

New York St. Louis San Francisco Düsseldorf
Johannesburg Kuala Lumpur London Mexico
Montreal New Delhi Panama Paris São Paulo
Singapore Sydney Tokyo Toronto

APPLIED PSYCHOLOGY
ADJUSTMENTS IN LIVING AND WORK

1234567890MAMM7987654

This book was set in Primer by Black Dot, Inc. The editors were Richard R. Wright, Helen Greenberg, and Barry Benjamin; the designer was Jo Jones; the production supervisor was Judi Frey.
The Maple Press Company was printer and binder.

Library of Congress Cataloging in Publication Data

Gilmer, Beverly von Haller, date
    Applied psychology.

    Bibliography: p.
    1. Psychology, Applied. 2. Psychology. I. Title.
[DNLM: 1. Psychology, Applied. BF636 G486a]
BF636.G53 1975   158   74-12053
ISBN 0-07-023210-5

PHOTO CREDITS

CREDITS FOR CASE MATERIALS AND LINE FIGURES

FIG. 10-2   Wittreich, W. J. Visual perception and personality. *Scientific Amer.*,
               1959, **200**, 58. Photograph reproduced by permission of publisher and by
               William Vandivert in the psychology laboratories of Princeton University.

FIG. 10-3   *No credit.*

FIG. 10-4   *No credit.*

FIG. 10-5   *No credit.*

FIG. 11-1   *No credit.*

FIG. 11-2   Van Ormer, E. B. Retention after intervals of sleep and of waking. *Arch.*
               Psychol., 1932, No. 137.

FIG. 11-3   Krueger, W. C. F. The effect of overlearning on retention. *J. Exper.*
               Psychol., 1929, **12**, 74. Reproduced by permission of the American
               Psychological Association.

FIG. 11-4   Postman, L. Retention as a function of degree of overlearning. *Science*,
               1962, **135**, 666–667. Reproduced by permission of the American
               Association for the Advancement of Science.

FIG. 12-1   Reproduced from data of the U. S. Department of Labor.

FIG. 13-1   Hovland, C. I., & Weiss, W. The influence of source credibility on
               communication effectiveness. *Publ. Opin. Quart.*, 1951, **15**, 635–650.

FIG. 14-1   *No credit.*

FIG. 14-2   Reproduced through the courtesy of the American Federation of Labor
               and Congress of Industrial Organizations.

FIG. 15-1   *No credit.*

FIG. 15-2   *No credit.*

FIG. 15-3   Courtesy of R. S. Ramsay.

FIG. 16-1   Sleight, R. B. The effect of instrument dial shape on legibility. *J. Appl.*
               Psychol., 1948, **32**, 170–188. Reproduced by permission of the American
               Psychological Association.

FIG. 16-2   Chapanis, A., & Lindenbaum, L. A. A reaction time study of four
               control-display linkages. *Hum. Factors*, 1959, **1**, 1–7.

TABLE 16-1   Woodson, W. E., & Conover, D. W. *Human engineering guide for*
               equipment designers. Berkeley: University of California Press, 1964.
               Courtesy of authors and publisher.

FIG. 16-3   Reproduced from data of the U. S. Department of Transportation.

FIG. 17-1   *No credit.*

FIG. 17-2   *No credit.*

FIG. 17-3   Courtesy of V. H. Vroom, & E. L. Deci.

FIG. 17-4   Dunnette, M. D., et al. Why do they leave? *Personnel*, May-June, 1973,
               25–39. Reprinted by permission of the publisher from *Personnel*,
               May-June 1973. © 1973 by AMACOM, a division of American
               Management Association.

FIG. 18-1   *No credit.*

CONTENTS

Some Precounseling Thinking. Guidelines Relating People and Jobs.
Vocational Selection—A Two-Way Street.
The Employer's Selection Problems. The Employee's Selection Problems.
Summary.

This second edition of *Applied Psychology* has as its central theme the many personal adjustments of the normal individual. It differs from the first edition in three ways. First, the material related to motivation and life-styles has been expanded. Second, the subject matter related to the growing emphasis in higher education on career development has been brought up to date. Third, the section on psychology in law, medicine, and the military has been omitted and replaced by chapters on personality and abnormal psychology. These provide a comparative basis for helping to establish the criteria for normal adjustment.

Since this text is written for the freshman or sophomore college student, technical material on methods and techniques has been omitted. The text is planned for use in regular classes and can be adapted to many continuing education programs.

Applied Psychology is based upon a broad spectrum of content in general psychology, with emphasis on applying established principles to the common problems of normal adjustment. Emphasis is given to the ways we can learn to adjust to an almost constantly changing physical, social, and economic environment. More and more, we are becoming a nation concerned not only with change in general but more specifically with our individual reactions to change. Thus, this text stresses those areas of psychology that deal with the adjustments we must make in satisfying personal needs and in planning individual life-styles. We deal with questions of motivation and techniques of making effective adjustments, and with the nature of individual development. We suggest ways to make the most of our abilities and ways to pinpoint and work around the limitations we all have. We cover immediate and long-range career planning and discuss selecting an appropriate psychological climate in which to unfold. Throughout, we deal with society's conditioning of women and their changing social and vocational goals. We also discuss the many variables that go into humanizing work and make it not only profitable but also more satisfying. Although the text touches on group and organizational structures, the adjustment of the individual remains paramount.

In order to facilitate reading, all research references have been placed at the end of the text without special notation. A summary is given at the end of each chapter. We have surveyed hundreds of research publications in the areas of experimental, educational, social, organizational, clinical, and coun-

PREFACE

seling psychology. These provided a background for applications of psychology to problems in the home, the school, the community, and at work. We hope the reader will find that psychology does make a valuable contribution to coping with the many day-to-day problems in living and work.

B. von Haller Gilmer

APPLIED
PSYCHOLOGY

THE BASES FOR
APPLYING PSYCHOLOGY

This is a book designed to help the individual with his or her ways of thinking about the *normal* problems of daily living and work. Only in a limited sense is this a how-to-do book. We hope, however, that this text does help provide the basic concepts necessary for thinking about how one can get the most out of living and work day-by-day. Most of us, after all, dislike having our future decided by others or by "the system," where we feel that we are being cast to fix potholes rather than to build highways. We often cannot avoid frustration and conflict, but we can at least come to understand these very common experiences and learn ways of adjusting to them. We believe that the printed page, impersonal as it is in so many ways, can provide a background of data helpful in making the psychology of adjustment meaningful. It is hoped that this text will help the student latch a little more firmly onto his or her inside feelings and come to terms with himself or herself in a personally and sociably workable way. Let us begin with a few questions and answers illustrating a sample of the content of the text.

SOME QUESTIONS AND ANSWERS

Q. "I want to apologize for leaving the class early yesterday," said the freshman as he dropped by after class. "When you said that a problem general to practically all students involved career planning, I felt as though I just couldn't take it again. Do other people find the subject of career planning actually painful, so much so that they try to avoid it?"

A. Yes, many do. Facing career planning is really complex (see page 304). Intellectually, we realize that we must plan and learn how best to make a living. Emotionally, we often find that just thinking about the problem may become unpleasant. Sometimes when we have been living with a problem for a long time only in a vague way, we need to get more knowledge about it. This is particularly true when the decision hour begins to build up tension. Career planning is a long-term process and we need to approach it step by step over a period of time. This helps us to avoid decision making "by chance or by crisis."

Career planning, which often includes specific training as well as general education, helps to ease us into the world of work, thus causing the decision-making process to become not only more realistic but also less painful to us. Some people delay too long in asking appropriate questions about careers. The pain gets worse as time goes on if we keep pushing the problem to the back burner.

Q. "Do I have what it takes intellectually to succeed in college?"

A. First of all, let us point out that intelligence is not all that is involved. Of the 50 percent of those who never graduate from college most drop out for reasons other than IQ. Intelligence is not the end-all, the be-all, or the do-all of human performance. We need a given amount of IQ for this, and not so much for that. Often other things are equally important in terms of specific skills and motivation. And let us not overlook the fact that success relates also to aesthetic and spiritual things, to the capacity to love, to experience joy and sadness, to show compassion and understanding, and to what we so often call "common sense." As we look at ourselves as "a whole person," it is often beneficial to get some counsel and guidance along the way. We shall give much attention to this. Talking things over with a professional often helps us to establish our individual value judgments and provides leads in our search for identity (see page 288).

Q. "I am middle-age and want to enroll in some college courses. Will I be accepted by the faculty and younger students?"

A. Yes, research indicates that continuing education has become quite popular, especially for those above twenty-two. Many people are going to college just on a part-time basis.

Middle age is a time of reevaluation; it is a time when our experience allows us to ask very appropriate questions. Often the answer centers on getting more know-how or just more general knowledge. Often in middle age we have less physical bounce; and it has been found that intellectual pursuits can help fill the gap (see page 183).

When we have the conflict between "flight from" and "fight with" in middle age, going back to school part-time is an effective way for some people to cope with the problem. This is noticeably true when we begin to feel that our tripping becomes less light and more fantastic.

Q. "As a co-ed, I am interested in knowing if women's roles are really changing?"

A. Studies show that a decade ago our culture and educational system drained a woman's motivation to seek a career. She was expected to marry and retire from the competitive world of business. But attitudes and work opportunities are changing—slowly. This is bringing on a new aspect of an old role conflict, namely, the problem of the working woman who also is raising a family. Statistics about women at work abound. Slightly over one-third of all jobs in the United States are held by women, but few reach top-level positions. For example, women hold less than 5 percent of full professorships in educational institutions and they constitute only 4 percent of executive officers in industry. But the future looks hopeful according to a study of the changing college environment: "The old stereotypes of male and female roles in our society are changing (see page 315), and the change is beginning to be emphasized on the college campus."

Q. "I realize that you cannot put people into pigeonholes, but is it possible to make some rough classifications of people?"

A. Yes, various people often do fall into profiles in a rough sort of way. For example, research in the early 1970s showed that there was a "behavioral profile" of the airplane hijacker (the exact profile remains highly classified) that was useful in screening airline passengers. The profile relates to dress, grooming, and personal behavior which describes "a typical group," that is, statistically speaking, more likely to attempt hijacking.

Not all potential hijackers react uniformly, but in a general way they show behaviors in common. They are people who appear less likely to be carrying cameras and similar items of magnetic detector signature. Suspicion is aroused when three or four people book a given flight who have similar behavioral profiles. It has been found that the behavioral characteristics of hijackers in our country may be different from those of other countries.

The profile used in the United States came from a computerized distillation of past hijackers and hijacking events, showing how they differed from other passengers. The federal government reports: "The profile has proved to be a most effective hijack deterrent tool."

One study of hotel tipping practices showed that men tipped better than women. A man with his girl friend tips better than a man with his wife. Women traveling alone tip more than women traveling in pairs. Clergymen have been found to be more generous than college professors; show business stars and doctors tend not to tip well. Says one old-time bellhop: "When being tipped by a man traveling with his wife, try to block off the wife's view. No matter what the husband produces, the wife generally thinks it's too much."

People of a kind seem to associate together. Scientists tend to socialize together and artists congregate in "colonies." Teen-agers assemble in peer groups. Even social misfits (as viewed by middle-class standards) tend to come together in their own tight little society, such as in the carnival or circus world. Here the individuals may capitalize on their physical handicaps such as the fat lady or the dwarf. The circus provides a place where an isolate, with some unusual skill honed to absolute perfection, finds use for it. Circus people want to have as little as possible to do with the world outside. As a nonperforming subgroup, roustabouts are for the most part alcoholics. The nightmare alley of the carnival has an orderly social system with its own behavior patterns and language ("donnicher" for toilet, "flat store" for a con game, and "slum" for cheap merchandise). At the top of the carnival caste system are the owner and administrators, the ride superintendent, and finally in prestige are the strippers, freaks, and other performers. Whatever their rank, carnies stick to certain norms of behavior where even children are taught not to associate with outsiders. Some customs are odd. Although male carnies permit their wives to perform as strippers, they do not permit them to be watched by other carnie men. Show owners set a limit on the amount by which any "mark" (victim) can be conned.

In short, people tend to fall together in personality clusters and this is important for each of us (see page 410). But regardless of the groups that each may be a part of, we need to stress individuality as a counterbalance to group behavior.

Q. "Under what condition do we tend to avoid helping others?"

A. Both laboratory and on-the-scene studies show that individual bystanders are less willing to help someone in a dangerous situation if they are surrounded by other nonresponsive onlookers. An individual is more inclined to help another person, even in a very dangerous situation, when he is alone. Here there is no "diffusion of responsibility." In other words, many of us who attempt to avoid involvement tend to disappear into the faceless crowd, as though this gives us some feeling of psychological protection (see page 40). There is some evidence which supports the belief that we can learn to help others by practicing behaving helpfully.

Q. "Why are people so aggressive?"

A. Recent research suggests a close relationship between biological and environmental causes of violence (see page 28). For example, boys are more likely than girls to inherit aggressive tendencies. The triggering of aggressive behavior can be influenced by environmental conditions. The mere presence of firearms can stimulate aggressive action. Some people seem to live in a "subculture of violence" where attack becomes a part of one's life-style.

Psychiatrists even say, for example, that some avid motorcycle riders express their aggression through the motorcycle syndrome. "Driving it is very physical, the machine is a part of me." Unlike the mentally healthy cyclist, the person with the motorcycle syndrome literally needs his machine; without it he has a deep feeling of inadequacy. For some it may be a compensation for feelings of weakness.

These questions are but a sample of the subject areas we are going to cover in the text. However, before turning to specific appliable subject content in the various chapters, let us talk in general about some basic areas and emphasize the importance of the scientific method in the study of human behavior. After giving a work example of the scientific way of looking at psychology, we shall resume with a discussion of the parts played by heredity and environment on development.

THE SCIENTIFIC METHOD

Most college students no longer see the "scientific method" as a foreboding term. *The scientific method is nothing more nor less than fact finding through observation, and a verification of conclu-*

sions based on the facts tested under controlled conditions. The final conclusions are held to be true only as long as the available facts support them. The scientific method as a means of controlling and altering environment and attitude is a valuable tool in applied psychology.

Let us illustrate the scientific method by describing a study in industry showing how a seemingly simple problem turned out to be very involved, opening up a large field of research that is still going on today.

The Classical Hawthorne Studies

In 1927 the Hawthorne (Chicago) plant of the Western Electric Company began a series of studies designed to ascertain "the relations between conditions of work and the incidence of fatigue and monotony among employees." The studies began with an attempt to determine the relationship between changes in plant illumination intensity and production.

The researchers started with varying factors such as lighting, temperature, humidity, hours of sleep, and the like in order to see their effect on the workers' output. There were studies to determine the effect of rest periods, a shorter workweek, and wage incentives and production. The results were surprising; they opened up a new field of research on employee attitudes, a field which has grown so rapidly in recent years that reviews of the writings on job attitudes record almost four thousand references. The Hawthorne studies led to a change of methodology from the direct to the indirect method of interviewing, and they led to new approaches in the study of leadership. Studies began to show the importance of social organizations and their effect on production. The problems of communication became apparent. The beginning of industrial counseling came as a result of these studies. Although it soon became clear that no specific relationship existed between visual illumination and production, this original problem opened up an array of motivational problems still being worked on in industry and in other organizational settings.

The illumination experiment was conducted in three selected departments. In the first department small parts were inspected. In the second, relays were assembled, and in the third, the work involved winding coils. For the control situation, production was measured under the existing lighting.

In the first department illumination was arranged so that the various levels of intensity averaged 3, 6, 14, and 23 footcandles. In this department the production of the workers did vary, *but not in direct relation* to the amount of illumination.

The illumination intensities in the second department were 5,

12, 25, and 44 footcandles. Production in this department increased during the study, but not entirely as a result of the changes in illumination.

Observations of the third department showed similar results, and the experimenters began to see the necessity of controlling or eliminating various additional factors which affected production output.

Here was a problem that was not so simple as it looked. The study was replanned, and a second experiment was conducted with more refined techniques. It was set up in only one department with two groups of workers participating, equated for numbers, experience, and average production. The control group worked under relatively constant illumination, and the test group worked under three different illumination intensities. Competition was eliminated between the groups by having them work in different buildings.

What happened? *Both* the test group and the control group increased production appreciably *and* to an almost identical degree. These perplexing results brought forth a third experiment in which further refinements in procedure were introduced.

In this experiment only artificial light was used to illuminate the working areas; all daylight was excluded. The control group worked under a constant intensity of 10 footcandles. The test group began with an illumination of 10 footcandles, and this was reduced 1 footcandle per period until they were working under only 3 footcandles of light. Despite the discomfort and handicap of insufficient illumination, this group of employees maintained their efficiency of work.

In a fourth experiment two volunteer girls worked in a light-controlled room until the intensity was reduced to that of ordinary moonlight. At this stage they were able to maintain production, they reported no eye strain, and they showed even less fatigue than when working under bright lights.

A fifth experiment was conducted with girls whose job involved winding coils; during this experiment there was no real change in production. At first the intensity of the lights was increased each day; the girls reported that they liked the brighter lights. An electrician then changed the light bulbs, but kept the same intensity. The girls commented favorably on the "increased illumination." Finally, in the latter part of this experiment the illumination was decreased. For this condition the girls said the lesser amount of light was not so pleasant, *but* they reported feeling the same way when the lights remained constant, even though the electrician was supposedly reducing the illumination!

The "Hawthorne Effect." The Hawthorne Studies described above (and another one given on page 397) have led to what is now known as the "Hawthorne Effect," which says that *the results obtained in some given experiment may be due in part or in whole to the experiment itself.*

A person may be motivated to work hard even under adverse conditions if he feels part of a situation as an important participant. For example, students who have participated in some new educational program frequently say they prefer the new programs. Certain learning results may even support their position. This makes the evaluation of the results of some research difficult.

NATURE AND NURTURE

It is well known that we cannot pass along our college education through the channels of inheritance. On the other hand, we do know that color blindness in males is inherited and dominant, but in females it is recessive; that is, the woman will probably not be color blind, but she could carry the characteristic on to her son. Genetics studies the mechanics of heredity. We speak of *genes* as the unit of inheritance; they are housed, so to speak, in chromosomes. These structures are found in pairs and are responsible for our hereditary traits. Half of an individual's chromosomes come from the mother, half from the father. If both genes in a pair are dominant, the individual will display a given trait. If one is dominant and the other recessive, the dominant will still prevail, although the recessive will be passed on and may show up in a later generation. In other words, we can think of the dominant gene of an opposing pair as one that takes over to produce a hereditary trait.

Phenotypes and Genotypes

Characteristics that are obviously displayed, such as eye color, are called *phenotypes* to distinguish them from traits that are carried genetically but not displayed. These latter we call *genotypes.* If both brown-eye and blue-eye genes are present in a baby, he will have brown eyes because brown eyes are dominant and blue eyes are recessive. Among recessive characteristics are blond and red hair, baldness, and susceptibility to poison ivy. Some dominant characteristics include dark hair, curly hair, and even immunity to poison ivy.

Behavior Genetics

What about the things we *do?* Did Sally inherit her mother's pleasing personality? Did Bill inherit his father's aggressive tendencies? Such questions relate to *behavior genetics,* and we find examples such as mating chickens in terms of their tendency for fighting or not fighting. One investigator bred aggressive cocks and hens and then compared them to chickens bred for their timid behavior. After only four generations, offspring of these two groups were still consistently different from each other although they had been given no chance to observe the aggressive or timid habits of their parents.

Selective breeding has been studied over many generations in cattle, horses, and other animals, and, of course, in an indirect and less controlled way in man. We speak of the behavioral characteristics of "high-strung" horses or of animals with "hot blood" as a description of their desire for sexual behavior.

It is a generally accepted fact that in human beings, an individual's phenotypical or obvious level of ability results from a developmental process that involves the interaction of inherited traits and the environment. Since "selective breeding" experimentation in human breeding is impractical, we can only turn to indirect data, for example, studies of resemblances of behavior between blood relations. Identical twins are much more alike than ordinary siblings. Cousins are shown to have very little similarity. In studies of identical twins reared apart, the resemblance of intelligence remained higher than for fraternal twins raised together. But, interestingly, the intelligence relationships between identical twins reared apart were lower than for identical twins reared together.

Parent-child resemblances are greater with blood parents than with foster parents, whether or not the child has grown up with his blood parents.

Another indirect way of getting at human inherited problems is to look at disease. For a long time we have known that hemophilia is inherited, and although there are treatments for such "bleeders" as individuals, the potential for the disease stays with the blood line. Let us look at another disease example.

Disease Example. One inherited disease now being studied is sickle-cell anemia, so-called because the red blood cells take on a sickle-shaped form. The disease is characterized by periodic attacks of acute pain, weakness, jaundice, and leg ulcers. In some people it is recessive, causing them to be carriers; in others it is dominant. The disease is not infectious and cannot be caught from others by contact. Just as some diseases appear to be limited to Caucasians (thalassemia, for example, a blood disease), sickle-cell anemia has been found for the most part in Negroes. It is estimated that two out of twenty-five American Negroes carry the sickle-cell trait, while the disease appears about once in 400 births.

Heredity and Environment Together

It is a generally accepted fact that human beings are a *product* of heredity and environment. Out of the product come both our individuality and our individual differences. If a person with high hereditary potential is placed in a poor environment, his measured ability will probably be low. If hereditary potential is low, even the best environment will be able to take the person ahead only so far.

One may conclude that heredity provides a potential, which may or may not be developed by environment. Let us look at some animal studies on heredity and environmental stimulation since good control studies are so difficult using human subjects.

It has been found possible to breed rat strains with different amounts of inherited learning ability. In one laboratory situation, the learning ability of a large number of rats was studied by compelling them to run mazes. The animals were divided into two groups. Group 1 was composed of animals that made few errors and were mated together. Group 2, composed of those that made many errors, were likewise bred together. Succeeding generations in each group were tested for learning ability and selectively bred for intelligence. By the seventh generation, there was little or no overlap in the scores of the bright and dull groups.

In other studies rats equal in heredity were placed in two groups by using the split-litter method. One group was reared in a very restricted environment. Each animal was isolated in its own cage with no opportunity to socialize with other rats. The cage was bare, and there was no opportunity either to seek out or to solve problems. The animals in the other groups were raised in a stimulating environment, called by one psychologist an "amusement park for rats." Here the subjects were given objects to play with; barriers and pathways provided opportunities for exploration.

When the animals grew up, they were tested for their problem-solving ability. The group that had grown up in isolation was found to be inferior to those raised in the richer environment. Furthermore, the superiority of the second group was found to be lasting. Similar studies with other animals has shown the same sort of results. However, this superiority in performance did not carry over into the heredity strain for succeeding generations.

To conclude, nature and nurture work together, but one of them may play a larger role than the other in producing some given behavior.

THE BRAIN

We talk about the brain in many ways—this three-pound, electrochemical unit of some 12 billion nerve cells. The human brain has powers of recuperation from even the most drastic emotional shocks; it is in command of a nervous system that can send message impulses at speeds that exceed those of many fast racing cars. The brain is our control center for behavior and experience. It aids in our learning and sets up our perceptions and dreams, our thoughts and feelings.

Higher Levels of Control

Highest brain control is in the cerebral cortex, which is divided into two hemispheres. Here we find areas related to the senses and to the principal motor areas of speech and various bodily movements. Most parts of the cortex, not specifically devoted to sensory and motor functions, serve as association areas to coordinate not only sensory-motor functions but also complex learned acts.

Evidence is beginning to show that the two cerebral hemispheres function in some ways as "two brains." For example, the right hemisphere can function independently and largely outside the awareness of the left hemisphere. It can read, learn, remember, emote, and act all by itself. The two-brain concept helps to explain how left-brain-damaged patients can be taught, how the right brain takes over, and vice versa. Interestingly, one half-brain can go unrewarded in a learning experience and interfere with the learning of the other half-brain which is rewarded. Studies even show that reaction time can be different for the two brains. Perhaps fortunately, in the normal brain there is good coordination between the two hemispheres, giving us maximum control and balanced experiences. In a crude sense, we can think of one hemisphere as a backup system for the other and vice versa.

Intermediate Levels of Control

Below the cerebral cortex we find levels of control for such vital functions as breathing and heartbeat, and for various reflex centers such as those that cause us to jump when we hear a loud, sudden sound. Here also we find control in the midbrain for equilibrium, posture, and muscle tone. Also in the thalamus and hypothalamus we find control centers for hunger, thirst, and sex. In these intermediate centers of control we also find sleep centers and regions that relate to aggression. Here there are centers for inhibiting emotional behavior and even for stopping aggressive behavior. Within the general area of the midbrain we have centers involved in "pleasure" and "displeasure," and even centers for boredom.

Lower Levels of Control

Most elementary, but important reflex coordinations are controlled by the spinal cord. Familiar here, of course, is the knee-jerk reflex. Here a tap on the tendon just below the kneecap causes the leg to automatically kick out.

The spinal cord, in addition to being a connecting center for some reflexes, serves as the connecting cable that conducts nerve impulse messages up to the brain centers and down from them.

Autonomic Nervous System

The automatic functions of the body are coordinated by a motor system we call the "autonomic nervous system." This system controls heart action, blood pressure, breathing, digestions, excretion, and urination. It also relates to sweating and various functions of the stomach. Interestingly, research now underway points to the ability of some people to learn through "biofeedback" to control such vital functions as blood pressure and heartbeat. Some subjects have been trained to achieve enough relaxation to gain control of migraine headaches by controlling blood pressure within the arteries of the head. Some people have learned to control high blood pressure, and even to learn mental control over relaxation.

THE CHEMISTRY OF BEHAVIOR

We hear much these days of the use and misuse of drugs in relation to behavior. Scientific researchers and organized crime are both concerned with the chemical modification of behavior. As related to the problems of adjustment, let us take a brief look at some of the 3,000 chemicals that are known to change behavior in one way or another.

Each nerve cell is a tiny chemical powerhouse, generating small electrical currents which go from cell to cell, providing a vast nerve energy network. This has been called man's "inner universe." It is now well established that communication within the nervous system is by means of chemical agents which relate to such functions as sex, appetite, sleep, mood, and generally all that we do and experience.

All living cells and bodily organs function as organized systems of chemical reactions. This fact is being brought dramatically to our attention through the "drug scene" we hear so much about. It has given new emphasis to the description that "life is chemical." There are chemical hormones that can stimulate sexual behavior and others that can block normal reproduction such as birth-control pills that have their effect on a brain center. Drugs have been used effectively to help cure mental illness, and there is some reason to hope for a chemical victory over such killers as cancer. But the ignorant or unwise use of drugs constitutes one of society's deadliest enemies. Alcohol can induce euphoria or bring on a loss of behavioral control; the opiates can relieve pain or "hook" addicts. Hallucinogens may bring on unusual conscious experiences or warp the mind to the point of insanity. More about drugs will be given in a future chapter (see page 165), but here let us mention a few of the more common varieties.

Serotonin and LSD

Most drugs act on the nervous system at the synapse, the functional connection between two nerve cells. Here some drugs excite nerve activity and others inhibit it. The normal brain chemical that transfers the nerve impulses across a synapse is called "serotonin." In its chemical makeup LSD closely resembles the serotonin molecule and this similarity is thought to be related to LSD's power. One theory holds that the LSD molecule can "fool" a nerve cell into accepting it as an impulse-carrying serotonin molecule, but that the signals get altered, since LSD cannot forward impulses in the same manner. For one thing, the drug appears to increase the number of impulses, hence amplifying sensations, which are exaggerated in the extreme, for example, an uncontrollable kaleidoscope of brilliant colors. For some people the effects of the drug rarely stop here; they become terrorized by the agony of a "bad trip." There are instances where the effects of LSD make subjects imagine themselves so indestructible that they may walk into a moving car; others believing they can fly have jumped from windows.

Psychoactive Chemicals

Whereas LSD overactivates the brain, the tranquilizers calm nerve-impulse activity. For example, phenobarbital is used medically in the treatment of anxiety and tension states, but excessive doses of the drug may even induce tension and anxiety. The *amphetamines,* such as Benzedrine, can induce mild euphoria, increased alertness, and alleviation of fatigue; but they can also cause insomnia, even convulsions. People who become heavily involved in the amphetamine "speed scene" may become violence prone. They may go on a run lasting for several days and then collapse in total exhaustion. The addicted amphetamine user seems to live only in the "now," as the past and the future recede from his mind.

Heroin

Few who begin the use of this drug escape addiction, for heroin is its own best salesman. Somewhat like barbiturates, although more extreme, heroin produces a floating euphoria accompanied by a trancelike stupor. After a time it causes a fundamental change in the biochemistry of the brain to the point where one loses any voluntary chance of staying off the drug. Thus the heroin addict takes the drug not merely because he wants to, but because he has to. Adjustment to the drug's presence is gradual, but so is adjustment to its absence. Thus if an addict is without a "fix," withdrawal symptoms soon appear—sleeplessness, vomiting, sweating, and cramps.

Marijuana

Said to be one of the least understood of all the natural drugs, marijuana has been known to man for nearly 5,000 years. Studies demonstrate that the drug can impair performance on simple intellectual and psychomotor tests. The physiological and psychological effects of a single inhaled dose of marijuana appear to reach maximum intensity within half an hour of inhalation, to diminish after one hour and dissipate after three. Studies have shown that marijuana users, when introducing friends to the drug, "teach" them to notice subtle effects on consciousness. Two investigators describe the case of one subject who said he had some memory problems while driving an automobile under the influence of marijuana: "My reflexes and perception seem to be O.K., but I have problems like this: I'll come to a stop light and have a moment of panic because I can't remember whether or not I've just put my foot on the brake. Of course, when I look down, it's there, but in the second or two afterwards I can't remember having done it. In a similar way, I can't recall whether I've passed a turn I want to take or even whether I've made the turn. So all this difficulty must have something to do with some aspect of memory." Two effects of the drug indicate some change taking place in the brain during a marijuana "high." First, there is simple forgetting momentarily of what one has done or is going to do or say. Second, there is a tendency to go off on tangents because the line of thought is lost.

Alcoholism

The inhibiting control of the higher brain centers are affected by alcohol, which is overall a depressant. Alcohol tends to allay anxiety and gives the drinker a temporary sense of well-being and elation. In the later stages, however, experiences are negative. Although many people can drink in moderation without alcohol interfering seriously with normal living, it is estimated that some 6 percent of the adult population are alcoholics, so classified because their excessive consumption impairs their normal adjustment. In general, the alcoholic is immature and has a difficult time facing up to his illness. He or she is apt to combine a drinking problem with other problems at home or at work. This person gets caught up in a kind of vicious circle of spiraling problems.

Let us consider ten self-directed questions. A majority of "yes" answers should make one seriously consider his drinking habits:

1. Do you lose time from study or work because of drinking?
2. Do you drink because it relieves shyness?
3. Do your friends comment on your drinking?
4. Have you ever felt sorry about something you did while drinking?
5. Do you "lower your environment" while drinking?
6. Do you crave a drink at a definite time of day?
7. Do you want a drink the next morning?
8. Do you drink alone?
9. Has a doctor questioned your drinking?
10. Do you turn to drink when frustrated?

In one study comparing twenty-six normal drinkers and twenty-six hospital-admitted alcoholics in a bar-and-lounge environment it was found that alcoholics ordered more drinks, preferred straight drinks, took larger sips, drank faster, but took a longer time between sips than normal drinkers.

MENTAL HEALTH AND MENTAL ILLNESS

"How do I know whether I am behaving in a normal or abnormal manner?" No doubt this question comes to each of us on occasion. The question relates to the fact that there is no clear-cut distinction between mental health and mental illness. What then is "abnormality"? The term "abnormal" refers to personality traits that deviate from established norms of effective personal adjustment and to behavior in society that deviates from established norms. There are three standards involved:

1. There is the *statistical* definition which includes as abnormal any pattern of behavior that departs markedly from the average.
2. There is the nature of *personal adjustment,* where any behavior that produces anxiety, lowers efficiency, and prevents us from coping with the tide of change is abnormal.
3. Sometimes we use a *cultural* definition. Here "abnormal" may mean violating the customs of a given society, and in so doing, creating a threat to the society.

One writer emphasized that there is no mysterious difference between effective and ineffective adjustment: "We are dealing with a continuum of adjustive-maladjustive behavior, with most people clustering around a central point or average." We shall devote Chapter 5 to some of the details about normal and abnormal behavior (see page 91). Here we cover the distinction between normal and abnormal behavior and what this means to each of us.

The Well-adjusted Person

The essential characteristics of the person who has achieved good adjustment appear below. (It is hoped that this text will help to foster the development of these objectives.)

1. Having a practical and realistic attitude toward oneself most of the time
2. Being aware of one's wants, motives, and ways to live
3. Feelings of self-esteem
4. Feelings of psychological security
5. Ability to give affection
6. Ability to accept affection
7. Ability to be productive
8. Knowledge of one's own stress levels
9. A drive to help control one's environment rather than passively accepting it
10. A drive to change when one becomes uncomfortable
11. Flexibility in behavior
12. Knowing when to worry and when not to worry

Some Indicators of Abnormal Behavior

Some signs that something has gone wrong with our living are as follows:

1. Excessive behavior, such as drinking, irritability, and impaired judgment
2. Disturbances of thought
3. Emotional disturances, such as apathy, excessive euphoria, or long-lasting depression
4. Disturbances in motivation
5. Too many psychosomatic disturbances

The enlightened person comes to realize that no one else can solve *his* or *her* problem. Adjustment is highly individual, and it relates closely to stress.

Looking at Our Own Stress Cues

Other people can often detect excessive stress in us before we note it in ourselves. Let us look at a few cues that most of us can perceive in ourselves. *Irritability* is an indicator that a stress level is being exceeded. Make a note of those things that irritate you only when you feel tired and you have a useful cue. *Bad decisions* made time after time may indicate excessive stress. We all, of course, have trouble sleeping at times, but when *sleeplessness* goes on night after night, stress may be related.

When annoyances seem to accumulate in a concentrated period of time, stress may be involved—the incessant talker, the rattle in the car, the proposed date that gets turned down. If we can take the confusion of four people in some setting, but feel overcrowded when a fifth person enters the situation, then we have a cue in numbers. If we can determine how long we can sit in traffic before getting tense, we have another cue to our stress threshold.

Cues to determining one's stress level relate to our defenses. Under what conditions do we refuse to admit some reality that is unpleasant? When do we experience a renewed anger just by thinking about things we can do nothing about? When do we look for socially accepted ways to let off steam? Cues to stress come to us more often in terms of *feeling* rather than in an intellectual way. How do we usually feel under this situation or that condition? In short, if we can establish *base lines* for our usual way of feeling or behaving, we have comparisons available to us to indicate excessive stress. And it is important that we determine whether we are "internalizers," turning anger and other feelings inward, or "externalizers," expressing our frustrations on people or things outside. The externalizer often gets quicker knowledge of his condition than the internalizer because the outside world has a way of biting back. If we are the type who pressure-cooks problems inside of us or seem geared to explode at a high adrenalin level, we should try to know it and make adjustments accordingly.

A PREVIEW

In Part I, beginning with Chapter 2, we open up with questions of motivation. Why the individual differences in our wants? What needs, drives, and incentives motivate us? What is motivational theory? The chapter continues with the new emphasis in environmental psychology by taking a look at the relationships between where we live and the life-styles we develop. Questions are raised about the adjustments we must make when we choose where to live versus the situation where we have relatively little control over such a choice. We emphasize the design of buildings in relation to the types of behavior which differing designs may evoke. The utilization of space is important not only where we work and live but also in terms of the movement of people. The chapter concludes with a discussion of what behaviors, good and bad, are generated when we crowd people together. Environmental psychology spells out some of the factors involved in establishing our individual life-styles as we relate our inner needs to environmental influences.

Chapter 3 deals with the origins and components of personality, and with various classifications of personality types.

We introduce the concept of adjustment in Chapter 4 and talk about problems common to all of us: feelings of inferiority, fear, and anxiety. We discuss stress and how it relates to personality, and we worry a bit about worry. How do we meet all our day-to-day problems? This question brings us to the contrasts between the positive aspects of adjustment and the negative aspects of our defensive reactions. We talk about apathy, stereotyped behavior, problem overload, and the complexities of adjustment.

Part II covers individual development and change following the sequence of adjustments through childhood, adolescence, youth, and middle age into the retirement years. What to expect along the way is projected as we cover both the physical and the psychological aspects of growth. Many practical questions are raised at each level of development: Why is the three-year-old so annoying? Are all teen-agers basically rebels? What are the typical questions raised in youth? Is middle-age revolt normal? How do early adjustment patterns help to program our personality of the later years?

Part III discusses the assets we need to enjoy a satisfying life. Emphasis is given to the fact we do not have to have everything to make a go of things. How we perceive the world and our life-styles is important. We raise questions related to learning and to problem solving: How can we develop efficient techniques of solving problems? How can we get more out of study? Why and how do we learn? This part of the text emphasizes how we can gain more from our education, learn the basic elements of good communication, and come to understand the nature and importance of learning and memory improvement.

Part IV opens up the many considerations of career planning, now receiving major emphasis in higher education. Here we talk about the part played by professionals in counseling and guidance as we work our way through the maze of career decision making. We deal with developing the skills we need to get ahead in business and industry and give helpful hints on adjusting to organizational settings.

Part V covers the human aspects of work ranging through such varied topics as fatigue, work efficiency, wage incentives, and merit rating. Men and machines are described, with the philosophy that machines serve man, rather than the reverse. We close with a description of the psychological aspects of supervision and management. We all work for someone and many of us will have someone working for us. Hence, adjustment becomes a two-way street in all our human relationships. We look hard at the ways of getting satisfaction from work and conclude with a consideration of how the individual unfolds in an organizational climate.

SUMMARY

Applied psychology is introduced with a sample of questions ranging from the sometimes painful aspects of career planning to reevaluations of middle age; from women's roles to questions about aggressive behavior. The scientific method is described as fact finding through observation, and a verification of conclusions based on the facts tested under controlled conditions.

We begin a description of the bases of applied psychology with an introduction of the influences of nature and nurture on the individual. There are genes as the units of inheritance which are housed in chromosomes. Characteristics which are obviously displayed are phenotypes. These are distinguished from genotypes, which are carried genetically but which describe the things we do and how behavioral characteristics are passed from generation to generation through selective breeding.

Heredity and environment function together to produce the individual. It is a process whereby heredity provides the potential, which may or may not be developed by the environment. Nature and nurture work together, but one of them may play a larger role than the other in producing some given behavior.

The brain is the control center for behavior and experience. There are higher levels of control for sensations and perceptions, and for the coordination of sensory-motor functions, for thinking, for learning, and for problem solving. The intermediate levels of control relate to such vital functions as breathing and heartbeat, and to hunger, thirst, and sex. At this level we find centers involved in aggression, pleasure, and displeasure. Lower levels of control involve reflexes. The autonomic nervous system is a system of controls for heart action, blood pressure, breathing, digestion, excretion, and urination.

Communication within the nervous system is by means of chemical agents which relate to such functions as sex, appetite, sleep, mood, and generally all that we do and experience. The drug abuse scene has brought dramatically to our attention the fact that "life is chemical."

Three standards are involved in determining whether any given behavior is "normal" or "abnormal." First, there is the statistical definition which includes as abnormal any pattern of behavior that departs markedly from the average. Second, there is the standard of personal adjustment, whereby any behavior that produces anxiety, lowers effeciency, and prevents us from coping with the tide of change is abnormal. Third, abnormality may be defined culturally as a violation of the customs which creates a threat to society.

The well-adjusted person is one who has a practical and realistic attitude toward oneself, who is aware of wants and ways to live. This person has feelings of self-esteem and of psychological security; can give and accept affection; a person who is productive and knows how to react to stress.

Indicators of abnormality include excessive behavior and mental and emotional disturbances; disturbances in motivation; and psychosomatic disturbances.

Adjustment is highly individual. It relates closely to stress and to learning the cues of one's own stress levels. Each person can learn to establish base lines for the usual way of feeling or behaving making comparisons available to us to indicate excessive stress.

OUR WANTS AND LIFE-STYLES **2**

Fat and thin people are all around us and those of us who are obese may wonder why our friend can remain so thin. We know that being obese in some people relates to hereditary factors and that some aspects of satisfying hunger relates to cues we get that trigger our desire for food. One experimenter has hypothesized that the "state of hunger" differs between obese people and normal weight subjects. For the fat person the internal state is irrelevant. Whether or not he eats is determined largely by *external cues:* the smell, sight, and taste of food, and the environmental situation. These factors affect anyone's eating, of course, but for normal weight subjects they interact with *internal cues* of feeling hungry. After eating the normal weight subject can pass by the pastry shop window unaffected by the sight and smell of the delicacies; not so the fat person. Even after eating a hearty meal he is still triggered in wanting food by these outside cues. What we "want" is not simple. Those things that motivate us may relate to our biological needs such as hunger and thirst and they may be triggered by outside environmental forces. In this chapter we shall begin with a discussion of the wants with which we are so familiar and proceed to a discussion of the numerous things that lead to understanding how we develop some of our life-styles.

People want many things. We want food, a place to sleep, money, and the feeling that we belong as a member of a group. We also ask why we want these and many more things. We ask why did we come to college? Why do I prefer doing one job rather than another? Why do most people work harder when they feel they are overpaid? Why do we sometimes avoid facing an unpleasant task?

Such terms as "wants," "desires," and "needs" describe the motivations that distinguish between the *positive* forces which impel us to work *toward* certain ends. Such terms as "fears" and "aversions" refer to *negative* forces which repel a person *away from* certain objects or conditions. Yet the two types of forces are similar in one respect—they both initiate and sustain behavior, and this we call *motivation.* "Wishing" and "wanting" describe the positive driving forces in us which direct our behavior toward "approach objects"; such an object would be the food sought by a hungry person. A situation or object that a person tries to avoid or escape from is called an "avoidance object"; an example would be a party that one does not wish to attend.

A BASIC DIAGRAM OF BEHAVIOR

There are three broad statements that we may make about human behavior. First, behavior is *caused.* Second, behavior is *motivated.* Third, behavior is *goal-directed.* These interacting forces are represented in Figure 2-1.

The individual

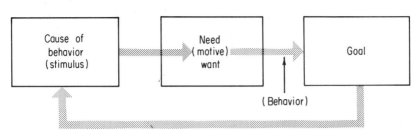

FIG. 2-1 Following the arrows of this closed-circuit model of behavior, we can see how obtaining a goal eliminates the cause of the behavior, which in turn eliminates the motive, which consequently eliminates the behavior.

In this closed-circuit model, attaining a goal eliminates the cause of the behavior, which in turn eliminates the motive, which consequently eliminates the behavior. When one's stomach is empty, the emptiness stimulates a feeling of hunger, and this feeling stimulates action in the direction of food. When obtained, the food fills the stomach, causing cessation of hunger impulses, and this in turn terminates the behavior in search of food. The description seems simple, but at this point the psychologist emphasizes that the closed-circuit conception has a limitation of which we should be aware. Whereas one can consume enough food to stop hunger and food seeking temporarily, it does not follow that one can consume a given quantity of prestige, for example, and feel satiated. This is important to remember if we are to understand the drives of people in school, in the home, and in industry.

Often human behavior does fit in with the system just described. Behavior may be an effort to eliminate tensions by seeking goals that neutralize the causes of tensions. For instance, a man thinks that he has a need for a new car. The more he considers the proposition, the more his tension increases. He explores the market and finds the car that will meet his needs. The more he thinks about a new car, the more he is influenced by advertising, and the more a desire to obtain one builds up in him. Finally, when arrangements are made to buy the car, the tension is resolved.

Understanding something of the general nature of human wants sets the stage for dealing with many of the problems to be described later in chapters dealing with development, work, and social and personal adjustments.

Fundamental Drives

Let us take a quick look at our physiological drives, which we relate to daily, to give us a start toward understanding some of the complexities of motivation. In *hunger* we eat both out of need, out of habit, and for some people because of the cues from the external environment mentioned in the opening paragraph of this chapter. In one experiment clocks were changed to present false time cues. It was found that normal weight subjects based their eating only on how they felt internally, but fat subjects ate almost twice as much when they thought it was 6:05 P.M. as they did when they thought it was 5:20 P.M. Other studies show that when the food is uninspiring and the eating situation is uninteresting, the fat subject eats little, but the normal subject seems less affected by such external circumstances that surround the eating routine. There may be some basis for the old adage, "The thin man eats to live, but the fat man lives to eat." Stanley Schachter, who has studied many aspects of eating behavior, believes that fat people are relatively insensitive to internal cues but highly sensitive to environmental food-related cues. This makes it difficult in the long run for people to stay on diets.

The act of drinking in response to *thirst* illustrates how the "osmoreceptors" in the hypothalamus of the brain functions to turn the water need on and off. These cells regulate thirst in a manner where dehydration produces changes in the tension of the walls of the osmoreceptors. These cells are sensitive to changes in the osmotic pressure of the blood plasma, changes that initiate excitatory nerve activity that results in the thirst drive. Thirst persists until the water level is restored. But as we all experience, drinking water does not reduce the felt need immediately. It takes from five to fifteen minutes for water to be made available to dehydrated body tissue.

Sexual excitement is a drive state in the human that shows a "systems arousal." Sex hormones in both male and female help sexual behavior as part of a system; for example, when the appropriate stimuli are not present, sex hormones alone are not likely to stir up the organism. During the early part of intercourse, breathing becomes faster and deeper. As orgasm approaches, muscles become tense, salivation is exaggerated, and the mouth opens. Inhibitions are relieved as the orgasm nears, and there is a tendency to become aware of one's surroundings as the sexual experience reaches climax. Clinical studies show that under some circumstances subjects report a feeling of well-being after coital orgasm; in some others there may be feelings of remorse. For some there is a difference in sexual behavior between those in love versus those for whom the act is only biological or professional. This emphasizes the point that sexual satisfaction relates not only to the "physiological" but also to the "psychological." Learning is an aspect of the "systems arousal" and relates to physiological conditions, stimulating opportunities, cultural conditioning, and even the availability of erotic literature. The touch, pressure, and temperature mechanisms serve to reinforce visual stimulation as they relate to patterns of behavior learned from experience. Habit often determines the way human beings express their sexual motivation and the kinds of outlet they prefer. The hypothalamus of the brain contains the "sex center" for both experience and behavior which serves in regulating the systems arousal.

Most drive mechanisms relate to active striving, *sleep* being an exception. Here the drive involves passive resting. Learning sleep habits is important and studies show individual differences in sleep patterns. Laboratory studies confirm our experience that a disturbed frame of mind interferes with good sleep, whether it be worry or some form of creative excitement. Studies also show that we can "catch up" on sleep, but we cannot "store it up" in advance.

INCENTIVES

In addition to the basic physiological drives it is useful to consider psychological incentives.

Need for Achievement

The setting of individual goals relates to *achievement* incentive and to standards for determining success. Some people strive for achievement and others do not. How well we rate our achievement relates to relative standards of comparison as well as to some absolute standard. Thus, some people who rate well by external standards may feel themselves failures by their own internal standards. From studies of a wide variety of college students one important conclusion has come which says in effect: "When the individual does not know his own capabilities, he looks to some external peer group for a standard, but when the individual has experience in some effort, he tends to judge his own performance by his own capacity." Some people like to set their own standards, for example, artists. Scientists, on the other hand, although they have clear internal standards of excellence, must also be judged by the scientific community. We know also that some well-adjusted people have a high drive to get ahead; other equally well-adjusted people may not have a high need for achievement. Thus again we need to emphasize individuality in personality and in the development of life-styles.

Need for Affiliation

Some people have a high need for *affiliation* with people and others do not. We know several facts from studies of the affiliation incentive. First, we tend to be attracted to others who we perceive to be similar to ourselves. Second, people tend to affiliate when it will enhance their own prestige. Third, expressing love for another person will inspire others to love. Fourth, sympathy and empathy are characteristic of people who are able to induce affiliation in others. Fifth, individuals seek their own popularity level when choosing friends in groups. Sixth, the presence of a friend reduces stress more effectively than the presence of a stranger. Seventh, fear of being alone or being rejected may relate to our desire to be with other people.

Incentive to Aggress

Most of us are aggressive in one way or another. We tend to fight back when attacked beyond some point of endurance. Those of us who "carry a chip on our shoulder" often let out with a verbal attack with slight provocation centering on our pet peeve. Sometimes our aggression is socially accepted, even applauded in certain circles. Usually, however, we are rejected in our show of aggression. When we cannot direct our aggression against another person, group, object, or against the establishment, we may turn our resentment inward. This may have its merits at times, but to become a habit tends to bring on feelings of self-depreciation.

Some theory holds that outward aggression has a "liberating effect" by reducing the stimulation for further aggression or to prevent "bottling" too many things inside of us. But how far can one go in being aggressive? Studies with children show that when they are allowed to be aggressive in certain situations, it is likely that there will be further aggression in another setting. Much childhood aggression, and the style it takes, comes through imitation of parents or other adults. The more verbal the aggressive responses made by parents, the more likely it is that the child will aggress verbally. Physical aggression is most likely to occur in children whose parents are physically aggressive.

Studies among adolescents and adults show that *extreme* aggression may relate to two personality types. At least this has been presented as a theory backed by some studies. First, we have the "overcontrolled" type of person who may present the image of a mild-mannered, long-suffering individual who buries his resentment under rigid but easily shattered controls. Such a person, under certain circumstances, may lash out and release all his aggression in one explosive act. Later he may revert back to his usual overcontrolled defenses. At the other extreme, we have the "undercontrolled" person who tends to let his aggressive responses out in small doses at different times and different circumstances, hence lessening the influence of tension buildup. Perhaps we should add that most of us most of the time work out our own individual pattern of self-control.

At the practical level we can say that certain circumstances have a way of unleashing some biologically sensitive aggressive incentive with the resulting behaviors becoming part of one's value system. We learn to note the people and things that aggravate us and we have the possibility of learning to distinguish between short-run adjustment reactions and long-run adaptive consequences. Some aggressive behavior that is not extreme, and is not adjusted to by mild reactions, may take the form of vandalism. Even here aggression takes on different forms ranging from stuffing gum into turnstiles and breaking street lights to more vicious destruction of property. Vandalism is sometimes vindictive where one tries to get even by destroying property of the establishment. Vandalism thrives in part because it is an anonymous way to release aggression.

Power Incentive

Some of us want power, some of us do not. The quest for power may be for or against the common good. People who seek out power, whether it be for control over people or property, do so in part for the satisfaction derived from the *act* of exerting that control. The power incentive can be thought of as an extension of the achievement motive that helps determine individual goals.

Incentive for Independence

None of us, of course, ever becomes completely self-reliant and probably many of us do not want to be. This is particularly true of those people high in the need for affiliation. Obtaining a workable balance between dependence and independence is difficult and important in our search for identity. Most us us learn the balancing process gradually through the rewards that come with independent behavior and the withholding of rewards that relates to too much depending. Studies show that in our North American culture, high school students play masquerading roles at times leading to an image of exaggerated needs for independence. Gradually, degrees of independence become important, manifested by what we do or don't do in making decisions or exerting extra effort. The dependent person is relatively satisfied with the status quo, is not looking for challenge, and has a low curiosity drive. Independence, of course, is the direct opposite of this. The independent person is motivated to work on something without help, often resisting assistance or suggestions. Studies show that independent people refuse to react to pressures of conformity.

In work situations it has been found that subjects with high independence scores are likely to be those most affected by how much participation they are permitted in making decisions at work. Those who participated with others in decision making were more satisfied with their work than those who had little participation. This did not hold for those with a low incentive for independence (see page 295).

Independence often comes at the price of being rejected, but the independent person realizes this. He or she seeks out opportunity to respond to choice situations even though these situations may engender resistance.

THE INTRINSIC AND THE EXTRINSIC

"Inner" and "outer" motivation relates to all of us. When a person is intrinsically motivated to do some activity, he does it because he *likes* what he is doing. The activity itself is its own reward. When we are extrinsically motivated to do something, we do it because it leads to an external reward, such as money, praise from someone, or even the avoidance of some experience we wish to avoid.

What can, and often does, happen to a person who starts out in some task because he is basically intrinsically motivated and then receives outside rewards? Studies in both laboratory and in real-life situations show that once subjects begin to receive money for doing an interesting activity, their intrinsic motivation to perform the activity tends to decrease. In theory, the "control" of the motivation can be made to shift from within to the external reward. But in another way, when intrinsically motivated behavior becomes dependent on external controls, it may be difficult to come back to "inner" motivation. The artist may come to depend on money for continuing to paint; the mechanic may find that winning the stock car race comes to mean more than the pleasure he gets from doing a fine tuning job on the engine. Of course, we sometimes find those activities that bring us both motivational satisfactions. Let us take a more extended look at theories of motivation useful to us in thinking about the many "whys" of behavior.

MOTIVATIONAL THEORY

The "whys" of behavior pull together essentially all of psychology—sensory stimulation, learning, needs, and unconscious motivations.

Need-Drive Theory

Drive theorists speak of *primary drives* for which the physiological states are identified (such as hunger and thirst) and of *acquired drives.* This theorizing is directly opposed to the nondrive theorists who say that all behavior is under the control of stimuli; for example, we get a "cue-stimulus" and answer the doorbell "out of habit."

Need-Hierarchy Theory

Maslow has proposed a system of need hierarchies wherein when one class of needs is satisfied, the individual is motivated by a higher need. This is a scheme for emotionally healthy people where it is assumed that man's inborn nature is basically good, but at the same time weak enough to be overcome by outside pressures. Maslow proposes a "ladder" of needs from lower at the bottom to the higher rung at the top. First come the basic *physiological* needs, such as hunger and thirst; without these, of course, man could not exist. Second are the *safety* needs, protection against danger, threat, and deprivation, for security and stability. When threatened or made to feel too dependent, the person's struggle for need satisfaction involves a search for protection. Third, when physiological and safety needs are satisfied, *social* needs become important motivators of behavior as the search goes out for belonging, human association and acceptance by one's fellows, for giving and receiving friendship and love. When social needs, like physiological and safety needs, are thwarted, the individual may become antagonistic, resistant, and uncooperative. This behavior is a result of need failure, not a cause of it.

In the ladder, on the fourth rung come two kinds of *ego* needs. On the one hand, we have needs of self-esteem where there are feelings of self-confidence, feelings of independence. And there are needs for status, recognition, and respect. Unlike lower needs, these are more difficult to specify. Finally, at the top of the need-hierarchy scheme is *self-actualization* or *self-fulfillment* where the person tries to realize his own potentials.

Emotion in Motivation

Emotion, of course, can be a strong motivation of behavior, ranging from love to anger. Two psychologists have advanced the theory that an emotional state depends both upon the state of physiological arousal and upon cognition appropriate to this state of arousal. Thinking about the emotion determines the way we label it. Knowing about the situation, and associating the circumstances with past experiences, brings cognitive factors into play. The same state of physiological arousal could be labeled "jealousy," "fury," "joy," or something else, depending on the cognitive aspects of the situation. Hence, one may have a desire to control the extent of his expression of "fury" but not be motivated to keep joy in check.

ENVIRONMENTAL PSYCHOLOGY

Environmental psychology is a study of the relations between the individual and where he finds himself in space. It studies how the physical aspects of where we live, work, and spend our leisure time affect our behavior and experience. This new and emerging discipline has been described by Joachim Wohlwill as involving three propositions. First, behavior occurs in some particular environment, which greatly limits the range of behaviors premissible in it. Second, certain qualities of the environment, such as under- or overstimulation, crowding, and psychological stress, may affect the individual. Third, behavior is in a variety of ways instigated by and directed at particular attributes and characteristics of the physical environment.

Human problems are basically the same wherever one finds himself; it is the environmental problems that differ. Man no longer exists for long in a fixed environment. Environmental change exists everywhere and has varying effects on each of us.

The Classroom and the Library

The college student comes in contact with examples of how a classroom layout can influence where people sit and how they interact. In a circle students tend to leave one or two seats vacant on either side of the instructor thus "isolating" him. In a classroom where the seats are arranged in a square or rectangle students generally sit in the back of the room if the instructor is near the front row. They tend to move toward the front when the instructor is farther away. When seats are arranged in a semicircle, the students sit to the side of one seat off center rather than in the center line in front of the instructor. In small seminar situations more people will interact verbally when seated around a diamond-shaped table than if the table is round or rectangular, provided the instructor does not sit in an end seat.

Studies with grade school children show that first graders behave differently under changed seating arrangements. When the traditional rows of desks are used and the teacher is up front, there is relatively little communication among the students. This teacher-centered spatial arrangement impedes natural communication between pupils in different parts of the room. It encourages shy children to be inarticulate and to rely on the teacher to be their interpreter. When desks are arranged in a hollow rectangle, there is more first-grader interaction. The situation is like that of a public lecture, in which adult discussion can be facilitated by the simple expedient of rearranging the seating pattern so that the usual rows of chairs facing the speaker give way to some kind of semicircular or horseshoe arrangement. A controlled study showed that children studying poetry talk more about it when the lesson is held in the library, with books around, than they will in an ordinary classroom.

In one college setting with graduate students it was found that when a 20 x 20 foot lounge was used as a seminar setting, there was more, and less formal, interaction with the instructor than when the same size room equipped with a rectangular table was used. These two settings were next door to each other. In a series of observations with twelve male adolescents (chosen because they were uncooperative, noisy, and outspoken) seated in a crowded room with desks fastened down in rows it was found that there was more class horseplay than when the same group sat around tables in such a way that the two most difficult members were separated. Adolescents who were used to boisterous behavior in a given spatial setting calmed down when put into a new physical setting, but gradually came back to their original behavior after they became used to the new arrangements. It may be that change itself is a part of the picture and spatial arrangements alone are not enough. As many homemakers will attest: "I just feel better when I move the furniture around from time to time."

The college library offers a good physical setting for "people watching." And formal studies probably highlight some of the things most of us have observed about our own library situations. A few things are noteworthy since we observe them over and over again. Where do people sit when they go to the library? First, most library users want privacy, and they seek it more by avoidance procedures than by offensive display. And it may not come as a surprise that most students go to the library to study their own materials rather than to use library books. A few, of course, seek private spots to have dates (see page 34). Second, people who come to the library alone prefer to sit alone. In one well-used room containing thirty-three small rectangular tables, each with four chairs on either side, distinct patterns emerged. When room density reached one person per table, the next person chose to sit in a diagonally opposite seat. At zero density the first occupants tended to sit one per table at an end chair. When one person occupies an end chair, the next person sat at the far end or in the middle of the table.

One study showed that when two people entered a library together conversing, 82 percent of them sat down side by side; 12 percent seated themselves directly across from one another; and only 6 percent sought more privacy. Library users employ various means of staking out their territory by leaving clothing, books, or personal belongings in "their" space. Surveys show that library room capacity is lowered by empty chairs staked out by students and faculty occupied elsewhere.

Movement of People

The commuter who rides a bus, train, or other public conveyance is well aware of the discomfort that comes with crowding. Seats are often designed for the average size individual, leaving the obese person to have to spread out of his given space. Even the small, thin invididual may experience discomfort. Says one petite lady: "It seems routine that the oversize person seeks out one of us smaller people to sit beside."

The problem of the movement of people even extends to crowding at subway platforms and other places where people gather to be moved. As studies at airline terminals indicate, "space for movement" runs into end limits. It has been found that complete comfort in going up and down stairs requires 50 square feet for each person, but when this much space is allowed during rush periods, jams occur. Hence, compromise has to be made between no movement and too few people moving.

OUR PERCEPTIONS OF BEING CROWDED

Much of our individual life-style relates to our closeness to others. Some people like to live under certain crowded conditions and not under others; some people never want to be in a crowd; and, of course, some of us like crowds at one time and not at another time. Crowding occurs when the number of people violates individual distance and *the way in which we perceive the situation.* In a night club we may not feel crowded although our individual spatial envelope is very small; the same amount of space in the classroom may make us feel very crowded. We may feel crowded under certain poverty-stricken living conditions, but enjoy crowding at an athletic event. Hence, crowding relates not only to space per se but also to the types of interaction that we find there. We may feel crowded when we seek privacy and cannot find it or when our spatial distance from others relates to what we are doing or would like to do.

Privacy

From time to time we seek out some form of privacy. Sometimes we just want to be alone where no one else can observe us. Often we search for solitude when we wish to think or when we are in a creative mood. Toilet procedures generally call for privacy and the spatial arrangements may or may not be available. Privacy relates to what we are used to. Physicians report that some patients are inhibited when asked to supply a urine sample alone in a laboratory setting.

They do better in a homelike facility. Degrees of privacy in toilet facilities relate to how space is arranged where one may be heard but not seen; where one can neither be seen nor heard; where one is neither seen nor heard nor is anyone aware of where one might be.

Privacy may be viewed as intimacy between one person and another or with only a chosen small group. At times we may seek privacy when we wish to remain anonymous; this is easy to find in the presence of strangers. Reserve is another form of privacy, allowing the individual to conceal certain things about himself. We speak of private conversations, private offices, and private thoughts. Studies show that people working in an open area feel less privacy than if there is at least some symbolic spatial barriers present. Even a line painted on the factory floor provides a degree of privacy for the machine operator as does the classroom seat where we place our personal objects on either side of us.

Social Distances

For the human input-output system distances are important. The lover may view intimate distance in a positive way. Under other circumstances the presence of another person nearby may bring on a sensory overload of sound, smell, and the heat from the other person's body. An unwanted person appearing at a given time may be perceived as being very close; in a conversation a whisper has the effect of expanding the distance. The bus or subway rider may defend himself or herself from the closeness of a stranger by trying to not move. If in actual bodily contact, the muscles in the contact area are kept tense, as though it is against social custom to relax and enjoy contact with a stranger. We keep hands to the side in elevators. We tend not to look a stranger close in the face both out of politeness and because at such a close distance features become distorted. Custom helps define accepted intimate distance. A wife can get by with invading her husband's "spatial envelope," but for a strange woman to do so may evoke a different reaction.

Keeping someone at "arms length" is more than an idle verbal expression. It keeps someone from touching us. Accepted close social distance is said to range from 4 to 7 feet. Here one's head size is perceived as normal and body details are not distorted. People who work together usually use close social distance and so do people who come together in a casual social situation. Far-away social distance, 7 to 12 feet, provides for social and work boundaries; this is one practical reason why desks are usually not "crowded" close together. "Proxemic behavior," as it has been called, is often arbitrary, but also becomes culturally conditioned. Many physical settings depend on custom—for example, where we place furniture in an office; it may even determine how we arrange a living room in the home. At such a distance we can either attract attention or shut it out. And there are other practical reasons for establishing social distances. Prolonged visual contact at less than 10 feet tires the neck muscles. Sophisticated people realize this and help provide comfort for the other person by maintaining a certain distance.

People who have studied the "anthropology of space" talk also about public distance, 12 to 25 feet. At 12 feet a person can respond in a positive way or can take evasive or defensive action if threatened. When we get much beyond such a distance, communication has to depend more upon the use of amplification systems—such as in a public election campaign—or upon nonverbal gestures and bodily stance.

CROWDING AND TERRITORIALITY

Crowding has been spoken of as "spatial invasion." All of us have experienced it, ranging from the lack of breathing room to the physical discomfort of close contact. Each of us tries to regulate his or her closeness to other people, and in many cases we can. When we have little or no control over the space surrounding us, we feel closed in and often react in ways to protect what we regard as our territory. Hence, the concept of *territoriality*—an area of space over which humans, and some animals, establish a sense of possession.

On a public conveyance we choose to sit with a friend, but we may take an empty seat if only strangers are present. Territoriality involves space, to be sure, but it also includes what we like to have within that space; friends are a part of our territory, but strangers are not. Events are related to territoriality. At parties, dances, and spectator sports we may not feel territory has been invaded even though spatially we come in close contact with others. How we express feelings or keep them to ourselves is determined by the occasion. In a crowded stadium at an athletic event we shout and show degrees of aggressiveness that would be frowned on in other settings. We behave in an opposite manner at a musical concert; we enjoy the private inner feelings which are enhanced by a closely packed audience. In both of these situations we have a measure of control over the occasion. At least we know what to expect in the stadium and in the concert hall. Crowding becomes unpleasant when it is beyond our control.

Most of us have limited choices as to where we live and work. Even with money and social status we may not have all the spatial freedom we would like. In most high-density areas it is difficult to create a life-style that balances the positive aspects of urban work with free-space living. We may live in the city and have a second home in the country, but getting from one to the other often means using crowded highways. If we spend too much time seeking our "tonic of wildness," we may miss some of the positive aspects of urban life. The search for a balanced life-style often means becoming realistic about compromise. The relation between man and his environment turns on psychological as well as physical things. As we seek out a physical environment to achieve our goals, we must often seek subgoals first in order to achieve primary ones. To achieve solitude, we must find the right time as well as the right place.

Territoriality for the human involves "mineness"—my property, my space, my time, my choice. Only up to a point can we protect our given territory. In this respect we humans may perceive our own situation better by observing our animal friends.

Territoriality in Animals

Just as people come together voluntarily in artists' colonies, college communities, and selected living areas, so do many animals come together in social groupings. And, like some people who become entrapped in a given spatial area, animals find themselves in territories to which they lay claim. Like some humans, the animal who feels a given space to be his decides whom he will allow to share it. A squirrel, for example, will tolerate a mouse in his territory, but may try to keep some other animal out. Both animals and humans defend their "psychological territory," which is something more than a specified area of earth, water, or air. Some animals compete for mates and man is no less subtle; a woman asserts that a certain man is hers. Animals, like man, may ignore NO TRESPASSING signs. The lion pays little heed to territorial rights anywhere in the jungle. Some naturalists state that the songs of birds at dawn are not primarily music, or invitations to mate, but basically warnings from one male to another to stay out of his territory. "I can protect my territory," says the skunk as he releases his unique sign of ownership. Yet, animal territory, like that of humans, can be invaded. Some ants play both defensive and aggressive games. Some species make war and even practice slavery whereby they use a form of "chemical propaganda." The slavemaker ants typically attack the nest of a closely related species. The defending workers are killed or driven off; the nest is invaded and the worker pupae are carried off. When the pupae mature, they become slaves in their new home.

Territoriality relates to problems in communication. The boy-girl engagement follows a sequential pattern of communication. The whale has evolved a social organization that stands at the pinnacle of life in the sea and his survival hinges on long-range communication. Whales produce a wide range of vocal signals which men have yet to completely decode. Low-frequency sounds have been measured to pulsate outwards for hundreds of miles enabling whales to find each other. Interestingly, pollution in the ocean has been found to disrupt whale (and other sea animal) frequency signals, thus reducing mating possibilities. Even the bond between parent and young has been found to be snapped by pollution toxins, leaving the young to be preyed on instead of cared for.

Migration and Space

Even migrating land animals maintain territorial range. Chimpanzees, gorillas, and other apes do not wander without some limits. Starlings that migrate widely come together in trees at night. Like man, animals have a home that takes on a special meaning of privacy. The friendly dog, which plays with its dog friend in the street, may become very possessive, even aggressive, when that dog enters "his" house. The compulsive urination of male dogs is said to be a way of staking out their territory, much as the library user puts a book on the table and the diner in the college cafeteria leaves some property (not worth losing!) in some staked-out eating space. The diner may even leave his lunch on his tray when he is forced to sit at a table filled with dirty dishes. He pushes them aside, letting the tray form a psychological barrier for his comfort in eating.

Space becomes a status symbol for animals just as it does for man. The size of the physical area around an animal that belongs to him alone is one indicator of the animal's social status within a group. Animals show a spatial hierarchy of status. For example, in a study of a flock of geese, the dominant bird tends to remain in the center of the flock, with the most important geese closest to him. The farther away from the center, the lower the animals rank. But in animals, as in man, the distribution of space is seldom uniform. Both seem to operate within some self-determined rules comparable to the way man sets up some of his spacing rules. A given environment helps to determine how closely we can approach neighbors, acquaintances, or strangers. But enough crowding can break down the rules.

CROWDING AND BEHAVIOR

From many sources we hear of the ill effects of crowding people into restricted quarters. We discuss the problem in terms of community delinquency and mental illness, and we ponder what increasing urbanization will do to the psychological health of the individual. Even studies in college dormitories show that crowding residents together too closely increases competitive behavior. Problems are lessened when the the architectural design permits more social interaction of small groups. A study of people living under crowded, poverty-stricken conditions found that failure to escape from the environment exaggerated mental problems already present. Striving to succeed under unfavorable conditions creates stress without any appropriate outlet. One problem is that disturbed persons set themselves unreasonably high or low goals compared to those of normal persons. These people may respond far more negatively to their living environment than those who find ways for upward mobility. Housing may affect behavior by contributing to or dissipating stress. People tend to avoid residents of poor housing. Such isolation can exaggerate stress and even lead to personality changes. People who live very close to each other tend to share common views and to reinforce one another's attitudes, particularly when there are common environmental problems to talk about. Ironically, we may get some feeling for the human aspects of the problem by turning to animal laboratory studies.

Animal Studies

In one study thirty-two domesticated albino rats were placed in a 10 × 14 foot four-chambered home. These animals were observed for sixteen months without any outside interference. They went through their activities in a normal manner. But what would happen if they were forced to continue to live in the same quarters as the colony expanded through birth of new members? At first the animals behaved as do all well-housed laboratory rats. Nests were prepared and the newborn were cared for. Gradually, as the colony expanded from thirty-two to eighty, social patterns of behavior changed. Some rats began to show neuroses. Some males gave up mating habits. They broke into nests and on occasion ate the young who had died from earlier neglect by the mother. Other males withdrew from normal social activities of the colony. Homosexuality became common. Happy family life, as best the experimenter could tell, was broken up. Five repetitions of the study showed the same results, with animals becoming withdrawn as overcrowding increased. Observed one psychiatrist, "One gets the uneasy feeling that we have heard of something not too dissimilar in our own human culture." It could be a mistake to conclude that family and community problems are a result of people having to live together under abnormally crowded conditions. The lack of enough living space may be just one of the many causes of psychological difficulty.

Some Influences on Styles of Living

From studies of animals and brain-damaged humans and from hormonal and anatomical data, there is evidence of predisposition to aggression, and environmental overcrowding relates to the release of aggression. Although we know that aggression can occur without crowding, we can often relate aggression to frustration which frequently has its source in overcrowding. To say the least, aggressive behavior relates to how we live. We become desensitized by accounts of massive doses of violence from newspapers, magazines, TV, and other media. Crime in the streets has become commonplace. Violence is part of our society. Children play with toy guns and tanks; adolescents and adults find violence institutionalized and glamorized in sports and entertainment. We have become used to violence and often try to escape from it through noninvolvement. Bystander apathy has become common in urban living.

Living under crowded conditions involves adjustments designed to conserve our psychic energy in several ways. First, we tend to shut out some of the sights, sounds, and smells bombarding us, ignoring unpleasant stimuli such as the sidewalk drunk. Second, we may restrict our emotional commitments to a small number of people we can relate to intimately. We often maintain more superficial relationships with others. In a sense we put both people and things into categories of priority. Third, we use various screening devices to isolate ourselves psychologically from the social environment. For example, we may refrain from saying "sorry" when we collide with someone on the street. Fourth, we tend to let others look out for the unfortunate person. In contrast to the person who lives in a rural area, or in a small town, and takes a personal interest in local charity, the city dweller leaves the problems of welfare to some impersonal bureaucratic institution. Part of the net effect is that the individual loses not only direct contact with others but also a feeling of responsibility for them. Fifth, as we try to protect ourselves from an overload of problems, we lose some of our feelings of sympathy. Of course, we can argue that if a city dweller attended to every needy person, and acted on every impulse to help, his own life would soon degenerate into chaos. Hence, living in the city adds to noninvolvement behavior. "Passing by on the other side," failing to help even the lonely traveler who was beaten and robbed, is of ancient origin. And this happened in wide open space. Crowding only adds to the development of life-styles of noninvolvement, and fear of helping others may not be the only factor involved. Let us look at a study.

Bystander Apathy—A Study. Two psychologists studied "diffusion of responsibility" in a *safe* laboratory situation with college students.

The subjects were led to believe that they were going to participate in group discussion dealing with personal problems in college life.

Each subject was taken into a cubicle off a long hall, seated privately in front of a microphone, and left alone to communicate only by intercom. Actually, though he did not know it, the individual was the only subject. He heard the voice of the experimenter over the intercom explaining the conditions under which the discussion would take place. He was told how many other participants were on the intercom system, each in a separate cubicle. In actuality, each subject heard only recordings.

The first "student" who spoke noted that one of his problems was occasional epileptic seizures that sometimes came on when he was under stress. "Conversation" among the students began and soon the first "student" reported that he was having a seizure. He said he was choking and going to die; he called for help and then began talking in an incoherent way. The real subject knew the "size" of the discussion group because he had been told before the experiment began. The number of voices he heard over the intercom system substantiated the size of the group.

The results of the experiment showed that when a given subject thought there was only one other subject in the group besides himself, 85 percent of the subjects left the cubicle very quickly to report the seizure while the victim was still on the air. The remaining 15 percent also reported the seizure, but they took longer to react.

The larger the group, the smaller the response. In three-person groups the seizure was reported immediately by 62 percent of the subjects. In six-person groups immediate responses were given by only 31 percent. Although *all* subjects in the two-person groups eventually reported the seizure, some 20 percent in the three-person groups and 40 percent in the six-person groups never did make a report. There appears to be a direct relationship between noninvolvement and the number of people around. The more the diffusion of responsibility, the more we are likely to "let George do it."

COMMUNITY SIZE AND LIFE-STYLES

We hear much of the social changes taking place across the nation. People are coming together with fewer restrictions on who lives where. With some exceptions, most small American communities find a class structure which is becoming more fluid. Both families and individuals are becoming more mobile—both up and down. Mobility in the smaller town is open for all to see, and although change is taking place, it still follows some patterns of yesteryear where "everybody knows everybody's place." Economic status still relates strongly to social status.

The Small Town

The system of position and class which governs American life is readily noticed in the town of only a few hundred population or perhaps up to 6,000 inhabitants. Here one notices the subtle interplay of education, money, profession, club membership, and business associations that mold the social pyramid. Although the distinctions between old families and new families is breaking down, some residuals remain. We still tend to put people into low, middle, and upper classes; but as one behavioral scientist put it, "Upward mobility in the community is much easier than it was back in the fifties." The distinctions between white-collar and blue-collar are breaking down. What a person can *do* is having more influence on one's community position than was true a few decades ago where position was largely ascribed to him by family connections.

One thing the person has who lives in the small town, or, of course, in a rural community, is a large amount of physical space. There is little in the way of traffic congestion in going to work, going to school, shopping, and dropping in unannounced on a neighbor. Community organizations are more on a personal basis where individual needs often tie in closely with community needs.

There are, of course, some negative aspects related to the life-style choices of being in an uncrowded community. Although space gives us more freedom of movement, and in some ways a large measure of privacy, living in a small community can change some aspects of the life-style we may prefer to live. We cannot hope for much anonymity. Our private living in Peyton Place is more open for all to see than it might otherwise be in suburbia or in the city. Choices of jobs for young people, and even for a variety of people to associate with, are often limited in the small town. While some people may prefer the slower-paced, more leisurely life-style of the smaller community, others may feel a need for just the opposite. In some measure effective adjustment for the individual relates to matching his understandings, skills, and desires to the opportunities which a given community provides.

Living in the Suburb

Descriptions of the suburb range from the "bedroom community" and "patches of green grass" to the "end of the traffic jam" where "children can be raised in more freedom." The community climate of the suburb is determined largely by economics. Since people at the same income levels tend to congregate together, the range of life-styles from rich to poor does not exist. The curve has been smoothed out; there is a great deal of sameness. Thus, some communities are made up almost exclusively of families with children; others may be retirement communities with no children.

One suburb may exhibit material abundance, the dream community where many aspire to live in a style of luxury. Another may provide a life-style where the conspicuous display of money is frowned upon. Even in a single neighborhood, an item which is quite acceptable on one block might be regarded as flagrant showing off on another. True, the suburb is filled with problems and conflicts, as is any other community, but here the family may have a little more control over its life-style than one might find elsewhere. Many suburbs have become a melting pot of people with a variety of interests and backgrounds. As a growing pattern of community living, suburbia is helping to set its own life-style.

What may be a threat to one community, such as the moving in of a minority group, may prove to an asset to another. Racial or ethnic discrimination and social or economic stratification, with their related fears and resentments, help determine community patterns. The community not only contributes to the security or insecurity of the individual, but is a place where behaviors can be manifested through informal organizations.

The Urban Community

Many people born in a city tend to live in a city all their lives. In fact, statistical data from long-distance movers show that most people move from one urban area to another or into a city for the first time. Life-styles in the large city are many and varied. With the exception of downtown luxury apartments most sections of a city are composed of many middle-income to poor neighborhoods of varying ethnic make-up. In other words, there is no single city life-style. Neighborhoods provide the life-style; thus, the city should not be evaluated entirely on the basis of size but also on who lives where.

There are neighborhoods where people of different socioeconomic and ethnic backgrounds "mix" and others where people "do not mix." There are neighborhoods where people are not only close physically but also close in terms of common behavior and attitude. Then there is the more spread-out neighborhood where one sees only acquaintances, with friends scattered over a wide area. We speak of "good" and "bad" neighborhoods in general terms, and for some this may be all they wish to know. It may or may not indicate something about the positive and negative aspects of life-styles. It is somewhat like oversimplifying the classification of schools as either "superior" or "asphalt jungle." We may even tend to ignore the possibilities of "in-betweens." Some people with a framework of middle-class values may tend to view life in the urban slum in negative terms. Yet there are those who live in slums who say they like many aspects of their way of life.

Studies indicate that some people resist being dispossessed from their slum dwellings even though a new environment may be "better." For some there is a feeling of belongingness that extends beyond the dwelling unit itself. The urban slum community has much in common with communities observed in old cultures where there are interpersonal kinship ties. Local friendships grow in importance with long-term residence. The street, local bars, and grocery stores serve as points of contact for communication. Social life in the slum has a flow between living quarters and the street.

View of a Life-Style. Whether we live in a rural section or small town, in a suburb or a city neighborhood, our perception of life-style relates to what we are used to. Some of us may want to maintain our present style, in part or in whole, and some of us may want change. An affluent life-style, attractive to many in theory may become a trap to someone caught up in it. There may well be strong family ties in poverty, and a feeling of neighborhood belongingness, which we wish to hold onto. This perception of values may cause the slum dweller to resent the interference of the well-meaning but often wrongheaded "do-gooder" who sees only the harmful effects of poverty and wishes to change them. Yet, the environment itself exerts an influence on the life-style of each of us. This is exemplified in the urban setting, which has been studied extensively and which has its effects on most of us, regardless of where we live. Change abounds; there appears to be no status quo.

SOME ENVIRONMENTAL CHANGES

We see urban development swallowing up a million acres of land a year, and cities expanding without ecological planning, built more for producing than for living. Whereas a decade ago local communities looked for new industries, many today do not want them if it means more pollution. Where, then, are we going to expand? Where are all the new people going to live? We are in conflict. Problems are enhanced when we realize that 80 percent of our population lives on 10 percent of the land, much of it now crowded. Slowly there has begun to develop the philosophy of "no growth," some observers proposing that both individually and as a society we need to change from the traditional "psychology of more" to a "psychology of enough." One thing is certain: Change is no longer allowing us to maintain the status quo.

We hear of the energy crisis and the swallowing up of large tracts of land for suburban subdivisions. We hear also of more positive trends—large areas of land being set aside for schools and parks, green-belt areas that break the spread of buildings, antipollution efforts to purify our air and water. At the economic level, in terms of dollars and cents, there are those who point out that an extensive no-growth policy can have negative consequences in terms of fewer jobs and shrinking tax revenues. New views are coming in for consideration. Says one corporation economist: "It may be evident that people are becoming somewhat disillusioned with economic growth as a means of solving all of our problems—now we are finding that growth itself causes problems." A psychologist defines some of these problems: "*More* is typical of our culture and this belief is manifested at all levels of our life. Wall Street is dedicated to its increasing search for growth stocks. The automotive industry depends on a bigger car market next year. Unions demand more wages for their members. Every Chamber of Commerce works determinedly toward making its town grow into a booming city. The family budget demands more pay. When *more* is still perceived as *not enough,* there is dissatisfaction."

The Individual and Change

There is much beauty and much blight in every large urban area, as we all know. We come together in cities in order to facilitate commerce and business, and even choose to live there in spite of all the hustle, bustle, and tensions. There is stimulation in the urban environment. Other people live in cities because they have little or no choice. It is in cities that much of our crime is committed and where the power structures of decision making are located. Sidewalks mean both crowds and places to play and socialize. Cities are places where we find extremes; in emergencies we are taken to hospitals, but almost anywhere we can be robbed. Here we find the finest in food and entertainment, and the extremes of poverty and wealth. Studies show that many of the positive aspects of urban living are largely individual, *under the control of the individual.* We can choose those things that bring us pleasure—the arts, sports, and various leisure-time activities. Of course, while the environment provides these opportunities, the choice of responding or not responding is largely ours. What of the behaviors of other people that bear directly on our well-being over which we have little or no direct control? Is it possible that physical aspects of where we live relate to our own behavior per se, as well as the behavior of others which affect us?

Can Planning Help?

Why do some people neglect to maintain their property? Why do they sometimes not even keep it clean? Is it possible that there is at least some observable relationship between planned space and crime? These are questions that led a team of architects and behavioral scientists in 1972 to study the physical layout of buildings as related to behavior.

The study began in St. Louis in order to try to determine why tenants allowed large, high-rise, low-rent apartment buildings to deteriorate, leading to vandalism and destruction. Although built at great public cost, these government-subsidized living units soon became slums. Some were even abandoned by their residents. The study was extended to include some failures of public housing projects in Philadelphia and New York City.

It was found that people tend to keep their own apartments in a housing unit in relatively good order and to maintain adjacent hallways which they feel are "theirs" fairly clean. As buildings get larger, taller, and more anonymous, they become neglected by the tenants. Lobbies, laundries, and mail rooms become stripped; excrement is often found in public hallways. The study also clarified the relationship between planned space and crime. For example, it was found that in public housing areas, high-rise projects had higher crime rates than those in some immediately adjacent projects which had similar patterns and types of tenants. A fourteen-story apartment had four times the number of crimes as did a two-story building in the same block.

As buildings get larger and taller, they become more anonymous, providing what researchers called "less defensible space." Angled corridors, blind public areas, and hidden places encourage crime. Empty staircases, required by fire regulations, provide criminals with alternate routes of escape. Designs of most projects in the past have included stylish interiors protected from sight of the outside public. This arrangement is prominent in exclusive, expensive apartment buildings, where privacy has been a major concern. But in public housing such "hidden" design allows criminals to operate with little or no observation of their activities. In contrast to the more affluent living areas there are no doormen or other personnel to guard the doorways, halls, and other areas which tenants do not regard as part of their territory. The study found that when more than six families live on a corridor the sense of possessiveness decreases; hallways are considered public territory. Under these conditions, crime flourishes.

On the positive side, the study found some evidence that "feelings of responsibility, pride, and territoriality" can be increased by architectual design of space which provides for more openness to outside observation. Open spaces with public walks, benches, and lighting facilities not only become social gathering places for residents, but tend to keep away intruders.

Bringing together the many elements that relate to our life styles underscores the need for both individual and social adjustments. We will take a look at the various aspects of adjustment in the following chapters on personality and adjustment.

SUMMARY

Our wants are triggered by both internal and external cues and we respond individually to each. Human behavior is caused, motivated, and goal-directed. Our basic drives are physiological and range from such active strivings of hunger, thirst, and sex to passive resting and sleep. At the psychological level our incentives include the needs to achieve, to join, and to aggress. We speak also of the needs for power and independence. "Inner" and "outer" motivation affects all of us. When intrinsically motivated, we like what we are doing; the activity is its own reward. When we are extrinsically motivated to do something, we do it because it leads to an external reward. Sometimes motivation can be made to shift from internal to external reward. When intrinsically motivated behavior becomes dependent on external controls, it may be difficult to come back to "inner" motivation.

Need-drive theorists speak of primary drives, determined by physiological states, and of acquired drives. This theorizing is opposed to that of nondrive theorists who say that all behavior is under the control of stimuli from which we get a "cue stimulus." Need-hierarchy theory proposes a "ladder" of needs from lower to higher rungs. Five need steps are involved: physiological, safety, social, ego, and self-fulfillment. Emotion can be a strong motivation of behavior, where an emotional state depends both upon the state of physiological arousal and on cognition appropriate to this state of arousal.

Environmental psychology is a study of the relations between the individual and where he finds himself in space. It involves three propositions. First, behavior occurs in some particular environmental context, which imposes major constraints on the range of behaviors permissible in it. Second, certain qualities of the environment, such as crowding, may exert generalized effects on broader systems of response within the individual. Third, behavior is in a variety of ways instigated by and directed at particular attributes and characteristics of the physical environment.

Much of our individual life-style relates to our closeness to others. Crowding occurs when the number of people violates individual distance and in the way we perceive the situation. From time to time we seek out different kinds of privacy, where both physical and social distances become important. Crowding is "spatial invasion" related to the concept of territoriality. Crowding becomes unpleasant when it is beyond our personal control. Territoriality involves "mine-ness"—my property, my space, my time, my choice.

Living under crowded conditions involves adjustments designed to conserve our psychic energy by shutting out some stimuli, restricting social contacts, and avoiding problem overload.

Life-styles relate to the size of our living community, its cultures, and to individual perceptions. Living style relates to "what we are used to." The positive and negative aspects of community living are largely individual—how much control the individual has, how well he or she can tolerate change.

CHAPTER

PERSONALITY 3

When we think of the term "personality," one useful association to make is that of "pulling it all together." Personality concerns each of us directly and intimately as we have indicated previously. We see our own personality in terms of not only what we are but what we would like to be. An individual's personality is evaluated by observing his or her normal ways of adjusting to various situations. We shall discuss this further in the pages that follow. In Chapter 5 we shall discuss abnormal behavior, which gives us a base of comparison for better understanding normal behavior.

Individual differences are revealed in so many situations, and are repeated so often in those people that we get to know well, that we are almost constantly observing personality differences. In a small-group situation, for example, we see one person who is aggressive and wants to run things. Another straddles every issue cautiously. A third may be oversensitive and feel a personal attack if anyone criticizes or questions his or her opinions. One person may be able to evaluate different points of view objectively; another will color them with his own prejudices. Important in the concept of personality is consistency of behavior. This consistency allows us not only to recognize an individual by behavior but also to help predict what he or she will do in a given situation. We see personality as external appearance and behavior, as inner awareness of self, and as unique patterns of measurable, fairly permanent traits; in short personality is something that involves the whole person.

THE WHOLE PERSON

The characteristics that make up personality include physique, intellectual and other abilities, interests, attitudes, beliefs, values, and expressive styles. In all these things we differ from one another. There is no such thing as an "average" personality. Personality has a quality of uniqueness; no one person is quite like another.

The Origins of Personality

We indicated earlier that the individual is a product of heredity and environment (see page 11). Genetic differences play a large role in individual differences in personality, as well as in physical characteristics. Our physiological system manufactures and secretes many chemical agents that affect behavior. Even a slight imbalance in the hormones secreted may produce changes in appearance, physique, temperament, and how we react to stress. Physiological variables provide the foundation and limitations for personality development. In much of this we have little control. In contrast, the roles played by the environment provides us with some measure of control. Through the process of socialization the person learns what to do and what not to do. Agencies of socialization change or the individual matures. First comes the influence of the family. Studies show that negative home atmospheres, rather than specific practices, produce poorly adjusted people. The personality development of a child depends both on how he interacts with others and how he sees that interaction. When the baby first discovers the difference between "me" and "not me," he or she is beginning to learn the concept of self. In the family, the child learns reactions that become typical in an individualistic sort of way.

In later childhood and in adolescence, it is the peer group (see page 160) and the school that become important; sometimes, of course, these two conflict with the family structure. As adults we tend to associate with people our own age and of a similar social status. In terms of influence, it is within the peer group that the child often finds persons to imitate and identify with. These people do much to shape personality development.

Influences on Personality. Change and our reaction to change force us to reevaluate our self concept. Four things are important in this connection. First, people respond at *different rates* to socialization. Any person's characteristic response continues throughout life, but at a decreasing rate. When we are young, social changes seem to increase "parent obsolescence." As adults we become more and more "other-directed" as the environment exerts more influence on our life-styles. We seem to get entrapped in both work and social "systems." Second, *opportunities* differ for each of us and this has an influence on the development of our personality. Third, we learn from *experience.* We learn not only what to do and what not to do but also what is most likely to work or not work. Having "been there before" influences behavior. Fourth, the *structures of impersonal systems* (schools, colleges, industries, governments) provide sources of frustration for each of us that, repeated, begin to affect personality.

Body Image. One's body is such an intimate thing that it has an effect on what we are in terms of personality. We look at our hands in relation to what they can do, at our eyes and mouth in terms of sense reception and behavioral expression, and at our skin in terms of the reaction it may evoke in others. We feel the tiredness of the body, and we perceive the body in terms of form and shape and, at least in theory, we type people accordingly (see page 61).

Our perceptions tend to stay linked to our bodies in varying degrees. We perceive ourselves as being beautiful or ugly, awkward or graceful, superior or inferior, all in varying degrees. Sometimes we clearly see how we affect other people; at other times, this perception is colored by wishful thinking. Probably one reason why some people like to view themselves on television tape, or listen to their own recorded voices, is that it lets them see themselves as others see them.

The way the individual perceives his or her body has psychological consequences. The male adolescent may become unduly self-conscious as he exaggerates the awkwardness of his movements. The beautiful girl may be motivated to become an actress, only to find later that other qualifications also are necessary for success. Because we are conscious of how we look and are aware that others react to us at least in part because of our physical appearance, our body image is an important part of our self concept throughout life. Studies show that among college students many initial dates are set up on the basis of body build. But as important as body image may be to us, continuing relations between individuals depend even more on that aspect of personality related to mood and mood changes, and to the ways we expend energy or, in other words, to our temperament.

TEMPERAMENT

As we so well know, some people are "more emotional" than others. Some people are patient and some fly off the handle, and some of us may do one or the other at varying times. But what do we do most of the time? This is one of the questions that led to the development of the Guilford-Zimmerman Temperament Scale. Let us take a look at this scale in terms of its nine dimensions. You might like to answer the sample questions below as they pertain to you or to someone else. Of course, the survey scale contains many items on each of the nine dimensions. Here we will indicate only a few to show that temperament is an important part of personality.

1. Do you tend to "let go" when you get frustrated? This dimension is called *general activity* and people range along a scale from "slow" to "energetic." People scoring high have a great deal of energy to release. They show their hostility in aggressive language or action, or in other obvious ways.
2. Do you make an attempt to "hold yourself in check"? This is the dimension called *restraint* measured on a scale of "impulsive" to "restrained." A low score suggests lack of control, related to impulsive behavior and split-second decisions based on emotion. A very high restraint score may mean that you are overcontrolled and lacking in spontaneity with others.
3. Do you feel you are self-sufficient? This is measured on the scale of *ascendance.* A low score indicates timidity; a high score, confidence in personal contacts.
4. Do you like to interact with others or prefer to go it alone most of the

time? This type of question is measured on the scale of *sociability*. The indicator ranges along a scale from "sociable" to "solitary." A high score means a liking for personal contact. A low score indicates a desire to work alone and to keep one's feelings inside most of the time.

5. How easily do you get "shook up"? This is measured on the scale of *emotional stability* and ranges from "easily upset" to "emotionally stable." A healthy mental attitude is indicated by a high score, indicating that you are relatively free from neurotic tendencies (see page 96). A low score suggests emotional instability and moodiness.

6. How sensitive are you to the feelings of others? This dimension called *objectivity* ranges from "oversensitivity" to "objectivity." A low score indicates the person who is touchy and easily offended. Extremely high scores may indicate lack of sensitivity to the feelings of others.

7. Are you a friendly person? On the scale of *friendliness* a high score may indicate a strong wish to please and a low score a tendency to react defensively or aggressively toward others.

8. Do you usually react without thinking? On the scale of *thoughtfulness* a low score indicates that you are not a good problem solver. A high score indicates that you may be good at analytical thinking and are thoughtful of others.

9. Are you typically a cynical person? A range from "critical" to "trusting" gets at the range of personal relations. A high score indicates a tolerance of others. A low score suggests a cynical attitude.

EMOTIONAL RESPONSES

One important thing to keep in mind is that emotional control does not come easily. You can improve your emotional control by becoming aware of what to exhibit and what to keep to yourself. Let us elaborate on some points.

Learning Emotional Control

When a parent picks up a child in order to calm him, two things happen. First, the child learns to feel security. Second, things can be explained to the child after the tears have stopped. Gradually the child learns that rules and regulations enforced kindly, firmly, and consistently help in dealing with frustrations and conflict. As adults we extend this learning of emotional control, noting first of all that the initial emotional upset is never completely under our control. We also soon learn that we cannot control emotion simply by deciding always to do the right thing or to stay away from all possible sources of emotional stimulation.

Emotional control involves the recognition of reality. Control sometimes involves our having only limited alternatives. For example, the choice may be between prolonged aggravation and facing the shock of quick ego loss. It may be a choice between taking refuge in nostalgia and facing an uncertain adventure. We learn to view emotional control from the standpoint of our normal daily habits, not just from the standpoint of controlling severe abnormalities of behavior. We learn to expect emotional responses under certain situations. We also learn to control emotion by becoming adjusted to the stimulus that produces it. While emotion inhibits clear thinking, fortunately it is also true that clear thinking inhibits emotion. How well we do all these things reflects our personality.

Release of Emotions

The person who likes to release his or her feelings through encounter groups certainly differs in personality from the individual who is more restrained in showing feelings. Let us first look at sensitivity training for those people who like to express their feelings openly in groups and then talk about those who do not.

The purpose of sensitivity training, or "encounter groups" as they are sometimes called, is to make people more aware of how their behavior is interpreted by others. The training involves small groups of fifteen to twenty people, known as "T-groups." These people come together to share experiences and to say what they really feel, free of conventional niceties. Professional sessions are well planned, although they give the appearance of being very informal. Most groups begin with an embarrassing silence followed by rambling conversation during which feelings begin to be expressed and the reactions of the members are aired.

Carl Rogers, who has made extensive studies of encounter groups, says that the group goes through four stages as training sessions progress. First, there tends to be confusion, even frustration, when the trainer lets it be known that he will not directly run the group. Some resistance to expressing feelings comes out in this initial stage. An individual who does begin to express his or her feelings may get turned off by others. There may even be questioning of the appropriateness of such expression. Second, members of the group begin to talk about problems they have run into outside the group. Gradually, real expression of feelings begins to emerge. These first feelings, expressed about oneself or some group member, are usually negative. Third, a climate of trust begins to develop as the various expressed feelings are accepted. Fourth, the session opens up; now the group insists that each individual be himself or herself, free of defensiveness. The group now drops all conventioal tact and politeness.

When sensitivity training is used as group therapy, where facades are discarded, emotions expressed, and pent-up hostilities cut loose, unpredictable things can happen. One person may remember another's critical attitudes long after a session in a negative way; another individual may benefit from criticism that shows him how he appears to other people. Sometimes a person's fellow student, co-worker, wife or husband, or even the very open person may find new emotional release disturbing.

Advocates of sensitivity training believe that it is valuable to know how others see you. Critics, on the other hand, believe it is harmful to expose oneself so openly. Some observers have made the point that whereas many people can survive critical attacks, some have personalities that should not be exposed to such encounters.

Restraints on Emotional Release

Society has a way of keeping us from expressing ourselves fully. How we release pent-up feelings reveals something of our personality and life-style. Sports and hobbies, even routine office, factory, or household chores help release feelings. Some people can express themselves through reading or writing or even by booing officials at games. Our verbal criticisms of others may be as much a release of our feelings as a means of letting the other person know our evaluations.

Emotional suppression can both help and harm us. Suppressing anger in an intellectual argument may be beneficial on occasion, but suppressing all feelings all the time can lead to difficulties of adjustment. Persons who do not allow themselves to feel things deeply are plagued by a sterile dullness in their lives. They often wonder why others seem to be having more fun. On the other hand, becoming emotionally involved with people, causes, organizations, or even spectator sports calls for keeping our involvement within tolerable limits. Through many harmless releases of energy, we become to some degree immunized to frustration and conflict. If emotion is properly channeled, we gradually learn to share in other peoples moods and to join in the group emotions of listening to music, experiencing the visual arts, and sharing religious expression.

THE ROLES WE PLAY

We reveal our individuality in many ways by the roles we play. Chances are that when you think of the word "role" you think of an actor. The word is borrowed from the theater, and with good reason.

For the actor there is the stage setting and the script with the lines to be spoken and the actions to be portrayed. In real life we also function in a given setting, and although the script is missing, words and actions are often prescribed. As with the actor, the personality you bring to a role determines significantly the way it is interpreted.

The learning of roles begins early and continues throughout life. This learning is achieved both through intentional instruction about ways of behaving—the rules of the game—and also through the roles we find ourselves in. The male child learns "to be a man" and the female to grow up "like a lady." Role playing which often involves conflicts between what others want and what we want, can cause noticeable emotional upsets. A woman with supposedly "masculine" interests, for example, learns this at an early age. How we resolve conflict is itself a part of personality. We can see this is the case of Ann Stewart. How would you answer the questions on page 58?

THE CASE OF ANN STEWART

Ann was the only daughter of a middle-aged couple who had married late and who lived comfortably in a surburban community. The Stewarts had very little social life in the community simply because Mrs. Stewart found it too much of a strain. Mr. Stewart was a successful industrial executive who was very self-sufficient. He enjoyed quiet, uninterrupted leisure while he was at home, but also enjoyed the social contacts which occurred on his frequent travels. Some of his trips took him to exotic places overseas, and he would occasionally invite his wife to go along. She would never agree to accompany him.

Mrs. Stewart was overly concerned about the health of herself and her daughter. She raised Ann with dire warnings about dogs, strangers, or health hazards that lurked around her, and she herself frequently consulted physicians regarding her own health.

Ann was an independent child who played quietly in her own room or yard. She learned early that it paid to remain clean and quiet even when she played with the other children in the neighborhood. She would be as clean when she returned home as she was when she went out. As a child, she often preferred to stay in her room, engaging in solitary play. When she was older, she read a great deal. One end of her bedroom was turned into a stage where she acted out the stories she had read or the fantasies she enjoyed. Nancy Drew was her constant companion during adolescence.

In high school, Ann was a good student who always knew the material assigned and did well in class. When her friends began having parties in the evening, her mother drove her to and from the party, but when her mother became aware that they were pairing off in couples, she refused to let Ann attend any longer. Ann was told that she was too young to date and was warned about the sexual exploitations of girls who did date.

One day when Ann was seventeen and a senior in high school, she accepted a date and prepared for it very logically. She did not ask for permission, but simply dressed herself appropriately, confronted her mother and told her that she had accepted the date and was going out, agreed to be back by midnight, and left the house. Her date picked her up at the home of one of her friends. Ann returned from the date by midnight, found her mother crying in the living room, announced that she was sorry her mother felt that way but that she was glad she had gone, and went off to bed. Ann continued to date occasionally although she was very selective about the boys she chose and did not date any one boy too often or over a very long period.

Ann and her father talked about out-of-town college, but he encouraged her to stay at home and attend a local community college. He reminded Ann that her mother might break down completely if she left the community. Ann agreed, but quietly resolved to transfer to an out-of-town college for her junior and senior years.

In college Ann liked her freshman courses, found them easy, and did well in all of them. She did not much care what her major was, but found courses in psychology and child development more interesting than any of the others. She thought of herself as the kind of a girl who would probably get married and never have a career of her own. Late in her freshman year she met Guy, who was a sophomore at a university, studying computer science. He was the first male who had really attracted her, and they spent many evenings together. They became closer during her sophomore year, often going to plays or movies or to parties with their friends. It occurred to Ann during her sophomore year that she really ought to develop some skill she could use and perhaps fall back on if she ever needed it. She selected business education as her major and began taking courses in typing and shorthand although she had neither talent nor interest in either. She found the courses difficult and boring, and particularly objected to the long hours spent transcribing her shorthand.

Ann remained in the community college for a third year in order to finish her secretarial courses and to take a few more courses in psychology and English in order to qualify for an associate liberal arts degree. She and Guy were married during the mid-semester break. They knew that marriage was financially possible for them because they expected Ann to be working soon and knew that she could support both of them while he went on to graduate school. Ann was a virgin when she married Guy, even though her mother didn't believe it and had accused her for some months of throwing herself at Guy.

Ann began to work as a secretary during the following summer. She also began to complain more and more often and to suffer occasional headaches and depressions. It seemed to her that the excitement had gone out of life. She and Guy no longer went to parties and movies. Ann felt that she was competing with *Time* magazine, the daily paper, or Walter Cronkite to get Guy's attention when she came home from work. She began to feel that they had nothing in common and that Guy "was so absolutely Guy, so efficient, so lacking in emotion." Ann also began to compare herself with other girls who had gone ahead to prepare themselves for careers. She looked down on secretarial work and envied the girls who were planning to enter other fields. She, however, had never really considered a professional career, though now she began to dream about being a teacher or a child psychologist. There were also financial problems for Ann was not used to living on a limited budget. It seemed to her that she needed many new clothes for her office job. She was annoyed by having to take the bus to work on the days when Guy drove the car to the campus.

"I don't think I ever faced up to what Guy was really like or what marriage was really like," she said. "I'd like to get out of the whole mess, but then what can I do?"

1. Take the "women's lib" point-of-view and comment on the way Ann was raised.
2. Why didn't Ann have more definite career plans?
3. What do you feel motivated Ann's decision to get married?
4. Was Ann's mother overindulgent, overprotective, or overpossessive?
5. Would Ann have been able to have a less frustrating life if she had some real salable talent?
6. For those persons who have no special talent, what issues become important?

Role Conflicts

Each person gets so many varied prescriptions of how he or she should behave that it is inevitable that conflicts should arise. When we are aware of an inconsistency between the roles that we have assumed, between opinions, beliefs, or attitudes, or between a particular role and the situation in which we find ourselves, we are inclined to try to do something to reduce that inconsistency. We may try to *change* our belief or attitude to bring it more in line with the role we play. We may *give up* one role that is in conflict with another. Or we may resort to the defensive behavior of *rationalization* to try to push the inconsistency aside (see page 83).

While some people find it difficult to shift from one role to another, as we all do at times, others enjoy varying their roles and their behaviors. We like to have some choice about the roles we play, but regardless of our positions, society seems to create certain roles for us. This is well illustrated in male and female role expectancy.

PERSONALITY AND CREATIVITY

Creativity is noticeable. We may be creative ourselves and sense it, or we may observe it in others. Creative persons—inventors, writers, artists, mathematicians, scientists, architects—have been studied extensively. In describing the creative personality, we should note that certain characteristics of creativity may lead either to success or to conflicts and discouragement. Let us also point out that most of us would probably not classify ourselves as creative. Special skills and talents do tend, however, to influence personality.

The Creative Personality

Creativity is frequently noticed in childhood. The seven-year-old, for example, who does not easily follow the structured requirements of the classroom and seems to "turn off" the teacher or ignore instructions, may be genuinely creative. And as one can observe, such reactions can create problems not only for the child, but also for parents as well. The creative person is self-motivated (see page 30). Once the individual has experienced the joy of discovery, which can range from fixing a motor or some appliance to organizing a successful event, he or she is more determined than ever to explore new paths and try new things. Creativity reinforces itself. As with any other personality trait, creativity shows individual differences. However, most creative people do have a number of things in common.

Some Things in Common. First, creative people are less conventional than others, regardless of field. Second, because they are less conventional, creative people tend to show independence of judgment. Third, creative people view authority as conventional rather than absolute. Fourth, creative people do not always know where the results of their efforts are going to lead them.

Depending on our personality type, we may be glad we are creative or conventional. Creative people like to deal with complex things, even becoming bored with simplicity. We can learn much about our individual personality when we examine the types of risks we like to take or to avoid. Basically, an examination of the roles we like and do not like to play tells us much about our personality.

Chances are that many of us have our own ways of viewing personality and personality differences. Theorists also have their views. Let us look at three different theories of personality.

THEORIES OF PERSONALITY

Many of us associate personality theory with developmental theory. For psychoanalysis in particular this makes sense since so much importance is attached to an individual's life history. Developmental theories do not deny hereditary factors, but rather emphasize personal experience. And again when we think of personality, chances are we think in terms of types and traits and the styles of behavior people show. When we think of the complexities of personality and all that it includes, we can see how useful it is to devise some systematic way of looking at it. The first theory we will consider is the psychoanalytic theory. Whether we disown this theory, endorse it, or accept it with reservations, we should recognize that it is one of the major influences on the twentieth century. It has colored not only the study of behavior, both as a science and as a profession, but also our philosophy, literature, art, drama, and our ways of looking at ourselves.

Psychoanalytic Theory

In brief, psychoanalytic theory sees the working of our minds and emotions as a product of the dynamic interaction between our instincts and the counterforces set up by the external environment. As a method of psychotherapy developed by Freud it involves uncovering the individual's conflicts, repressed memories, sexual hangups, and many such difficulties. Its aim is to help the individual understand and reeducate himself or herself.

Freud developed the psychoanalytic theory from the study of poorly adjusted people. He saw the primary source of behavior as sexual with the generating energy being what he called the *libido,* an instinctive pleasure-seeking drive. He used the term "sexual" in this context to refer to any type of physically pleasurable activity. As for personality, Freudian theory divides the personality structure into the *id* (a division of the psyche from which come impersonal impulses that demand immediate gratification); the *ego* ("the self" that is in contact with the external world); and the *superego* (the conscience, or moral standards of society). The theory deals with personality development caught up in all its conflicts as we pass through the various stages from infancy to old age. As both theory and practice, psychoanalysis has undergone many changes by such analysts as Alfred Adler, Carl Jung, Erich Fromm, and Karen Horney.

Adler gave emphasis to the universal feeling of *inferiority,* stressing the social rather than the biological determinants of personality. For him, the prime source of motivation is the innate striving for superiority, to "perfect oneself." Jung introduced the dimension of *introversion-extroversion* which has led to the identification of such factors as social introversion, thinking introversion, and depression on the one hand, and the happy-go-lucky mood on the other. Jung described the introvert as being subjective with an interest in ideas and a lively imagination; he may be sensitive and idealistic. The extrovert was described as oriented toward the world of things and events, tough-minded, realistic, and practical. But the division between the two personalities was never meant to be rigid. Most people are a blend of extrovert and introvert.

Fromm says man is a product of society. When he cannot cope with society he suffers, becomes unreasonable. He emphasized that social conditions reach beyond family influences, a good society being one in which human needs are met and despair is avoided. Social systems thus help form personality. Horney brought in an emphasis on compliant, aggressive, and detached types of people; she makes *anxiety* the basic concept rather than the sexual and aggressive impulses described by Freud. Man has "neurotic needs" for affection and approval, for self-sufficiency and independence. They are neurotic in the sense that they come to dominate the person.

Type Theories

It seems natural, even if incorrect, to classify people as though they came out of some mold. Early theories of personality as determined by body build are oversimplified for modern psychology although there are residuals of such thinking. Sheldon speaks of the round, soft person as an "endomorph," one who is fond of food, apprehensive, insecure, and conformist. The "mesomorph," in whom muscle and bone predominates, is characterized as the adventurous type who can withstand discomfort. The nonadventurous "ectomorph" is fragile in body build. Controversy about such classifications has stimulated much research. Freud has spoken of the "erotic" type, gregarious and self-dramatizing; the "obsessional" type, critical and skeptical; and the "narcissistic," or self-satisfied, type. He regarded these types as normal modes of adjustment, but when adaptation failed, they could become maladjusted.

Trait Theory

The use of such descriptive terms as happy, resourceful, aggressive, and dependent is a common way of talking about personality. Such traits, or typical ways of behaving, go into many descriptions. In the

English language alone, some 18,000 terms have been compiled that serve to distinguish people behaviorally. According to trait theory personality can be described by its position on a number of scales, each of which represents one trait. We have both *common* traits by which we compare one person with another and *personal dispositions* that give each of us individuality. The trait approach to the study of personality lends itself to experimentation where traits are reactions, not something a person possesses. One psychologist emphasizes that "it is important for the student of personality that when psychologists describe personality in terms of traits or types, they may be using identical terminology but may have completely different theories as to what traits exist and how these traits are organized within the individual."

THE USEFULNESS OF THEORY

Let us emphasize here something we all know about theory, whether it concerns predicting the weather or trying to explain how the brain works. Theory gives us a guideline to interpret observations and facts so as to arrive at generalizations and make predictions. In theorizing, we set up assumptions not only to explain our data, but also to relate to them in a practical way. We may predict that it is going to rain in our general area because the barometer is falling, but we are not certain what part of the area will receive showers. The Weather Bureau includes not only barometric readings but also other data. Using these data, it can come up with a statement about the statistical chances for rain in any given area. Like personality theorists, weather forecasters use statistical, atmospheric, and other indicators to guide their thinking. Like psychologists, they drop theories, modify theories, and come up with new ones as they discover fresh data.

    What about theories whose results are difficult to check? An example: studies show that most adults can repeat a series of seven numbers immediately after the series is read. However, if these persons are asked to repeat the numbers thirty minutes later, most cannot do so. In the first instance, we are dealing with short-term memory (see page 282), a type of immediate memory span quite different in process from long-term memory. Behind these basic observations lies a theory of two-stage chemical memory storage. According to this theory, immediately after every learning trial, a short-lived electrochemical process is established in the brain. Within a few seconds or minutes, this process decays and disappears, but before doing so, it triggers a second series of impulses in the brain. These impulses are chemical in nature, involving the production of new proteins and the induction of higher enzymatic activity levels in the brain cells. In theory, this process provides the more enduring long-term memory.

This theory of memory is possibly of interest only to the people doing research in the area. Personality theory likewise is of more interest to the specialist than to most of us. But like the weather, we do find theories of personality valuable in helping us understand the sources and workings of our own personality.

SUMMARY

An individual's personality is evaluated by observing his or her normal ways of adjusting to the situations that life presents. Individual differences highlight the study of personality, but important in the concept of personality is consistency of behavior. We see personality as external appearance and behavior, as inner awareness of self, and as unique patterns of measurable, fairly permanent traits. The characteristics that make up the whole person include physique, intellectual and other abilities, interests, attitudes, beliefs, values, and expressive life-styles.

Genetic differences play a large role in individuality and give us potential. Through the process of socialization we learn what to do and what not to do. Agencies of socialization change as the individual matures. Reevaluations in our self concept change as we respond to different rates of socialization; as opportunities differ for each of us; as we learn from experience; and as we are influenced by the structures of impersonal systems. Our body image remains an important component of our self concept throughout life.

Much of personality is revealed through our temperament, measured along the Guilford-Zimmerman Temperament Scale of nine dimensions. We have *general activity* ranging along a scale from slow to energetic. The dimension of *restraint* is measured on a scale of "impulsive to restrained." Self-sufficiency is measured on the *ascendance* scale; a low score relates to being timid and a high score to confidence in personal contacts. *Sociability* scales out from sociable to solitary. *Emotional stability* ranges from easily upset to emotionally unstable. Sensitivity is measured along a scale of oversensitivity to objectivity along the dimension called *objectivity*. Other scales include *friendliness, thoughtfulness,* and *personal relations.*

Emotional control involves the recognition of reality. We learn to view it from the standpoint of our daily habits and to expect emotional responses under certain conditions. We learn control by becoming adjusted to the stimulus that produces it. How well we do these things reflects our personality. Some people like to release their emotions in public; others do not. Advocates of sensitivity training believe that it is valuable to know how others see you; critics believe it is harmful to expose oneself openly. Emotional suppression has both positive and negative aspects.

In many ways we reveal our individuality by the roles we play; and the learning of roles begins early and continues throughout life. Role conflicts appear for all of us. Some people find it difficult to shift from one role to another; others enjoy varying their roles and their behaviors. The personality of the creative individual illustrates the point that people can have certain characteristics that may lead to success or to conflicts and disenchantment.

Psychoanalytic theory attempts to explain mental phenomena as interaction between urging forces within the individual and counter-forces set up by the environment. Type theories attempt to classify people as if they came out of a mold: the "endomorph," "mesomorph," "ectomorph"; the erotic, obsessional, and narcissistic types. Trait theory emphasizes typical ways of behaving.

ADJUSTMENT

Oftentimes it is the urgency of a problem that makes us want to know more about the processes of adjustment. This book is devoted to the many aspects of personal adjustments and the relations we have with other people. Sometimes we mistake pessimism for realism and feel that as individuals we can do nothing to change the people or the world around us. Basically, most of us wish to seek out our own individuality; we want to be more than just a statistic in some computer storage unit.

WHAT IS ADJUSTMENT?

As we know, behavioral adjustment is the process of trying to bring about a balance between needs, stimuli, and the opportunities offered by the environment. It consists of attempting to satisfy needs by overcoming both inner and outer obstacles and by fitting oneself to circumstances, like the student who wants to get along with the group. While physiological adjustment involves adaptation to the environment, we can think of behavioral adjustment as a kind of "psychological survival." Learning about adjustment means analyzing two things: our internal makeup and our interpersonal, or social, behavior that results from having to live with other people. We can think of adjustment in two ways: (1) the *process* by which man and his environment are kept in balance and (2) the individual's efforts to fulfill his needs. In response to hunger we eat and thereby restore the balance between bodily needs and the food energy available to meet them. We seek a comfortable balance between the extremes of hot and cold environments and do things to bring this about. In attempting to be stimulated but not overwhelmed, we go through sequences of behavior in response to stress. When circumstances change, we discover new ways to satisfy our wants. This pattern is the process of adjustment.

In this chapter and in the remaining chapters, we shall detail the many aspects of the concept of adjustment. It is a concept that develops gradually in our understanding. Let us here note that good adjustment does not necessarily mean conformity to some norm. In fact, one can think of adjustment as being sometimes a two-way process whereby one works to change the norm, or standard, of behavior rather than change one's individual behavior to conform. Giving value to honesty and behaving accordingly is an example of where we may be bucking the norm in some given situation. Mindless conformity is, of course, just the opposite of healthy adjustment. Yet, some conformity is a part of good adjustment. We certainly stand less chance of an accident if we conform to well-researched traffic regulations. Even for the pedestrian, statistics bear this out in terms of the direction from which we may be hit by a motor vehicle. For example, pedestrians crossing at intersections are twice as likely to be hit by a car turning left as right. In part, the automobile's design is responsible, requiring the driver to make some adjustments different from turning right. For the pedestrian, good adjustment means looking just a little farther to the right. Safety regulations are related to both the pedestrian and the driver. If one person conforms and the other does not, the chances of an accident increase. This example illustrates the idea that adjustment is only partially within the control of the individual. Each of us must determine when he or she is in control and when not.

In many social situations, knowledge is essential to adjustment. But in large measure, effective adjustments are within us and relate to feelings of self-worth and the ability to give and receive affection. Knowing when and when not to be flexible in our behavior is important, and our values, goals, and attitudes become a part of the adjustment process. Adjustment is an ongoing process, not a static thing. It centers so much on the question, "Who am I?" and changes as we change. We shall talk later about self-identity (see page 288) and other aspects of personality, but here let us extend our thought to personality and some of the differences in value orientations that relate to the adjustments we make. We may adjust in varying ways to different types of people as well as to different situations.

PERSONALITY TYPES

We find the *dominating* type of person who wants to run things and perhaps people. There is the *individualist,* who has a great need for doing what he or she wants to do and is often (though not always) willing to pay the price for nonconformity. Then there is the group-oriented *social type,* who strongly wants the acceptance of others. This person thinks of adjustment as the ability to meet the demands and expectations of the group to which he or she belongs. We have also the *ideologue,* who is committed to a set of ideas or ideals, who is willing to engage in struggles, not for power over others but because he or she sincerely believes that power is essential to furthering a cause. Another is the *professional rebel* whose adjustment consists of being different in many ways. These are only rough classifications and are not, of course, mutually exclusive. One may be an individual-its in one situation and a social type in another. Although we are all individuals, likenesses in value orientation give direction to the adjustments we seek.

TYPES OF RELATIONSHIPS

Adjustment involves four types of relationships. There is the *intra-personal* relationship, which consists of the individual's attempt to understand his own desires, abilities, and frustrations. There is the *person-to-person* relationship, such as the communication that takes place between student and counselor. When several people interact, for each person a *person-to-group* relationship is involved. Finally, there is a *person-to-object* relationship, such as driver and car or typist and typewriter. In effect, adjustment means opening up to experience in each of these four directions.

We are, of course, familiar with several typical adjustments; let us mention a few by way of introduction, beginning with physiological adjustment. Body temperature regulation is an automatic type of adjustment. The human body operates with maximum efficiency at an internal temperature of about 100 degrees Fahrenheit and maintains this level within 1 or 2 degrees. If the external temperature becomes too high, the body meets the emergency in a number of ways. The capillaries in the skin dilate, exposing a larger amount of blood to the cooling influence of the body surface. Also the skin secretes perspiration, the evaporation of which lowers the heat of the body. When the environment becomes too cold, the capillaries contract, driving blood from the skin. These adjustments are made without voluntary control. However, individual choices aid the physiological adjustments. When he is warm, a person will avoid physical exercise, retire to a shady place, dress lightly, or enter an air-conditioned place; when he is cold, the opposite occurs.

We adjust to hunger by eating and give reflex responses to being burned. We make sense organ adjustments by moving our eyes or turning our heads toward the source of sound. We make adjustments to a complex set of stimuli in driving an automobile. Sometimes, of course, we find a problem situation to which we cannot adjust immediately on the basis of reflex, past experience, or habit. This type of problem solving is an example of intellectual adjustment. And, in some ways, social adjustment may be the most complicated of all. The social contacts of groups of people require subtle and delicate adjustments. Learning what to do is quite involved, as we shall see in much of our discussion throughout this text.

SOME COMMON PROBLEMS

Let us briefly describe two college students the reader probably knows. They are hypothetical, but probably not too far removed in their problems from most of us. These descriptions were provided by an experienced counselor to help us illustrate some typical adjustment problems of college students.

Harry is nineteen, Sue eighteen. Both are from middle-class backgrounds, healthy, and intelligent. They are normal in terms of the three criteria separating the normal from the abnormal. First, in the statistical sense their behavior does not depart markedly from the average. Second, their behavior does not deviate from normal types of effective personal adjustment or produce enough anxiety to lower efficiency or to prevent them from coping with change. Third, in terms of a cultural definition, where "abnormal" may mean violating the mores of a given society, both are normal; they do not behave in ways that are a threat to society.

Harry describes himself as being work-oriented; while he expresses interest in the social sciences and the humanities, he prefers to deal with problems related to things, with some interest in human relations that relate to work and getting along with people. Harry finds it hard to study, preferring to spend his time in athletics and tinkering with cars. He is enough of a realist to know that he must get an education in order to make a living. His awareness of his own motives, feelings, and desire for security causes him to worry about not being a better student.

Sue is an excellent student interested primarily in the arts. She wants to be a teacher and also to get married before finishing school, and herein lies a conflict. On a questionnaire scale of descriptive adjectives she sees herself as appealing, moderately attractive, poised, and spontaneous, but overly sensitive. Sue is aware that in terms of job opportunities women are handicapped, and this relates to some anxieties she has about the future.

Although different in abilities, personality, interests, and ambitions, Harry and Sue have problems common to most of us: feelings of inferiority, fear and anxiety, stress, and worry.

FEELINGS OF INFERIORITY

Counselors report that of all the problems they hear described by college students, the most common is *unfavorable self-evaluation.* And it can be added that attitudes of inferiority are so common among adults that we regard them as a normal aspect of living.

Why are feelings of inferiority so common? One reason is that our culture is *success-oriented.* We expect to win at games, get to the top in business, exert social influence. And many of us have to prove something to someone.

From the time of birth the individual is compared and contrasted on every level—looks, intelligence, muscular strength, academic and social accomplishment, and a host of other things. Each of us, in his or her struggles to win, picks "an ideal" as a standard of comparison. We do this even knowing that it may be unfair. In looks we rate ourselves with the model or entertainer, in athletic ability with the professional. In academic pursuits we have parents or an older brother or sister to match in accomplishment. We feel inferior in the classroom because the teacher knows more than we do. In most areas, someone else excels. In other words, the "ideal" does not exist, but we fail to realize this. Instead, we try to measure ourselves by our mistakes rather than by our accomplishments.

Another reason why all of us have feelings of inferiority is that we know more about our own feelings than anyone else does. We often see only the surface feelings of others, and we observe only their many cover-ups through the roles they play. In being ourselves, we come closer to our problems and see our failures. We are aware of what people think of us, and this disturbs us.

One psychologist characterizes a feeling of inferiority as an emotional reaction to an assumed failure. At the level of theory he has proposed that personality development is a continuous series of reactions to inferiority, whether real or fancied. He views inferiority feelings as essential to psychological growth. These feelings become detrimental for good adjustment only when they become excessive or when a person strives for success and fails repeatedly.

Indicators of Inferiority Attitudes

There are six common ways to recognize feelings of inadequacy in everyday life. Up to a point, they can be counteracted.

One common indicator of inferiority is a marked *sensitivity to direct or implied criticism*. A student may devote much effort to prove that his solution to a problem is correct. On the other hand, he may more profitably search for a better method of attack. If a better method is found, reinforcement sets in to help offset the attitude of "I can't do it."

A second indicator of the inferiority attitude is *reference of all criticism to oneself*. A whispered comment or chance laughter by others, which may actually have no relationship to the anxious person, may cause him to feel that he is being attacked. *Seclusiveness* is a third indicator of an inferiority attitude. In the extreme instance, the individual will cross to the other side of the street to avoid meeting people. He will not join with students gathering in the hall. He feels that he is not wanted. A note of caution, however, is needed here. The fact that a person does not chat in the hallway is not in itself an indication of feelings of inferiority. There may simply be more important things to do.

Fourth, the person with feelings of inferiority characteristically *overresponds to flattery.* This seems to help him improve his own feelings of adequacy. Anyone who supports his ego will be given a welcome reception. But again, let us point out the need to draw a line between overresponse and liking to hear good things about ourselves. A teacher's appreciation of a favorable comment about himself may be in no way related to inferiority. The chances are that such appreciation is normal in the educational climate since, in general, the professor gets mostly negative feedback from students. Those who do poorly drop the word that he is a poor teacher. Those who do well, and who honestly think he is an excellent teacher, rarely if ever tell him so. Hence, it is only human nature that he may respond with good feelings to indirect flattery.

A fifth indicator of inferiority feelings is a *poor reaction to competition.* The person is not a good loser. Every contest he enters, whether a game of skill or an attempt to impress a friend, is played most seriously. He prefers, however, to compare his skill with that of someone he can defeat. He likes obscure games in which he has a high degree of competence; he avoids more conventional situations in which winning is somewhat a matter of chance.

Sixth, a *tendency to depreciate others* indicates an attitude of inferiority. Pointing out the faults of others not only helps to minimize one's own defects, but also involves some projection. When we feel inferior, we want, perhaps unconsciously, to know that we have company.

Excessive Feelings of Inferiority

Most of us probably keep our feelings of inferiority within reasonable bounds, but for some people feelings of depression go along with severe inferiority. There is no prediction of moods from outward events. Friends and relatives often do not realize the extent of the depression. While normal feelings of inferiority relate to comparisons with the ideal, such comparisons carried to excess turn to envy. The individual makes comparisons about his weaknesses, rarely about his strong points. Most such people actually have a number of accomplishments, but they themselves do not realize this fact.

The person who lacks confidence to a great degree not only fails in adjusting to many normal problems, but also makes his life miserable. His fear of himself often is severe enough to cause him to repress his talents and abilities. Outwardly, this person may display ability, but actually he holds back because of fear of failure; even mild risk taking is shunned. Said one counselor: "If I can get the client to better understand the nature of fear and anxiety, he or she may come around to taking the chance of a possible failure."

FEAR AND ANXIETY

Fear is a common example of a response to a situation in which the person is unprepared for the interruption; sudden, intense, unexpected stimuli catch him unawares. Since fear keeps us from *not doing* things that have some element of calculated risk taking, it relates closely to feelings of inferiority. Fear has a specific *external* cause—the rattle of the snake, the creaking of a door. At a more general level is anxiety, the emotion of dread or uneasiness, a feeling that something is threatening. It involves fear and feelings of depression, and at times it is free-floating. Anxiety is generated *within the individual,* who is apprehensive but cannot attach his feeling to any specific cause.

Normal and Abnormal Anxiety

Anxiety is by no means the exclusive property of either the student or the neurotic. Anxiety is for all practical purposes a universal problem. Anxiety seems to thrive in a climate of uncertainty, and particularly in situations dominated by hostility. It shows up in such physical symptoms as ulcers and breathing problems associated with such psychological reactions as fear and feelings of depression.

The nonspecific aspects of anxiety are interesting to observe in one's own feelings. Said one student as she came out of a counseling session: "I feel like a free-floating anxiety looking for something to tie onto."

Normal anxiety includes, as we all know, those anxious moments before going into an exam. It entails a sense of helplessness when one is unable to find a solution to a demanding problem. Like other emotional tensions, normal anxiety can act as a drive. A person may react with moderate anxiety because his lack of skill in dancing prevents him from taking part. This may motivate him to learn to dance in order to overcome shyness or inconvenience. It may help in fighting that urge to flee.

Abnormal anxiety is manifested in varying degrees. At one end of the scale it involves feelings and behavior which keep the person from functioning efficiently; at the other end it may involve panic. The chronically anxious person is in a state of stress because of some internal conflict which cannot be reduced by defensive behavior (see pages 80–84). He or she has the usual complaints of headaches, backaches, and upset stomach; cannot think clearly or concentrate;

and feels tired all the time. Further, this person has a feeling of failure and dread without knowing why. These panic states are usually brief, though their duration is variable and they may last anywhere from minutes to days.

Anxiety and College Success. Most college students seem to be affected by anxiety. Let us look at some studies.

In one study it was found that 90 percent of a group of college sophomores who had been chosen for good health and academic adjustment had psychological problems intense enough to warrant assistance in solving them. In most of these cases anxiety played a major role.

From several studies comes the conclusion that practically all students suffer from test anxiety. The A student, with strong needs to achieve and to stay at his high level, often has more anxiety about an exam than does the person who is below average. One investigator found that at the lowest and highest levels of academic talent, anxiety has little effect on academic performance. The lowest-ranking students do poorly in college regardless of their level of anxiety. Superior students are sufficiently bright to overcome any adverse effects of anxiety. One practical way to hold down anxiety is to keep busy. Hence, bright students learn to cope with their anxiety through hard work and are reinforced by the resulting academic accomplishment. For a few students, the struggle to get ahead seems to be mostly a game of mistakes.

But what about the average student? Research shows that within the middle range of intellectual ability, anxiety interferes markedly with successful college performance. Since most college students are average, chances are that some students who could get through a given college program successfully fail because anxiety gets the better of them. For these students college counseling and guidance programs are most helpful.

Anxiety and Counseling. Investigators put anxious freshmen into a group counseling situation and compared their academic performance at the end of the first year with that of a control group of anxious freshmen who were not counseled. The result of this study are shown in Figure 4-1. Here we see that the anxious but *counseled* students showed a significantly greater improvement over their own mid-semester grades than the noncounseled students. (The counseling sessions began in the middle of the semester.) Also, note that those who came regularly to the counseling meetings made the greatest improvement in grades.

Other studies show the payoff that comes from attending individual and group sessions in counseling and guidance. So important is this college service that we shall later devote detailed attention to it (see page 287).

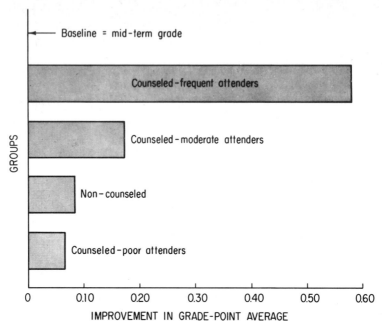

FIG. 4-1 How counseling benefits anxious college students. The counseled group had three subgroups—frequent, moderate, and poor attenders. Those who came often to counseling meetings showed the most improvement in grade-point average.

THE NATURE OF STRESS

It is natural that when a problem arises, we search for *the* cause. Often we overlook the fact that most of our everyday problems do not fall into a simple cause-effect pattern. Our researcher has emphasized that stress is a cumulative process related to the wear and tear of daily problems and to our adjustment to short-range, long-range, and ultimate goals. He maintains that stress is a normal counterpart of living; it is our reaction to it that is important. Often our tensions, conflicts, and frustrations stem from our struggles to play the role of someone we are not, and many times we fail to heed our own cues of when we are exceeding our individual stress levels.

Let us illustrate how stress can build up over a period of time. One psychologist made a study of parachute jumpers at various time periods in the jumping cycle—the night before the jump, the morning of the jump, upon reaching the airfield, during the training period immediately preceding the jump, and at the time of being strapped to the jump equipment. Ratings were also made at the time of boarding the aircraft, during the aircraft's ascent, at the ready signal, upon stepping toward the jumping stand, upon waiting to be tapped to jump, during the free fall immediately after the jump, after the chute had opened, and immediately upon landing. The peak of threat occurred not at the moment of jumping, but at the point of the *final decision* to jump, when the jump could no longer be avoided and the parachutist could no longer turn back. Ratings made along scales of "approach" feelings and "avoidance" feelings showed that up to the moment of the ready signal for jumping, approach feelings *declined* and avoidance feelings *increased*. The pattern was reversed following the jump signal. This study gave emphasis to the point, probably observed by the reader in a less dramatic situation, that the moment of ultimate decision carries the most threat when there is a gradual build-up of stress involved. Studies also confirm that students under the pressure of taking a crucial examination feel increasing stress as the time of the examination nears.

Stress and Personality

Stress harms certain people while causing others to thrive. What may be an *overload* of stress for one person may not be for another. Researchers have found two behavior patterns related to the "fit" between the person and his psychological environment. The Type A person is characterized primarily by excessive drive, aggressiveness, ambition, involvement in competitive activities, frequent vocational deadlines, pressure for vocational productivity, and an enhanced sense of time urgency.

Type B, the converse pattern, is characterized by the relative absence of the interplay of psychological traits and situational pressures. The Type B subject is more relaxed and more easygoing, seldom becomes impatient, and takes more time to enjoy avocational pursuits. He is not easily irritated and works steadily, but without a feeling of being driven by a lack of time. He is not preoccupied with social achievement, and is less competitive in his occupational and avocational pursuits.

The Type A person is likely to *overload himself;* the Type B person is not. This "role overload," as it is called, which requires a person to do more than he is able in the time available, is related to coronary disease and to job satisfaction. For example, the Type A person has been found to have significantly higher blood cholesterol levels than the Type B person with the same diet. Research data strongly indicate also that "striving without joy" may lead to an increased risk of coronary disease. These data are based upon three separate studies involving various occupational groups where mortality ratios due to coronary heart disease and levels of job satisfaction were correlated. The subjects included professors, scientists, managers, journalists, workers, and other occupational groups. The studies imply that the ability to adjust to stress seems related to personality factors. One indication of how we individually react to stress relates to what we worry about and when. One individual may worry considerably *before* he makes some decision; another person may worry afterward. And, of course, there are those of us who worry most of the time.

WORRY

Worry is persistent nonadjustive "thinking" which is not always negative; it may stimulate us to seek some solution to a problem. It is in some ways the verbal conterpart of nervousness. The worrier "spins his wheels" by going over his troubles again and again without getting any closer to a solution. When worry is concerned with a minor and *specific* problem, it is likely to disappear when the difficulty is solved or when the person directs his attention to something else. A very difficult type of worry to overcome in a reasonable period of time is related to the error we have made that will affect some future event. Examples are numerous: the unmailed letter that makes us realize we have failed to meet an important deadline; the last-minute awareness that we are lacking a credit for graduation; or inadvertent publication of possibly offensive material. Sometimes worry is caused by the small things that get called to our attention again and again. For example, one large food distribution company reports that of some 125,000 complaints a year from consumers, about 10,000 have to do with a particular product, such as its condition or use, but three times as many complaints involve premiums that do not come as soon as expected. Most people, it seems, ignore the printed notice of six to eight weeks for delivery.

The uncertainty of whether our explanation of some difficulty, or even solution for it, will be accepted by some other person involved adds to the persistence of worry. One thing we do know: Persistent worry cannot be relieved merely by telling the worrier not to worry. As one well-adjusted instructor said: "I can solve problems, but I cannot solve worries. I try to convey this to my students."

Steps in Reducing Worry

It is safe to say that it is impossible to get rid of *all* worry. As a matter of fact, the solutions to problems often come because of worry. Or observe sometime what you think about when you do not have a worry over a fairly long period of time. It is quite possible you will raise the question, "What is or is not a worry?" This leads to a second question, "What is my individual threshold for worry?" Analyzing worry as a process generally allows us to cut down on the *frequency* of worry and to some extent on the *degree* of worry. Bearing in mind that the steps given below in relieving worry do not always work, you may still wish to try them. Chances are you will discover that you have been using these steps from time to time; it is important to become aware of what does or does not work well.

First, set a *time to consider the worry.* What is the cause? Often worry is vague and without specific cause. Taking time out to analyze it may help find the cause. If there is no cause, this fact may help us get rid of the "ghosts." Putting off looking at worry does not reduce tension.

Second, *talk the worry out with a good listener* (see page 246). Worries tend to become exaggerated when bottled up inside. An impartial observer can help us go through the stages of (1) trying to make our worry more objective by expressing it; (2) being asked questions about the cause; and (3) getting some participation in the worry.

Third, *seek reliable information* about the area of the worry. Some worry is unnecessarily generated through ignorance, misinformation, or misconceptions. Sometimes people who seem to operate at a high crisis level, frequently using such words as "urgent" or "demanding," may tend to exaggerate our worry level. By talking the problem over with someone in whom we have confidence we may discover different solutions to try or we may at least find new ways of thinking about the problem. Seeking information in itself is a conservative exercise that helps to cut down on wheel spinning.

Fourth, *do something active about the source of the worry.* For example, low grades may be helped by guidance and efficient study. Social worries may be lessened by some group activity.

Fifth, realize that some worries have no solution. If the conditions are impossible to remedy, turn to *other types of behavior* to occupy yourself; sports, hobbies, amusements, and work help reduce stress brought on by "no-solution" worry. And we *all* have these kinds of worry.

Sixth, *counseling centers* are good places to go to when professional guidance is necessary. One must remember, however, that most centers are overloaded with work and some prethinking about one's problems can be helpful (see page 293).

From a personality standpoint some of us are "worry worts," even arranging our worries in order of magnitude. If we have no real cause for concern, we tend to fall back upon a lesser feeling of just being uneasy.

THE PROCESSES OF ADJUSTMENT

The more stress a person is exposed to before he learns to cope with it, the harder it is to effect good adjustment. One may think of behavior going through four stages of adjustment. First, the individual has some motive which is pushing him toward a goal. Second, he meets some baffling difficulty or frustration. He tries to overcome it, but cannot do so readily. Impelled by the motive, which is still unsatisfied, the individual makes various attempts to fulfill it. This process results in the third stage of adjustment involving trial-and-error behavior, or what we generally call "varied responses." Finally comes a solution which, in whole or in part, satisfies the motive that started the adjustment process. In this chapter we shall describe how all this takes place.

We can think of human behavior as having three components. First, behavior is directed toward effectively solving problems, and for most of us this is what we usually do. We may not think so because when we solve a problem, it no longer bothers us; hence, we tend to forget that we even had a problem. This *integrative* behavior we call "good" adjustment. In contrast, behavior can have a second dimension, which we call *nonintegrative.* This occurs when we do not see the whole picture and are, therefore, left with some conflicts. For example, we may not notice some positive aspects of the situation. A person may work so hard at reducing some immediate anxiety that he fails to see how well he is doing in other areas. Third, behavior may be *nonadjustive,* causing the person to remain in a continuing, restless, and unresolved state of anxiety. In these three descriptions we are dealing with classes of responses, not types of people. Put another way, people differ in the degree to which their behavior is integrative, nonintegrative, or nonadjustive. The very healthy person shows ineffective behavior at times, while the severely maladjusted person is effective at certain times.

COPING BEHAVIOR

The phrases "I have to learn to cope with my problems" and "He can't cope with the situation" are descriptive of the specifics of adjustment. One psychologist has stated that when we run into a situation in which there is no automatic response, ready-made answer, or well-established habit to fall back on, we must "cope" as best we can. For example, the cultural shock of moving into a new and strange social environment, such as college, requires us to get experience in dealing with the newness. The problems with which we have to cope range widely from refraining from offending someone to dealing with actual danger.

Meeting a Crisis

Some people who get upset over little things often come through in crisis situations. Studies of reactions to fires, earthquakes, and tornadoes show that the majority of people conform very closely to a "disaster syndrome"; people behave much the same in one disaster situation as in another. They follow a *sequence* of behavior, as follows:

1. *Behavioral bankruptcy.* The individual has no reactions "on tap" to deal with the situation. He is stunned into silence and immobility.
2. After extricating himself, his family, and his neighbor, the individual goes into a *state of shock;* he becomes extremely passive.
3. *Extreme curiosity.* People go "sightseeing" to watch the rescue work.
4. Increased perception as to the *cues to danger.* It is in this stage that we find the beginnings of coping behavior.
5. Increased *interpersonal communication* and "togetherness." People appear to get comfort from others. Antagonisms and prejudices seem to vanish in this phase of the behavior sequence.
6. *Compulsive rituals and superstitious practices* commonly begin to emerge. For example, following the atomic attacks on Hiroshima and Nagasaki, many Japanese rubbed onions on their heads to prevent bombs from seeking them out.
7. *Planning* finally gets underway. People begin to organize aid, restore communications, and ward off further disaster.

Perception of the Situation

Many of us tend to handle daily situations which are psychologically threatening by *overreacting.* The salesman may worry about the inept remark he has made; the instructor may tend to read too much into the critical remark of the student. Even the tone of a verbal statement can be reassuring or threatening. It is how the individual perceives the situation that is important. Let us illustrate with a study.

Three-word sentences were flashed before subjects. They were asked to interpret the sentences under two different conditions. The experimental group was "threatened" by being asked to describe a complex picture which was presented so rapidly that the subjects could not see it well. Their sense of failure was intensified by criticism from the experimenter. The control group was shown the same picture with adequate exposure time and without any disparaging remarks being made. Later, both groups were again tested for their ability to perceive three-word sentences shown rapidly. In the post-frustration test the experimental group perceived less well than the

control group. The threatened subjects tended to *misperceive* innocent stimulus words as aggressive words. This classic study, performed a quarter of a century ago, has been substantiated a number
of times, leaving us with the generalization that *effective coping
behavior has its beginning in the process of perception.* How often
we may misread some letter, some remark, even some bodily movement as hostility! When we are very strongly anticipating success in
some endeavor, even the least threatening feedback may be distorted.
When this happens, we may react in a variety of defensive ways.

DEFENSIVE REACTIONS

"If you wait patiently, everything will turn out all right." This
statement may sometimes be true, but usually problems are not
solved so easily, much as we should like to think they are. This kind of
statement is typical of the person who depends too much on someone
else or who rationalizes his behavior and shows other common
defensive reactions.

Defensive behaviors fall into various descriptive types and
classifications, many of them arbitrary. In effect, a defense mechanism is a coping process which operates to some extent more in the
mind of the individual than in reality. It is a response that enables an
individual to avoid or lessen threat; it is a substitute or partial
adjustment. Defensive behaviors deal with problems that lie somewhere between effective solution and no solution. We all fall back
from time to time on defense mechanisms, and since we all use them,
in the statistical sense they are normal. Used in excess they may be
harmful when they prevent us from searching out better solutions to
our problems. On the positive side, they serve, at least temporarily, to
reduce our anxiety, to allow us to "play for time" in working out a
better solution. These substitute adjustments are described below.

Dependency

Statistics show that dependency is used more often than is its
opposite, self-reliance. Dependency shows up in several ways in what
people *do not* do. Chief among these failures is unwillingness to make
decisions or to exert extra effort. Dependency is sometimes characteristic of the person who appears satisfied with the status quo and is
willing to "let George do it"—even though George will get all the
credit. This mechanism is related to conformity in behavior; it is less
threatening to agree than to be different.

The dependent adult is much like the dominated child who
constantly wants to be reassured. Dependency can be a roadblock to

individual productivity. For example, technical or professional obsolescence can result from the individual's failure to appraise himself, particularly when other people may be overprotective with him.

Projection

In this reaction, the individual attributes to others motivations which he recognizes in himself. Thus, the dishonest or greedy person may judge others to be just like him. Projection is not only a poor judgment; it is also a false belief. The individual who employs projection perceives in other people the motives and traits about which he is sensitive and anxious himself. The man who pads his expense account may ease his guilt by saying that it is a part of the "culture of the organization" ("everybody does it"). The young person who does not feel he is being listened to may project his feelings against "the system."One favorite whipping boy in our technological age is the computer, certainly a boon to the person who likes to lay blame on some relatively inanimate object. This is somewhat comparable to the attitude of the baseball batter who looks critically at the bat when he strikes out. Projection can be considered logical to the person using it on the ground that it "makes sense." The extremely rigid person, unwilling to admit his lack of flexibility, may project against the person with new ideas in the belief that this person is naive, poorly informed, or irresponsible. At an extreme level, projection can be thought of as a defense mechanism for the paranoid individual who believes that someone else is seeking to injure him, when in reality he has thoughts of injuring that person.

Identification

Identification is the reverse of projection; a person claims as his the admirable traits of others. It is common in grade school for the student to identify with a favorite teacher, or for the high school quarterback to identify with the pro. Identification may be good or bad, depending both on the individual's goals and on those of the person with whom he or she identifies. In identification we tend to copy the other person's actions and even his attitudes. We can also think of identification as a method of reducing tension by "taking on" the achievement of another person or group of people.

Identification can be an important aid in training. The beginning employee is in a stressful situation because he does not know what is expected of him just when he wants to make a good impression. Thus, the new worker may identify with the worker at the next bench; the copilot may identify with the pilot. As stated above, this may be good or bad, depending on the interaction of the person with his work climate and on the goals of the organization. People join clubs, lodges, and unions in part for the satisfaction of identification. In the same way, we identify with our possessions. Owning an expensive home or car tells us that we are "successful." Identification, like other defenses, is rarely adopted deliberately, nor is the person usually aware of it as an adjustment. Identifications sometimes lead to difficulty; the person may identify with the wrong values or the wrong crowd.

Compensation

Compensation is a very common defense mechanism, for most of us feel inadequate in so many ways. When achievement of an original goal is blocked, we may substitute a second goal and reach it instead. For example, the small person may develop a deep, husky voice as compensation. A student who has high ability in mechanical skills but who is weak in speaking and writing may compensate by becoming outstanding in tuning an engine. Compensations serve not only as substitutes for some other achievement, but also divert attention from our inadequacies. Thus, they help us by reducing some of the expressed or implied criticism that produces anxiety.

Compensation, like identification, may be pushed too far. College counselors report that many failing students have been pushed into inappropriate programs of study to satisfy the compensatory needs of their parents.

Overcompensation

Frustration often leads to overcompensation, providing for the individual some measure of ego-protection. Failure in the classroom or in a business deal may make a man attempt to regain his self-respect by bragging about earlier accomplishments. Whereas compensation may lead toward an effective adjustment, overcompensation may bring about obnoxious behavior. Common examples are talking too loudly, showing off, or insisting on holding to some position that is unreasonable. In the long run, overcompensation may increase anxiety rather than reduce it.

Reaction Formation

Reaction formation consists of attempting to conceal motives by publicly displaying attitudes that are their direct opposites. A feeling of hostility toward another person may be covered by excessive thoughtfulness in dealing with him. We may well suspect the presence of this defense mechanism whenever "righteous indignation" occurs out of all proportion to the circumstances. One counselor reports the case of an athlete who used every opportunity to extol the virtues of his coach, whom he disliked very much. Sometimes we may resolve conflict by strengthening one of the motives. The shy person whose past experience has caused him to feel anxiety in face-to-face communication with other people may react by displaying gruff and aggressive behavior.

One of the difficulties in recognizing reaction formation is that different people may react the same in a given situation but for diverse reasons. One person may display highly moral attitudes and preoccupation with socially approved objectives as reaction formation, while another reacts out of real concern. Again, the intensity of the reaction can clue us in to its sincerity. If it is irrational, it may be reaction formation. Another guide is that reaction formation usually occurs under fairly special circumstances. We can think of reaction formation as an exaggerated expression of some behavioral tendency exactly opposed to some "repressed" impulse. Genuine expressions of an impulse are not usually extreme, nor are they compulsive. One clinician says that we often reverse emotion in speech; instead of expressing hostility toward another person, we express love. Presumably, the stronger the hostility, the more intense the positive expression of love.

Rumor

For some people the starting or spreading of rumor may be considered defensive behavior. Rumors may be started deliberately for political ends or they may be intentionally inspired, serving competitive need to build one's own ego. Rumors tend to flow best horizontally, and they spread more widely when they are ambiguous. Knowledgeable people are less likely than the uninformed to transmit rumors, particularly in a crisis situation. Errors in relaying rumors are in the direction of what one expects to hear rather than what one actually hears. This relates to the factor of set in perception (see page 235), where the perceiver selects certain aspects of the environment and ignores others. There is a tendency for the person with a "high crisis quotient" to like rumors, particularly those that relate to negative things about groups or organizations. Rumor is also fostered by expectation.

Rationalization

So common is rationalization that we may tend to overlook it as a defense mechanism. At times we all go through the process of justifying our conduct or opinions by inventing socially acceptable reasons; rationalization is a wishful-thinking defensive reaction. The person tries to find an "out" by coming up with a plausible excuse for failure.

Rationalization is not reasoning, although it may have such an appearance. Reasoning is the process of seeking a true answer to a problem, whereas rationalization justifies an answer that already has been determined by desire, without reasons, intent, or purpose. It is, in effect, an attempt to "make sense" out of feelings and behavior in conflict situations. Rationalization shows up in a variety of forms to help us believe what we want to believe rather than what is true. These forms range from "sour grapes" to those "unfair objective exams." Of course, rationalization may sometimes help us protect ourselves from anxiety when we are in an anxiety-producing situation. In the long run, however, it is no satisfactory substitute for reality.

Intellectualization

We may try to cope with some problem and wind up overplaying objectivity. Intellectualization is the defensive maneuver by which the person tries to remain untouched emotionally by some threatening event; he becomes overly analytical and detached. Science students sometimes fall prey to this mechanism because it is an extension of the objectivity they are taught to value. The unattractive person who is not sought after by the opposite sex may intellectualize his or her position by an attitude of staying free by remaining detached.

Scapegoating

The displacing of aggression onto some object, person, or group is scapegoating and is usually harmful to both the individual and the recipient; it is sometimes related to prejudice. In scapegoating we often find agreement with other people seeking out defensive behavior. And, in college, we have an ever-present situation whereby the student can join with others in blaming the educational system for his lack of progress. One socially undesirable effect of scapegoating is that a minority group can become the focus of attack in which large numbers of people are willing to participate. The individual may feel less personal guilt when he or she is part of a group focusing on some other group.

APATHY AND STEREOTYPED BEHAVIOR

The effective solution of problems involves *action,* and so does the substitute adjustments of defensive behavior. In contrast are two other forms of adjustment characterized by inaction on the one hand and by behaving with oversimplified and fixed responses on the other. The first is *apathy* in which our behavior is listless and indifferent. The second is *stereotyped* behavior whereby we fall back on some "programmed" set of responses which we tend to repeat. Like defense mechanisms, these are comfortable forms of adjustment. Life situations are conducive to their use even in those of us who like to believe we are well adjusted. We get tired of fighting back, particularly when resistance makes the situation even more threatening. We learn that aggression or counteraggression is not always the sole or best response to frustration. We also find that our defensive plays do not always work and that we need some virtually "automatic" behavior to keep us going. The person who has given up smoking will say that he often lit a cigarette when he didn't have another way to respond to some stressful situation: "It took me a long time to find out what to do with my hands when I was made to feel uncomfortable."

Apathy

We often feel that the solution to individual and social problems is hopeless, and hopelessness induces apathy. One of the difficulties we have is deciding between the calm resignation of hopelessness and the defensively maintained feeling that there is no real problem in the first place. When the odds are too great, the resolution too remote, the punishment for aggression too severe, the defensive response not on tap, apathy results. Fortunately, most of us never reach a state of complete apathy, such as has been found in studies of some war prisoners who were victims of prolonged degradation and deprivation with the result that they became utterly indifferent to their surroundings.

An environment filled with persistent frustration can breed apathy. Through the news media, television, and from personal observations we see so much of the negative that we tend to become apathetic to situations which we believe are beyond our control, and even to those capable of control. Apathy, in the extreme and at critical times, can become a threat to mental health.

Stereotyped Behavior

While the efficient problem solver keeps his behavior flexible and searches for new ways to attack his problems, the opposite is true of the person who behaves in a fixed, repetitive way. His responses are stereotyped, that is, rigid, unchanged by circumstances. This type of person may try to categorize groups of people by neat labels whether these labels apply to individuals within the group or not. His behavior can become so stereotyped, so rigid, that effective alternatives no longer exist. Some people seem to program their responses so narrowly, in order to avoid conflict and frustration, that they do not allow themselves any openness to experience. Of course, we are tempted to seek the simple solution when we become overwhelmed with problems.

AN OVERLOAD OF PROBLEMS

Let us introduce the concept of overload by some common examples. Driving into a strange town, we ask directions for getting to a given hotel. Our informant, who knows the area by heart, tells us, "Go three blocks, turn right until you come to Forbes Street, and then take a left until you come to the Museum. Here you go etc., etc." He has given us *too much* information to process, so we probably say, in effect, "Point me in the right direction, and I'll take it from there." Many studies confirm the generalization that the human brain can remember and process just so much information in a limited amount of time. And there is quite a difference in processing the familiar and the unfamiliar. No doubt, you have had the experience of trying to follow your friend's car to his home for the first time. You had difficulty in keeping up with your friend, who felt he was proceeding at a painfully slow pace. Why? The answer involves the programming of perception, judgments, and decisions for the leader who knows the way. His sensory inputs, information processing, and physical movements have become virtually automatic. He has learned the route well, thus reducing the demand put on him. For you, almost everything was new; whereas he made decisions automatically, you had to make conscious choices.

Even under the best of circumstances, where there may not be a disturbing emotional involvement, it is easy to overload our problem-solving mechanisms. But what about personal problems that entail conflict, frustration, and all those depressive feelings involved? And often it happens that before we get one problem solved, we are hit with another, and still another. It is here that our system becomes overloaded. If we have a background of understanding the nature and complexity of adjustment processes, we can learn effective ways of coping. If, on the other hand, we are ignorant of these processes, we may be overcome by the avalanche of problems we face. Most problems, even the apparently common ones, are in reality quite complex.

COMPLEXITIES OF EFFECTIVE ADJUSTMENTS

Problem solving involves setting alternate goals, and good mental-health practice means that we know the probable costs of reaching our primary goals—costs in terms of personal and social insecurity from time to time, the struggle against indifference, and the threat of failure that goes with the promise of success. Information, relevant and available, is essential to effective adjustment. Yet, we know that at times we may suffer from too much information. Further, very imaginative people may multiply their problems into a vast array of possibilities. To solve problems effectively, each of us must consider his or her own personality and motivational characteristics, level of need achievement, and tolerance of ambiguity, uncertainty, and hostility. We should try to search for alternatives in decision making and to anticipate the consequences; this is important for a healthy personality. Basically, we must learn to weave our way through an understanding of even such a "simple" problem as waking up tired.

There are many reasons for waking up tired, ranging from the purely physical to the purely psychological, to any mix in between. Here are some general things to consider. Some people just need more sleep than others. One person may get up early and feel fresh and vibrant (perhaps bog down at 4 P.M.) while another reaches a peak of efficiency later in the day. Our "biological clocks" differ; some of us are "morning types" and others "evening types," and there are physiological reasons for the differences. Habit has a lot to do with it.

A restless night (and we all have them)—with aches, bathroom trotting, disturbing noises, or a roommate who snores—can leave one feeling tired. Sleeping pills or too much alcohol can have a "hangover" effect. Poor physical condition, stemming from faulty nutrition, is a factor. Low thyroid activity can cause morning fatigue. Poor ventilation or too warm a room can be bothersome.

Psychological factors in tiredness are frequent. One is just the matter of one's sleep patterns. If you have become a habitual late sleeper, it takes some time to get into the habit of earlier rising.

Although we may think of sleep as part of a twenty-four-hour clock, its patterns can be changed. Studies show that army recruits who need eight hours of sleep at home can manage with six or less under certain military conditions. But a person who cuts his sleep to four hours or less for several nights may get his system out of control. The college student studying for exams may break his sleep pattern enough to change certain kinds of behavior. He may go without sleep one night. The next day his attention may wander a little, or he may feel like lying down, but nonetheless he may function normally in taking exams. Staying up night after night, however, causes irritability, and judgment and reflexes become impaired. Although we can to a degree "catch up" on sleep, researchers say that we cannot "store" it up.

Other psychological factors that relate to fatigue are boredom, anxiety, and worry. If you go to bed worrying, it can be reflected in morning fatigue. If you dread the problems of the day, you may well wake up tired. Or even if there is nothing in the day ahead that disturbs you, just having no incentive to get up can make you feel tired from the moment of waking.

Finally, we can say that the experience of fatigue involves

perception. When a task does not involve the expenditure of a great deal of physical energy (which can bring on tiredness), and yet the individual feels tired, we must look elsewhere for the cause. One's interests, activities, and emotional states affect his perceptions. The student who cannot continue with his lessons because he is "so tired" often finds that the weariness vanishes when he turns to an activity that interests him.

The complexities of adjustment, whether they involve effective problem solving, substitute defensive adjustment, or nonadjustive activities are important to anyone interested in knowing why he acts and reacts as he does. By learning something about his own behavior patterns, he can shape his life, direct it, and not feel himself merely tossed from one situation to another.

COPING VERSUS DEFENSIVE BEHAVIOR

We have discussed in this chapter two opposite behavior systems; here, let us contrast them to emphasize the complexities of adjustment. In contrast to defensive behavior, in which some threat is reduced largely in the imagination, coping involves active mastery; it is essentially the same as adjustment, as we have implied. One of the reasons coping behaviors seem so complex is that they are so individual; every person copes differently. Some people learn how to perceive their wants and life-styles with a minimum of distortion, while others have difficulty in doing so. Some people are very intolerant, while others are quite open to new experiences. And some react with calm and deliberate thought to serious problems, yet fly off the handle when faced with a minor inconvenience.

We can think of coping as a *system*, composed of accurate perceptions, a memory bank of relevant experiences, and behavior strategies programmed for efficiency. Such a system involves planning to see that appropriate alternatives for action are included. Coping is a positive process; not so defensive behavior, which is negative in many ways. Coping is a forward-looking process, in contrast to the backward look of defensive, substitute adjustments. Defending the past, for most of us, is not as productive and satisfying as is relating to the future in a practical way. This will become increasingly clear as we take a look at maladjustment in the following chapter, which deals with abnormal psychology.

SUMMARY

Learning about adjustment means making analyses of two things: first, our internal makeup; second, our interpersonal or social behavior that results from having to live and work with other people. We can think of adjustment as the process by which the individual and his environment are kept in balance; bring about the effectiveness of one's efforts to meet needs. The concept of adjustment develops gradually in all of us.

Adjustment involves a four-way function of relationships: intrapersonal, person-to-person, person-to-group, and person-to-object. Adjustment involves solving such common problems as feelings of inferiority, indicated by sensitivity to criticisms, reference of criticism to oneself, seclusiveness, overresponse to flattery, poor reaction to competition, and tendency to depreciate others. Within limits all of us show fear and anxiety, quite common in the college student who functions in a highly competitive environment. Anxiety is a universal problem which thrives in a climate of uncertainty, and particularly in situations dominated by hostility.

Stress is a build-up process, related to the wear and tear of daily problems and to our goal seeking. Reactions to stressful situations relate to personality. What may be an overload of stress for one person may not be for another. The Type A person is characterized by excessive drive, aggressiveness, ambition, involvement in competitive activities, vocational deadlines, pressure for productivity, and an enhanced sense of time urgency. The converse personality, Type B, is more relaxed and easygoing, seldom becomes impatient, and takes more time to enjoy avocational pursuits. While the Type A person is likely to overload himself, the Type B person does not.

Worry is a characteristic of all of us; it is negative in excess and positive when it stimulates us to seek solution to a problem. Although it is impossible to get rid of all worry, we can reduce it by setting a time to consider it and talking it out; by seeking reliable information and doing something active about it; and by engaging in other types of activity.

In contrast to coping behavior we find an array of defensive reactions, so common that we can think of them as normal. For most people they include dependency, projection, identification, compensation, overcompensation, reaction formation, rumor, rationalization, intellectualization, and scapegoating. Failures to cope effectively with problems can lead to apathy or to stereotyped behavior.

Effective adjustments involve avoiding problem overload and setting goal alternatives. Information, relevant and available, is essential to effective adjustment. Most people motivated in self-understanding come to grasp the complexities of adjustment, whether they involve effective problem solving, substitute defensive adjustment, or nonadjustment activities.

ABNORMAL PSYCHOLOGY 5

Writers in the field of abnormal behavior emphasize that there is no mysterious difference, no cutoff point, between normal and abnormal adjustment. We are dealing with a continuum of behavior, with most people, whom we call "average," clustering around a central point. Most people achieve a moderate level of adjustment, while a few at one extreme lead very fulfilling lives and a few at the other extreme are severely maladjusted. The phrase "well-adjusted" is often used to indicate good mental health. Characteristics shown by the well-adjusted person include a realistic and accepting attitude of oneself *most of the time.* This involves feelings of self-esteem and security. It includes the ability both to give and accept affection, and the ability to be productive. The mentally healthy person knows something about his or her own stress levels and shows flexibility in coping behavior. This person knows when and when not to worry. He or she avoids *extreme* behavior, such as excessive drinking and irritability or excessive emotional and thought disturbances.

Problems of adjustment vary in degree. At the "normal" level are nervousness and worry, feelings of inferiority, and defensive behaviors which we have previously discussed (see page 69). At the "abnormal" level we have the neuroses, psychoses, sexual deviations, and antisocial behaviors which we shall describe below. Somewhere in between we find people who are not really abnormal but who certainly are not functioning well. The hypochondriac is an example. Let us talk about the case of Henry S.

THE ILLS ARE PHYSICAL—THE ILLNESS EMOTIONAL

It's a normal morning for Henry S., a middle-aged salesman who lives in a Boston suburb. He takes some pills for his ulcer and bladder, and he regularly takes a laxative. He breakfasts on prune juice and warm water. Then he straps on his back brace, swallows the day's first tranquilizer, and sets off for work.

Henry's coworkers long ago stopped asking "How are you?" The reason was simple. When someone asks that question, Henry tells them. This answer is as pungent as his aches and pains.

On some days, Henry leaves work early for doctors' appointments. At the moment, he is being seen by an internist, an orthopedist, a chiropodist, a neurologist, an opthalmologist, and a genital-urinary specialist.

None of these doctors can find anything wrong with him. But that does not mean that Henry is not sick. For Henry is a hypochondriac. This means he is excessively preoccupied with his body and constantly demands attention for his physical complaints. Hypochondria is an emotional illness that ranges from mild forms of anxiety to more severe disturbances. Henry, and the many like him, are not fakes. Hypochondriacs experience real discomfort.

Psychiatrists estimate that up to 10 percent of the 200 million hospital outpatient visits in the United States a year were made by hypochondriacs. They are estimated to consume up to 20 percent of the nation's 80 billion dollar annual health budget.

Many hypochondriacs are middle-aged people in their crisis stage. They often get into a life-style of the person in revolt (see page 184).

SOME FACTS AND FICTION

In his book *Essentials of Abnormal Psychology,* Benjamin Klein-muntz summarizes some differences between fact and fiction about mental illness:

Fiction: The abnormal are very different and therefore attract immediate attention to themselves.

Fact: (1) With few exceptions, the mentally ill are indistinguishable from the rest of us.

(2) They tend to talk about their illness as does the person with some physical illness.

(3) There is no sharp dividing line between normal and abnormal.

Fiction: You cannot treat mental illness.

Fact: Except in rare cases, behavior changes for the better are possible under proper professional treatment.

Fiction: Mental health can be preserved by avoiding facing problems, by the "power of positive thinking."

Fact: "Positive thinking" is a result of normal adjustment rather than an agent of it. Personality disorders are a consequence of a life-long pattern of faulty learning.

Fiction: All mental illness is transmitted genetically.

Fact: Facts are not conclusive. Present data indicate that hereditary factors predispose persons to some disorders, especially among the psychoses. Actual illness is precipitated by environmental stress.

Fiction: Masturbation causes insanity.

Fact: (1) In terms of statistical criteria of abnormality, masturbation is normal.

(2) However, guilt and anxiety associated with the act which is deep-rooted can cause excessive worry and feelings of guilt.

Fiction: A person can rid himself or herself of unpleasant thoughts and memories through willpower.

Fact: (1) There are some neuroses (depression, obsession, compulsion) and many psychoses in which the primary symptoms are unacceptable and abhorrent thoughts.

(2) Persons with these thoughts cannot banish them from their minds, however hard they try.

Fiction: When someone is recovering from a mental illness, it is best not to discuss the treatments he or she has had.

Fact: (1) There is nothing more disconcerting to the former mental patient than to be ignored, or

(2) to be treated as an object of curiosity.

(3) One should show the same concern and use the same discretion in inquiring about his or her experience and present condition as one would with a person who is recovering from physical illness.

Fiction: Patients in mental hospitals speak in words that cannot be understood.

Fact: (1) Only a small proportion of hospitalized patients are incoherent or incomprehensible.

(2) Most people in mental hospitals speak as logically and articulately as other people do.

Fiction: Many hospitalized patients try to commit suicide.

Fact: (1) Suicide is seriously attempted by depressed persons and drug and alcohol addicts.

(2) Only a negligible group of other mentally ill patients threaten or attempt to kill themselves.

Fiction: It is easy for most people to recognize the type of person who is likely to have a behavioral disorder.

Fact: (1) Prediction of mental illness is difficult even for a professional.

(2) One exception: extreme cases where one's history is well known.

Fiction: Mental health specialists try to teach self-control to their patients.

Fact: (1) Psychotherapy does not consist of lessons in the ordinary sense that educators use the term; instead:

(2) Specialists try to restructure habits and coping practices.

Fiction: Emotional self-control is the best cure for the mentally ill.

Fact: Emotional self-control is neither a symptom nor a cure for recovery of mental health. There are probably as many cases where overcontrol is as prominent as loss of self-control.

CHILDHOOD AND ADOLESCENT DISORDER

In Chapters 6 and 7 we shall talk about the day-to-day aspects of child and adolescent behavior. Let us here describe a few problems that are severe enough to be called "disorders." We do not feel that this text should suggest specific solutions to these problems, since they should be dealt with first hand by the professional. We shall mention several fairly common childhood problems that one is likely to observe from time to time.

Food refusal may lead to nutritional deficiencies. A common way to refuse food is dawdling, where the child takes two or three bites but does not chew or swallow the food. This child simply may not be hungry, or too busy to eat, or may be trying to avoid what follows the meal—naptime, bedtime, or having to sit on the toilet.

A more serious form of food refusal is vomiting. If we assume the child is not physically ill, chances are the child is trying to make the parents anxious. Refusal to eat can become the basis of a power struggle between parent and child.

Obesity from overeating has four common causes. First, overeating may develop in the child of five to eight years of age as he or she attempts to replace immediate members of his family with friends. Failing, the child becomes lonely; consolation is found in eating. Second, many psychoanalysts believe that maternal overprotection is at the root of obesity. Overfeeding symbolizes the parent's attempt to atone for her own loveless childhood. According to this theory, the mother equates food with love, and lavishes it on the child. Third, family patterns of abnormal food intake are responsible for childhood obesity. Here the child acquires the habit of overeating by imitation, encouragement, and even pressure from parents and relatives who believe that being obese is a sign of good health and nourishment. Fourth, obesity in the child may have the same cause as in the adult, that is, some children overeat because they respond to external cues for eating rather than to internal visceral states (see page 24).

Enuresis is usually psychogenic in origin. This failure to control urination is most common at night and is more frequent among boys than girls. It may vary from slight bedwetting to complete bladder emptying. In most cases, it stops around puberty, but occasionally it may continue throughout life. Enuresis is commonly related to arrival of a new sibling, separation from family or loved ones, or extreme sensitivity to the inability to compete. Shyness and mild anxiety usually go along with enuresis. When the difficulty is not symptomatic of a more serious personality disorder, the child usually gains control spontaneously as he or she develops and is praised for success.

Infantile autism is rare, but has received much public notice; it usually has its onset during the first year of life. The first noticeable sign is failure of the child to make anticipatory movements and postures prior to being picked up by an adult. Language takes on a strange parrotlike quality because the child seems not to talk to anyone in particular or to expect a response to his or her sounds. The autistic child will sit motionless for hours staring into space, as if deep in thought. Some believe that the disorder may be caused by brain damage. The treatment and prognosis for autism have not been favorable, in part because of these children's extreme detachment from relationships.

School phobia is a common disorder of adolescence, usually occurring between the ages of twelve and eighteen, although it may begin earlier. Child guidance clinics report this extreme fear of going to school to be one of their most common problems. The younger child pleads to stay home, cries, trembles, and comes up with a variety of aches and pains. At the younger ages, it is traceable to fears of separation from mother and anxiety about going to strange toilets; even eating in the school lunchroom creates fear. For the adolescent, school phobia is usually a symptom of a larger neurotic personality behavior pattern. Here the adolescent tends to avoid unpleasant situations because he or she has no skill in coping with them. The school just happens to be one among many of these situations. The adolescent is more disturbed than normal (see page 150) and tends to be demanding, especially at home. Pouting is characteristic, and negativism is common. The adolescent attributes fear of school to any of a series of incidents which are exaggerated out of all proportion to their actual importance. Treatment varies with the individual, but basically it is aimed at having the youngster achieve some insight into the difficulty. Clinics usually try to get the phobic person back to school and away from the pleasant home situation in which he or she seeks refuge.

NEUROSES

Anxiety is the main characteristic of neuroses; it has a disruptive and disorganizing effect on the individual. Anxiety neurosis occurs when defensive behaviors (see page 80) are functioning inadequately, or not at all. Although no two anxiety attacks are alike, they generally are marked by episodes of extreme apprehension and restlessness, accompanied by periodic attacks of hear palpitation and excessive sweating. Panic reactions, where breathing is difficult, sometimes occur. Other symptoms of an anxiety attack include nausea, stomach distress, or instant severe headaches with stiffness of the neck and shoulders. A decision about even minor matters may precipitate major crisis for the anxiety neurotic because he or she is so insecure. To the neurotic, misery is real, not imaginary. The neurotic suffers in taking even the usual risks of life.

With the passage of time, the well-adjusted person solves his or her conflicts; not so the neurotic, who tends to cling to ineffectual behavior, unsatisfactory as it may be, because it temporarily lessens the anxiety.

At the intellectual level, the neurotic may know that the anxiety is unreasonable, but this helps little. Some people stay in a chronic state of anxiety, but for others it is only a temporary effect produced by specific events in their lives. Some anxiety is out in the open, such as extreme anxiousness in taking tests. Other anxiety may be hidden, coming out in a psychosomatic disorder such as a migraine headache.

Kleinmuntz describes a case of anxiety neurosis where the client's past history became available. His anxiety attacks were almost always precipitated by such stressful circumstances as lecturing before a group or being teased by fellow workers. These settings served as an excuse for his incompetence. His reasoning, although possibly not a conscious level, was a convenient alternative to facing up to the possibility that he might not pass muster. Ironically, however, in John's case this "insanity bit," as he called it, became an occasion for further anxiety.

THE CASE OF JOHN L.

John L., a laborer at a United States Steel plant, age twenty six, came to the Veterans Administration outpatient clinic because he feared he was losing his mind. Even before going into the army he had been having what he called "panic attacks" in which he would become dizzy and weak, and then completely immobile. During his two years of army duty, he experienced these attacks, especially while lecturing the troops on the dismantling and assembling of weapons. Afterward he showed great concern about their opinions of a "goofball" like him "trying to tell them how to do something."

Following his military service, he accepted a laborer's job at the steel mill, and while acknowledging that he was not intellectually challenged by the work, he explained that he would attend college and then seek other employment as soon as he overcame his "insanity bit." However, he feared being unable to compete with others even in his present job, and he frequently complained that his coworkers teased and harassed him.

One day, during lunch break, while being ridiculed by some of his associates, he had his first real anxiety attack at work. He reported that something seemed to snap in his ears, after which everything sounded louder than usual, and he held his hands over his ears until he fell to the ground. Once down, John became afraid that he might never get up again; but he jumped up suddenly and reassured everyone around him that he was all right. The first anxiety attack lasted about sixty seconds, but thereafter he had a constant fear of its recurrence, and he sought help because he was afraid that he was losing his mind.

Psychotherapy, conducted on a twice-a-week basis for about six months, disclosed that although his anxiety had a long history, the immediate causes of his military and postservice attacks were related to his marriage just before entering the army. His wife was a vivacious young woman, who, in sharp contrast to John, was self-confident and outgoing. During therapy, he began to understand the relationship between his anxiety and his lack of self-confidence as a lover, provider, and person. He had to learn also that his apprehension about future attacks was very much related to their actual occurrence.

It must be remembered that anxiety neurosis should be distinguished from normal apprehension or fear, which occurs in realistically dangerous situations.

OBSESSIVE-COMPULSIVE NEUROSIS

Obsessions are composed of persistent and repetitive intrusions of unwanted, *irrational thought,* often coming at an inappropriate time. They cannot be banished voluntarily. Petty worries are common examples—"Did I turn the car lights off?" "Did I turn off the stove?" Such persistent thoughts, even tunes that recur for no apparent reason, represent common mild obsessions. Quite common is the irritating TV commercial or jingle that persists in spite of efforts to banish it from memory.

The neurotic's obsessions are different. Not only are they more insistent, they are so disturbing that they interfere with the individual's adjustment. They are often psychologically painful, since they center on morbid thoughts of obscenity, murder, suicide, or death. In the extreme, these obsessive thoughts can disable the individual.

Compulsive symptoms, at a normal level, hit most people. Common examples include paying excessive attention to unimportant matters, fussy tidiness, and sometimes fastidious dress for oneself or children. A compulsion is an *irresistible behavior pattern* that may or may not grow out of obsessive thoughts—the compelling urge to express oneself or to repeat some behavior over and over again. At the abnormal level, compulsions often take the form of rituals such as washing one's hands over and over again. Here the individual engages in the behavior, unaware that it is an obsession. The compulsive act makes little or no sense to the individual intellectually, but if he or she does not perform it, intense anxiety results. In exaggerated form, compulsion reactions become *manias.* For example, we frequently hear of *pyromania,* the compulsion to set fires, and of *kleptomania,* the compulsion to steal.

Obsessive ideas and compulsive acts may occur separately, but usually the two are combined.

DISSOCIATIVE REACTIONS

As the term implies, "dissociative reaction" is a condition characterized by a disunity of one part of the individual's personality with the other. The neurotic may block out certain aspects of life as an escape from anxiety and stress. Not uncommon is the behavior of sleepwalking, called *somnambulism,* where a mild dissociation takes place. Here the individual gets out of bed and goes through various acts, almost as if looking for something specific. The sleepwalker may wander from room to room, or leave the house and go for a short walk. On command from some authoritative voice, the person will stop what he or she is doing, or even return to bed spontaneously. If questioned closely without awakening, the sleepwalker may only mumble something that is probably related to some daytime event or conflict. Sleepwalking is common in children, who like adults walk in connection with dreams. These dreams are almost always forgotten, as are the sleepwalking episodes themselves.

Less common is dissociation through *amnesia,* the loss of memory commonly involving one's name and address or other facts about one's personal life. The individual may still be able to function normally in routine ways to provide the simple necessities of life. Actually, amnesia is an attempt to escape from oneself.

Amnesia is a psychological flight from reality. Sometimes amnesia may be accompanied by an actual physical flight whereby a person may wander off for days or even weeks. The person may be discovered by others or "wake up" without help, unaware how he or she got there. Such episodes are called *fugues,* from the Latin word meaning "to flee." Although there are records of fugues lasting for long periods of time, they frequently last only for days. The national police network for missing persons often locates such people. The search may be helped by giving a description of the individual's skills. During a fugue the person retains both basic skills and knowledge.

The most extreme form of dissociation is *multiple personality.* Although very rare, it has been dramatized so effectively that many people believe it is quite common. Robert Louis Stevenson's famous story *Dr. Jekyll and Mr. Hyde* shows a dual personality of which one part is selfish, the other generous; one aggressive, the other quiet. As in the story, so in actuality an individual may at different times be two entirely different people. Not always, but usually, one personality is completely unaware of the other.

A true clinical case, also widely dramatized, is *The Three Faces of Eve.* Here we find the struggle between Eve White—sweet, retiring, dignified, and motherly—and Eve Black—vain, irresponsible, and mischievous—both inhabiting the same body. Eve White is unaware of Eve Black's existence, but not the reverse. During the months of psychotherapy a third personality, Jane, appears. It is she who is able to reveal the trauma of early childhood that had produced the dissociation of personality in the first place. Jane finally helps to banish both Eve White and Eve Black, leading to the synthesis of all three into a normal, integrated personality.

CONVERSION REACTION

In a conversion reaction, sometimes called "conversion hysteria," the individual transfers an emotional problem into a physical disorder. This is a form of protection against an anxiety-arousing stress situation. The term "conversion" was coined by Sigmund Freud to convey the idea that there is a transformation of psychic energy into body symptoms. In many cases, these somatic symptoms resemble real physical disturbances. The patient may become temporarily blind, deaf, or paralyzed. There may be prolonged coughing or sneezing spells. There are even conversion reactions that produce symptoms of pregnancy.

"Writer's cramp" is a common symptom. For example, a management official time and again had difficulty writing his name when it involved signing contract agreements. He blamed the difficulty on writer's cramp. After he was given a new job that did not involve responsibility in labor relations, the writing difficulty disappeared. However, life is not so simple. In this case, writer's cramp was replaced by a new physical complaint that went along with his new job in sales. The man got a stomachache each time he went to lunch with a customer!

NEUROTIC DEPRESSION

In contrast to the normal person who becomes depressed under stress of the loss of a loved one, financial reverse, failure in a course, loss of a job or demotion, the neurotic has a tendency to blame himself or herself, or feel guilty in some way. It is as though, for the neurotic, the danger of "coming apart" increases. With the normal person, lessening or getting rid of the difficulty brings relief from depression; not so, the neurotic. Getting rid of the cause does not remove the depressed state. The normal person becomes aggressive in becoming adjusted to his or her problem rather than depreciating oneself as the neurotic does. Normal depression clears up quickly, whereas neurotic depression may last for weeks or months. It can clear up with or without treatment, but it is likely to recur. The following case history illustrates the point.

THE NEUROTIC FATIGUE SYNDROME

A public relations man for a well-known corporation began appearing at the office in a more or less haggard or distraught condition. He claimed to his associates that he was not sleeping well at night. It was obvious that he was less alert during the daytime than he had been previously. Several times during the day he would sit back in his chair to rest or he would even go to the lounge for a short nap. When he also complained about slight nausea and lack of appetite, others in the company encouraged him to get medical and then psychiatric assistance.

While undergoing psychotherapy, he reviewed his enthusiastic approach to the public relations field some twenty years earlier. He felt he had all the qualifications to move quickly toward one of the top public relations posts in the nation. To reach this goal, he had traveled extensively and worked long hours both in the office and at home. He had known all along that he was sacrificing family welfare for his own vocational aspirations. It was only when he passed his fiftieth birthday that he became dimly aware that he was never going to be the success in his field that he had dreamed of being. This dimly sensed realization was apparently responsible for the insomnia. Both the insomnia and the anxiety over not reaching a top position were responsible for the generalized fatigue reaction. Gradually, the fatigue syndrome subsided as his individual goals were reevaluated.

Individuals with fatigue complaints which last over a long period of time talk freely about their troubles and frequently demand attention and sympathy. College students often complain of fatigue, and quite justifiably. Most students work hard, and under different forms of stress related to various motivations for achievement. Gradually, most of us learn that top achievement is a nice thing to have, but is not absolutely essential for feelings of self-worth. Trying too hard can make anyone—student, laborer, or executive—anxious and chronically tired.

In some measure, the neurotic fatigue syndrome helps the

person reduce some problems to a size where he or she can better cope with them. Prolonged tension and the aches and pains that accompany it can be very fatiguing. They can interfere with sleep and leave the individual prone to rest a good bit in the daytime. This in turn increases the chance that one will not sleep well at night. Excessive tiredness is difficult to diagnose because the symptoms run down and because fatigue also occurs in normal states. One starting point is a good medical examination. Only in severe cases is psychiatric attention called for.

PSYCHOSES

Authorities in the field of the major maladjustments speak of two general categories of psychosis. First, there are those psychoses associated with brain damage, such as behavior changes that accompany senility, those related to alcoholism and other drug addiction, and brain damage by tumors. Some psychoses may have a genetic base, for example, schizophrenia which we shall discuss below. Second, there are some psychoses in which there is no evidence of brain damage, such as paranoia which we shall also discuss. Some persons with tangible brain damage may recover after the cause of the damage is removed. For example, someone whose psychosis is associated with an infection, like syphilis, may show some behavioral improvement as the infection is cleared up, even though brain damage itself is irreversible (see page 13). Such a recovery of function may occur, if damage has not gone too far, because of the brain's facility to compensate for destruction of some of its cells by having neighboring tissue take over.

Although neurotic and psychotic symptoms overlap in part, neurotic persons seldom become psychotic, even in the face of extreme pressures. Psychotic behavior usually develops suddenly. Sometimes there are borderline symptoms between the neurotic and the psychotic which are called *prepsychotic.* In most cases, however, psychotic reactions are clearly recognized by others. On the other hand, the patient rarely recognizes that anything is wrong. To the psychotic, there is little distinction between the real world and the unreal, inner world of fantasy.

Psychotic disorders are marked by four conditions. First, the disorders are accompanied by *disorientation* as to time, place, and person, and by *inappropriate behavior,* such as profane language, indiscriminate sexual overtures, and extreme physical aggression. Second, the disorders are accompanied by *delusions.* These false beliefs usually center on sin and guilt, delusions of persecution and grandeur, and sometimes feelings that one is being eaten away by some disease. Third, psychoses commonly involve *hallucinations,* such as hearing voices. Fourth, *exaggerated emotional disturbances* are characteristically found among psychotic patients.

Let us look briefly at three of the most common psychotic disorders: schizophrenia, paranoia, and manic-depressive reactions.

SCHIZOPHRENIA

It is estimated that schizophrenia, commonly called "split personality," accounts for over one-half of the psychotic population. There are four main types.

Simple Schizophrenia

This type is characterized by disturbances of thinking and attention. Human relationships are impaired. The individual insulates himself or herself from the realities of life, apparently trying to solve problems by giving up. This disorder frequently begins in adolescence and progresses gradually. Rarely do such persons find their way into hospitals. They may live out their lives as drifters and often as prostitutes. The simple schizophrenic has a low level of feelings about both self and others. This person has few, if any, hopes and aspirations. He or she builds a life around undemanding routines requiring little contact with other people.

Hebephrenic Schizophrenia

This type is characterized by delusions related to some part of the body, such as "softening of the brain." Often there are delusions of grandeur. Such persons also show unpredictable behaviors such as giggling and silliness. Most of them deteriorate rapidly, in contrast to the simple schizophrenic, to earlier forms of behavior, reaching a point of lack of control over urination and defecation.

Paranoid Schizophrenia

Here the disorder is characterized by delusions of persecution: "They are out to get me." The individual apparently tries to hold himself or herself together by blaming difficulties on others. Such patients often complain that other people control their thoughts by radio or some other means. The delusions of the paranoid schizophrenic are changeable and transitory, and differ somewhat from those of the true paranoiac which we shall describe below (see page 104).

Catatonic Schizophrenia

This disorder is characterized by a waxy flexibility. If one raises the arms of a catatonic to an upright position, the patient may keep them there for an hour or more. The normal person finds this virtually impossible to do. Try it!

Part of the clinical picture is a shift from stupor to extreme excitability, a condition in which the patient may be dangerous. While in stupor, the catatonic will do the opposite of what is requested. An offer to shake hands may lead the patient to put his hand quickly behind his or her back.

It is the interpersonal side of the schizophrenic's thinking that is especially confused; this person cannot anticipate what to do next. However, thought-disordered schizophrenics have been found to be only slightly less stable than normal people in the way they interpret objects, but much more unstable and inconsistent in the way they interpret people.

The visual hallucinations in schizophrenics have been likened to the projection of motion pictures on the wall—that is, striking intensification of color and light. Such experiences, however, are more rare than auditory (sound) hallucinations. One theory is that the biological system underlying visual memory storage is less susceptible to derangement than the system underlying auditory memory and images. Auditory stimulation, even though more frequent, is far shorter and less intense than that of the visual world. Schizophrenics react much more slowly than do normal people, and they are quite handicapped in making decisions.

PARANOIA

Delusion of persecution is the distinguishing characteristic in paranoia. "They are talking about me" and "I am being plotted against" are typical and often-stated views. However, paranoids have sufficient judgment and self-control to both avoid hospitalization and function socially. Here they differ from the paranoid schizophrenic. But in extreme cases the person may be a homicidal risk and must be hospitalized. Paranoid individuals may be very intelligent and well educated, but they are completely convinced of their delusional system and cannot be shaken from it. Aside from the delusional system, the paranoiac's behavior may be normal, logical, and coherent.

Paranoiacs are uncooperative and often do not respond well to psychotherapy. They are suspicious of doctors as well as people in general. Some individuals with noticeable paranoid tendencies do maintain good contact with reality except for their suspicions. Some try to isolate themselves from the world, yet are still able to carry on business functions. Some paranoid states are transient and of short duration; others last a lifetime.

MANIC-DEPRESSIVE PSYCHOSIS

All of us have our ups and downs in mood, but the psychotic patient gives an exaggerated picture of this normal behavior. The term *"manic"* is used to describe three main symptoms: extreme euphoria, heightened psychomotor activity, and flight of ideas. Left on his or her own, the patient may indulge in alcoholic or sexual excesses or possibly get involved in wild business ventures.

In the *depressed* stage, we find dejection and a feeling of hopelessness, accompanied often by feelings of guilt. Some patients manifest only the manic reaction and others only the depressive reaction. Still others show some alternation between the two.

In the manic phase, there is overactivity and constant talking, with rapid shifts from one topic to another. Depressive symptoms are just the reverse, and the patient becomes indifferent to both the physical and the social environment. The manic-depressive may swing from warmest kindness to near-ruthlessness. The exaggeration of moods in manic-depressive reactions often does not appear to be brought on by external situations. However, in any given individual there is a predictable pattern of events. Modern psychotherapy can do much for the manic-depressive, occasionally even clearing up the illness in a matter of days or weeks. However, the symptoms do tend to recur.

Four Subtypes

Manic-depressive psychosis is better described in terms of its subtypes. There is the *manic* subtype, whose elation, excitement, and hyperactivity can be described by those who know the person well, even to pointing out the little peculiarities of his or her life-style. For example, the manic subtype may become a nuisance to friends, calling on them at odd and inconvenient times.

The *depressed* subtype is revealed not only by extreme depression but also by a slowing down of psychomotor activity. An observer may get the feeling that the person is isolated from the environment.

The *circular* subtype is characterized by alternation between manic and depressed episodes. This up-and-down swing may follow a fairly smooth change from one extreme to another in one person. In another individual the picture is one of a gradual rise to the peak of the manic phase with a gradual decline to normal; then after a period of normality the depressive phase sets in. Some patients show irregularities in the up-and-down swings.

A fourth subtype called *involutional melancholia,* is marked by extreme anxiety. Here the person is preoccupied with something being wrong with body organs. Expressions of feelings of guilt are common. The depression often centers on the "decline of the self."

In the manic-depressive psychoses we should point out that the manic attack should not be confused with joy. The apparent elation may well be an attempt to escape from the feelings of depression rather than being something pleasurable. In a manic phase, the individual appears to have unlimited energy, and may be too excited to even eat or sleep. Of course, exhaustion follows. In depression, anguish is often expressed by crying and verbally depreciating oneself.

Psychiatrists frequently use drugs to treat the disorder; "downers" are used to reduce manic behavior, and "uppers" are used to bring the person out of his or her melancholic mood temporarily. Under medical supervision, drugs are used at times to ready the patient for some form of psychotherapy. Self-administration of drugs may be quite harmful to the manic-depressive person.

SEXUAL DEVIATIONS

Most writers conclude that "more than with most other disorders, the line between abnormal and normal sexual functioning is blurred." There are many common misconceptions about sexual behavior. One often hears that sexual offenders are typically homicidal sex fiends. The facts are that homicide associated with sex crimes is rare indeed and the offenders are usually mentally ill as well as sexually deviate. Only about 5 percent of those convicted as sex offenders inflict physical injury on their victims. Another common misconception is that sexual offenders are "oversexed." Just the opposite has been found to be true among those arrested by police and studied. Are sexual offenders usually repeaters? The studies say not. Only about 7 percent of those convicted of serious sex crimes are arrested again. Most repeaters are less harmful offenders, such as "peepers," rather than criminals of serious menace to the community. But let us look at sexual deviations not as crimes but as behavior disorders. And let us keep in mind that sexual deviation is defined as any method of obtaining sexual satisfaction which is disapproved of by society.

Homosexual Behavior

Said to be the most common of deviations, homosexuality involves erotic relationships between members of the same sex. It has come increasingly to public attention through various "gay liberation" organizations on some campuses and in larger communities. Homosexuality has been discussed throughout man's recorded history. Contrary to some popular opinion, there are no particular physical or personality characteristics by which all homosexuals can be immediately identified. Some males do affect high-pitched voices and effeminate manners, but more do not. Some male homosexuals may wear lipstick and nailpolish and otherwise fail to conform to the conventional attributes of manhood, but many do not. Similarly, some female homosexuals may wear "mannish" clothes and no makeup, but many are very feminine in appearance. And contrary to some popular belief, homosexuality is not classified as a mental disorder.

The term "gay world" may carry with it the association of pleasure, but in actuality it is the opposite because stable relationships are difficult to establish. This may relate to the fact that many homosexuals cluster in certain residential areas of large cities, establishing a fluid society that operates in its own little world of customs, value systems, language, gesture, dress, and communication techniques. Furthermore, the disapproval of society puts tremendous pressure on homosexuals; until quite recently, most of them have been forced to keep their affinities hidden. The homosexual tends to see his or her problem as being "social" rather than "individual."

Male Homosexuals

There are male homosexuals and female homosexuals. There are male homosexuals married to women, but whose preferences are for men. There are those who are exclusively homosexual and are repulsed by women. There are still others who are bisexual and enjoy sexual contacts with men and women. And there is a distinction between "latent" and "overt" homosexuality. Latent homosexuality consists mainly of fantasies and manifests itself in the pursuit of interests commonly associated with females. Overt homosexuals are males who are fully aware of their same-sex preferences. They express them by engaging in homosexual acts—mutual masturbation, orogenital, and anogenital contacts. Aside from limitations imposed by nature, full same-sex erotic enjoyment can be found in either a passive or an active capacity.

There are unhappily married men homosexuals, lonely and isolated, who may grab a few moments of impersonal sex in a toilet stall, and who try to keep their deviancy a secret. There are those who are more candid in their recognition of homosexuality as a life-style. They tend to read widely about homosexuality and discuss it within their circle of friends. There are the so-called gay singles who are open participants in a male homosexual subculture. These people are often in their early twenties, and are frequently supported by older male lovers. They are usually well educated, have effeminate manners, are careful of their appearance, and keep immaculate, well-furnished apartments. They often speak of marrying the men they love. One other type prefers teen-age boys as sexual objects. They are known to cruise the streets in search for boys thumbing rides.

Female Homosexuality

Historically called "lesbian," the female homosexual often engages in sexual relationships with other women because of the inaccessibility of men. It is commonly found among female prisoners, but there is less coerciveness in the relationship than among male prisoners. Although the lesbian is characterized as wearing a plain felt hat, tweedy clothes, shirt and tie, and short-cropped hair, according to many studies nothing could be more erroneous. Most female homosexuals are indistinguishable from other women. Whereas mutual masturbation, or other physical practices, is expressed in male homosexuality, feminine homosexuality is often confined to the psychological level. There may be no physical manifestation at all beyond tender embraces.

Homosexuality is not thought to be a biologically caused condition and heredity has been ruled out. Current theory holds that male homosexuality results from an excess secretion of estrogen, a female sex hormone, and that female homosexuality results from abnormally high androgen levels, the male sex hormone.

OTHER SEXUAL DEVIATIONS

There is "across-dressing," or *transvestitism,* found among a few male and female homosexuals, who adopt the general characteristics of the opposite sex. The male transvestite may wear louder dresses, higher heels, use more cosmetics, and wear longer false eyelashes than most women. Women transvestites go in for rougher slacks, shorter hair, and behave more gruffly than males. There are some *transsexuals* who have undergone surgery in the genital area to transform them as nearly as possible to the opposite sex. Christine Jorgensen is a celebrated case; she lived as a male until surgery and now lives as a woman.

There are other sexual deviations, such as *pedophilia,* in which the sex object is an immature child. These deviates are considered dangerous; their cravings often result in murder, inspired more by fear of identification than by brutality.

When animals are used for the achievement of sexual excitation, we speak of the deviation as *bes iality.* This form of contact is found mostly among adolescent males in rural areas where a variety of animals are available. They soon grow out of it as women become more available. On the other hand, some males turn to animals when rejected by women.

More commonly we hear of *fetishism,* where sexual interest is focused on something inanimate, such as an article of clothing. The mere sight of, or contact with, the object brings sexual gratification. Fetishists are usually males. Like *voyeurism* (looking at the genitals or other part of a sex object's body), it does serve a normal excitatory function during the play period preceeding heterosexual coitus.

We frequently hear of *sadism,* where a pathological motive leads to the infliction of pain upon another person. This pain may be of a physical or verbal nature, or both. The physical punishment commonly includes kicking, biting, or whipping; there are instances where murder has been committed. At the verbal level, the sadist uses abusive language, teasing or threatening the subject. The type and frequency of sadistic practices vary widely from one individual to another and even within the same individual from one situation to the next. Mild sadism may be expressed during sexual intercourse through punching or biting the sex partner.

In *masochism* the deviate attains sexual pleasure by having pain inflicted on himself. Whereas most sadists in our culture are men, masochism is predominantly found in women. But these descriptions are not always clear-cut; sadistic and masochistic behaviors are often present in the same person. This deviation is called *sadomasochism.*

Impotence refers to the condition in males where an erection cannot be retained long enough for intromission, or where potency has been occasionally lost. Worry and fatigue may temporarily impair sexual potency. Sexual unresponsiveness in the female is known as *frigidity,* and, as in the case of male impotence, there are degrees of frigidity. This may range from a diminished sexual drive to active resistance to any sexual activity. Early impotence is said to result from psychological conflicts, and frigidity from feelings of insecurity, disgust, or even hostility. Studies of marriage partners indicate that the female may be introduced to sexual relations for the first time in an atmosphere of haste, dissatisfaction, and sometimes disillusionment that can lead to frigidity. Although frigidity in the female is the counterpart of impotence in the male, it is more common.

Prostitution is considered a form of sexual deviation different from the aberrations described above. It is a business relationship. The buyer is usually male, although in a few cases one finds a female buyer. Prostitutes often become the targets for a wide range of unusual practices, even physical punishment. Kinsey reports that in most cases the female prostitute does not become sexually aroused during a professional contact. At the organized level, prostitution involves a large percentage of drug addicts, mentally deficient girls, and antisocial personalities. Most girls drift into prostitution, rather than make a conscious decision to become a professional. It becomes a way of life from which it is difficult to escape. The organization on the street involves pimps who line up business, pay fines, and put up bail for the prostitutes to get them back on the street. Some pimps set nightly quotas and punish "their" girls if they do not meet the requirements. Prostitution has a class structure that ranges from the flophouse to the high-rise apartment. It is sometimes highly organized with money interests investing for a "cut" of the fees. But for the individual girl, basic loneliness is a big problem in this sexual deviation.

ANTISOCIAL BEHAVIOR

Many common names describe antisocial behavior: arrest, desertion, excessive drinking, failure to support, child neglect, cruelty, delinquency, thievery, irresponsibility, pathological lying, unsocialized aggression, and the more generalized terms of sociopath and psychopath. Benjamin Kleinmuntz, after an extensive review of antisocial behaviors, concludes that traditional psychotherapy in the form of the "talking cure" has largely failed with antisocial personalities. "This is due, because, in part at least, of *their* superficial emotionality, disparaging attitudes toward treatment, lack of insight, impulsive acting out, and general lack of motivation for treatment." He points out that there are exceptions to this viewpoint. Behavior therapy holds some promise. Let us close this chapter with a look at various types of psychotherapy.

PSYCHOTHERAPY

In less disturbed cases, treatment may be restricted to counseling therapy. Two different approaches are generally used. First, there is the *directive* approach, where the psychiatrist or clinical psychologist, using diagnostic tests and interviews, attempts to learn about the past history of the individual and how this may relate to his or her present problems of adjustment. In *nondirective* therapy, the intention is to let the client arrive at his or her own concept of self in therapy sessions where one feels free to be and act himself. The clinician makes the client feel understood and accepted. The client learns to view personal problems in a new light.

In the more disturbed cases, more is involved in therapy than counseling. Here we shall talk about psychoanalysis, rational-emotive therapy, and behavior therapy.

Psychoanalysis

This is the most widely known form of psychotherapy in the popular sense. It involves uncovering the repressed experiences from childhood that are assumed to be beneath adult neuroses. The major aim of psychoanalysis according to Freud is to help the individual become conscious of the repressed self so that miseries, conflicts, and anxieties can be banished.

In the classic situation, the patient attends four or five hourly sessions per week, lying on a couch, verbalizing thoughts. Dreams and fantasies are discussed and emotions are expressed. These weekly sessions may last for two years or longer. Patient and analyst dig ever deeper into the *id* (the more primitive part of the unconscious) in the attempt to remove the patient's neurotic fixations. Encouragement is given to developing new interests and redirecting the *libido* (pleasure-seeking drive) into more mature activities where the rational aspect of the personality, the *ego,* takes hold. Psychoanalysis has been modified by many therapists over the years.

Rational-Emotive Therapy

In contrast to psychoanalysis, this form of therapy is based on the theory that the individual has enormous control over what he both feels and does. He can also *intervene* between his environmental input and his emotional output. Here the intellectual process is stressed.

This theory, which can also be practiced as a "cognitive-emotive-behavior" therapy, teaches individuals to understand themselves and others, how to react differently, and how to change their basic personality patterns. Three things are brought to bear in getting the person to learn control over his or her emotional processes. First, the person attacks irrational beliefs by disputing them. Second, once the irrational beliefs are eliminated, at least to a degree, one is now free to *establish new* beliefs and appropriate behaviors. Third, gradually one learns control over emotional processes; this increasing control can, at least potentially, lead to personality change.

This therapy has been described as an A-B-C approach, where one begins with "C," the upsetting emotional "consequence" that the individual has recently experienced. Typically the person has been rejected in one way or another, such as not being accepted by his or her peers as he or she sees it. This is called "A" for the "activating" experience which the person wrongly believes directly causes "C," with such typical feelings as anxiousness, worthlessness, and depression. Gradually the individual learns that an activating event (A) in the outside world does not cause or create any feeling or emotional consequence (C). How then is C caused by A? The theory holds that C is really caused by an intervening variable called "B," the individual's "belief" system.

This theory relates closely to three variables conventionally used in experimental situations. First, we have the *independent* variable, the factor under experimental control to which the changes being studied are related, so named because we can change it "independently." This variable is often the stimulus. Responses which occur "depend" on these changes, and we call them the *dependent* variables under investigation. For example, let us say we are interested in knowing the relationship between the illumination of our study light and how long we can read before our eyes get tired. The light source, which can be varied in intensity, is our dependent variable. In other words, the dependent variable in the experimental situation is the "outcome" variable. But something else is involved. How we respond to the change in stimulus may relate to how sleepy we are to begin with, how interesting or boring the reading material is, and other possible factors. This makes our problem more confusing because we are now dealing with something in between. We speak of these "in betweens" as *intervening* variables. They come between the stimulus and the response, thus accounting for one response rather than another to the same stimulus. In the rational-emotive approach to personal problems, the intervening variables are our "beliefs" (B).

Behavior Therapy

A recent movement has been toward psychological treatment that involves applying the principles of learning to behavior modification. Joseph Wolpe defines this approach briefly: "Behavior therapy, or conditioning therapy, is the use of experimentally established principles of learning for the purpose of changing unadaptive behavior. Unadaptive habits are weakened and eliminated; adaptive habits are initiated and strengthened."

Behavior therapy assumes that behavior disorders which can be learned can also be unlearned, by either weakening the responses or learning new responses. For example, obese persons, who are otherwise normal, have been successfully trained to imagine that they are vomiting when they experience hunger—a way to "harness" the obvious fact that nausea removes the appetite. At the abnormal level, behavior therapy views neurosis more as a collection of bad habits that can be unlearned than as unconscious conflicts, which psycho-analysis maintains underlies neurosis. Behavior therapy emphasizes correcting disturbed behavior rather than searching for elusive causes of neurosis.

The technique in behavior modification starts with a gradual *desensitization.* By talking with his client, the therapist first determines just what stimuli bring on feelings of anxiety. For example, let us suppose that the client is fearful of flying in an airplane, presumably because he or she has learned to associate planes with accidents and death, or injury. The therapist then establishes a hierarchy of stimuli according to how much anxiety each elicits. First, the stimulus might be a plane in a magazine picture. Second, the stimulus could be a plane overhead. Third, the stimulus situation could be checking in at the flight counter; and so on until the last and most threatening stimulus, actual flight.

When the hierarchy of stimuli has been established, the therapist asks the client to lie or sit on a comfortable couch. In a soothing voice the therapist instructs the client to relax each part of the body. "Feel the tension in your left shoulder. Now begin to relax it slowly. Relax. Feel your shoulder become very limp and loose. Relax." After a period of time the client becomes totally relaxed and virtually free of tension. The therapist now instructs the client to imagine vividly the least threatening stimulus on the hierarchy while remaining calm. If this is done successfully, the therapist moves on to the next stimulus item and so on. Thus, the stimuli which the client formally paired with anxiety are *now paired with relaxation* by way of classical conditioning (see page 261). Hence, the phobic person has been "desensitized."

In closing, let us reemphasize the point that abnormal psychology offers the individual a base of comparison for understanding normal adjustments in living and work.

SUMMARY

Problems of adjustment vary in degree. At the normal level are nervousness and worry, feelings of inferiority, and defensive behaviors. At the abnormal level are the neuroses, psychoses, sexual deviations, and antisocial behaviors. Fact and fiction about mental health range widely. Among the lesser childhood and adolescent disorders are food refusal, obesity, enuresis, infantile autism, and school phobia.

Anxiety, the main characteristic of the neuroses, has a disruptive and disorganizing effect on the individual. The neurotic suffers in taking even the usual risks of life. Neurotic obsessions are persistent and repetitive intrusions of unwanted, irrational thoughts coming at inappropriate times. Neurotic compulsions show irresistible behavior patterns that may or may not grow out of obsessive thoughts.

The neurotic may block out certain parts of his life as an escape from anxiety and stress through dissociative reactions; an extreme example is the multiple personality. Through conversion reactions the neurotic transfers an emotional problem into a physical disorder. In contrast to normal depression, which arises from stress and lasts temporarily, neurotic depression may last for days or weeks. It can clear up with or without treatment, but is likely to recur.

There are two general categories of psychosis: those associated with brain damage and those without evidence of damage. Psychotic disorders show four basic things. First, the disorders are accompanied by disorientation as to time, place, and person, and by inappropriate behavior. Second, the disorders are accompanied by delusions. Third, psychoses commonly involve hallucinations. Fourth, exaggerated emotional disturbances are characteristically found among psychotic patients. The most common psychotic disorders include schizophrenia, paranoia, and manic-depressive reactions.

Sexual deviations, more than most disorders, show the line between the normal and abnormal to be blurred. They include both male and female homosexuals, transvestites, and transsexuals. Other deviations include pedophilia, bestiality, fetishism, sadism, masochism, sadomasochism, impotence, and frigidity. Prostitution is considered a form of sexual deviation different from other aberrations. And there are antisocial behaviors which range from child neglect to unsocialized aggression.

Common methods of psychotherapy include psychoanalysis, rational-emotive therapy, and behavior therapy. Abnormal psychology offers the individual a base of comparison for understanding normal adjustments in living and work.

TWO

INDIVIDUAL
DEVELOPMENT AND CHANGE

THE PRACTICAL 6
ASPECTS OF CHILD DEVELOPMENT

As the adult looks back to his childhood, hazy as it may be in many respects, two conclusions emerge. First, love is an essential ingredient in the parent-child relationship if the individual is to better his chances of good adjustment. Second, the child's development must be managed in an effective way. Children must not only be given opportunities, but they must be disciplined at times. Good upbringing does indeed involve some knowledge and planning as we try to get the individual off to a good start. That is what this chapter is all about.

Human development follows an orderly process but not a smooth one. It demands an almost constant adjustment. The newborn infant comes with well-equipped sensory mechanisms for vision, hearing, and the other sensory "inputs" which tell the infant that he or she is seeing things in the world around and hearing what the parent is saying. Feeling the warmth of milk is also an input for the infant, as is some harsh voice which may bring about a startled response, which we can think of as "output." To be sure, sensory mechanisms develop toward being able to make finer and finer discriminations, just as the motor outputs need time to mature. These outputs include not only the waving of hands and kicking of feet but also those muscular responses involved in gurgling, laughing, and crying. The inputs and outputs are coordinated by the nervous system, which matures in a well-programmed manner.

The human personality is molded by both biological predispositions and the process of socialization, such as the friendliness or coldness of those caring for the infant's needs. These "outside influences" of socialization help mold personality from the beginning. Genetic differences play a large role in developing individual differences in personality, as well as in physical characteristics. The person learns what to do and what not do do as the process of socialization takes place. These agencies of socialization change as the individual matures. The family is the first setting for socialization, followed by the influences of friends, school, church, and later the occupational group.

No subject area of human behavior relates basic science to practical, everyday problems as frequently as does child psychology. Questions range from "Does the newborn infant have a personality?" to "Should the child be spanked?" "How should sex play among children be handled?" "How can the parent help the child get rid of those 'naughty' words?" "What should be done about the timid child?" These and dozens of other questions will be dealt with in this chapter, with answers provided from literally thousands of formal studies of children and from many practical writings. For the parent and for the teacher, knowing what to expect in the growing child is helpful in coping with most of these problems. For the student, much can be learned about human behavior by watching how children grow. Since most students eventually become parents, we shall talk about problems as parents face them.

WHAT TO EXPECT

For the newborn infant "my day" falls into a sleeping-feeding-tending sequence. Around eighteen weeks of age the baby can sit up with support, and by the end of the sixth month he or she is showing some motor coordination, beginning to be a little more sociable, and expressing various emotions, such as fear, disgust, and anger. The child is now ready for the playpen.

Around the first birthday, motor behavior is moved into the "Wave bye-bye" stage, and such vocalizations as "Mama," "Dada," and "Nana" are heard. Socially the child may still be a bit shy around strangers; some temper is showing up, which will become quite noticeable in another year as the child begins to display a little more independence.

Great Explorer

The eighteen- to twenty-four-month-old is a great explorer, getting into everything and seemingly too big for a playpen. Both boys and girls are coming to understand their environment better and imitating the behavior of others. At this age the child piles blocks in a mass, later making a tower of three or four blocks. All this indicates that the child is beginning to have constructive ideas, however simple they may seem to the adult. By the time the child is three years of age, ideas sometimes outrun conventional words. In asking to be weighed, the child may get on the scales and say "pound me."

The Negative Stage

The stage of the "city manager" arrives around two to three years of age when the child is beginning to show domineering ways, alternating between temper tantrums and showing affection; shifting from exuberance to shyness, from being eager for food to rejecting it. Such *negativism* is quite normal, even though the routine includes "no-no-no" even to reasonable requests and a repertoire of biting, pulling, and hitting. Some children of this age ask for privacy on the toilet. Lingering in the bathroom can be expected.

The two-year-old has a listening vocabulary of several hundred words, which grows rapidly. "Tell me the story of so-and-so," you will hear him ask over and over again. He will detect even the slightest variations in his favorite stories. Emotional upsets are found commonly between the ages of two and three years.

Better Adjusted

It may be hard to believe, but the self-centered, negativistic child of three can grow into a child with some self-control, ready to accept suggestions and learn social conformity, and fortunately this happens within the brief span of about a year. By four years of age the child is beginning to show a sense of humor and is dramatizing events and happenings in an interesting manner. "Natural" baby talk is disappearing and will continue to drop out if not encouraged. By four years of age the child has become more cooperative and sociable in play with other children of his or her own age. Taking turns in riding the tricycle is a concept much better understood. But before one concludes that the child is now ready to settle down, just wait!

Off Again

As the child approaches the fifth birthday, he or she becomes a bundle of energy, both physically and mentally, and races here and there. Imagination is becoming extensive in scope, ideas shifting rapidly from one thing to another. Socially, boys in particular are becoming more aggressive, boasting of their abilities, being bossy at times, and "hating" everything. However, they are not returning to the stage of negativism they went through two years earlier, even though it seems so at times. The four-to-five-year-old is quite a talker, exaggerator, show-off, creator of make-believe, and user of naughty words. Number concepts are beginning to appear, and the child is becoming a little more "other-directed." Although he plays more cooperatively with others, quarrels among children of this age can be expected. He will tell you he can count from 1 to 10, but, "I can't count down a missile."

By six the child has become better "housebroken," more manageable. He or she appears to be taking things a little easier, consolidating gains made earlier. One may even detect some politeness on occasion! Although still talkative, the child speaks with more thought behind what he says. Questions center on practical matters: "What's it for?" "How does it work?" Emotionally the child is becoming better adjusted, though he or she may pick up certain fears easily. Bad dreams and nightmares are not uncommon. By the fifth or sixth birthday sex differences begin to make their appearances, boys showing interest in tools and mechanical gadgets, while girls are interested in domestic things. But these sexual differences in tastes do not arise spontaneously. Cultural influences have a bearing on interests; boys are given tools and encouraged to use them, and girls are given dolls and encouraged to play house. It is not only that our culture seems to program sex differences at an early age, but that children are reinforced in the roles they are expected to play (see page 146). Our culture even calls the little girl a tomboy if she enjoys roughhousing or shows ability in using tools. The six-year-old is becoming clever in sizing up situations and people, and in getting some understanding of self. After a week in school one boy put it this way: "I can't read, I can't write, and they won't let me talk."

Just after the sixth birthday, the child becomes temporarily rather trying. He or she is impulsive, compulsive, bossy, and full of indecision, starting projects and not finishing them, yet often pursuing activities from one day to the next. As the child approaches the seventh birthday, indecisive behavior of just a few months back begins to give way to more organization.

Back to Better Adjustment

Children of seven begin to calm down somewhat. They are a little more reflective and do not branch out into so many new adventures. One can reason with them with a fair degree of success, and they even like to please. Emotionally the seven-year-old has more control over its temper, but also has up-and-down swings of mood. Nose picking, tattling, and alibiing have become part of the behavior pattern. At seven the child is ready to take on more responsibilities.

By eight the child is "no longer a baby." The boy at this age likes to play different roles from time to time—from being a "woman hater" to utilizing the "wolf whistle." Girls are a little more realistic in understanding sex differences. Boys and girls show much the same developmental trends in behavior. The eight-year-old is a good observer. Boys and girls like to attack problems that take some effort to bring about a solution. The use of tools, sewing, and drawing interest the child at this age, but preciseness of mental and physical control is still lacking. As one psychologist stated it, "The child's level of aspiration at this stage in develoment is higher than his or her level of skill."

Some individual sex differences are quite marked in the age range from nine to ten. Each sex seems to show some contempt for the other, although when they get together, kissing is not uncommon. Both sexes are becoming more self-sufficient. They have more staying power in sticking to a task and are more positive in their likes and dislikes. The ten-year-old gives an impression of being an adult in the making, but in spite of many grown-up ways, development, both physically and psychologically, has a long way to go. Socially, girls tend to develop a little more rapidly than boys.

In some respects the best total picture of psychological development can be had by taking a look at problems related to physical habits—walking, talking, thinking, and the like. This we shall do in the following sections as we deal with some very practical questions.

EATING, SLEEPING, AND TOILET TRAINING

One might expect that such basic needs as eating, sleeping, and elimination get off to a good start in development. Unfortunately, many children develop feeding problems, and some develop undesirable sleeping and toilet habits. Both good and bad habits begin early. Where do they come from? Bad habits are acquired in the same way as good habits, for both come through learning.

Eating

One of the strongest of all drives is that of obtaining nourishment, but this in itself does not assure good habits of eating. Resorting to pressure methods of feeding may bring on difficulties. Most children, like some adults, have times when they eat little simply because they do not feel like eating. Studies have shown that parents' food dislikes are often reflected in the behavior of the child. One investigator found that among children who presented feeding problems, 47 percent of the foods disliked or refused by a member of the family were also disliked by the child. Many foods are not liked by the young child on first trial—he must learn to like them. This learning may be enhanced by giving new foods early in the meal when the child is hungry and giving them in small quantities at first. Give the baby only one new food at a time. If the mother takes a "This is good and you're going to like it" attitude, the child is more likely to think the food really is tasty.

One of the most difficult things for parents to recognize is that mealtime should not be the time when unpleasant subjects are discussed. Even too much conversation can distract the child and cause him to play with his food. But of all the "don'ts" the most important one centers on not getting the child emotionally upset at mealtime. Both appetite and digestion can be disturbed by an emotional climate.

Change in Eating Habits

One of the most noticeable changes in eating habits occurs around one year of age. During the first several months of life the infant seems always to be hungry at mealtime. About the time the child begins walking, food becomes less important and he becomes more choosy about what and how much he eats. Allow the child some choice in what he or she eats during the second year, because this seems to be the time in his life when he is beginning to have some say-so for himself. Expect changes in taste from month to month.

On the average the baby can sit up well without slumping sometime after six months of age. This is a good time to start feeding in the high chair. Not until the child is around a year to fifteen months old can he or she begin using a spoon. Using the fork comes somewhere around two to three years of age. As the child progresses from spoon to fork, table manners will improve. But even the child best trained in table manners will revert occasionally to some cruder form of eating.

Sleeping

In many respects we can think of sleep as a habit. The child used to a quiet environment may have sleep disturbed by noise. But in most homes a noiseless environment is almost impossible. As long as the child feels safe, he or she can soon learn to sleep well under any normal conditions. Taking the youngster on trips where one must sleep in a new bed each night, under different noise conditions, may be good experience.

The amount of sleep needed by children varies from individual to individual. But on the average the newborn infant sleeps about three-fourths of the time. By one year of age the average child is sleeping a little over half the time. Gradually the amount of sleep needed decreases. The average five-year-old sleeps about eleven hours. By eight years of age the child will sleep ten hours or less.

Crying out, grinding teeth, and even walking in one's sleep are not usually regarded as abnormal. These types of behavior generally occur when the child is overtired, overexcited, or puzzled about some problem. Some suggestions for developing good sleep habits are:

Maintain some regularity at bedtime.
Avoid inducing sleep by rocking or walking.
Avoid excitement before bedtime.
Let the child take some harmless toys to bed with him.
Let the child sleep alone in bed, if possible.
Don't be taken in by his or her many and varied tricks.

Toilet Training

Toilet training should be delayed until the child has matured to the point at which he or she is beginning to have some ability to restrain bowel movements and urination. Many writers say that ten months is early enough to start bowel training; bladder training may be started around fifteen to eighteen months. Training readiness is indicated when bowel movements begin to occur at about the same time each day and when the baby begins to strain. Children are ready for bladder training when they begin paying attention to the puddle made on the floor or listening to urination while waiting for a bowel movement on the toilet.

Encouragement in learning to use the toilet comes about in two ways: First, the apparent satisfaction that goes along with not messing up the diaper serves as an indirect influence in training; second, the feeling of accomplishment that goes along with the learning serves as reinforcement. But expect accidents in toilet habits as a matter of course—children often misjudge the time-distance relation back to the house!

WALKING AND OTHER MOTOR SKILLS

Crawling, creeping, walking, jumping, running, riding tricycles, using the hands and fingers in dressing and undressing, and other motor skills follow somewhat an average trend in development in all children. However, children often vary as to the ages when specific skills begin to be evidenced. Some even reverse the order in which specific performances appear, and certain children are late bloomers in development.

The development of locomotor behavior which leads to walking comes about gradually. At birth the infant cannot hold his chin up, but in about four weeks he or she can do this for brief periods of time. In the second month the chest can be raised, and at four months of age the infant can sit in an upright position if given support. The average baby can sit alone around the seventh month, and the development of this skill is followed by the ability to stand with help a few weeks later.

Walking

Walking, with some aid, follows after the period of crawling and/or creeping. The baby usually can stand alone before he or she learns to walk by himself at about fifteen months of age. Of course some babies walk much earlier than this, and some later. As a general rule, the child who is advanced in his ability to creep before ten months, as compared with the average child, will walk before fifteen months. However, some babies become so efficient in their creeping that this in itself may delay walking. Some children never creep at all, some never even crawl around on their abdomens, but just sit around until they grow enough to stand alone and, later, to walk.

A number of factors, such as weight, illness, and motivation, may play a part in determining the age of walking. If the baby is carried around much of the time or has become very efficient in creeping, his desire to learn to walk may be delayed. Can the "age of walking" be hastened through training? The practical answer is "no." Many experiments lead to this answer, most of the studies having been made on twins, with one twin receiving training and the other being left alone. Walking is one skill the child will "grow into" through maturation. The same holds true for riding behavior. Most children can easily learn to ride a kiddy car around two years of age and a tricycle about six months later.

Grasping

If you observe a child about six months of age trying to pick up a block, a peanut, or any other small object, you will most likely be impressed by his or her inability to use the fingers successfully; the object is grabbed in an awkward way with the palm of the hand. Through maturation the infant goes through stages of scooping the block in with the whole hand, followed by a crude manipulation of the fingers and thumb in grasping. It's not until the child is about one year of age that one can pick up the block with the thumb and two forefingers without resting the hand on the table. Such observations remind us that motor skills develop slowly and that we should not try to force the child to be precise in movement while growth is still playing the major role in development.

Undressing and Dressing Skills

On the average, children begin to show an interest in learning to undress themselves at about eighteen months of age. At two years the child does a rather good job of it—scattering clothes all over the place.

Dressing involves more motor coordination than does undressing, but certain parts of the process, such as slipping on shoes and holding an arm or leg for the clothing to be put on, start at about eighteen months of age. By two years of age the child can help put on his or her coat and by three the child shows interest in buttoning clothing or tying shoes, but without much success. Four-year-old children can do a rather good job of dressing with only a little help. Between five and six years of age they begin to tie shoelaces, which is, by the way, a very difficult motor skill to acquire.

EMOTIONAL BEHAVIOR

The newborn infant shows no definite emotional responses, but gradually through growth and learning, distinct forms of emotional expression appear. First comes excitement, noticed readily in the one-month-old child. By three months of age the child may exhibit delight as he or she smiles or distress when movements are hindered. A few weeks later, anger will appear as an emotion. Some mild unhappiness is usually noticed by the time the child is six months of age; some fears appear by twelve months. At two years of age the child has quite an impressive array of emotional responses: fear, anger, jealousy, distress, excitement, delight, joy, elation, affection.

Fear

Fear is produced by so many situations that we are likely to conclude that all fears are inborn or unlearned, but this is not the case. The child who is sent to bed with some threat may come to fear the dark. A child who observes a member of the family showing, or even talking about, fear of an animal may become afraid of it without having personally been frightened by the animal.

Although the baby learns most of his fears, there are a few things he will naturally be afraid of: strange and unexpected situations and objects, thunder, lightning, and sonic booms. Once babies get used to these happenings, so that they are no longer strange and unexpected, fear may cease.

There are no simple and direct rules that all parents can follow in obtaining effective emotional control over the fear of their children, but several helpful suggestions can be made. First, one should keep reminding himself that *most fears are learned.* Removing certain stimuli will prevent some fears from becoming established. Preventing disturbing associations for the child insofar as possible goes a long way toward keeping fears at a minimum. Second, it is important that the child be made to *feel secure,* free from threats, too-frequent punishments (psychological as well as physical), and sudden, unexpected situations. Third, *fear is associated with injuries,* so give the child comfort when he is hurt. This kind of comfort will not lead to spoiling. Finally, *set the child a good example,* not an example in "bravery," but the example of not exhibiting or talking of fears. It is comforting to remember that most fears, except the very severe ones, pass away with time.

Anger

Anger in most children should not be taken too seriously. As the child grows older, outbursts of anger become fewer and longer. The most common causes of anger for the first few years include restrictions of movements, interference in play activities, and direct conflict with authority. With increasing age, anger responses become more specifically directed at the obstructing person or object, frequently taking the form of fighting.

Around two to three years of age temper tantrums are rather common ways of expressing anger, and closely associated with tantrums is the negativistic behavior we spoke of earlier. *Negativism* is a form of anger in which the child refuses to cooperate, often doing the opposite of what he is told. It is so typical that psychologists regard it as normal behavior. As the child gradually learns more and more effective habits in getting along with other people, anger responses diminish. But the child who is frequently given in to when he becomes angry is likely to resort to more fits of rage because they get him what he wants.

Studies show that among parents who are tolerant with their children fewer anger responses are found than among those children of critical parents who are unreasonably concerned as to whether they are "good" or "bad." By the time the child starts to school, he or she usually learns one way or another that anger does not pay off too often. As with adults, children show anger more frequently when they are tired, in need of sleep, or overstimulated. If the general psychological climate is one in which one frustration piles upon another, anger may well erupt with the least provocation.

Jealousy

Most children show some jealousy, particularly when a new baby comes into the house. One can prevent the child's jealousy somewhat by telling him or her in advance about the new member of the family and getting the boy, for example, to feel that it is *his* baby sister. Letting him help in little ways with the care of the baby and letting him show off the new arrival give him a feeling of participation in a family project. He is less likely to feel that his psychological territory has been invaded.

Reassurance to the older child that he or she is still loved pays better dividends in decreasing jealousy than do punishments, scoldings, and reasonings. The fewer comparisons one makes between jealous children, the better. Not much "natural" jealousy comes from children over five or six years of age. Jealousy between brothers and sisters arises not so much from discrimination between them with regard to gifts and privileges as from unfairness in the general attitude of the parents toward them. The girl who claims that she didn't get as nice presents as her brother may be using this as an excuse to point out unfairness shown in more subtle ways. It is not uncommon for the child who feels insecure to set up a defense for his feelings by exhibiting jealousy against a brother or sister. It is also quite common to have a younger child jealous of an older one who has more possessions and is permitted to do more.

Sex Play

Practically all children handle their genitals at one time or another. Such behavior begins around six to eight months of age. Most children, boys in particular, around three to six years of age will masturbate somewhat. Calling attention to the activity in a direct disciplinary sort of way may only make matters worse. Getting the child interested in something else, a toy or some other activity, may lessen the problem. Children sometimes masturbate because they need to urinate, because their clothing may be irritating them, or just out of boredom and lack of anything else to do. Nervousness is not caused by masturbation, but sometimes children masturbate because they are nervous.

Sex Questions

Giving children honest answers to their sex questions, although lessening to some extent the behind-the-barn type of sex experimentation, does not mean they will not engage in some sex play among themselves.

Child psychologists offer a few suggestions that may be helpful in handling sex play among children.

1. Don't let children play alone in a closed room for long periods at a time without casually dropping by to see what they are doing.
2. When interest in what they are doing begins to lag, have some other interesting things for them to try.
3. Don't cause the child to feel that there is something mysterious about sex. Children who have their sex questions answered truthfully and within the bounds of their understanding are less likely to be secretive about sex.
4. As far as possible, try not to let children get a sense of guilt about sex.

Other Annoyances

Perhaps there is no other subject in child psychology on which there is so little agreement as there is on the question of what to do about *thumb- or finger-sucking.* Fortunately, however, most researchers agree that it is not a habit to worry about too much. Nearly every infant puts his thumb, or fingers, in his mouth. Since the child always has his thumb with him, it is natural that the thumb finds its way into the mouth. Preventing thumb-sucking from becoming a habit involves recognition that sucking behavior is natural and should be allowed to continue. Substitute something else for the infant to suck on and he may leave the thumb alone. If one can prevent thumb-sucking for the first year, the chances are it will not become a habit. Even if it gets started, most children are over the habit by four or five years of age, and usually before permanent teeth start to come through.

Nail-biting is an emotional type of response found more commonly in high-strung children. Scolding or punishing the child for biting his nails won't break the habit; in fact, it may only increase tension. It is necessary to get at the cause of tension and remove it before the habit can be broken.

Stuttering in children learning to talk is not uncommon. After all, speech is a very fine skill that has to come gradually and many little things can upset the smooth progress of acquiring it, especially when the child is in an emotionally charged environment. Let the child who stutters have plenty of time to say what he or she is attempting to say. It is wise not to interpret the child's repetition of the same words over and over again as stuttering. Most children who stutter for a time will outgrow it if their attention is not called to the stuttering. For a few the problem may be serious, requiring professional attention. Tension and anxiety are inseparable from true stuttering. Calling attention to the stuttering only increases the sense of inadequacy.

The Pleasant Emotions

We read and hear so much about fears, angers, and other emotional problems, and have so many opportunities to see them dramatized, that we tend to forget that there is another side to our emotional life. Very little is said about *joy, laughter,* and *happiness,* perhaps because these responses are rarely, if ever, problems. However, there is a great deal that both parents and teachers can do, directly and indirectly, to help develop this side of the child's emotional life.

Enjoyment of good music, the other arts, science, work, literature, social contacts, and play—all comes about through learning. Good music should not be forced on the child. Children should be given the opportunity to hear it. Releasing energy through enjoyment is one of the best ways to keep down emotional tensions that produce problems.

LANGUAGE AND UNDERSTANDING

In one sense, language begins with the birth cry of the newborn and continues to develop with such sounds as "ma-ma" and "da-da," which are sometimes proudly interpreted to mean "mama" and "daddy." In the stricter sense, however, language begins when *meaning* becomes attached to words. In this sense the baby really doesn't speak his first word until he is about a year of age, often older. At first a single word may carry a number of meanings. For example, "milk," given with varying inflections and gestures, may mean, "I want milk," "There is milk," "I spilled my milk," or "I want more milk." After a time the baby passes from the single word to phrases, such as "All gone." Finally, language develops to the stage at which ideas are conveyed by whole sentences.

Vocabulary Growth

Here are some rough estimates of the growth of spoken vocabulary in the average child:

At 12 months	3 words
At 15 months	18 words
At 18 months	22 words
At 21 months	120 words
At 2 years	275 words
At 3 years	900 words
At 4 years	1,500 words
At 5 years	2,000 words
At 6 years	2,500 words

Increase in size of vocabulary is, of course, only one aspect of the child's language development. Ability to pronounce words clearly lags far behind vocabulary growth. Not only are new words added to vocabulary, but old words become used with fuller meaning. *Listening* vocabulary grows larger and faster than *speaking* vocabulary.

Learning to Talk

Children learn a language largely through imitation. Speaking clearly and correctly to the child aids in learning good speech. Pushing the child into talking, even after he or she has some speaking vocabulary, may make him become stubbornly silent. When the child is given too much attention, when every need and whim are anticipated, talking may be delayed. Silence itself can indeed be reinforced. In cases of delayed speech, a careful study of rewards and punishments, in nonspeech matters, almost always results in improvement in speech.

It is quite common for children seemingly to drop words from their vocabulary as new words are added. It isn't so much that they forget the words as it is that a change in the need for using certain words comes with increasing age. The preschool child (and exceptions are few) seems to take on those words which to the adult may seem useless. When the child gets into the second or third grade of school, bad language increases, particularly in boys. Fortunately, children grow out of these habits as they grow out of bad manners, which they will pick up somewhere between six and eight years of age. Our culture seems to be one that expects girls to have better language habits than boys.

Understanding

By the time a child is three years old, his sensory perceptions are well organized. Some children can give good descriptions of what they perceive, feel, and understand. Experience with concrete situations is an essential aspect of the early development of understanding in the child. Such experiences are often used in describing related events. For example, when the "crazy bone" of a three-year-old was stimulated for the first time, the child described the tingling sensation as "My fingers are singing." Apparently the child perceived a relationship between the nerve sensation, a new experience, and auditory perception, which had familiarity and therefore was meaningful. Another described the perception as feeling like ginger ale. When his foot went to sleep, one five-year-old said, "My foot is fizzing."

One of the most difficult concepts for a child to grasp is that of *time*. Since time is a relatively abstract concept, this is to be expected. For the five-year-old a favorite TV program may have meaning in terms of "late afternoon" or "after dinner." The average child is seven to eight years of age before he or she can tell time on a clock to the quarter hour, and the concept of "month" or "year" comes even later.

Thinking

The thinking of children is not unlike the problem-solving process of the adult. It is natural that children should confuse the real with the imaginative and should fail to see certain cause-and-effect relationships in the manner of the adult. A child may say, "Clouds are alive because they move," or he may have the idea that thinking is done with the mouth.

Much of the mental life of the preschool-age child is based on make-believe activities which, as a mode of early adjustment, allow him to carry on thinking without much effort. In the growth of understanding, make-believe, fantasies, and other imaginative activities play a significant role. Around four to five years of age imagination reaches a peak. Fantasies may serve the child as escape (just as they sometimes do for adults), or they may provide the basis for constructive ideas. Out of childhood make-believe come useful habits of thinking. Through fantasy the child is also provided with a good means of emotional release. As far as five-year-olds are concerned, they are not lying when they say that they were chased by a bear. If a child turns out to be a liar, it will be for reasons other than early understanding through make-believe!

ABILITIES, INTERESTS, AND PLAY

General mental ability, mechanical ability, ability in music, and other psychological characteristics are found to conform to the same principle of distribution as do physical traits.

General Mental Ability

We hear much about the IQ (intelligence quotient) score which is a measure that allows us to compare any one child with all other children, regardless of chronological age. It is important not to get too enthusiastic or too depressed when you first learn the score of your child. The teacher or psychologist can explain both the advantages and the limitations of tests and test scores. Present-day psychologists and other professionals are giving some new critical attention to methods of testing, IQ testing included, while beginning to pay more attention to processes in intellectual development. While one child may possess the mental equipment necessary for responding to conventional test situations, another may find himself behind in responding. Another may be very good at response and thus may seem more intelligent. Even slowness in muscular development may make a child appear inferior when in fact his mental prowess is quite keen.

Modern school practices give particular attention to school readiness, grade placement, and curriculum modification, emphasizing the individual and his particular rate of development. Psychologists are now giving more attention to the environmental aspects of intelligence. We now know that the standard IQ tests, which are geared to the culture of the middle-class child, can actually penalize bright children from a ghetto culture. Language barriers, often found among Puerto Rican and Chicano children, add to the problem of intelligence testing. The failure to perform on some test may be due to a lack of expressive capacity rather than lack of general ability. How the child approaches some test item or problem relates to the kind of competence highly regarded in the child's particular culture. When children are compared within a given subculture, the tests may prove useful. It has been found, for example, that some children in Nigeria score very high on general intelligence tests when the items are relevant to their local culture. It is certainly safe to say that no ethnic origin, no culture, and no part of the world has a monopoly on intellectual ability or special talent. Intellectual ability is found to be universal when we define intelligence as the ability to acquire new information, to profit from experience, to adjust to new situations, and to adjust to one's own cultural climate. Intelligence is the aggregate of all the learning experiences of any individual. We get a useful view of intelligence as we observe a sample of mental growth in children.

As an illustration of the nature of mental growth, let us consider the development of the ability to generalize and recognize abstract ideas. The ages and accompanying descriptions are of the average child in a middle-class North American culture.

At the age of three and one-half years the child can identify the *longer* of two sticks or the *larger* of two balls. (Length and size are abstract ideas, although for us adults these ideas are so simple that we may forget they are abstractions.) At four years of age the child can point to the longer of two lines drawn on paper, thus using the same concept in a more abstract setting. At four and one-half years he or she can select drawings of faces as *pretty* or *not pretty*. At five children can distinguish between *heavy* and *light*. By six years of age the child can tell the *difference in composition* between two objects, such as wood and glass. Not, however, until the average child is seven years old can he or she describe the *similarity* of two objects, such as a peach and a pear.

Many research studies made on the nature of mental growth have given us answers to a number of practical questions. They indicate, for example, that superior children grow at a more rapid rate throughout the growing period of their mental development, continue to develop for a longer time, and reach a higher level at maturity. Children of high intelligence generally excel in school achievement. They have a wider range of interests, do well in sports, read more books, and are better adjusted emotionally than the average. Long-range studies show that they are highly successful in later life. Of course, some individuals of superior intelligence run into problems as children, and others do as adults.

In contrast to the mentally bright children and those of average intelligence, we find the mentally handicapped children. Many slow children can be directed through proper home handling and schooling to make satisfactory adjustments to life. Since this is a problem requiring special attention, we offer no advice here. Suffice it to say, however, that with proper training these children can acquire a number of important skills.

Special Abilities

In addition to general mental ability, children often exhibit special abilities. Through aptitude tests we are able to measure potentials in the arts, mechanical skills, and other special talents (see Chapter 9). Interests are important in developing abilities.

One reason we find so many individual differences in interests is that we all have individual differences in abilities. Children change their interests for much the same reasons that adults do, although they change more often. Whereas adults soon get set in their ways and follow through on their interests routinely, children are bombarded with so many changes in their environment, so many new acquisitions of skills, and so many opportunities for trying out new activities that they show many shifts in their interests.

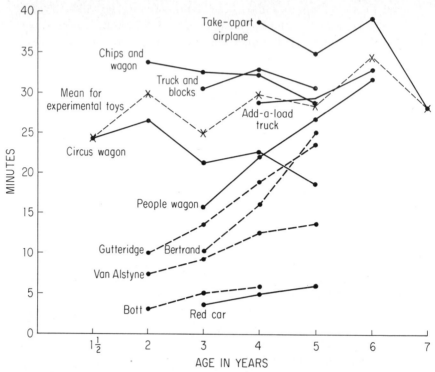

FIG. 6-1 Results of five studies with more than 900 boys and girls dealing with how long children concentrate in play with toys. The dashed curves show the results of the researches of four experimenters using toys available on the market. The solid lines show toys designed and redesigned to meet needs at different ages. Toys ranged from a very simple "red car" to a complicated "take-apart airplane." Some toys decline in interest with age ("chips and wagon"), while others gain in interest ("people wagon").

Play

We characteristically associate toys with play. Toys date back to 3,000 B.C.with dolls and miniature carts found in the ruins of ancient cities. Toys offer the opportunity for the child to respond to his or her environment and, in an elementary way, to act out feelings toward that environment.

     Many interests are developed through play. Whether it be playing with rattles, blocks, or dolls, pretending to be a cowboy or an astronaut, learning to jump rope, or making mud pies, playing is more than just fun; it is "work" for the child. Through the study of attention spans in children we know that play also satisfies needs. Figure 6-1 shows the tendency for attention spans of children at play to increase with age. The increase, however, is not regular. Also, a toy that may be a good attention holder for a two-year-old declines in its appeal as the child grows older. Some toys, of course, are beyond the age range of the child.

Every good toy should contribute to the mental, physical, and aesthetic development of the child. Toys should be selected for *child appeal* rather than parent appeal. Thus the three-year-old may play with a given toy for a certain amount of time, the four-year-old for a longer period of time, and the five-year-old for the longest period of time. If when the child is six years of age the toy has lost its appeal, then it is no longer satisfying a need. The closer a toy comes to satisfying the particular needs of the child, the higher will be the play value of the toy. The length of time children will concentrate in play depends on the selection of the right toy for the right age.

SOCIAL DEVELOPMENT

A few years ago a study was made of the personnel records of seventy-six companies to find out why they had fired some four thousand of their white-collar workers. The reasons given varied, of course, from individual to individual, but when all the cases were analyzed, two main categories stood out: "lack of competence in their jobs" and "inability to get along with other people." Even more surprising was the relative number of persons fired for one or the other of these reasons. Those let go for lack of competence totaled about 11 percent, while *some 89 percent* lost their jobs because of inability to get along with other people.

Development of Social Responses

One study illustrates how individual social behavior may be acquired indirectly through the influences of the environment. An experimental comparison was made between the social responses of children who were organized into "autocratic" and "democratic" clubs. As time went on, the children who were treated in a rather dictatorial way exhibited more aggressive domination in their relations with one another and showed less give-and-take than did those subjects who lived in the more democratic climate. Individual expressions of resistance, hostility, demands for attention, and competition were more than twice as frequent in the authoritarian group. The children in this autocratic group were less spontaneous and friendly in their relations with their adult leader than were those in the permissive club.

When children join a social group they *take into the situation* many attitudes and habits which they have learned at home. These may be such as to reinforce the habits acquired outside the home, or they may come in conflict with them.

The boy becomes noticeably more social as he grows older and at the same time becomes more independent. He must learn a balance between these two, must learn to share his toys, yet at the same time not be taken advantage of. He must learn some reserve, yet avoid becoming timid. He must learn cooperation, yet be able to carry on an activity by himself. He must learn to respect the rights of others, yet not develop a submissive attitude. He must learn to resolve his own conflicts, yet avoid overaggressiveness. This is a tightrope hard to walk. Girls often mature in social responses more rapidly than boys.

Friends

One way in which parents can help the child to have friends is to give him or her a chance to be with other children around their own age. Selfishness among young children comes naturally, cooperation gradually. There may be many reasons why a child fails to make friends. It may be that some of these questions are related to the problem: Is he a "mama's darling"? Have the parents prohibited his noisy friends from coming around? Was she pushed too hard into being sociable? Good teachers recognize that often an unpopular, sometimes lonely child has to be worked into a group activity where he or she can warm up to the situation. The lonely child has a hard time expressing why he or she is lonely. This is also true of some adults. One person put it this way: "I feel most alone when I am misunderstood."

By the age of two years children may begin to show preferences in friends among several children, and a year or so later strong attachments between two children may be noticed. Such attachments may last only a few days or weeks, or they may last for years. Some companionships may become so close among two or three children as to limit the widening of their social contacts.

Quarrels among children are frequent, and so are aggressiveness, teasing, bad manners, and impoliteness. These types of behavior, however, rarely have a long-term bad effect on social development. In contrast, prejudice instilled in the young may restrict opportunities later.

Leadership

Leadership differences may be noticed in children even at the preschool age. There are no set rules for helping the child develop leadership.

Several children who are leaders may differ markedly. One child may become a leader because he or she gets around, is constructively aggressive, or is resourceful in ideas for play. Another may have the knack of running things behind the scenes while the other persons feel important. A child may be a leader in one situation and a follower in another. It is not always the child who makes the big splash that leads the group. Behind him or her may be the idea child, quiet and mild.

Development of Values

In some respects the values the child acquires are imposed on him, and often they come in indirect ways. Some come from parents, some from school situations, and some from one's peers. Values also relate to identification and to social class determinants. Goal setting relates to our value system. For example, a child raised in a middle-class home, where self-sacrifice and long-range educational planning are part of the environment, is likely to be motivated by these values. In such a home, self-discipline is taught and an effort is made to subdue immediate gratifications. The person growing up in this climate strives to learn the appropriate social as well as technical skills and struggles for improvement. When achivement is a dominant goal, failure is an ever-present threat.

In contrast, a child growing up in a poor environment may be deprived not only of material possessions, education, and opportunity, but of other values that relate to goal seeking. The person who is guided by middle-class values may find it difficult to understand or even communicate with those whose values differ markedly. But it is characteristic that some children, as well as adolescents and adults, revolt against their original class value structures.

The feelings, attitudes, strivings, and even complacencies of many adults are more easily understood when we look into their backgrounds for determinants of values. There is considerable difference in values between those who have a background of struggle against poverty and those raised in affluence. One of the problems in subcultures where there has been laxity of parental control is that the individual may evade, try to destroy, or make a game out of control exercised by others, particularly by legal authorities. The standards of success or failure set by any given adult may well be traced to values learned in childhood. It should also be noted that a child or young person may have good intelligence, even special abilities, and still function within a value system that decreases motivation for achievement. We sometimes see this in college, where attending class on a regular basis and doing the required work may not be part of one's habit structure.

THE GROWTH OF PERSONALITY

When we think in terms of personality growth, we may find it useful to break behavior down into reactions of dominance, indifference, submission, self-confidence, inferiority, sociability, and the like. The big job involves understanding the integration of habits, skills, interests, abilities, emotions, and perceptions into a whole concept we call "personality" (see Chapter 3). How does it grow?

The shy, timid child is heading more in the direction of becoming too self-centered than in the direction of sociability. It is doubtful if an introverted child can be transformed into an extrovert, and it would perhaps be undesirable to attempt such a transformation. However, children who seem to be headed toward withdrawal can be helped by being given more opportunities to be with other children of their own age, size, and abilities. The more studious type of child may be encouraged to get out and develop interests that will involve cooperation with others. The socially minded child may be encouraged to settle down more to schoolwork.

Children raised in a family in which the parents are aggressive, autocratic, and hard-headed may take on dominance instead of becoming submissive as one might expect. Submissive persons may have many creative qualities and they may be well adjusted and easier to get along with than the upward-mobile person. Research on the past lives of people who have shown extreme tendencies of submission show that related causes may include physical defects, real or imagined; unfavorable comparisons with other persons; friction in the home; ridicule by others; lack of opportunities to learn; and rigid parental discipline. Among the causes of dominance, investigators have found such contributing factors as early assumption of responsibility; parental training; absence of discipline in the home; superior mental or physical ability; and some unusual skill, frequently in athletics.

Self-Confidence

Another way to come to understand the nature of personality traits and how they grow is to pick a very desirable trait and see how it can be destroyed. For this we shall use self-confidence. How many of the dozen questions below would you say are involved? Here let us address the parents.

1. Are you babying the child rather than encouraging him or her to do things on his or her own?
2. Are you making the home climate tense rather than relaxed?
3. Are you expressing more disapproval than praise?
4. Are you pushing the child beyond his abilities rather than realizing his limitations?
5. Are you aloof rather than friendly toward the child?
6. Are you riding the child on weaknesses rather than trying to correct them?
7. Are you holding up a superior child as an example rather than comparing the child to someone nearer his or her own abilities?
8. Are you demanding perfection rather than showing tolerance?

9. Are you providing the child with unnecessary worries rather than making the child feel secure?
10. Are you setting an "I can't" example rather than exhibiting self-sufficiency yourself?
11. Are you overprotecting the child rather than teaching him or her responsibility?
12. Are you telling the child to withdraw from situations one should be made to face?

To illustrate a positive approach let us show how parents can help the child develop *self-confidence in problem solving.*

1. Be sure that the problems are within range of the child's abilities at any particular growth level.
2. It is well to let the child work on only one big problem at a time. Several coming all at once lead to frustration.
3. Be patient; solving problems takes a lot of trial and error. A part of this process involves learning what *not* to do.
4. Be cautious in judging the child's accomplishments in terms of adult standards. Expect the child to regress in the ability to solve problems.
5. Don't get in the habit of solving problems for the child.
6. See that the child receives reinforcement when problems are solved.

It may be beneficial to remember that practical child psychology deals with essentially all the *kinds* of problems we face as adults. In biological development, time is on the side of the organism, but in psychological growth time always seems to be running out.

SOME SHORT-ANSWER GUIDES

Many books have been written about practical child psychology in terms of answers to practical questions. The description already given in this chapter deals with the more general questions of interest to parents and teachers. Let us here add some others, bearing in mind that many pages can and have been written on each of them.

When does the infant smile at me?
There are two kinds of smiles, the "reflex" smile and the "social" smile. The first may be noticed at birth, the latter in about six weeks.
Should the child be cuddled?
Yes. Most parents naturally do not go to extremes in showing affection.
Does the newborn child have a personality all his own?

Yes. Some are placid and serene, while others are more or less restless.

When does the child begin to learn?

He or she is ready to start learning at birth.

When does the child begin to make choices in eating?

About the second year. When children lose interest in food, take them out of the high chair and forget about feeding until the next meal.

Should the sleeping child be awakened to be played with?

No.

Should the baby be rocked or sung to sleep?

No harm can come of this other than it will become an expected habit. Rocking or singing can soon become reinforcers (see page 335).

Can the child be put to bed too hurriedly?

Yes, hurry and excitement delay the onset of sleep.

Should the child be put to bed with toys?

One favorite soft bear or doll—or blanket.

Is training necessary to get the child to stay dry at night?

As the child matures, the bladder will gradually "train itself."

How can toilet training and other habits be affected by physical illness?

Temporary regressions are not uncommon even in the healthiest of children.

When should the baby be put into a playpen?

Around three or four months of age. When the baby learns to walk alone, it will "want out."

Are mechanical baby walkers advisable?

No.

When is telling the child "no" necessary?

When the child is good at walking and has developed some skill at using the hands, a few "no's" are necessary to prevent accidents.

Can the three-year-old be trusted not to run into the streets?

No.

Should we expect the child to be awkward while learning new motor skills?

Yes. Be patient. Feelings of confidence and satisfaction go along with achieving something new. And remember, some skills develop late.

When does handedness begin to show up?

Whether the infant is going to be right-handed or left-handed, or in some cases ambidextrous, cannot be determined for several months after birth. Some children do not settle down for four or five years.

Is the left-handed child really handicapped?

No, the southpaw soon becomes adjusted to the right-handed world.

Should you try to influence the child's handedness?

Let the child determine which hand he or she prefers. It takes time for dominance to show up, a time that varies from child to child.

Should children be taught rhythmic dancing?

Yes. It helps the development of motor skills, self-confidence, and social poise.

Will the child slip back at times in the development of motor skills?

Backsliding in sports, art, language, and other skills can be expected.

How can the child learn not to fear lightning?

Sit with the child by the window while a storm is going on.

How can fear of the dentist be prevented?

Start casual visits to the dentist early, before any work needs to be done. Two to three years of age is not too early.

Can the child learn caution without fear?

The child should learn caution in crossing streets, approaching strange animals, and keeping away from open fires, not fear of these things. Safe experimentation makes the child more, rather than less, cautious.

Should the child be spanked?

There is little agreement from authors on the "yes" or "no" of this. They do agree generally that children learn to behave well not through threats and punishment, but through respect.

How can parents help the child learn to talk?

Children pick up words from us, so we should speak correctly and clearly.

What things may delay early talking?

Coaxing, lack of patience, anticipating every wish, and too much attention.

Should "baby talk" be encouraged?

No. It may seem cute, but will soon become a social handicap for the boy or girl.

Can children learn two languages at the same time?

Yes. There are some advantages in being able to understand and speak more than one language. Getting mixed up can be expected.

Do children project their feelings through make-believe?

This is quite common in preschool children. It provides some insight into the child's thinking and feeling.

Should the child be told the truth about Santa Claus?

Yes, after the make-believe stage is over. The child usually gets wise about the seventh or eighth year.

Is it normal for the child to have a hard time paying attention?

Yes. Averages show three-year-olds show sustained attention for *eight* seconds, five-year-olds for *seventeen,* and six-year-olds for *twenty-eight* seconds. But when needs are being satisfied, attention span can expand. See Figure 6-1 (page 136).

Why do children ask so many questions?

Out of curiosity, to establish social contact, to get attention, to show resistance, to learn the "what," the "why," and the "when."

When should the child be given an intelligence test?

Many authorities say to wait until the child is at least three years of age.

Who should give the child an intelligence test?

Only a competently trained person. Ask a counselor for advice.

How can parents help the child develop ability at problem solving?

1. Keep problems within the range of the child's abilities.
2. Let the child work on one problem at a time.
3. Be patient. Problem solving involves trial and error, and this takes time.
4. Be cautious in judging accomplishments by adult standards.
5. Do not solve the child's problems for him too often.
6. Analyze *your* problem-solving habits.

What can we predict about interests?

Children change their interests for much the same reasons that adults do, but more often. Interests run along with the development of abilities and with repeated exposure to things.

What can be done when interest lags?

1. Show enthusiasm yourself.
2. Don't press the irritable or tired child.
3. Participation stimulates interest.
4. Give help in getting over snags.
5. Encourage "helping" you.

What should be done about laziness?

Most children (and adults) are lazy from time to time. If laziness seems a way of life, then ask these questions:

1. Is the child bored?
2. Is the child daydreaming excessively?
3. Is the child happy?
4. Is the child being disciplined the wrong way?
5. Is the child trying to cope with too many problems?
6. Is the child in good physical condition?
7. Are you supplying motivation correctly?

Such questions often lead to a *cause* that may be corrected.

Should boys and girls be encouraged to play together?

This is something that takes care of itself—at all ages!

Should the child play alone?

Yes, at times. We must learn to live with ourselves as well as with others.

What are some arguments as to why the child should have a pet?

1. A dog, cat, or other animal provides something alive that is more nearly the child's own size.

2. Helps teach responsibility.
3. Gets used to animals.
4. The child learns some caution, some give-and-take with a safe animal.
5. The child learns something about giving as well as receiving affection.
6. A well-trained dog can be a protection.
7. Children often become interested in nature through pets.
8. Provides companionship.

How can interest in good music be fostered?

By listening to it.

Should the child read comics?

Yes. The good ones help motivate reading.

Should the child be teased?

"Kidded," yes; "teased," no.

Does the child sometimes regress in his manners?

Yes. Children have their ups and downs, but eventually training takes over.

Does generosity come naturally?

Generosity must be learned gradually. Sometimes the child swings a bit far in giving things away, but he soon learns where sharing leaves off and give-and-take begins.

Is nursery school or kindergarten necessary for the child?

It is helpful for the child, but not necessary if he or she has children his own age to be with.

Are there individual differences in adjusting to school?

Yes. Children vary greatly in this, and for many different reasons; the chief factor involved is their degree of independence.

Is the "only" child at a disadvantage?

Not really if there are other children in the neighborhood.

What about feelings of security in the adopted child?

All the principles of good child psychology relative to raising your "own" child apply to the adopted child. There is no special age at which the child should be told that he is adopted, but he should be told, preferably as soon as he is capable of understanding.

When the young child takes things, should this be interpreted as stealing?

Children two to three years old will take things that do not belong to them. This can hardly be called stealing. The idea of property rights is not clear to the young child.

What should you do about stealing in the child who knows better?

Again we suggest trying to get at the cause:

1. Is the child lonesome?
2. Is the child using the money to buy friendship?

3. Is the child jealous?
4. Is the child seeking revenge?
5. Is it a defense against insecurity?
6. Does the child want special attention?
7. Is the child getting some kind of approval—satisfaction from his gang?
8. Is there some kind of emotional frustration which is not coming to the surface?
9. Do *you* have "hotel towels" at home?

What are some basic summary principles in raising children?
1. Give the child every chance at good health.
2. Help the child learn to solve his own problems under proper guidance and discipline.
3. Give the child a chance to become adjusted to one situation before thrusting him or her into the middle of another.
4. Be constant enough in your behavior to let the child know what to expect from you.
5. Stay emotionally well adjusted yourself.
6. Keep the home situation as free from quarrels and conflicts as possible.
7. Hold on to that sense of humor.
8. Try to enjoy the child instead of thinking of him as a problem.
9. Be friendly with the child.
10. Have patience!

And remember—when you feel that it is the child who is the problem, it may be well to consider that the problem might be elsewhere.

An Orderly Sequence

Children follow an orderly sequence in development. Some are more rapid in motor development and slower in verbal development. The reverse is true in other children. Some are slower in all steps of development, and others develop rapidly step by step. There is a wide range of individual differences in growing up. No child is exactly like another. It is difficult to compare unlikes. Sequential development is the same, but growth does not necessarily proceed at the same rate at any given time. Understanding these generalizations is helpful in answering many practical questions.

Raising Boys and Girls—A Cultural Difference

Our North American culture decrees that a girl can seek affection, but a boy is discouraged from doing so. If he seeks help, he is a sissy. One college counselor put it this way, "The girls from the women's college come into the office with their problems, and sometimes cry. The boys come in and fight against revealing their feelings, and this slows down the problem-solving process." The roles we play affect these differences (see page 122).

In our culture girls may shed tears. This is even expected. They may let off steam in ways that are denied to boys. A father tells his son, "Don't cry," "Get up, be a man," "There is nothing to be afraid of." When little sister is afraid, she is soothed. We hear the parent say, "She can ride as well as a boy," but rarely do we hear, "My boy can cook as well as a girl."

The press for masculinity often begins before it has any real meaning. Many fathers (not all) equate roughness and toughness with being a male. Often boys are called upon to prove their masculinity in athletics, even fighting, whether or not they are so inclined.

In their earlier years boys spend most of their time in a woman's world. In the home and in the school women set their standards ("Be nice, like your sister"). These standards sometimes conflict with those that prevail in the man's world; yet the father says raising children is a mother's job.

Boys, as well as girls, need reassurance in the trials and tribulations of growing up. Girls get reassurance from Mother, but often boys do not get if from Father. A father should try to involve his son in some of his activities. Just having the son near him assures the boy of his father's affection. Problems in adolescents sometimes can be traced to early boyhood in which the child felt father rejection. In our culture living in a man's world does not come so readily for the boy as living in a woman's world does for the young girl. But she too soon runs into conflict as to her role in our changing culture.

SUMMARY

Human development follows an orderly process but not a smooth one. Personality is molded by both biological predispositions and by agents of socialization. Child watchers find that managing the developing child can be facilitated by knowing what to expect at different stages of development. We find the negative stage around two to three years, phasing into a better adjusted stage at four and back to an off-and-on hyperenergy stage at seven. Individual sex differences are marked by age nine or ten.

Both good and bad habits begin early, many centering on eating, sleeping, and toilet training. How these problems can be managed relates closely to the basic principles of learning. There are individual differences even in the motor skills—crawling, creeping, walking, jumping, running, riding tricycles, and using the hands and fingers in dressing and undressing.

Emotional development follows a pattern from the general to the specific; from general excitement to the specifics of fear, anger, and jealousy. Sex play and sex questions develop gradually and predictably. Annoyances, such as thumb-sucking, nail-biting, and sometimes stuttering occur as if programmed. Releasing energy through the pleasant emotions comes gradually but less noticeably.

Language begins when meaning becomes attached to words; learning a language comes largely through imitation. Understanding comes gradually as the child deals with concrete situations. So does ability in thinking, which is not unlike the problem-solving process found in the adult.

General mental ability, mechanical ability, ability in music, and various psychological characteristics conform to the same principles of development as in the more noticeable physical traits. Currently schools are giving more attention, at least in theory, to problems of school readiness, grade placement, and curriculum modification to emphasize individual rate of development.

Interests at play are receiving attention in research centering on need satisfaction at different development stages. Studies emphasize how social behavior may be acquired indirectly through environmental influences. Values often develop in indirect ways and relate to identification and to social class determinants.

At center stage in the growth of personality is the development of self-confidence, which is understandable and to a large extent manageable as children follow an orderly sequence of development. Some children are more rapid in motor development and slower in verbal development; others show the reverse. There is a wide range of individual differences in growing up.

CHAPTER 7

ADJUSTMENT PROBLEMS OF ADOLESCENCE

In adolescence the problems of identity begin to emerge strongly, and it is not uncommon for the adolescent to become something of a rebel. Adolescence is a stage of conflict between dependence and independence in which it is difficult to reconcile a world that "ought to be" with the world "as is." It is also a time of positive growth, however erratic it may seem to the adult. Adolescence is more than just childhood extended. It may be described negatively as the "un" stage—*unbalanced, unstable,* and *unpredictable.* It may also be described positively as a time when a low threshold for boredom is counteracted by an even lower threshold for stimulation; it takes very little to ignore adolescent enthusiasm. Adolescence is a period of transition between childhood and adulthood, a time when a few bad decisions can lead to delinquency or a few lucky breaks to a good start in working toward a future.

Adolescence extends from the time preceding sexual maturity to the age of independence. For boys, who mature somewhat later than girls, we regard preadolescence as the period roughly from ten to thirteen years of age, early adolescence from thirteen to seventeen, and late adolescence from eighteen to twenty-one. For girls, preadolescence falls between ten and eleven, early adolescence from twelve to sixteen, and late adolescence from seventeen to twenty-one. It is, of course, somewhat arbitrary that we separate adolescence from early youth. In reality, some adolescents are more mature than some older people.

SOME PROBLEM AREAS OF ADOLESCENCE

The following comment indicates some of the problems faced by adolescents: "I think of myself in relation to others, how I stand up by comparison. I may put on a show of self-confidence, but it's only a cover-up. Everywhere I face nothing but competition—from my classmates, my teachers, and my parents."

What are some of the problems of the adolescent and early youth? Before we turn to studies, let us give a sample of what some people say about themselves:

"I am concerned about physical attractiveness."
"I want to wear the right clothes."
"I dread making a decision."
"I am lost with time on my hands."
"I want to be different, but not too different."
"I am unhappy with my name."
"I have conflicts about premarital sex."
"I worry about what is real love."

"I wonder what is involved in living together without marriage."
"I frequently distrust adults."
"I sometimes think about running away from home."
"I worry about venereal disease."
"I worry about those arguments at home."
"I even have thoughts about suicide."
"I seem to drift without planning."
"I am concerned with learning too much too soon."
"I am worried about experience coming at too high a price."
"I wonder what will happen if I drift without motivation."

We do not have specific answers to many of these questions, but we do feel it may be useful to talk about some of the things we do know from studies and from counseling experiences. We shall cover areas that range from "square" to "risk taking" and try to provide some ways of thinking about the conflicting problems of adolescence and the more positive aspects of youth, in spite of the many negative things that get in our way.

Maturity

For the teen-ager, maturity has the advantages of freedom—a chance to bring aspirations in line with ability—and an increased feeling of security. The disadvantages are that one is held accountable for his or her behavior, that one is alone in an unfriendly world, and that there is little guidance from others.

Intellectual maturity, growing strongly between sixteen and twenty-five years of age, is indicated by such behavior as making up one's own mind, taking responsibility, and learning the difference between compromise, rigidity, and mindless conformity.

Social maturity is sort of "psychological weaning," with no clear-cut ages defined. It is indicated by such behavior as self-reliance, examination of prejudices, and the ability to amuse oneself. It also involves freedom from conformity to fads.

Emotional maturity also has no age boundaries. Some adults never get beyond adolescence. Among the indicators of growing up emotionally are the ability to adjust to stress, become selective in what to worry about, and discover harmless ways of letting off steam.

Mature adult morality is stable. It does not vary with the environment and is indicated by tolerance, understanding, and adjustment to rules and laws. The teen-ager wants this kind of morality also, *but now.* Adolescent morals are often lofty, often idealistic. The teen-ager wants to solve the world's problems overnight. He or she typically responds to problem situations by saying, "It's not fair."

The adolescent is puzzled by what he or she sees as changing moral standards—sexual revolutions versus old-fashioned morals. Something about the life of swinging singles bothers both males and females. One university reports that freshmen chose in large numbers to live in a co-ed dormitory, but before the year was over, they asked for rooms in dorms separating the sexes. One senior dorm counselor says: "As I see them mature, their attitudes become a little more conservative."

Academic maturity comes slowly. One finds both the "under-achievers," whose performance falls below their potential, and the "overachievers," who exceed expectation. Many of the problems of dropouts center on failure to reach academic maturity—failure that can be overcome in the right climate. Basically, however, there is no "normal" age range for attaining academic maturity.

EMOTIONAL BEHAVIOR

Emotionally the adolescent is more of a problem to himself than to others. He or she faces new roles faster than they can adjust to old ones. It is important in understanding the development of human behavior to realize that most of these emotional problems are *normal* in the statistical sense.

There is a marked *sex difference* in both interests and problems in early adolescence. Girls, maturing more rapidly, have more problems than boys. They are more concerned with school, family, and social adjustments, and with personal appearance. Boys are more concerned with money problems and career planning. Both groups increasingly become concerned with emotional problems, particularly those who were unsuccessful in dealing with childhood problems. Older adolescents are often concerned with problems related to getting into college, and once in, staying there. Some wonder if they should go to college at all, or whether they should combine college with work, a growing practice in our changing culture.

Normal Emotional Expression

Normal adolescent emotions differ from those of childhood and adulthood in many ways.

1. Emotional responses are often intense and out of control. The adolescent gives way to feelings of the moment. He or she reacts out of proportion to the reason for the behavior.
2. Responses shift rapidly from one extreme to the other—from joy, pride, and hope to despair and gloom, from self-confidence to self-destruction, from success to failure and back.
3. There is a lack of control at times. Typically girls weep or giggle; boys grin or become silent.

4. Moods become drawn out in duration. When outward expressions are inhibited, moods take over. Emotional feelings seem to get bottled up inside, where they may smolder for days.
5. Oversentimentality is characteristic of teen-age emotions—for school, for family, and for peer groups.
6. Steam is let off in the wrong places and at the wrong times.
7. In contrast to many of the outward expressions of emotion, the adolescent keeps some things quiet. For example, feelings of possessiveness may not always be shown as open protection of territory (see page 36), but some things are hidden away—candy and other food, and even unusable prize possessions of no real value. Secretiveness is characteristic of the adolescent.

Nervous Habits

At puberty there is likely to be an increase in nail-biting. This nervous behavior decreases as the adolescent becomes more conscious of his appearance. Substitutes, such as finger tapping, hair twisting, or cigarette smoking, arise. Nervousness in girls may take the form of giggling or overreacting to mild stimuli; such behavior usually lessens after puberty. Boys tend to display exaggerated behavior in such acts as "burning rubber off the tires."

The nervous habits of adolescent college students have been studied extensively. One may conclude that worries, shifts in mood, and the more acceptable emotional feelings take over from earlier overt emotional expressions. The college freshman must deal not only with old nervous habits, such as nail-biting, but habits of thought as well. Moods of exhilaration and depression alternate, varying with environmental influences (the big weekend versus examination periods).

Research indicates that increased emotionality, and the many habits which are displayed during adolescence are attributable mainly to social factors. Chief among these are unfavorable family relationships, restraints imposed by parents, and situations in which the individual feels inadequate and where expectations of mature behavior exceed actual performance. For the college freshman, coming to understand and learning to cope with a new psychological climate is especially difficult. Once he or she learns more about "the system," nervousness decreases considerably.

Fear and Worry

One observer put it this way: "Adolescents have the same worries and fears as adults, only more so." Possibly one reason why we hear so much about teen-agers' fears of social relationships is that they are more likely to talk about their feelings than they are to analyze fear itself.

Social fears include such situations as meeting people, being alone, being in a crowd, reciting in class, making a speech, or dealing with members of the other sex. Excessive self-consciousness makes the teen-ager easily embarrassed if he or she is teased about someone of the opposite sex, or if he or she is observed in clothing not like that of the group. The male overemphasizes status; such overemphasis may even lead to delinquency. The female appears more at ease in mixed gatherings.

Shyness in adolescents reaches a peak around fifteen years of age. It is often prolonged and intensified if the individual is forced into situations in which he has to display a weakness. By the time the adolescent is in college, he or she has acquired enough skill to make a good appearance, and hence fears decline. It is at this stage that worry, the mental counterpart of fear, increases. Most worries center on anticipated situations, clustering around schoolwork, feelings of inferiority, and loss of prestige. In addition, there are worries about conforming to changing cultural patterns. Says one counselor: "In their quieter, more reflective moments many adolescents really fear to try the new in social relationships, although it appears on the surface to be the in thing to do."

Adolescents worry about prejudices, the degree of worry reflecting the amount by which one is hurt. One study found that black and white adolescents have essentially the same types of worries, but blacks show more defensive behaviors and make more conscious attempts to appear adequate. Blacks show more of a tendency to withdraw from social contacts in integrated settings.

Worries in early adolescence relate a great deal to lack of understanding on the part of parents and the inability to communicate with them about problems of physical development, sexual revolution, religion, money, and "what is expected." Worries become a little more "other-directed" as adolescents grow older. Worry sometimes even extends into thoughts of suicide. Here we find a multitude of studies and some reassuring statistics about the infrequency of suicide in adolescence and youth, in contrast to a higher rate found in later life.

Depression and Suicide

We all have mild feelings of depression at times, but normal depression clears up quickly and without any form of treatment. Feelings of depression in adolescence are characterized by restlessness and boredom. The individual alternates between total disinterest and intense preoccupation with some activity or event. These extreme shifts in mood bring on physical fatigue and difficulty in concentrating, which often affect school performance. Acting out takes several forms—

temper tantrums, running away, defiance, rebelliousness, and delinquency.

Extreme depression, however, can prompt suicide, but this does not mean that all extremely depressed people turn to self-destruction. Many factors are involved. First, suicide is most difficult to predict. Second, it occurs very infrequently in the population at large. It may seem to be a bigger problem than it actually is because one instance in a community is often dramatically publicized. Third, suicides claim our attention when they are near us. Fourth, many suicide "attempts" may be for reasons other than genuine self-destruction. Fifth, statistics show, in spite of popular belief, that there is a trend toward the diminishing of suicide among youth.

Suicide in adolescence is usually precipitated by some specific problem or event. Conflicts within the family, particularly those turning on some disciplinary action taken, are commonly related to suicides or their attempts. Like adult suicide, the suicidal adolescent, whose success at taking his life is often unintentional, usually has a previous history of either talking about or attempting self-destruction. It is seldom possible to predict an adolescent suicide attempt or its consequences except in instances where the adolescent verablizes his or her intention.

One writer has proposed the following "danger signs" of possible suicide. First, the possibility should be considered when the youngster begins to exhibit depression, accompanied by declining school performance and prolonged periods of rebellious behavior. The possibility of drug taking (see page 165) should be watched. Second, the risk of suicide is enhanced when there has been a recent and marked breakdown in previously existing communication channels. Third, note seriously any attempts at suicide, even though they may turn out to be mainly attention seeking. Attempts to hang or shoot oneself have greater lethality than aspirin overdosage or superficial scratches of the wrist.

Anger

Adolescents, like many adults, become angry when mechanical things fail to work or in other impersonal situations. But the most effective stimuli in evoking anger are social—unfair treatment, unjust accusations, unwelcome advice. Among college students, high on the list comes *thwarted self-assertion.*

The most frequent response made by the angry adolescent is talking. Boys swear and lash back with sarcasm and ridicule. After such explosions the teen-ager often becomes sulky or engages in behavior annoying to the individual with whom he or she is angry (e.g., whistling under the breath). Male adolescents may kick and throw things, girls cry. Gradually language responses substitute for more direct acts. Studies show that college girls exhibit more frequent verbal responses to anger than do boys, who engage in more physical combat.

The frequency of anger responses in adolescents is quite individual. It is related to such factors as college climates, parental restrictions, and in particular the degree of realism present in dealing with problem solving. For many people annoyances take over in place of anger with maturity. *Jealousy* often grows out of anger, and *envy* may take over. This is particularly true with the adolescent girl. In both jealousy and envy, the typical adolescent reaction is verbal.

The Pleasant Emotions

There are two reasons why more attention is given to the undesirable emotions of fear and anger and less to the more positive emotions of joy, pleasure, delight, and affection. First, fear and anger are usually exhibited in *specific* ways. One has a fear of failing an examination. One is angry about a regulation that he or she perceives to be unfair. On the other hand, pleasure, happiness, and the like are generalized feelings, difficult to pin down. Second, fear and anger often bring on a sequence of problems which must be dealt with. No doubt a part of the reason why adolescence seems to be the *un* age, a time of storm and stress, is that negative behavior is so easily observed. It often creates community problems. Part of the problem is that adolescents are expected to be disturbed.

For the teen-ager with abilities, with a sense of humor, living in a favorable home and school climate, the pleasant emotions may outweigh the negative behavior. Some of the disturbing emotions may even have in them a source of enjoyment, i.e., they provide excitement. They may even help provide certain required amounts of stress.

Emotional Control

Achieving emotional control during adolescence can be most beneficial to adjustment in adult life. Applying the *problem-solving process* helps us to see the cause-effect relations in behavior. This, in turn, enables the person to gain better control in expressing emotion. An individual who maintains an *appearance of calmness* in the face of anger- or fear-producing situations has taken the first step toward real calmness. Also, we can control an emotion by *becoming adjusted to the stimulus* that produces it. Since emotion is a nonadjustive reaction, procedures that give a person more adjustive power over his or her environment will lessen emotional reactions. Though emotion inhibits clear thinking, it is also true that *clear thinking inhibits emotion* to some extent.

Many studies support the conclusion that counseling can help the adolescent objectify and think through his problems. Though guidance may not itself solve the problem it encourages problem-solving behavior. Sharing problems makes the adolescent more aware that he or she is not alone with his or her problems. Learning that many emotional problems are "normal" aids understanding. Guided group discussions are most beneficial in this respect.

SOCIAL BEHAVIOR

Many researches, ranging from studies of industrial work groups to those of retirement communities, emphasize the importance of providing opportunities for social interaction. Although most disturbing emotional problems of the adolescent come through social contact, no other individual needs people more.

Changes in Social Behavior

Changes in social behavior and attitudes are related more to sexual maturation than to chronological age. It is to be expected that when boys reach sexual maturity, they will break away from the old gang and begin to enter into activities with girls. They show more interest in personal appearance and in competitive sports in which they can "look good."

In early adolescence social experimentation centers on organizing activities, selecting leaders, and creating on a small scale a society modeled after that of adults. Lounging around and talking occupy much time. In late adolescence three social worlds become important: family, school, and friendship groups. For some, a fourth world may come into being: the work group. In attitudes, by the time the adolescent reaches college, there is a trend toward liberalism as the individual acquires more information and becomes less provincial in his thinking. For some students such broadening experiences may be emotionally disturbing as well as stimulating.

Conformity

In terms of conforming to group norms the adolescent goes the much-maligned organization man one better. He or she conforms not only to group dress and group behavior but also to group opinions. Although the adolescent is becoming liberal and somewhat idealistic in certain social attitudes, he or she is more conservative where age mates are concerned. They want to be different and to conform at the same time. This leads to the formation of "in groups" that are different from the outsiders. The gang wars in many of our large cities combine the desire for togetherness with frustration and hatreds.

Whereas one adolescent may find a certain amount of security and ego satisfaction in a school situation, another youth, usually under-privileged by middle-class description, finds gangs. Frustrated people often identify readily with violence. In the gang, the adolescent can both be different and conform to gang conduct at the same time. It is important to remember, however, that numbers of adolescents are individualistic in many ways, despite their conforming behavior.

The desire to receive approval of the group sometimes leads the adolescent into trouble. With time, self-confidence increases and the urge for approval changes toward seeking recognition for effort expended. Until he feels accomplishment, reinforced by the recognition of others, the older male adolescent may switch his attention-getting behavior from off-color jokes and clownishness to expressing radical points of view. It must be recognized that acceptance takes time. The female adolescent is a little more reserved in her social expression.

Social Perceptions

Most children are lacking not only in social insight but also in self-insight. Hence, social perception is first noticed during adolescence. The perception of the status of others develops during the high school years; the perception of one's own status comes later. Freshmen college counselors report that one of the most bothersome problems at this age is, "Who am I?"

Perception of the class status to which one belongs is often confusing. The adolescent is part of a family that is a member of a socially ranked group. He or she is influenced both by social position and by pressures from this group and must often play socially approved roles not of his or her own choosing. The idealistic attitudes of adolescents predispose them to disappointment, disillusionment, and even cynicism.

The adolescent's self-evaluation is gradually determined by the perception of his or her *relative* position in two different kinds of groups. First, where does one stand in some peer group to which one belongs? Second, how would the person rate himself in a group to which he does not belong but wants to join? For example, the premedical student may evaluate his intelligence by comparing himself with his fellow college students. Here he has more evidence on which to base his judgment than when he compares himself with "great doctors," a group to which he aspires to belong. And what about the female who also aspires to be a physician? Where will she find her identification?

Adolescents have a tendency to perceive themselves in comparison with the "ideal." Girls who try to rate their own physical attractiveness may feel badly when they use the movie star as a model. Boys often feel inferior when they fail to compete with adults. Gradually the adolescent learns to perceive himself or herself in relation to many social groups. Older college students are found to be more cynical that younger ones. This may be, in part, because there is sometimes a thin line between cynicism and wisdom.

Social Groupings

The group affiliations of late childhood gradually break up during the preadolescent period. The need for belonging to a group becomes more important during adolescence. The close parent-child relationship, which served as a source of security for the child, becomes strained during the transition to adolescence. The possibilities of groupings are many: kinships, friends, neighbors, classmates, and special-interest peer groups of various sorts.

Groups may be charted in three ways. First, groups are characterized by rules of behavior accepted by a majority of the group. This *group norm* spells out the attitudes and actions expected of members. Second, in voluntary groups *cohesiveness* is important. Here one sees the group's policing power over its members. The greater the cohesiveness of a group, the greater is the amount of conformity to its norms. A nonvoluntary group (for example, an Army reserve unit),

FIG. 7-1 Basic structure of an adolescent group. Note how the lines of communication flow toward leader L. A mutual pair (U-V), the chain (R-Ro-M), the clique (clusters), and isolates (W and B) may be seen. Three socioeconomic classes are shown. These adolescents lived in a town of 4,500 population, near a large city.

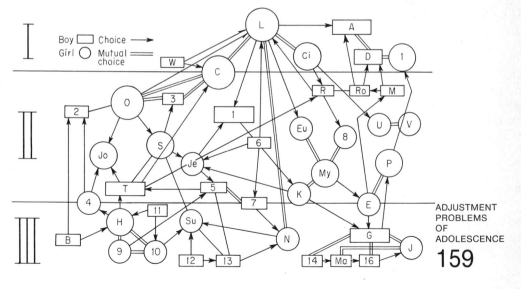

i.e., one which persons are forced to join, may have absolute power. Third, control over members involves a *monitoring system,* under which deviant behavior may be punished.

There are three characteristics of group membership: (1) the *rank status* in the group; (2) the degree to which the new member *values membership* in the group, membership being valued more highly when it is difficult to get into the group; (3) the influence of the *perceived legitimacy* of the group norm, i.e., the impact that norm will have upon a new member.

There are marked individual differences as to how people fit (or fail to fit) in a group. Figure 7-1 pictures the basic structure of adolescent groups, showing the isolate (W and B), the pair (U-V), the chain (R-Ro-M), and the *clique* (clusters). The leader is designated by L.

Many of the problems of the social behavior of adolescents can be understood by seeing where each person fits into a group. Peer group clusters have been studied extensively. In many respects investigation of groupings reveals the nature of adolescent social needs.

Peer Groups

The peer group, sometimes referred to as a clique if the members are closely knit, is usually a small, informal, and somewhat exclusive affiliation of individuals in a face-to-face group. It has been defined as a "social group approximately equal in age and status to one's own category, such as a group of college sophomores." It has a common set of values but no formal rules. Members of a clique satisfy their feelings for belongingness in ways that make them think and act alike. Sometimes loneliness helps force the individual to conform to the behavior of his group.

A special peer group or clique, a term long used by sociologists, may or may not be associated with a geographic location. Cliques are, however, made up of individuals who are brought together daily in some practical way (e.g., car pools). Adolescents usually fall into school cliques, recreational cliques, and institutional cliques (e.g., Scouts, church groups). Cliques begin to form around the fourteenth year of age. Initially consisting exclusively of boys or girls, they develop later into mixed groups, with the sexes being equally represented.

The typical adolescent *crowd* is composed of several cliques that join together in some "gathering." Activities involving both sexes have more organizational complications than those organized on a single-sex basis. For example, cross-clique dating sometimes requires approval by members of the cliques to which the boy and girl belong. Girls cliques are more closely knit than are boys', with more resistance to change. This makes it difficult for a new person coming into the school or neighborhood to gain acceptance.

Adolescent peer groups come into existence informally, with individuals simply getting together to do things. Congeniality based on interests or special aptitudes provides a basis for peer group formation. Studies show that cliques hold together well because their selection system makes sure that the individual will "fit." One researcher found that being together consumes 64 to 99 percent of young adolescents' leisure time.

Typically the adolescent peer group tries to avoid supervision of its activities by adults, engaging in such pastimes as gossiping, dancing, dating, going places, watching television, *and* eating. Influence of the peer group structure on adolescent attitudes and behavior is enormous for both good and bad.

On the positive side the clique offers its members:

1. Opportunity for satisfying the need for belonging.
2. Opportunity for release of emotional tensions in a friendly climate.
3. Opportunity for development of social skills.
4. Opportunity for reinforcement of one's own personal importance.
5. A status power structure providing prestige in the eyes of his or her peers.
6. Incentive to behave in mature ways.
7. A source of protection in striving for independence.
8. Trial-and-error experiences in developing human relations skills.

On the negative side the clique:

1. Restricts development of individuality of its members.
2. Tends to encourage hostility of members of "out groups."
3. Creates competition of "keeping up with the Joneses," or "down with the mob."
4. Creates conflict of allegiance between parental authority and clique mores.
5. Amplifies the development of class segregation.
6. Sometimes disrupts organizational harmony of school or campus.

Minority Problems

Recent research on black children and adolescents and on other minority groups is opening up new understandings of early motivation and academic success. Three negative things have come to light. First, minority group members in general have low expectancies for success, except where some special talent may be evidenced at an early age (see page 135). This low expectancy relates especially to academic success. Second, minority children, when compared to white children, find fewer academically successful racial models to follow. This is in marked contrast to professional sports where athletes offer many outstanding models. Third, young minority persons often develop a syndrome of hopelessness as they see their handicaps increase and chances of achievement bog down.

On the positive side, some minority members find high-achievement motivation once they make a distinction between lack of success due to discrimination and that due to personal inadequacy. One theory holds that when discrimination is a root cause of lack of motivation, group efforts to remove discrimination increase motivation more than emphasis on self-betterment. The same social values and cultural motivators that are stimulating in the life-styles of one individual can actually be obstacles to another person. This is especially true if the values are not related to his or her cultural norm.

In writing on the changing educational climate related to the identity trauma of blacks, Doris Mosby makes several points. First, the national stereotype of the black is changing toward a more positive image. Second, the pride of blackness as a state of mind is being reinforced in the home. Ancient heritages and physical traits are being judged by new and different standards of merit. Third, the home is beginning to confront, challenge, and condemn the previous black cultural image.

INTERESTS AND ATTITUDES

One of the oldest continuous research programs in psychology has been the study of male and female interests. The research begun by Strong in the 1920s, and expanded by a number of scientists, emphasizes the importance of early interests and experiences in career development. Although interests change for many reasons, vocational decision making is nevertheless influenced by adolescent interests. Measures of the interests of high school and college students show that some one-third change between 15.5 and 16.5 years of age, one-third between 16.5 and 18.5 years, and one-third between 18.5 and 25 years.

Although interests are influenced by sex, age, physical development, and the climate of opportunity, it is useful to take an overall look at adolescent interest patterns, particularly since interests are so highly individual.

Sex Differences in Interests

In recreational activities girls show interest in less vigorous endeavors. Boys prefer competitive activity requiring psychomotor skill.

They go in for organized sports. These sex differences lessen in late adolescence.

Girls are more verbal than boys. They spend more time on the telephone (though this observation will probably be doubted by some parents) and express themselves more in writing. Girls often keep a record of their social and emotional life in a diary; boys rarely do so. By the senior year of high school conversations among boys center on ball games, dates, television, records, and money. Girls give more attention to books, dates, and parties. One study of the college bull session found that men discussed an average of 3.4 topics as compared with 5.7 for women. Men tend to dwell longer on one topic than do women. College women talk most about dates, clothes, food, and dancing. Men talk about sex, about topics directly or indirectly related to careers and about sports.

The author, who has studied career decision making in over one thousand college seniors of both sexes, concludes that women are concerned primarily about the dual role they must plan on of raising a family and making a living. This is part of our increasing concern about the roles of women in our culture. Men are concerned primarily about two factors: knowing when all the alternatives have been covered for decision making, and knowing how best to relate abilities and interests to job climate and opportunities.

If it is any comfort to the reader who is finding difficulty in relating his or her abilities, interests, personality, and goals in a practical way, let us note that the problem is widespread. Our investigations show that over half the seniors we have studied are not sure what they really want to do. Vocational interests change frequently during adolescence. This may be good. It helps the person explore possibilities in something of a laboratory situation before having to make final choices. For those who would pressure the adolescent (possibly for the better) to think about his or her career, one should be mindful that it is easier to try to exert influence than it is to make judgments and decisions.

There is some evidence to support the position that girls are discouraged from showing intellectual interests in our society, although this attitude seems to be changing slowly. In spite of our increasing need for the better utilization of women's brainpower, our culture discourages women from more than casual interest in science, mathematics, and those activities involving decision-making processes. The male role centers on a vocational career, expressed by interest in money and success. The role of the female centers on domestic activities and marriage as a career. While girls have an interest in money as a means to an end, boys have a broader and more varied experience with money during childhood, which is amplified in managing financial affairs in adolescence. One research study concludes that as girls grow up, they discover that women are not supposed to excel intellectually. By the twelfth grade their growing concept of the "woman's role" prevents them from competing with men. Social pressures by her peers help mold the girl student into the stereotype of feminine charm—to be feminine she must shudder at a column of figures. For the young girl in our culture the marriage-go-round is a primary goal, although tempered somewhat by the newer attitudes generated by women's liberation movements.

The Struggle for Woman's Identity

In 1963 when equal pay for women was made law in the United States, reactions ranged widely, highlighting the role conflict of women. This conflict began to be expressed in the early 1970s as "women's liberation." The stereotypes of male and female roles in our society began to be questioned. In the area of abilities we became more conscious that our society was not using the vast amount of talent that women could contribute. We became increasingly aware that women were not being given an equal chance with men in jobs and in pay. Although women are now going into many "men's" jobs, the proportions are still small, and statistics indicate that most female college graduates who work still go into traditional women's jobs—teacher, nurse, dental assistant, lab technician, library work, and the like. More opportunities are opening up for better utilization of female talents, but progress is slow. Legislative debate continued for two decades before equal pay for women became law in 1963, and controversy rages still.

Social pressures, in the form of conflict between the home and the job, restrict both the single and the married woman. Some of the conflict centers on individual identity. Says psychologist Erik Erikson: "Young women often ask whether they can have an identity before they know whom they will marry, and for whom they will make a home. Much of a young woman's identity *is* already defined in her kind of attractiveness and in the selectivity of her search for the man (or men) by whom she wishes to be sought." Another on-the-scene observer writes: "I don't know what immutable differences exist between men and women apart from differences in their genitals; perhaps there are some other unchangeable differences; probably there are a number of irrelevant differences. But it is clear that until social expectations for men and women are equal, until we provide equal respect for both men and women, our answers to this question will simply reflect our prejudices." Strains and inconsistencies are built into some of the expected roles of the woman in our culture, and it often reaches uncomfortable proportions by adolescence and early youth. It even plays a part in the molding of interests, and in the ways males and females get together.

THE DRUG SCENE

In Chapter 1 (see page 14) we talked about drugs as they relate to the chemistry of behavior. Here let us say something more about the misuse of drugs since in adolescence many people are introduced to drugs for the first time. The search for indentity in adolescence and youth may lead to the dead end of drug abuse.

Drugs are everywhere, from the gym locker to the home medicine chest. Our drug problem involves a wide variety of uppers and downers: those that are psychoactive (affecting the mind), those that are legal, and those that are illegal. Researchers and clinicians say that most users, like alcoholics, do not feel that they have a drug problem, and herein lie the dangers of drug abuse. There is no single type of drug user. Drug use cuts across all economic, ethnic, and social classifications and includes the hard-to-identify secret user. The rise of illicit drug use by young people is one of society's most puzzling problems.

Parents, Peers, and Marijuana Use

A study of 8,000 New York State high school students revealed some interesting data. First, it was found that adolescents whose parents and friends used psychoactive drugs are most likely to use marijuana themselves. Second, peers were found to be more influential than parents in determining whether a young person will use drugs.

The adolescents studied came from eighteen high schools. In general, drug-using parents were found to enhance but not initiate drug use among their children. The highest rate of adolescent marijuana use detected in the study (67 percent) was found among those whose parents and peers both used drugs. Children of non–drug-using parents were less likely to take up drugs than those whose parents used drugs. Interestingly, the link between parental and adolescent drug use has been almost exclusively limited to mothers; it is strongest when a daughter considers her mother a drug user. Among adolescents who reported their mothers' use of tranquilizers, 37 percent were marijuana users, compared with 24 percent who said their mothers did not use drugs.

The study observed that 15 percent of the students, both male and female, whose friends say they have not smoked marijuana use it themselves, while 79 percent of those whose friends have used marijuana 60 times or more use the drug. The percentage of adolescents who have used marijuana sixty times or more increases from 2 percent among those whose friends have never used marijuana to 48 percent among those whose friends are sixty-time users.

Theories about Drug Abuse

Theories of *personality* in drug usage focus on psychological needs. For example, one view holds that very insecure people have underlying emotional problems and conflicts that predispose them to turn to drugs. Such individuals may use heroin or other opiates to relieve anxiety, to drop out from society, or to fulfill self-destructive wishes. This is opposed to *interactional* theory, which stresses that one learns to use a drug as he learns any other behavior. Therefore, opportunities for a person to use drugs are generated by his or her association with users. The adolescent drug user finds support and reinforcement from friends; he or she becomes a member of an ingroup. One *sociological* theory holds that youth may turn to drugs to show their opposition to the life-styles of the establishment. Thus, large social gatherings of youth at music festivals and other happenings often involve drug usage and free sexual practices as a dual social pattern of protest.

SOME QUESTIONS AND ANSWERS ABOUT DRUGS

Let us give some brief answers to some commonly asked questions. The answers are summarized from federal government sources.

What Is Drug Abuse?

Drugs become an "abuse" when taking them interferes with a person's health or ability to do well in school or to earn an appropriate living; or when there is disruption of the person's individual or social adjustments, or both.

What Is Compulsive Drug Abuse?

Whereas *habituation* is the desire to repeat the use of a drug as an escape from tension, or for euphoric experiences, compulsive drug abuse involves *addiction*. Here there is a physical dependence upon a drug; the body exhibits a need for the drug beyond the psychological aspects of habituation. One can become addicted not only to heroin and other "hard" drugs but also to sedatives, certain tranquilizers, alcohol, and stimulants in very large doses.

What Is Drug Tolerance?

One speaks of drug tolerance when a person has to increase the dose constantly to bring about the same effect.

What Is Drug Dependence?

This is a state in which you "have to have it." It involves physiological or psychological dependence, or both, which results from chronic, periodic, or continuous use. Not everyone who uses a drug becomes dependent upon it. Alcohol is a common example. The majority of persons who drink do not harm themselves or those around them. But the problem is that many people fail to see the harmful effects growing with usage. It is estimated that several million Americans are alcoholics and refuse to admit it.

Can Drug Abuse Cause Mental Breakdown?

Yes. Some drugs can produce irreparable brain damage. For example, studies show that alcohol can have a direct toxic effect on the brain cells by disturbing circulation and depriving the cells of oxygen. Stimulants, such as amphetamines, can produce long-term biochemical disruption of the central nervous system, but it has not been proved conclusively that they cause permanent brain damage. On the other hand, sniffing glue has been found to cause brain cells to die. And brain cells do not regenerate once they are destroyed.

Can the Effects of Drug Abuse Be Passed on to the Unborn?

Heroin-addicted mothers have given birth to babies who show withdrawal symptoms. Not enough is known at present about the genetic effects of drugs to make a generalization. But it is regarded as extremely risky to take any drugs without careful medical supervision during pregnancy.

Where Does One Go for Help about Drugs?

In large urban areas, there are drug information clearing houses. Elsewhere, information can be obtained through the family doctor, mental health professionals, and counselors in schools and colleges. Inquiries can be directed to the National Clearinghouse for Drug Abuse Information, Box 1701, Washington, D.C. 20015. Many college libraries contain material from federal sources that is frequently updated.

FOUR DIMENSIONS OF SELF

The following statements were made by four adolescents.

"I'm just an average, healthy American girl—I have many interests—I am smart, but I could do better in my schoolwork if I studied a little harder."

"My parents think I'm too slow even when I'm going as fast as I can. They think I'm too irresponsible—I guess they would like to trade me in for somebody like my cousin."

"Other people think I'm a stupid jerk—some think I'm bright and some think I'm dull—I'm fairly quiet and a little shy."

"I would like to be a person that can look back through the years and feel satisfied with everything I have done."

We no doubt all get involved with three basic questions: "Who am I?" "Where am I going?" "What will it cost me to get there?" And we probably have difficulty in coming up with precise answers to these questions. Let us take a look at four dimensions of the self as viewed by adolescents. The college student may wish to extend the thinking here to apply to his or her own problems.

The Basic Self Concept

This is the concept proper which is the individual's perception of his or her abilities and status. It is the perception of the roles to be played in the outside world. This concept is influenced by one's physical self, personal appearance, dress, and grooming; by abilities and disposition, values, beliefs, and aspirations.

The rapid changes that take place during adolescence in height, weight, body build, facial appearance, and voice bring about changes in the adolescent's body image. Such matters as not having clothes like the other youngsters and not having a home where one can entertain friends without feeling embarrassed decrease one's conception of his or her own importance. They bring on feelings of social incompetence. They make more difficult the problem of appraising true ability and worth.

The self concept is enhanced when there is intellectual ability to meet problems. The slow reader, for example, may find difficulty in learning, thus causing negative self concepts to operate in learning situations. Even for the person with intellectual abilities and good learning habits, the self concept still has its ups and downs.

The Transitory Perception of Self

The adolescent's self-image may at one time be compulsive, compensatory, and unrealistic and at other times insightful and practical. One's self-perception at any given point in time may be determined by some "inner-directed" mood or by some "other-directed" influence. Many adolescents do not recognize the source of their self-perceptions or their transitory nature. They are optimistic or pessimistic, elated or depressed, satisfied or dissatisfied in an all-or-nothing way. They are sometimes able to switch rapidly from one extreme to the other. Since there is some tendency for the adolescent to focus more on problems than on accomplishments, the transitory perception of self is largely negative.

The Social Self

"To see yourself as others see you" may or may not be valid. At one time, when in an optimistic mood, the adolescent perceives that other people see him in a good light. When depressed, he perceives that others depreciate him. When others think him stupid, or socially inept, there is a tendency for him to amplify his feelings of insecurity: "How could anyone like me?" More positive views on the part of others may enhance his perception of his social self somewhat, but they play a lesser role when he is down. "There are more ways to get feedback from a loused-up social situation than from doing things right." This perceptive college freshman may have something in this statement!

The Ideal Self

The concept of the ideal self, the kind of person the adolescent hopes to be, involves questions of standards and comparisons. It involves relating levels of aspiration to levels of ability. It also involves opportunities for self-realization.

When the ideal self is set at an unrealistic level, frustration is increased. When it is set below one's level of ability, motivation may become lacking. The adolescent's level of aspiration tends to go up with success and down with failure. This up-down movement is more exaggerated than that usually found in adults. The ideal self of the adult has evolved slowly through experience. Lacking such experience, the adolescent depends a great deal on identification with someone else as the ideal—an older brother or sister, a parent, or a teacher. This ideal person may stimulate either emulation or resentment, sometimes both.

The concept of self is molded by reward and punishment, praise and blame, and by the feelings of accomplishment that come with solving a problem. During preadolescence, parents and peers both influence the self concept. This situation changes gradually until the young person's self-evaluation is determined by what age mates think. Later, peer groups and other organizations provide a climate of influence. *Finally the adolescent discovers that the self must be determined individually.* He or she has to learn the hard way that achieving identity is a long, difficult process. One learns that such identity comes through thinking, feeling, and decision making. It thrives on social interaction. And in the end, the question "Who am I?" still remains.

THE POSITIVE SIDE OF ADOLESCENCE

So much of the development of the adolescent is a sequence of meeting new problems before old ones are solved that it is easy to view this period of growth negatively. But the positive side involves learning to react appropriately to stress, which is a normal part of living.

One investigator did a series of experiments with laboratory rats. He kept one group immobilized for extensive periods of time and found that they struggled desperately to get free. They needed to engage in all the activities that *normally* provided their required quota of stress. When deprived of these problem situations (some of which were quite stressful), they became ill in their efforts to maintain health. Another group of rats, with the same hereditary background (litter mates), which were allowed to engage in stressful situations, lived longer, healthier lives.

From his many studies of stress on human beings as well as animals, this researcher concludes that the individual has to learn to react to stress. He points out that when the individual chooses goals, he or she should not attempt primarily to avoid stress, which is a natural part of life, but rather should watch his or her own stress level. Knowing this level comes through experience. Human beings, like animals deprived of a wide variety of stress situations, do not learn how to take care of themselves. We said essentially this in Chapter 4 on adjustment (see page 74), but we must reemphasize here how important it is to learn to react well to problems.

Facing too many problems too rapidly in an unfavorable environment may be unhealthy. With exceptions, of course, adolescence is a stage of development in our culture in which to discover oneself and gain independence in a semisympathetic environment. Adolescence provides a setting in which at each age group the individual problems have much in common. One may think positively of adolescence as a laboratory for experiences, for learning by trial and error, and for developing good problem-solving habits at the thinking level.

DATING

Changing Patterns

Male and female of any generation have, of course, always gotten together for basically the same reasons—companionship, mating, sex, and sometimes just to keep from being alone. But while the reasons have not changed significantly over the years, the patterns have. In some circles "gatherings" have supplanted the formalities associated with "dating," where boy calls girl, and for sound, logical reasons. Such reasons range from more freedom of exploration by both sexes to less dependence on tradition: "I'm going over to——. Come along."

The concept of dating, regardless of the current in-words used to describe it, still includes "paired association of members of the opposite sex without references to the intent to marry." It is, in effect, an exploratory or search process with a variety of motives. Even the settings for getting together have changed. Gone are the rumble seat days of the thirties and the love-in arrangements of the sixties. Settings and getting together today center on two things. First, pairing off is more spontaneous. Second, there is less separation of role behaviors by couples; duties, for example, are no longer automatically labeled "masculine" or "feminine." And the in-words come and go very rapidly. "Grooving" gave way to "digging." Tomorrow's in-words are difficult to predict. Words, of course, reinforce our ways of feeling, thinking, and behaving, and we sometimes come back to conventional words for purposes of communication. Both "dating" and "courtship" seem to fall in this category. Dating, for its many and varied reasons, contrasts with the concept of courtship, which involves obligations to carry through to marriage.

Dating as a form of social behavior has been viewed by cynic, critic, promoter, and researcher. Some content that dating is a barrier to happiness in marriage and that on dates the girl must learn to protect herself against the boy's sexual advances. Others believe that it is a form of social behavior largely dominated by a quest for thrills, sometimes through deceit in the pretense of love and devotion. And still others say that it is a built-in trap to promote marriage. Many have wondered what alternatives might take the place of this widespread custom.

The advantages of dating have been equally touted. Dating is partly educational, helping us learn to adjust to members of the opposite sex and gain poise and ease in social situations. It helps us learn to control behavior, evaluate personality types, and build up concepts of right and wrong. Dating is a means of mixing and having a good time socially, while defining the roles of the sexes.

Attraction

After some purely trial-and-error procedure, some double dating, some pairing off from a gathering, or some computerized search, people really come together through some mutual attraction. From a variety of studies of "liking" and "disliking" come some useful generalizations. First, there is a tendency for people who like each other to mingle in groups, thus providing pairing-off opportunities. Second, empathy plays an important role as we come to share the other person's feelings. Third, the greater the similarity of attitudes, the greater will be the attraction. Fourth, people tend to associate with others whom they perceive as similar to themselves, though when persons are secure about being liked, they are willing to associate with others who are dissimilar. Fifth, the highly defensive person tends to be attracted to someone like himself, although he may say just the opposite. Sixth, the nondefensive person is more outgoing and adventurous, and hence has the opportunity to become a member of several groups. Seventh, agreement in thinking is a factor in staying together, when offset with a small amount of in-fighting. Studies show that happy couples "think alike" more often than do unhappy couples. Studies of divorced people also show that when physical attractiveness was the primary reason for marriage, the give-and-take of reciprocation was lacking. Eighth, attractiveness relates to reinforcement (see page 260). We tend to like persons who give us rewards at the right time. Ninth, popularity among college students relates to the psychological climate (see page 408). Tenth, attraction relates to similarity of interests over a fairly wide range.

Blind Dates and the Computer

"Just another evening wasted; I'll never go out on another blind date." Yes, *you* probably have said the same thing on some occasion.

Several mixer-weary students concluded that college students *do* know what kind of people they enjoy dating. They also agreed that blind dates are fine up to a point, but that there must be a better way than the usual trial-and-error system. Why not use a computer? This was the beginning of Operation Match.

Operation Match began with the construction of questionnaires, which were sent to many college students. The data were analyzed statistically. During the first year some 200,000 college students across the country were matched, with a follow-up sample of 8,000 of them in a validation study. Through refinement of the questionnaire and programming, much of the gamble can be taken out of the blind date by using the computer for matching couples on the basis of their preferences.

The student is asked to fill out a vital statistics and personality inventory on an answer sheet which comes with "the test." Thus, placed in the computer memory file are vital statistics of sex, race, religion, age, and interests. Also included are responses to questions about attitudes and how one reacts to specific situations. Data programmed into the computer include general and specific information about one's academic record, social standing, and even political affiliation. Physical appearance is added to the picture, as are self-evaluations of such qualities as "talkativeness" and "emotional responses." Not only does the male, for example, describe himself, but he records on an answer sheet what he wants his date to be like. Each client is sent a list of possible dates from which he or she can choose. The matching is based on responses to items which have been found to be valid for "good matching."

Reactions of students have been generally favorable to computerized date matching: "It got me out of a rut." "I met some other adventuresome people." But sometimes the wrong number may get punched in. In a system of "1" for male and "2" for female, there have been reports of the mistake of "1-1" matching! Conclude the originators of Operation Match: "If you live in an area with several thousand college students, the number of possible matches for dating is several million. You yourself have a choice of several thousand dates, and be modest—that's too many to check out." In another study, of sex differences in dating aspirations and satisfaction with computer-selected partners, it was found that women have higher aspirations for a dating partner than do men. Women register a high degree of satisfaction less frequently than men following the first date.

Computer matching has spread widely and beyond college populations. "Getting together" has brought technology in to help, but the psychological problems involved have changed little.

LIKING AND LOVING

Psychologist Zick Rubin has opened up a research field related to constructing a measure of loving and how it might be distinguished from liking. A "likable" person is someone who is viewed as good or desirable in a number of ways. We not only like people to whom we are attracted, as described above, but we also like people who are intelligent, competent, and trustworthy. We try to choose people whom we like to work with and to do things with. Of course, we may like a given person for some reason, but wonder if it can lead to love. Rubin has put loving and liking on a scale, which at least helps to try to objectify the differences. The scale, which has been used with college students, spans a wide range of thoughts, feelings, and behavioral predispositions. Although everyone has his own definition of loving and liking, the scale does provide us with some practical leads. The "love" scale includes items that seem to tap intimate feelings (e.g., "I feel that I can confide in [name] about virtually anything"). It tries to identify the things that make up the components of attachment (e.g., "If I were lonely, my first thought would be to seek [name] out"). There are also "caring" items (e.g., "If [name] were feeling bad, my first duty would be to cheer him [her] up").

Items on the "liking" scale center on such dimensions as adjustment, maturity, and good judgment. Examples include, "I think that [name] is unusually well-adjusted"; "In my opinion, [name] is an exceptionally mature person"; and "I have great confidence in [name's] good judgment."

Students put these items under love: "It would be hard for me to get along without [name]." In contrast, the "liking" items include such statements as "I think [name] is one of those people who quickly wins respect"; and [name] is one of the most likable people I know."

Admittedly, these distinctions are somewhat arbitrary, and items in one list often shade into the other. Then, too, liking and loving should, ideally, go together if the individual is to be truly happy. In other words, everyone must make up his or her own list.

Although the classic date is becoming outmoded for many college students, the problems of liking and loving still exist. The strategies of selecting the right person relate to one of the most important decisions most of us make—marriage.

MARRIAGE

Factors in Selecting a Mate

Unhappiness in marriage is largely a matter of personal relationships between husbands and wives which result in conflict—being too critical, too emotional, too impatient. Happiness centers on common interests, common friendships, and common levels of aspiration.

Selecting a mate is a decision-making process involving *maturity* of judgment. Some signs of such maturity include:

1. Knowing the difference between romantic ideals and practical reality
2. Freedom from adolescent kinds of behavior
3. Understanding the realities of socioeconomic status
4. Setting realistic goals
5. Having insight into human relations
6. Freedom from being "other-directed"

The success or failure of a marriage is determined by the quality of adjustments husband and wife make to each other. The adjustive histories of childhood are important because the relationships in marriage have much in common with those experienced between a parent and a child. For example, the immature, dependent wife may expect the same kind of indulgence from her husband that she received from her father. The husband who had a rebelliously hostile attitude toward his parents may be overdominant with his wife.

Sexual compatibility is important in marital adjustment. Satisfactory sexual relations may be either a result or a contributing cause of a generally successful marriage. Married couples who are relatively free of anxieties and hostilities are usually compatible in sex.

Marriage involves both short-term and long-term decisions and factors of choice, personality, education, religion, age, and the stresses of living with children. There are several generalizations related to the success or failure of marriage.

1. Young people who are socially well adjusted before marriage tend to enjoy successful marriages.
2. Understanding the process of making choices increases the chances of success.
3. Men and women with a high level of education have better chances at success in marriage.
4. Religious differences are not a major source of marriage failure. Sophisticated people have weighed this factor heavily in the selection process; this filtering has prevented some marriages from taking place.
5. Most people marry someone of approximately the same age. However, it has been found that age differences do not contribute in any great degree to happiness or unhappiness in marriage.
6. The optimum age for success in marriage (as seen from statistical studies) is between twenty-one and twenty-nine for women and twenty-four and twenty-nine for men.
7. Early marriage may fail if the primary reason is fear of waiting too long to be married.
8. Although the expressed desire for children increases the chance of happiness in marriage, the actual presence or absence of children is apparently not a factor.
9. Being tied down by children too soon brings on frustration and conflict.
10. Couples who communicate effectively at the emotional level as well as at the verbal level tend to be better adjusted than those who do not.

Difficulties in Marriage

One student of the psychology of divorce has said: "To expect marriage to last indefinitely under modern conditions is to expect a lot." Whereas divorce was once socially unacceptable, today it is tolerated in spite of the unhappiness it may cause. Yet, most people who marry say that they plan to stay married. A 1972 survey of a sample of 2,500 college-age students showed 97.8 percent said that they planned to marry in spite of any difficulties that might be involved. Researchers seem to be toning down their criticisms of romantic love as a primary basis for marriage.

Love is a strongly felt emotion, but it is an emotion. Among many couples it lasts a lifetime. In contrast is the statistic that roughly one-third of marriages contracted in our society end in divorce. Added to the causes of difficulty in marriage discussed in the last few pages are two new ones: increased individual autonomy and rapid social change. One sociologist suggests that the faulty initial perception of who would make an appropriate marriage partner may contribute to divorce, but that the divorce rate in America would have climbed at least as rapidly without romantic love as with it. We hear so much about the negatives in marriage that we tend to forget the positives. And sometimes the positives have to wait for a "second time around."

ATTITUDE AND KNOWLEDGE SURVEYS

An Attitude Survey

One study of the attitudes which college students expressed before marriage centered on premarital sex. Whereas a number of students thought that it was all right for them to live in coed college dorms, or share summer beach houses and winter ski resorts in mixed groupings, many of these same students said that they would not want their sons or daughters doing the same thing. In another study, a follow-up of several hundred young married former students, a majority of them expressed conservative views on sex relationships before marriage that did not involve real love affairs. Sex as an expression of love was approved; sex for its own sake was not. Controversial views were expressed about using the pill before marriage. Incidentally, in another survey among noncollege population, including both young and older people, some ignorance about the pill was found. Few respondents knew that the pill functioned on a brain center to inhibit female sex gland functions. More important, a number of teen-agers believed that birth control methods in general, including the pill, prevented venereal disease.

A Knowledge Survey

For a time following World War II, syphilis was in sharp decline. However, with the advent of oral contraception, and its attendant freer attitudes about sex experiences and decreased need for use of condoms, the incidence of syphilis has risen sharply. This disease is caused by a microscopic organism (the spirochete) which is transmitted by an infected individual, usually during sexual relations. The spirochetes multiply rapidly, and within two or three weeks a sore develops at the site of the infection. This sore disappears within about one month, even though untreated.

Some few weeks later a copper-colored rash resembling smallpox emerges, sometimes covering the whole body. The microorganisms may attack any of the organs of the body. If not treated properly, the infection can eventually lead to the disease of *paresis,* which includes rapid mental and personality deterioration. The diseased person may be unable to spell or count; his sense of time may become distorted; he may become confused about persons or places. Depression may be so severe that it leads to suicide.

How much do teen-agers know about this problem? Surveys show that many have never heard of the symptoms. Of those who have, as we have said, many erroneously believe that the pill prevents not only pregnancy but V.D. as well. Health communications of various kinds have not been able to clarify the facts. Even an antisyphilis publicity campaign, with such slogans as "Birth control DOES NOT control V.D.," has had little success.

SUMMARY

Adolescence is a stage of conflict between dependence and independence, a period of transition between childhood and adulthood during which maturity comes through ups and downs. It is a stage of emotional unbalance, of nervous habits, of fear and worry, when emotional expressions are often intense and out of control. It is also a stage of gradually learning to solve problems; here, counseling can be helpful.

The adolescent needs social experimentation and approval. Self-evaluation is gradually determined as the adolescent perceives how he or she is rated by peers. The need for belonging to a group becomes very important in adolescence. Peer groups come into existence informally, typically avoiding supervision by adults. Interests are highly individual although influenced by sex, age, physical development, and the climate of opportunity. It is in adolescence that role differentiations come on strongly, with particular emphasis on woman's struggle for identity. Strains and inconsistencies are built into some of the expected roles of women, often reaching uncomfortable proportions.

For many people the misuse of drugs begins in adolescence. Both ignorance and, in some measure, the search for identity in adolescence and youth may lead to misguided ways. The role of drug-using parents has been found to enhance but not initiate drug use among their children. Theories of drug use include, first, personality and psychological needs; second, interactional theory, which stresses learning through association; and third, sociological theory, which holds that youth may turn to drugs to show their opposition to the life-styles of the establishment. Questions of the drug scene center on abuse, habituation and addiction, drug tolerance and dependence, and about where one can go for help.

The dimensions of self include the basic concept, the transitory perception of self, the social self, and the ideal self. The concept of self is molded by reward and punishment, praise and blame, and by the feelings of accomplishment that come with solving a problem. Finally, the adolescent discovers that the self must be determined individually. Adolescence provides an interactional situation in which, at each age group, the individual problems have much in common, and learning by trial and error plays a major part.

Changes in cultural traditions and in attitudes are bringing about changing patterns of dating as a form of social behavior. Regardless of how, adolescents, like adults, come together through some mutual attraction. The nature of liking and loving becomes important.

The success or failure of a marriage is determined by the quality of adjustments husband and wife make to each other. Sexual compatibility is a significant factor in marital adjustment. Other factors relate to decision making, choice, personality, education, religion, age, and the stresses of living with children. Success in marriage hinges on a decision process of selecting a mate with maturity of judgment. A knowledge survey on sexual relations showed that many teen-agers are ignorant of birth control information and venereal disease.

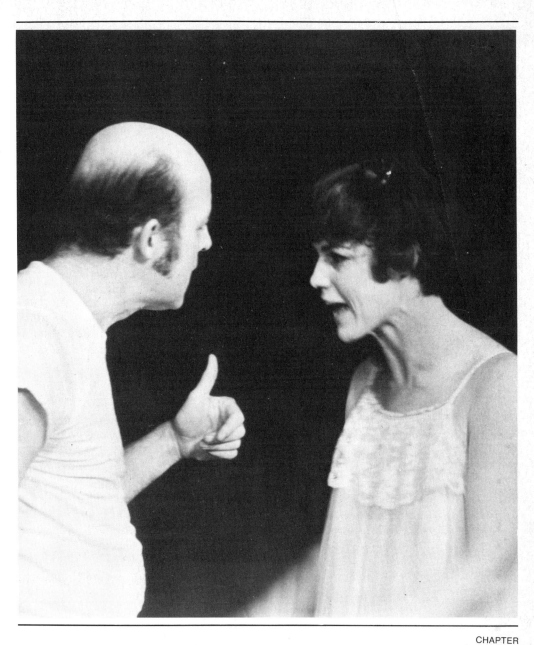

YOUTH, MIDDLE AGE, AND BEYOND

8

Beyond the psychological uncertainties of adolescence we find the beginnings of effective, and noticeable, adjustments of youth. For a quick look, let us think somewhat arbitrarily of youth as covering the twenties and early thirties, with middle age gradually approaching. We customarily reserve the sixties and beyond as involving preretirement to retirement.

Psychologically, we may think of youth as a period involving some agonizing indecisiveness in life-style and career planning. In some respects the crisis of youth hinges on realizing that "we can't have it all ways"; we must make some choices. Middle age is more upsetting as one reaches "a point of no return." Old age has been described as "a triumph of hope over experience." The three ages of man have also been spoken of as youth, middle age, and "how well you are looking."

YOUTH

Psychological needs change with age, and these changes affect our attitudes toward work, toward living, and toward understanding. Early youth is the stage in which the individual straddles adolescence and maturity. It is a stage in which traditions are created within a few weeks and lost just as quickly.

Desire for Change

Youth is aware of change and welcomes it. Adolescence, with all its random trial and error toward adjustment, has given way (with some exceptions) to better-planned behavior. The man just out of college, entering a career in technological development, sales, or management, seizes every opportunity to get ahead and generally has the stamina to take the competition. The young woman may want to earn her own living before settling down to family responsibilities, or to get an early start on a well-adjusted life-style that may or may not include marriage. Both people want and expect challenge, for this is the path to experience and recognition. This attitude contrasts with that of old age, in which for most people change is unwelcome and often resisted. The dream of better days ahead is over, and the world is narrowing. Competition is shunned because few have the stamina to keep up the pace. Boredom begins to take over as time becomes more difficult to fill.

Problems of Youth

The problems of youth are numerous and varied. However, in contrast with those of adolescence, the problems facing youth are better defined. The college student in his or her graduating year must decide whether to take a job or to continue with formal education. When the young man begins working, he must somehow adjust his need to get started early with his desire to raise a family at a time when he can least afford it financially. Particularly for the young woman, the best years biologically for having children come at about the same time that both husband and wife have to work in order to establish a home of their own. Youth sometimes spends money before learning how to make it.

On the job youth must look for an opportunity where anticipations can be realized and enthusiasms rewarded. One may not succeed at first. But youth has one big advantage: Disappointments are soon overcome by hopes for a better future. Dissatisfaction with one job may be remedied by taking another. The opportunities for youth in our changing, expanding economy build up attitudes of both confidence and defiance—just the reverse of the feelings of the older person. A youth at the worker level, regardless of his limitations in education, is optimistic about the future. His physical strength and vitality to some degree make up for his lack of training and experience. Desires that are not readily fulfilled today may be tomorrow. The more highly educated youth shares in this optimism, but with a greater sense of reality. Understanding the problem lessens that satisfying feeling of confidence in the future. This caution is characteristic of the college sophomore, who begins to sort out emotional and intellectual problems with some sophistication.

Search for Opportunity

Moving up socially and economically is a problem which the sophisticated student plans for. Recent research emphasizes that upward mobility depends not only on training and aspiration but also on opportunity. Workers often feel that pull and luck spell advancement. In contrast, for the more thoughtful individual, getting ahead is a game in which education, formal or otherwise, is essential for understanding how opportunity can often be made. There is some tendency for people to advance during their careers, but for most people the advancement is not very far. The skilled industrial worker finds himself basically a commodity, the demands for which fluctuate with the economy and with technological change. Above the skilled level the individual is in many respects more on his own.

Do opportunity and income increase with age? Economists answer both "yes" and "no." In managerial jobs and in the professions earnings do increase with age. This is not true in the lowest-paid manual jobs. For such work, a man reaches his peak in his early twenties; after that he goes downhill.

In early childhood career thinking involves a fantasy stage in which interests are generally unrelated to potential capacities and change rapidly. The child wants to be a fireman, doctor, teacher, or astronaut without considering how or why. Following this period, in early adolescence, comes the stage of *tentative choices.* Here there is some vague relationship between interests and vocational preferences, but career planning is little more than daydreaming. In the late teens comes a third stage of more *realistic planning,* when school or work alternatives are forced on the person.

Not all people have a choice in selecting their careers or jobs. Opportunity, economic responsibilities, intelligence, and various other circumstances enter in. One person may have to quit school early because of a family problem. Another may stay in school longer only because work opportunities may not be available. And one reason students with some types of technical training (e.g., computer programming) never finish their formal education is that their services may be in such demand that they cannot turn down an offer. The same is true of many jobs related to the health field.

Change

Technology is spreading irresistibly and bringing with it new problems. For some persons, automation expands the world of career choice; for others, it closes opportunity. Change, along with accommodation or resistance to it, is bringing about the retraining of the worker to give him new skills and is causing the manager to wonder how he can best use the computer in decision making. Unskilled jobs are becoming a smaller and smaller fraction of all jobs, making for some less than a bright future.

It may be well to remember that throughout a lifetime a person may have several careers. The man who is twenty years old may expect to make at least six job changes during his working life and to retire earlier than his father did. Choosing an occupation ranks second in importance only to the selection of a mate in marriage. How and where a person will spend even his or her nonworking hours is influenced by such choice. Most important, occupational choices must be made carefully because in many cases there is no going back. True, some people change their occupations, sometimes for the better. However, for most people in our culture, the general area of vocational choices lasts for a lifetime, although specific jobs may be changed several times.

From many studies on the relationship between fathers' and sons' occupations come several conclusions. First, college students' stated choices tend to coincide with the occupations of their fathers more often than would be expected by statistical chance. Second, the greater the father's income, the more likely the student is to gravitate toward a money-making career. The more money currently earned by the father, the more the student expects to be earning in the future. Third, sons tend to enter and remain in occupations similar to those of their fathers. Fourth, when occupations of fathers and sons are compared according to level (e.g., corporate vice-president or foreman), sons whose fathers are at very high levels tend to enter lower occupations, and those whose fathers are at lower levels tend to enter higher occupations. Mothers influence daughters in career planning, just as fathers influence their sons.

Abilities and Choices

There is a rough correspondence between an individual's intelligence and the intellectual requirements of the occupation he prefers. It is very difficult, of course, to get an exact measure showing the relationship between interest and *actual* ability. However, there is much evidence showing a relationship between interest and *perceived* ability. The activities which are most highly preferred are those in which the person believes himself or herself to possess the greatest ability. This is certainly a type of finding useful to the student in trusting (to some extent!) self-perception.

Many data from test scores and from practical situations support the position that verbal and quantitative scores are related to choice of work. Persons with abilities related to an occupation tend to choose that occupation. One follow-up study of over two thousand high school students found that those who entered the mechanical, electric, and building trades had their highest scores in mechanical reasoning. Those who succeeded as clerks had superior knowledge of grammar and spelling.

One psychologist, who has been following thousands of students in their career development, has come up with the following practical theory about vocational development: "The process of vocational development is essentially that of developing and implementing a self concept: It is a *compromise process* [ITALICS ADDED] in which the self concept is a product of the interaction of inherited aptitudes, neural and endocrine makeup, opportunity to play various roles, and evaluations of the extent to which the results of role playing meet with the approval of superiors and fellows."

MIDDLE AGE

The transition from youth to middle age is a gradual process. For some people who have prepared themselves "to go all the way" middle age is taken in stride. For others, middle age peaks in a crisis described by someone as "a time when what makes you tick needs winding." The middle-aged person is introspective. He is resigned and rebellious at the same time. Middle age attracts less attention than youth and inspires only little research. It is recognized, however, as a time when one thinks that decisions in the past have sometimes robbed one of choice in the present.

Needs In Middle Age

Middle age is a time of determining whether the man or woman is a success, as measured by the goals set for themselves in youth. In occupations such as engineering and science, in which long professional training is essential to productive activity and economic independence, persons who have not yet been admitted to full standing may identify themselves as being young. A laborer, on the other hand, who may be the same chronological age as the newly licensed company lawyer may feel himself old at thirty-five. A steel worker or miner may feel he has reached his economic peak just at the age when the young business executive and accountant are ready for promotion and their best work. Needs in middle age center on self-evaluation—questions of status become important. In terms of behavior some people act in middle age as if they were living through a period of "emotional second adolescence." It is important for family harmony for younger people to realize that parents have problems of psychological adjustment also. Let us take an overall look at these problems in the male and in the female.

Middle-Age Revolt in the Male

Along with decreases in physical stamina and sexual activity, such signs as receding hairlines indicate the passing of youth, a stage soon to be followed in some people by what the psychoanalysts have termed "middle-age revolt." This usually comes earlier for the worker, later for the manager or professional man; but it comes to many in terms of lost dreams and failure to meet cutthroat competition. This revolt comes when the man cannot plead the inexperience of youth or the frailties of age. The middle-ager sometimes expresses guilt feelings of failure and blames himself for not having gone into the right job. He frequently wonders whether he married the right woman. Middle age begins when the phone rings on Saturday night and you hope it is a wrong number.

The man in middle age may see his weight climbing and his hair thinning. These easily observed changes disturb him. When youngsters call him "Sir," and the lone courtesy candle appears on his birthday cake, the middle-aged man is quite ready to magnify his problems. His ego suffers another blow when he moves into the bifocal stage and he finds that his insurance rates are going up. It is in this stage that the middle-aged man sometimes begins to take out his aggression against his family and his job. During this period of emotional second adolescence, the middle-aged worker may be difficult to deal with and the manager may be hard to work for. The professional begins to take stock of where he stands.

Middle-Age Problems in the Female

In the preceding chapter we indicated that our culture has fostered some prejudices against women, particularly at the economic level (see page 164). The female in middle age must cope with both psychological and physiological changes. Many strains and inconsistencies are built into the system that casts them in various roles. The insistence on glamour in our youth-oriented society is one example of the pressures on the middle-aged woman.

Most of us have a feeling for the concept of role. We see it being played out all around us—at home, on campus, and at work. Understanding middle-age problems relates to three general classes of roles. First, we have the *prescribed role* which is expected of us in any given situation. Throughout history it was generally accepted that man was head of the household; thus, the role of woman fell beneath him. Second, we have the *subjective role.* Here both male and female perceive their own positions, and what we perceive may be in conflict with what we would choose. Third, we have the *enacted role,* in which the individual behaves in some given way. Sometimes we play roles in a given way because we have to, or because we want to, or because we feel we should. The "have to" role often is the one that hurts.

When we run into role-playing situations that point up inconsistencies between roles that one has assumed, or been forced into, we sometimes revolt. Some unanswered questions may bother us. Are personality differences, at least in part, sex-related? Are women, in general, more docile and dependent than men? Are men more success-oriented than women? Do some roles come more naturally for females? The current emphasis on the liberation of women is raising anew some basic problems about sex differences and the roles we all play. The "biological" and "social" seem to come together naturally when our thinking turns to questions of sex differences. One thing we do know is that menopause is not only real but forms a base for middle-age revolt in the female, comparable to, or even stronger than, the revolt in the male.

Some women use menopause as a reason to go from one physician to another looking for medication. They search out diets, exercises, and sometimes the occult. The biological change becomes further complicated in our culture by the exaggeration of psychological conflicts. The woman in middle age often sees her beauty and sexual attractiveness fading and social success becoming more restricted. As children grow up and go out on their own, there is psychological loss of maternal influence. The muscular cramps, dizzy spells, and "hot flashes" that accompany the change of life for the female add to the emotional problems of middle age.

There is a physiological basis for the emotional problems that start in the late thirties. For example, there is some breakdown of hormones produced by the adrenal glands, along with other biological changes. Middle age in the female, as in the male, is characterized by periods of anxiety and depression. It is a time when both sexes refuse to accept a revised self image. And let us repeat what we have indicated about the male: the emotional upsets of middle age in the female are normal; most women are affected by them. But there is also the positive side. By the time of middle age, we have already established some habits of self-control that not only support us, but also give us some understanding of the frailties of human nature.

Status

In middle age, status becomes very important. At this stage the man or woman wishes to be looked up to by youth for advice and asked by the aged for help. Rules and procedures in the organization make status differences quite visible by making it clear who gives the orders and wields influence. Allied with status is self-esteem. Whether one will attempt to persuade others depends in part on his estimate of his own competence. The higher one's status, the more control he or she has over what happens on the job. More status means more opportunity to participate in decisions.

Studies show a general tendency to overestimate one's own job and to underestimate the job of others. This often brings about confusion. The waitress may see herself as having more status than the short-order cook when she tells him what orders to fill. Not only does he resent taking orders from a female whom he regards as having lower status than his own, but he sees himself not as a cook but as a chef.

Status confusion also arises because a person with high status in one situation may be low in the pecking order somewhere else. The superintendent of a small-town branch office who is "Mr. Big" may find himself virtually without status when rotated to a staff headquarters position. The bookkeeper in the small operation may lose status when advanced to the position of one of many computer programmers, even though the latter job pays better.

People react differently to status symbols. One person who gets a job title change without additional authority, responsibility, and compensation may feel no status enhancement whatsoever. In fact he may resent being so treated. Another person may prefer a title change which makes his job sound more important; he may even wish not to have additional authority and responsibility.

The Negative and the Positive

In terms of problems the middle-aged person worries over the delinquencies of youth, the insecurities of old age, and the devastations of disease and war. He or she is concerned with the decay of democracy, with holding down his job, and with balancing budgets. One of the costs to the middle-aged person in terms of energy is exacted by his or her community responsibilities, in which one can contribute much in the way of skills and wisdom. However, for many people who have reached their limits on the job, community activities provide for lateral growth, which partly satisfies the drive to attain success.

Caught in the period between being "still young" and "already old," the middle-ager shoulders psychological burdens which are often kept hidden. To talk too openly about them would possibly lower the person's status, even if he or she could get anyone to listen.

Guilt feelings of failure are typical of the middle-ager. We feel we have not advanced far enough in our job or profession. We are concerned that we have not made adequate economic provision for our family in the event that something happens to us. The middle-aged person feels that the doors of opportunity are closing fast. He or she is concerned about status when noting the high divorce rate among peers. In much the same way that the adolescent magnifies his problems, so does the person in middle age.

But there is a *positive* side to middle age. Certain hazards of life have passed; for example, there is more tenure on the job for those who planned ahead. These people are also in positions of dignity and power. They have more knowledge, skill, and wisdom than they had in youth. Anxieties have decreased. Now one can get more satisfaction from the "simple life." Marital companionship may be closer than ever if the couple can survive the biological and psychological changes that take place during middle age.

CHANGES IN MIDDLE AGE

Physically, both men and women find their most difficult adjustment in middle age during the change of life. In women this period, with its loss of child-bearing capacity, is called "menopause" (see page 185). The average age for menopause is about forty-five years, but it varies greatly with heredity and general health conditions. Early puberty usually means late menopause and vice versa.

The physical aspects of the male climacteric are quite different from those of menopause. It comes later, usually in the sixties or seventies, and occurs at a very slow rate. Psychological change, however, occurs during the forties in terms of the revolt we have spoken of.

Self Concept in Middle Age

For some two decades the young adult has become used to himself or herself. The male knows much about his assets and weaknesses, and has learned to play various occupational roles accordingly. The female has learned to play even more roles. But gradually, following the middle-age revolt, roles begin to change, and so does self concept. To replace the roles of parent, social affiliations widen; citizenship activities expand; homemaking and hobbies are intensified. However, the person who has played few roles is less likely to expand interests. It is particularly important for adjustment that one be able to shift emotional attachments as well as ego involvements. As one psychologist put it, "The individual must withdraw emotional capital from one role and invest it in another one."

Revision in self concept comes gradually. Changes relate more to physical than to intellectual abilities. Because the individual feels that there is a cultural demand to "stay young," the man judges himself in terms of appearance, dress, and youthful activities. Women who find earlier roles ending, whose husbands (if successful) are emphasizing work and community activities, and whose children no longer need care often express feelings of uselessness. Boredom is sometimes added to the "three B's" of bridge, bonbons, and bourbon. The poorly adjusted woman has the exaggerated idea that she is losing her sex appeal and that her husband may turn to other women. The unmarried career woman also undergoes change. Realizing that her career (particularly in glamour fields) is in danger from competition with younger women brings on stress. The realization that her chances of marriage are dwindling enhances the problem.

Because men continue to work, they feel the effects of role change less than women. Competition at work disturbs the man who never felt himself too successful even in youth. Some men in their forties or fifties have symptoms similar to those of the female menopause. They complain of anxiety, depression, irritability, and fatigue. They are conscious of having to cut down on their intake of food and drink, and at a time when financially they can best afford some luxury. Some adopt the attitude that if you are over fifty you are entitled to indulge yourself.

Changes in Interests

The shift in the direction of cultural pursuits is characteristic of both men and women in middle age. There is a tendency to turn from interests that deplete the energy reserves to reading, art, and music, from participative roles to observer roles.

Well-adjusted middle-aged men and women become generally more conservative. The less fortunate are conscious of the lack of money. The man who has been comfortably well off in earlier years is less concerned about making money than when he was younger—assuming, of course, that there are no marked demands on him by children and relatives. The middle-aged woman, however, finds money of more concern, because it means security to her. In middle age there is a change in attitude toward the use of money. Studies show that middle-agers consider extravagance more serious than do college students.

Some of the frictions between youth and parents relate to reactions to interests. One reason why solutions are hard to come by centers on *communication of feelings.* A comparison of college students with middle-aged business and professional men revealed that the older group responded more quickly to emotion-provoking stimuli. The older men were less calm and easygoing than the younger, but they were more reserved in expressing their feelings. Younger men had more frequent periods of excitement, restlessness, and "blueness" than did the middle-agers.

Success and Failure

Some people enter middle life with a background of success revealed by various types of recognition. Others enter the prime of life with a past history of failure. In either case there is no quarrel with the criteria of evaluation. But what of the man who feels himself a failure while others applaud his successes? What about the man who questions the standards for judging success and failure? What about the woman who felt handicapped just because she was female?

For most adults the early forties are a period of evaluation. The man examines his career to see how he rates according to goals established in youth; the woman looks at her career or marriage in terms of earlier alternatives.

In a culture such as ours, which both idealizes and rewards youth, some pressures act to prevent people from admitting to themselves that they are becoming older. Add to this the fact that our culture encourages youth to set aspirations beyond the bounds of realization. One can see how when evaluation comes, it comes with a jolt.

A person's criteria of success may be greatly different from those of his or her colleague. We cannot establish universal criteria, and the generally accepted definitions of success seldom satisfy any one person. Sometimes individual criteria for personal success do not satisfy society in its abstract, mass personality. A man may hold a position of authority, with responsibility and prestige; he may be making a good salary; yet in his own judgment, he is a failure. In constrast, the world at large may think a man a virtual failure, while he himself has reached a peace of mind which can fairly be called success. Through thoughtful career planning in youth, this middle-ager attempted to balance the levels of ability, of opportunity, and of aspirations within a critical set of limits to achieve success in work and in personal life. He gradually learned that repeated frustrations lowered his aspirations, and he also learned that repeated successes raised them. But when he sought to keep in balance his levels of ability and levels of aspiration, he found he was walking a tightrope.

Many people who pass the middle-age test find their most psychologically rewarding years are ahead. There are others who age without growing up.

THE PSYCHOLOGY OF AGING

One of the problems that middle-agers face is caring for aged parents. One of the problems elderly people face is loss of independence and sometimes having to move in with children and in-laws. And some may have to play by new government rules in order to participate in various aid programs. At best, getting old creates a new set of problems for both the individual and society. In the remainder of this chapter we shall discuss the psychological aspects of these problems. A household made up of children, adolescents, youth, and old age certainly provides a laboratory setting for studying human relationships.

Decrease in Performance

From a rapidly increasing amount of research come some generalizations which add up to saying that aging is associated with a gradual decrease in the performance of most bodily organs. The speed of this change varies, however, from one organ system to another, even in the same individual. For example, muscle strength decreases 50 percent between the ages of thirty and ninety, while the speed of an impulse passing down a nerve fiber is reduced only 15 percent in this same time span. Among production workers only a slight decrease in productivity occurs after age forty-five. The decrease does not become substantial until age sixty. As for office workers, little if any decline occurs prior to age sixty, and the subsequent decline is minor.

Researchers looking for suggestions of changes in mental function resulting solely from age have found virtually no changes in the fifties that were inevitable. Some persons in their sixties and seventies show loss of memory, reasoning, and decision-making ability, *but many do not.* It may be that the brain does not become exhausted so much by overwork as by what happens during the process of working. The individual may become worn out from the emotional stress accompanying the effort. Of course, there may also be decline in the ability of the brain through disuse.

Individual Differences in Aging

Individual differences among older people are extensive. There are attitudinal sex differences which are significant. For example, a study was made of 590 men and 770 women, over the age range of twenty-one to sixty-five, on the need for affiliation, achievement, and power. Among men, need for achievement dropped with age, but need for power rose. Among women, need for affiliation and need for power dropped.

The older person finds that he is sometimes in conflict with himself. He has a craving to straighten out the affairs of others and to express himself on every subject. After all, he does have experience and a store of wisdom. But he also is aware that on occasion he may be wrong. He knows a listener may get bored with his recital of endless detail. He wants to be thoughtful but not nosy, helpful but not bossy, and in the end he hopes to have some friends. Older people react in various ways to this conflict.

With advancing age there is a tendency for behavior to return to an earlier pattern and a simpler level of function. This is one reason why it is advantageous to build up good habit patterns early in life. The idea that the single person, "alone in the world," will face an unhappy old age is contrary to experience. Not having had companionship over the years, he or she may be better adjusted to the declining years than a married person who loses the spouse. There are no traits found only in aged people, no "typical" description of old age, in spite of some overgeneralized stereotypes to the contrary. Literally thousands of studies of vision, hearing, muscular strength, reaction time, psychomotor coordination, and various job performances have shown great individual differences at every age. In general, *physical aging comes earlier than mental aging.* The reverse sometimes occurs, however, in those people whose personality is such that they believe they are growing old. Such people may say they are losing their memory, when in actuality they probably put little or no effort into learning something in the first place. Psychological aging in some sense is a defensive mechanism, possibly useful at times.

Interest in money represents a highly individual type of behavior. Such interest, which may have waned some in middle age, generally is revived in old age for those who seek security or who wish to leave property to their children or grandchildren. However, some elderly persons seem unconcerned about money above a subsistence level. A few like to accumulate or manage money as a game. Enjoying the manipulation of large sums of money may interest some, while others use its manipulation more symbolically. One former vice-president and treasurer of a large corporation living in retirement said he looked forward each month to a meeting of his local shuffleboard club. Much discussion of finances was always in order—what to do with a balance of $55 in the treasury!

PRERETIREMENT—A CHANGING PATTERN

There are mixed trends in the thinking about earlier and earlier retirement. On the one hand, automation is pushing toward the earlier retirement of those people who are being replaced by machines and in those situations where there is need to spread jobs around. There are pressures to retire men early to give the new generation a chance. On the other hand, some people are just beginning to reach the peak of their skill, creativity, and wisdom as early retirement forces a change. Psychologically, there are, no doubt, some people whose personality favors a do-little kind of life; but the many studies of boredom and of how people spend their leisure indicate that having little or nothing to do may bring on problems.

Leisure time (free time after subtracting working time, sleeping, eating, and other essential activity) has increased from three hours in 1870, to five hours in 1910, and up to eight hours in 1960. It has been estimated that it will not be long before half of the twenty-four-hour day is leisure time. What do people do with this time? Most surveys show entertainment to be well in the lead. Almost three-quarters of leisure time is so invested. To some, leisure time is a myth. It may be better thought of as time for creative expression. Planning for leisure may be psychologically the same in some respects as planning for retirement.

Criteria for Retirement

"Aging, true physiological aging, is not determined by the time elapsed since birth, but by the total amount of wear and tear to which the body has been exposed. There is, indeed, a great difference between physiologic and chronological age." These words of Hans Selye, who has worked on the problems of aging and the stress of life for over three decades, give us a key to the problem of how long any given individual should continue to work. Measuring physiological or psychological age is most difficult. Forces other than "the good of the individual" have set standards. After all, chronological age *is* easy to determine, and it does give us a universal standard.

The magic age of sixty-five for retirement came about originally as a base for social security legislation. It was lowered to sixty-two for women shortly after the Social Security Act was passed. One may question the logic of this type of differentiation. It could hardly have been made because women outlive men by some four years. Under various conditions and with some options one, of course, may, and in some instances must, retire before sixty-five or sixty-two. The trend, however, toward lower retirement ages continues to increase. Most Americans never retire. They are either forced out of work or they die before retirement. Of those who retire, some 25 percent try to find new work. There is not a great deal of retirement moonlighting, particularly among those receiving social security.

Preparation for Retirement

Most of those who work up to the last possible day, then face the problem of no longer being employed, feel the retirement impact. Some organizations now have planned programs of preretirement counseling, seminars, and easing-up practices in which the person gradually gets used to doing less. Such job decompression programs are helpful for some people.

Social attitudes toward old age are generally unfavorable, causing some people to delay, even resist, preparation for approaching old age, except for building up financial reserve in pensions. There is realization of the chance of having physical handicaps, but usually less attention is given to the psychological aspects of a feeling of uselessness, inactivity, loneliness, and boredom. One elderly woman in England reported that she was sorry when it was no longer necessary to queue up for buying groceries because "I had someone to talk to."

It is possible to predict in middle age, even sooner in some people, what kind of adjustment the person will make in old age. For those who have sought change, or at least showed only token resistance to it, and who have health, financial security, and companionship, old age can be a time of happiness. For some it is a time for enjoying the results of one's labors. It is a time of independence, when the person is no longer driven by ambition and regulated by work. It is a time to enjoy the prestige of wisdom, the loyalty and devotion of family. In a community where leisure is a status symbol of success, the elderly have priority. But, one may ask, what are the chances that these favorable factors will fall my way?

Individuals who are psychologically tough and resilient have learned patterns of adjustment that are useful in their declining years. They are, by and large, people who see themselves as active agents in their own progress, who are not willing to leave their future in the hands of others. These are the people who prepare for retirement psychologically as well as physically and economically. They are the individuals who see that preparation during middle age can lessen the impact of retirement. They are the people who understand that in some settings the older person can be hit by a "youthquake" and still survive.

Preparation for retirement involves a measure of prethinking about the questions one should consider months in advance of actual retirement. Many questions center on physical health and financial problems. Social Security offices across the country have written material, kept up to date, dealing with a wide variety of questions and answers in these areas. Here we wish to consider three factors and add some questions that may help persons think ahead on problems of psychological adjustment to retirement.

Three Basic Factors

Planning for retirement is quite individualistic, but for all of us three basic factors may well be involved. First, we need to look at our individual *personality* (see page 50). The relatively lazy, procrastinating type of person has less difficulty in filling time than does the person who has lived a life of hard, time-consuming work. The upward mobile individual may find that he or she really has no place to go. The indifferent person may not pay too much attention to prethinking on retirement; whatever will be, will be. The person who could always spend leisure time puttering around may find this trait an advantage in retirement. Second, how well one adjusts to retirement relates to previous *life-style.* The person who needs stimulation from others for motivational purposes has built a life-style accordingly. The loner has developed a behavior style more in line with self-motivated activities. Some people need to feel out new situations gradually. Here partial retirement strung out over a period of time may lessen retirement shock. This is the concept involved in job decompression where one gradually slows down from the pressures of the work environment. An analysis of life-style can help determine those aspects of behavior that will have to change with retirement. Third, our *previous habit of riding with change* is related to adjustment in retirement. Persons who have thrived on change, who have repeatedly sought out new types of situations to adjust to, have an advantage over those who have strongly resisted change.

Some Personal Questions

From formal studies, and from people who have described their years of getting ready for and living in retirement, we present some questions for prethinking about psychological adjustment to retirement:

Where do I want to live, and where can I afford to live? For some persons, or couples, the retirement community may be the answer; for others, remaining in the same place may be best. Again, the question relates to the concept of matching the individual with the psychological climate (see page 409).

How can I occupy time without getting too bored, and also get some satisfaction from what I do? One retiree exemplified the problem: "The most useful thing I do all day is going down to the corner for the newspaper."

What roles that I have been used to will I have to give up?

What new roles should I consider?

What goals do I keep? What new ones should I establish?

Which past skills should I keep up? Which ones should I let go?

Regarding retirement as a new or modified career, what planning is involved (see page 193)?

What types of new friendships do I need to establish?

Will continuing education help me to remain alert?

Where do hobbies and sports fit into the changing scene?

Should I look for new interests?

Other questions may center on how long all those "little jobs" will last, how much traveling one really wants, and how realistic one has been in analyzing those retirement community ads. Questions also center on doing things at a slower pace and engaging in appropriate voluntary work. Planning for leisure has been said to be psychologically comparable to planning for retirement. Such nationwide organizations as the million-member American Association of Retired Persons (215 Long Beach Boulevard, Long Beach, California 90802) provide current information on many problems related to preretirement and to life-styles in retirement, ranging from the up-to-date descriptions of the pros and cons of retirement communities in various regions to the current problems of the destitute elderly. Attention is given to legislative efforts related to aging. These periodicals also help the elderly feel that they still belong.

RETIREMENT

Problems in retirement range widely: from boredom to bucking attitudes against age; from loss of relatives through death to the breaking up of friendship cliques; and from loss of independence to deterioration in influence credit.

Self Concept

Several factors influence self concept in old age: (1) the history of one's habit structures; (2) acceptance or rejection of the cultural stereotype of aging; (3) feelings of success or failure in life; (4) the cultural climate in which one is spending most of his or her time. This cultural climate includes living arrangements, club affiliations, and the amount of independence one has in decision-making processes about his or her way of living. Finally, self concept is influenced by the criteria used for getting old. Some may use chronological age. Others evaluate themselves in terms of failing eyesight or hearing or a tendency to fatigue easily, and still others use sexual potency as the indicator of their point of no return. For some getting old is indicated by an increase in the poverty of loneliness.

Studies show that subjective age is closely related to morale, rigidity, and fantasy behavior. It is also related to treatment by others and to the ability to get around. Among institutionalized people, negative attitudes seem to be the result of institutionalization rather than of age per se.

Personality Differences

One man in his seventies described retirement in these words:

> I began planning for retirement when I was nearing sixty. My wife was involved in each decision made about it. Preparation involved three main problems—financial, physical, and mental. The most frequent question asked me after I retired was, "What do you do to keep busy?" Well, I never find the time to do all the things I want to. If you are married you find you are not retired. You have gone on a "Honeydew vacation"—"Honey do this, honey do that."

A woman gave the following description:

> My husband retired at sixty-two when his company merged. For the first few months it was wonderful, just like we were on an extended vacation. But then things became different for him. He gets tired of watching television and he can work around the house just so much. Although successful in the business world he has not succeeded in adjusting to retirement. As for me, a woman never retires anyway.

From many descriptions and studies of retirement one generalization stands out: People react to retirement according to individual patterns that may be more marked in maturity than they are in childhood, adolescence, youth, and middle age. Some retire and like it, some tolerate it, and some fight it. Aging may come gracefully or it may come in anger.

In a statistically analyzed study of male aging and personality at the University of California, five clusters of persons were found.

Among the well-adjusted were the "mature" men who understood the developmental processes reasonably well. They accepted themselves realistically and grew old without regret for the past. These men were relatively free from neurotic conflict, and they had little difficulty in spending their time in psychologically satisfying ways.

Next in order came the "rocking-chair type." These men welcomed freedom from responsibility. In some ways retirement gave them what they had wanted for a long time. Old age provided the opportunity to indulge in their passive needs. As one observer put it, "The rocking chair is a great institution. It is a way of sitting still and moving at the same time."

In the middle of the fivefold classification from well-adjusted to nonadjusted came the "armored" men. These individuals maintained a well-functioning system of defenses against anxiety by keeping busy. Always doing something keeps down worry and anxiety. No doubt this type of reaction in older persons is related to successes they had earlier in life.

Among the poorly adjusted came the fourth type, the "angry" men. These people were bitter over failures to achieve their life goals. They blamed other people for their disappointments, or they attributed defeat to the organizational climate.

Finally, the study factored out the "self-haters." These were the people who turned their resentments inward. They blamed themselves for their misfortunes. This unhappy group of retired people were depressed rather than angry.

Changing Role Patterns

Many persons "practice" for retirement by giving up work and starting again, and by trying out various life-style arrangements. Some people go for full disengagement from work while others prefer a more gradual approach. Some people find that taking a long trip right after formal retirement is one way of easing out of old routines. Breaks in life-styles can give one new directions. Studies show that even women who have never worked outside of the home find part-time jobs in retail stores or similar places a satisfactory way to "make the break."

As they approach old age, most people restrict their social roles, reducing the number and variety of their contacts. Old friends are lost; new friends do not quite take their place. Said one successful seventy-year-old retiree: "I soon found that I had to come in balance with the new roles I had to play, based mainly on a very low level of involvement." From many writings about the problems of retirement one central thought emerges: Formal disengagement from work means abandoning life's central roles; this results in a reduced social

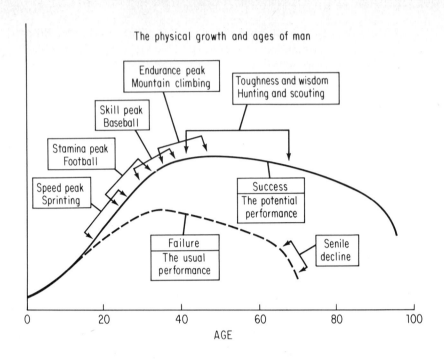

The physical growth and ages of man

Endurance peak
Mountain climbing

Toughness and wisdom
Hunting and scouting

Skill peak
Baseball

Stamina peak
Football

Speed peak
Sprinting

Success
The potential
performance

Failure
The usual
performance

Senile
decline

AGE

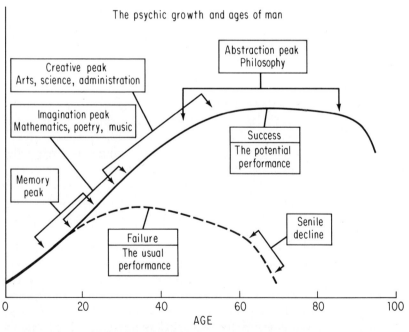

The psychic growth and ages of man

Abstraction peak
Philosophy

Creative peak
Arts, science, administration

Imagination peak
Mathematics, poetry, music

Memory
peak

Success
The potential
performance

Failure
The usual
performance

Senile
decline

AGE

FIG. 8-1 Possibility and actual performance. In these two graphs the solid curve indicates the physical or psychological potential of normal people, with peak periods for various activities. How most people fail to measure up to these potentials is indicated by the broken curve.

life. For those with a past history of being able to adjust well, there is little or no crisis or loss of morale, following retirement. Role change in retirement relates to one's own personality, life experience, habits, health, and energy status. There is, after all, an art of retirement.

INDIVIDUAL POTENTIAL

In concluding Part Two of the text covering individual development, let us ask the question: How many of us in childhood, adolescence, youth, middle age, and beyond really perform anywhere near our potential? In Figure 8-1 we see one projection which suggests that most normal people fail to measure up to their potential either physically or psychologically. In some measure, this may mean that we fail to take stock of the many assets we have.

SUMMARY

Adjustments of youth are effective and noticeable. Psychologically, youth is a period involving some agonizing indecisiveness in career planning. Youth is aware of change and welcomes it. On the job, youth must look for opportunities where anticipations can be realized and enthusiasms rewarded; where dissatisfaction with one job may be remedied by taking another; where physical strength and vitality to some degree make up for the lack of training and experience. Typically the college sophomore attempts to sort out the emotional problems from those that are intellectual.

Change characterizes our society, with its positives and its negatives. The choice of a vocation is not an event that happens suddenly, but rather is a process extending over a period of time. In youth, development is a compromise process in which the self concept is a product of the interaction of inherited aptitudes, neural and endocrine makeup, and the opportunity to play various roles.

Middle age is a "crisis" stage for both male and female. For men it is a revolt centering on lost dreams and feelings of guilt, a period of taking stock of where they stand, a period of second adolescence where one revolts both against one's spouse and against one's job. In terms of a statistical criterion, male revolt is normal.

Middle-age problems in the female center on both physiological and psychological changes; role change enhances the problems of muscular cramps, dizzy spells, and "hot flashes." Middle age in the female, as in the male, is characterized by periods of anxiety and depression, where status becomes very important. The self concept in middle age develops gradually from negative revolt to positive realities.

Many people who pass the middle-age test find their most psychologically rewarding years ahead. Others age without growing up. Middle age is a time to reevaluate the criteria of success and failure.

Beyond middle age one finds the positive as well as the negative; some compensations for losses accompany aging. With a decrease in muscular strength and psychomotor performance often comes an increase in social perception and wisdom. Preretirement brings on a changing pattern of life-style marked by individual differences. Preparation for retirement involves prethinking and preplanning related to three basic factors: personality, life-styles, and previous habits of coping with change. It is important to prepare for retirement psychologically as well as physically and economically. Personal questions center on doing things at a slower pace and planning for more leisure time and a change in life-style where there is less social interaction.

Problems in formal retirement range widely: from boredom to bucking attitudes against age; from loss of relatives and friends to loss of influence and independence. The problem of self concept relates closely to personality, changing role patterns, and a realistic evaluation of individual potentiality. At the positive level we can remind ourselves that at any age we can and should take stock of our assets as well as our liabilities.

THE ASSETS WE NEED

MAKING THE MOST OF OUR ABILITIES

9

We all feel at times that we do not have all that it takes to get where we want to go. At other times we believe that there is no job that really demands all our capabilities. This is fortunate, since none of us is physically, mentally, or emotionally anywhere near perfect. Thus, we are normal workers in relation to the jobs we can do successfully and handicapped workers in relation to the jobs we are physically, mentally, educationally, or emotionally unable to perform satisfactorily.

How we feel about our general intelligence and special abilities relates to the standards we have set for ourselves or to those imposed upon us. It also relates to our individual patterns of adjustment, as we discussed in Chapter 4. In contrast to the well-adjusted person, who concentrates on what he can do, the individual low in self-esteem dwells on what he can't do.

Why are attitudes of inferiority so common? In part, it is because our culture is so success-oriented, as we described earlier (see page 189). We tend to use the "ideal" as our standard, evaluating ourselves not by our abilities and accomplishments but by our limitations and mistakes. Of course, we also appreciate the accomplishments of the many who stand out, from Nobel and Pulitzer prize winners to outstanding artists and captains of industry. But we sometimes forget that the world is run by the majority of us. We have, perhaps, put too much emphasis on the IQ as a number, failing to realize that beyond a given level, personality, motivation, opportunities, education, and training contribute more to occupational success and failure than does general intelligence. Since we have become so test-conscious in our American culture, let us now discuss psychological testing as it relates to general intelligence and to special abilities.

PSYCHOLOGICAL TESTING

Many readers of this text are familiar with intelligence tests, since they may have taken them, possibly even several times. They may be less familiar with special ability tests. We think of the intelligence test as providing comparative data on our ability to acquire new information, to profit from experience, and to adjust to new situations (see page 134).

Range of Intelligence

Most people are normal or near normal in intelligence and these are the people with whom we usually associate day-by-day. The two extremes are the mentally retarded at one end and the mentally gifted at the other. Compared to the normal range of 90 to 110 IQ, the lower extreme includes persons with an IQ below 70. In between we have borderline cases.

At the other end of the intelligence range is the gifted person. We speak of the "very superior" in the 130 to 140 IQ range and the "genius" as above 140. It is important, however, to emphasize that IQ is not everything. We all have seen the gifted person, perhaps very verbal but lacking totally in artistic, psychomotor, or mechanical ability. He or she may not have the qualities or skills many jobs call for. General intelligence, as measured by conventional intelligence tests, does not always relate to the job to be done. Beyond a certain point other things may count more toward success, particularly in a nonverbal work-oriented climate.

Kinds of Tests

Tests come by the thousands. There are individual and group tests of the paper-and-pencil variety and there are apparatus-work-sample tests. There are performance tests, those involving speed versus power, and subjective-objective tests. There are proficiency and achievement tests. Increasingly important are the "behavioral objectives" tests that diagnose the things we can do readily and those in which we are deficient. The functions measured by tests include intelligence, aptitude, ability, achievement, interest, personality, and a variety of skills such as musical, mechanical, and artistic. Since so much of the practical world relates to special abilities, let us consider some of them.

SPECIAL ABILITIES

Specific jobs require specific skills. Salesmen and teachers, for example, need verbal ability; engineers need mechanical comprehension and dexterity in using their hands. Accounting emphasizes numerical ability, and the scientist needs to understand complex things, be oriented toward theory, and often be able to work with apparatus. The professional football player needs not only psychomotor skills and physical stamina but also split-second cognitive abilities for reading defense shifts. Special abilities relate to coordination, to verbal and quantitative things, to spatial comprehension and other things. Some of these abilities are discussed below.

Psychomotor Abilities

Let us begin by describing the clumsy person, who technically may be described as having "motor difficulties" or in need of remedial "perceptual motor learning." He can be the child who always gets chosen last in games, who is slow learning to ride a bike, and who cannot seem to catch a ball. He may even be handicapped in writing with a pencil. Whether or not he outgrows his clumsiness (and many do not) he has taken a lot of psychological punishment from his peers and has built up various compensations as he tries to work around his handicaps. But the clumsy person is not alone, at least statistically. It is estimated that some 20 percent of all school-age youngsters have psychomotor handicaps. And it is important to remember that they are not "just stupid." They vary over the entire IQ range. Although we do not know why, more boys than girls suffer from psychomotor difficulties. The causes may range from birth injuries to a lack of oxygen supply to the brain during the prenatal state. The perceptual-motor handicapped person often has an excellent hereditary background in terms of his or her gene structure. One authority says: "The prognosis for these kids is pretty good, if we catch them young enough. We give them writing help, have them practice tightrope walking and teach them to turn somersaults on padded mats. We try to add a little to their self-image."

The application of psychomotor skill ranges widely, from threading a needle to flying an airplane. The ability to use one's sensory-motor equipment efficiently is necessary in many job situations and in many walks of life—for example, in dentistry, surgery, science, engineering, and in the various skilled trades.

Athletic Ability

Many of us associate athletic ability with the word "psychomotor," and with reason. Psychomotor behavior, honed to a fine edge, is exhibited to us year-round when we observe sports. There are exceptions, but in general there is a positive relationship between success at sports at the professional level and intelligence. The learning and problem-solving involved in football offers a common example. Studies show that two factors are important in athletic success. The first is general good health, combined with initial psychomotor ability in running, jumping, and throwing. Second, in spite of many instances of all-around athletes, learning in terms of professional proficiency is usually specific. The person capable of a professional career in either baseball or football must choose between them. Both may play golf, but as an amateur on the side.

Mechanical Ability

Psychomotor competence, of course, relates closely to mechanical ability, which is actually a combination of skills. In addition to the ability to perceive mechanical relationships, strength, precision, speed of movement, and the ability to combine all of them are needed. Complex tests of mechanical aptitude have proved to be more successful than simple ones. Mechanical ability is not really correlated with general intelligence, but this does not mean that intelligence is unnecessary for mechanical work. It means rather that sheer mechanical ability is distributed among people without much regard to the things that intelligence tests measure. Many intelligent people have great mechanical skill, and some have none. For success in a mechanical field, both special ability and general intelligence are necessary, but these two components must be measured separately. Such talents as music and art fit a similar pattern.

Musical Ability

"You have it or you don't have it" is a slightly exaggerated statement we can make about our potential in the area of music. In music perhaps more than in any other human activity, the existence of special talent is clearly recognized. Most great musicians have exhibited their ability at a very early age. The measurement of musical ability involves such things as sensitivity to pitch, intensity, time, and appreciation for rhythm, timbre, consonance, and volume. Manipulative skill is obviously essential in both vocal and instrumental music. Of course, one may have little or no performance ability to enjoy music. As a matter of fact, listening to music is our biggest national hobby.

Artistic Talent

Talent for drawing, painting, sculpture, or architectual and other design is also rather specific. Many of us cannot draw a straight line or paint a picture, regardless of our desire to express ourselves artistically. We have graphic arts scales for measuring drawings and measures of art judgment or "appreciation" resting on the ability to make fine discriminations, as well as measures of feeling and insight. But missing are valid measures of the creative aspects of art. Work samples are our best indicators.

Success in most special ability pursuits requires varying degrees of creative, innovative, and problem-solving ability.

Creativity

To be creative in any given area requires more than just some specific talent in art or science. From studies of creative people two generalizations can be made. First, the creativity involved in solving some difficult problem results from a tremendous preoccupation with that problem. Second, the creative problem solver must have a great tolerance for ambiguity. And for most people creativity comes at a price. So often the innovator is out of step with his times and therefore often rejected (see page 59).

The creative person is self-motivated. Statistically speaking, he or she is in the minority. Most creative productions are contributed by a small number of people. We know several things about such people. First, creativity is often noticed in childhood. Second, the creative child (or college student) may get "turned off" at school. Third, creative people are less conventional than others, regardless of field. Fourth, they usually show independence. Fifth, they do not always know where the results of their efforts will lead. Sixth, creative people tend to live within themselves; they are often hard to live with.

TRAINING AND EDUCATION

As we know, we may have potential in some area that never gets developed. Here training and education enter in, and there is a distinction between the two. *Training* relates to the teaching of specific skills. *Education* is broader and less specific; we learn things that relate to proficiency in future situations. Learning to type or mastering the specifics of mechanical drawing exemplify training. Learning anatomy or the principles of psychology are considered to be educational. We speak of both driver "training" and driver "education." The first, the specifics of building up psychomotor habits, is training; what we learn about traffic laws and safety principles involves education. Many college programs, of course, combine training and education. "Career education," for example, is a balance between work-oriented training and academic preparation.

Many organizations give on-the-job training to the graduate of high school or college because in many instances an individual's educational experience seldom prepares him for a particular job. Most of us continue to get an education all our lives as we observe, read, study, and accumulate information. Sometimes we also need to be trained or retrained in something. The artist or the engineer may learn some new technique. The businessman may take a course in computer programing for the purpose of education; someone else may take the course to become a programmer. Although somewhat artificial, the distinction between training and education is useful at times in relating our learning to our goals. We sometimes engage in continuing education because we want to know what is going on; we may seek a training program because some ways of doing things are better than others.

Toward Growth of Self-Confidence

When the clumsy youngster learns to ride a bike, and becomes proficient at it, some bit is added to his or her feeling of self-confidence. The artist who sells a painting and the author who gets a good book review finds his or her self-confidence enhanced. But what if the painting goes unsold and the book gets bad reviews?

Self-confidence comes through self-understanding and relates closely to what we do with our abilities and how we learn to work around our disabilities. It is also important to recognize that we all tend to slip back at times, to feel inferior to others. It is difficult to continually keep our strong points in mind; perhaps we shouldn't even expect to do so. Self-understanding, and hence self-confidence, comes, as Carl Rogers says, from "being open to experience." This is the opposite of being defensive. Our personal self-evaluation is determined gradually as we come into contact with competition. One reason the adolescent has so much difficulty in developing a positive self-image is his tendency to compare himself with "the ideal." Girls who try to rate their own physical attractiveness may feel inferior when they use a cover girl as a model. Boys often make comparisons with adults and come off second best. As we become more sophisticated, we become more realistic; the loss of idealism is a price we come to pay. Perhaps this is one reason why older college students are found to be more cynical (or wise!) than younger ones.

One must learn to trust his own experiences, as we have indicated in Chapter 4 on adjustment. He must be able to separate his real self from some role he may be playing. Although we are all influenced by early experiences, behavior is not irrevocably set. One of the beneficial effects of college experience is that it makes us aware of new possibilities for change and growth. Self-understanding is aided by both training and education, but it is still difficult to achieve. It is easier to understand another person's motives than our own.

Gaining self-confidence demands that we start somewhere. The college setting offers opportunity in the competitive environment of the classroom. Here we can always find room for improvement. "Learning to learn" has a payoff not only in the acquisition of good study habits but also in its contribution to the growth of self-confidence.

EFFICIENCY IN STUDY

All too frequently students finish their schooling without having learned how to use their study time well. To complete one's assignment in a minimum amount of time with a high degree of success, permitting sufficient time for leisure reading, sports, relaxation, and various extracurricular activities, is one important mark of a successful adjustment to college life.

That many students oversimplify the problem of how to study efficiently is shown in the frequently heard remark, "I didn't study hard enough." Statements like this imply that study efficiency is entirely a matter of putting forth extra effort. "Try harder next time and you will make out all right," is the pat solution. Certainly effort is important, but many students spend a great deal of time in study and accomplish much less than others who spend less time. The reason may well be that the effort of the time consumer is poorly directed. True, differences in ability may be a contributing factor, but on the other hand, there is ample evidence that a person of average ability who uses his time well often surpasses in accomplishment a more capable but less efficient individual.

You should not make the mistake of assuming that study efficiency is a topic of importance for only the poor or average student. All students, regardless of their grades, can profit from an analysis of effective study principles and their application. Indeed, surveys show that the study methods discussed in this chapter help good students as well as poor ones. Significantly, the best students profited even more than the poorer ones.

HOW GOOD A STUDENT ARE YOU?

Before reading further about the various conditions that you can manipulate and control to increase study efficiency, it is helpful to appraise yourself. The following questions allow us to differentiate between efficient and inefficient students. Read the questions and answer each one "yes" or "no" as honestly and accurately as you can.

1. Do you have several definite, strong reasons for going to college?
2. Do you have several good reasons for knowing the material in each course you are studying?
3. Do you have difficulty in finding time for study?
4. Do you have a daily study plan or schedule of work?
5. Do you adjust your study time to the difficulty of a course?
6. Do you usually spend time trying to be as relaxed as possible when you study?
7. Do you frequently strive to analyze your work and try to find out just where you are weak?
8. Do you frequently use the facts learned in one course to help you in the work of another course?
9. In preparing for an examination, do you try to memorize the text?
10. Do you often write the answer to a question, only to find that it is the answer to some other question on the examination?
11. Do you take your notes in class just as rapidly as you can write?
12. Do you sit up late at night before an exam studying?
13. Do you usually skim over a chapter before reading it in detail?
14. When you find a word in the textbook which you do not know, do you usually look it up in the dictionary?
15. Do you usually skip the graphs and tables in your textbook?

16. Do you stop at the end of each section of study material and review in your own words what you have read?
17. Do you usually study every day in the same place?
18. At the end of an assignment, do you quiz yourself in a fashion similar to that used in quizzes in class?
19. Do you read rapidly, always seeking the main ideas, and without speaking the words to yourself or pausing over words?
20. Do you make frequent use of artificial memory aids?

On page 224 you will find the answers which characterize the good student as compared with the poor one. Score your responses. Each disagreement with the key points to a bad habit or attitude which you should try to correct. Analyze your responses and make a summary of your weak points. Keep the summary before you as you read the remainder of this chapter. Doing this will make it apparent why a particular habit or attitude is undesirable.

MOTIVATION FOR STUDY

Despite an earlier statement that effort alone will not lead to efficient study, you should not minimize its importance. It is a basic requirement and one of the most difficult to cope with. Marshaling one's efforts presents a problem in motivation. From a future chapter on learning, you will see the importance of motivation in changing behavior (see page 257). Learning will not take place unless there is an underlying reason or motive to learn. In dealing with techniques for efficient study, we must face the learning problem. Indeed, the title of this section might well be "Learning How to Study."

If you attack your assignments in a lackadaisical fashion, doing little more than sitting with your book open before you in the hope that something will eventually "sink in," you are not going to make much progress. If self-analysis reveals lack of motivation, you should try to determine the cause. What are your goals in life? Is there any relationship between these goals and what you are doing in school? Are you attending college simply because your parents want you to, or because your friends are in college? Are you studying subjects in which you are really interested? A careful consideration of such questions will usually lead to answers from which you can plan an intelligent attack on your motivational problem.

Why College?

Why go to college? One observer put it this way: "If a person has to ask this question, then he will probably have difficulty understanding the answer."

When asked why they are going to college, many students reply that they want to land a good job, be distinguished citizens in their communities, and make good salaries. Surveys have shown that there is a significant relationship between these goals and college performance. On the average, those who make the best grades make the best incomes later on. The trend among employers is to offer the best jobs to those students who have made the best grades in shcool. Employers assume that the person who has learned to study efficiently, and thus to make good grades, will transfer his efficiency to the new job. Other measures of success besides salary are related to good grades.

Students with motivational problems sometimes say that they cannot get interested in books and ideas having to do with the nature of man's culture, his discoveries, ideals, art, and music. Generating such curiosity is to a considerable extent a matter of talking and associating with others who already have some enthusiasm about these things. If you need stirring up, cultivate contacts with teachers, lecturers, writers, and good students, and you will most likely become infected with their enthusiasm, curiosity, and intellectual inquisitiveness. Wisdom is related to motivation. Wisdom comes from the awareness of timing, recognition of change, and knowledge of one's own limitations as well as strong points.

SETTING UP A STUDY SCHEDULE

Although motivation is a prime requisite for effective study, there are those who, despite a strong interest in schoolwork and a high degree of natural ability, find it difficult to perform well academically. When teachers and counselors look into the causes of such academic failures, or near-failures, they often find an absence of an organized study routine. Efficient workers almost always have a set time and place for doing their work. If you think that you do not study enough, a schedule that outlines definite times for study will help. The student who protests scheduling his study time on the grounds that he will not have time for other activities is fooling himself. A schedule does not deprive one of time for nonstudy activities; it simply ensures that each type of activity gets its fair share of time. It is interesting that busy students who have outside jobs and engage in many extracurricular activities often make better grades than those who are much less busy. If you ask such a student how he finds time for study, he will invariably tell you that he has learned to organize or schedule his time. Having so many things to do forces him to allot a certain amount of time for each activity. Regardless of how busy you are, planning is likely to improve your efficiency.

In preparing a schedule, you should list all the activities of the day, whether class lecture, laboratory, students' activities, outside work, recreation, meals, or just plain loafing. In setting aside times for study, make them as specific as possible. Don't, for example, set aside two hours on Tuesday evening for studying; make it a time for studying a *specific subject.* Also, schedule a study period for a particular class as *close to the class period* as possible. The amount of time you give to a subject depends on individual circumstance. If you know that a subject is difficult for you, you will naturally schedule more time to study for it. These time allotments may, of course, change, depending on your experience with the schedule. You may find that preparation for an economics course requires more time than you had estimated, and that an English course requires less time. Make the change, but then stick to it until further experience tells how it is working out.

PHYSICAL SETTING FOR STUDY

It is highly important that the student study in the right setting *for him.* Motivation and scheduling are *preparatory* to the act of study. If the act is to be effectively carried out, it must take place in the proper environment. Reading should be done in diffused or indirect light. Green and blue lights should be avoided. Natural daylight of uniform intensity is easiest on the eyes. One's desk or table and chair should be so situated as to facilitate concentration. Sitting by a window that affords outside views is not a good practice because of possible distracting influences. Don't study in a lounge chair. Instead, use a hard, straight-backed chair and sit with the feet on the floor, shoulders squared, and book firmly grasped. These may be good suggestions for one person, but not for another. Some students prefer the comfort of lying down, with papers and books all around and a soda nearby. This may prove to be an efficient situation for study—but not for everyone! We must consider individual differences. What are your habits? How efficient are you?

In general, anything likely to produce excessive relaxation should be avoided during any kind of learning. There is much experimental evidence to substantiate this advice. For example, in one investigation, subjects exerted a mild muscular tension while learning. The tension was produced by gripping a hand dynamometer, an instrument designed to test the strength of grip. The subjects did not try to maintain their maximum grip. Instead, they merely exerted a continuous squeeze of moderate intensity. The results showed that those subjects who maintained a little muscular tension during learning were the most efficient in learning and in recalling what they had learned. Another experimenter found that mental work is done more efficiently during hunger contractions than at other times.

These and related facts show that learning is facilitated by bodily tensions that are not too strong. Intense contractions of the muscles or intense hunger would serve as distractions to effective learning. The applicable conclusion for study is that one should maintain a firm body posture but not permit himself to become strained as he studies.

Many students report that on occasion they have sought out some quiet isolated spot for studying an especially difficult assignment. Much to their surprise, they discovered that they did not accomplish nearly so much as they expected. The common experience of many is that work is done more rapidly and with less effort where there is some background of more or less regular noise. These observations are what one would expect in the light of what has been previously said about the effect of muscular tension on learning. Moderate intensities of noise produce some muscular tension, usually of such slight magnitude that it is not noticed. Nevertheless, this unnoticed tension is likely to increase speed in learning.

MAKING AN ASSIGNMENT MEANINGFUL

Everyday experience and laboratory experiments in the psychology of learning and remembering attest that meaningful material is learned faster and remembered longer than meaningless matter. You can demonstrate this to yourself by doing the following exercise.

Read twice the following list of nonsense syllables, close your book, and write down as many of the syllables as you can. Then determine your recall score and record it.

KUB, WIB, RIX, POZ, GIG, LUP, MOR, VEB, BEX, DOV,

FEL, GEB, HIC, JOM, NEB, BOC, GOK, CEX, REB, TOC

Next, read over twice the following list of related nouns and write them down in the proper order. Calculate your recall score and record it alongside the first.

TREE, GRASS, DOG, CAT, MAN, WOMAN, ELEPHANT,

CIRCUS, HOUSE, TENT, BRICK, MORTAR, POLICE, JUDGE,

PREACHER, CHURCH, LAWYER, DOCTOR, STUDENT,

TEACHER

Finally, read the following sentence; calculate and record your recall score.

YOUNG HENRY WHOSE FATHER IS A BUSINESS EXECU-

TIVE THINKS HE WOULD LIKE TO BE A POLICEMAN

WHEN HE GROWS UP.

Compare your recall scores for the three types of material. A comparison of the findings will show the relative learnability of meaningful versus meaningless material.

Perhaps you are saying, "The results of the experiment are clear enough, but what application do they have to the study of an assignment in English or psychology?" Oddly enough, many students try to learn textbook assignments as so many meaningless statements. This they do when they memorize material and try to repeat it verbatim. This kind of learning may be retained for a short period, but it will never become a real part of one's mental equipment. It is much better to study for the purpose of getting ideas that make sense in themselves and are related to other ideas.

Getting the Meaning Four Ways

With an assignment before you, how should you treat it so that it will be meaningful? The first thing to do is to *skim the assignment.* Read over the material rapidly before starting intensive study. This bird's-eye view will provide a general idea of what the assignment is about and will add greatly to the meaning of the parts to be examined later. As you skim through the material, pay attention to the section headings; they tell you how the material is put together and what the main subject of each section is going to be.

Another obvious, but usually neglected, practice that contributes to meaningful study is to *use a dictionary.* Don't pass over unfamiliar words. Whenever you encounter a new word or expression, look it up in the dictionary or mark it for later investigation. You thus clear up the meaning of an otherwise obscure word or passage and you add a new word to your vocabulary.

Meaningfulness is also enhanced if you *relate new facts to old problems.* When you meet a new fact, ask yourself how it affects your attitude on some issue or belief with regard to some proposition. For example, do the facts and principles of perception support the common belief that what we see, hear, and smell are entirely a matter of the structure of the eyes, ears, and nose? Do the facts and principles of learning support the old adage, "Practice makes perfect"? Does your study of habit formation give you an understanding of why habits are so hard to break? Talk these questions over with fellow students.

You can also make what you have studied more meaningful if you *summarize in your own words.* No amount of mechanical copying of text material will aid learning so much as a preparation in your own words. In summarizing, try to hit upon the essential material, neglecting the anecdotes and illustrations. They tend to stick of themselves. Emphasize the principles in preparing your summary.

RECITATION

Reciting to oneself after having read a section of material is a widely recommended study procedure, yet one that is much neglected because it is time-consuming. You can easily fool yourself into believing that what you have just read is understood and remembered, but generally this is not true. To make certain that you remember and understand, stop periodically and check yourself by trying to recall what you have just read. In other words, *recite.* When this is done, errors and omissions should be carefully noted. Then a little later, recitation is once more in order. In preparing for examinations, recitation should be paramount in one's study procedure.

Experimental studies have shown that recitation is a great help in preventing forgetting and thus increasing remembering. Actually it is profitable to take time away from "studying" and spend it on recitation, for learning is better when part of the study time is spent on recitation than when all of it is given to reading. In one well-known experiment, when all the subjects devoted all their time to reading, recall of the facts in five short biographies averaged 16 percent after four hours. When 60 to 80 percent of the learning time was devoted to self-recitation, recall after four hours was nearly twice as great. Check by a fellow student helps.

The advantage of recitation over passive reading is that the student is forced to maintain *an active attitude*—to react and become involved in the subject matter rather than merely trying to absorb it. Recitation serves to keep his attention on the task. He cannot let his attention lapse by daydreaming if he is trying to recall something.

REVIEW

There is no doubt that frequent review is essential to efficient remembering. Experimental studies of forgetting show that the greatest loss in retention occurs right after learning. From this fact we may infer that the best time for review is immediately after studying. One experimenter found that when a class lecture was listened to by students but never reviewed, the class recalled only 25 percent of the content after eight weeks had elapsed. But when the lecture was immediately followed by a five-minute review test, the amount of recall after eight weeks was 50 percent better.

Reviewing immediately before an examination is also highly desirable. This review should be intensive, since the examination may cover an extensive amount of material, and it should emphasize recitation because, in effect, this is what is called for when one is examined. If you can recite well what you have learned from study just before an examination, you need have no fears about the outcome of the test.

It also pays to have one or two reviews between the first review and the one just before the examination. The more frequent the review, the greater the degree of overlearning. You will see from the chapter on learning that *forgetting is checked by overlearning*. Put this basic principle into practice when organizing your study technique (see page 276).

TAKING LECTURE NOTES

Overall efficiency in study can be facilitated by taking notes in class. Good note taking is a skill that surprisingly few students have taken the time to acquire. Some instructors, by their poorly organized manner of presenting material before a class, make note taking difficult for the students, but by and large, the fault lies less with the instructor than with the student.

In taking notes, keep in mind that your main task is to *organize* what the instructor is offering. Do this by trying to identify the main points. Don't be led astray by an interesting illustration and an amusing anecdote. Always keep in mind the point that the illustration or story is supposed to make. Condense the teacher's discussions into simple phrases or sentences. And to make them more meaningful to you, do the condensing in words of your own phrasing. A good note taker is *not* a stenographer, who merely records. He is a sum-marizer—one who *evaluates* material that will be useful to him in the future.

Even the best of note takers miss some salient points. They write down short phrases which seem meaningful at the time but do not make much sense later on. Therefore, notes should be reviewed after class. With the lecture freshly in mind, the missing items can usually be inserted and the meaningless ones deleted or corrected. If a review of your notes shows lack of organization, it pays to rewrite them completely. The organization and review will stand you in good stead by furthering your understanding of your notes at some future time.

Taking notes in most courses can be greatly facilitated by using a system of abbreviations. If you use such a system, make it consistent. Many students, especially in the early months of college before abbreviations have become automatic, have found that a page set aside in the notebook for abbreviations is an aid to the mastery of the system. The use of a system of abbreviations is particularly desirable if the student is the kind who complains that he misses part of the lecture because he gets too wrapped up in note taking. In general, the use of abbreviations and other forms of condensation helps one to listen and write at the same time.

MORE ON STUDYING

Let us add a few suggestions from several successful students.

1. *Study in the same manner as you will be expected to reproduce material.* Memorize more for objective exams and study broad ideas in outline form for essay exams. We shall expand on this in the following pages.
2. *Study the teacher.* Some teachers (often intentionally) will all but give away exam questions on pretest lectures and reviews. One professor may emphasize one subject that another will gloss over.
3. *Review notes with a classmate.* Often someone else will pick up points that you miss.
4. *Do not cut classes.* Even if you are not paying close attention in class, some things still get through that would have been missed if you were absent. The other person's notes are usually poor substitutes for your own; and one other point—some who teach feel badly that they cannot hold the interest of an audience enough even to get them to class. Physical attendance is easier to monitor than is psychological attendance.
5. *Do not overintellectualize in review.* Review should be just what the term implies. Too much thinking at this stage often leads to confusion.
6. *Do not fall behind in your work.* In some students this leads from a feeling of anxiety to that of panic.
7. *Help the other fellow study.* Explaining a point to someone else helps fix it in your mind.
8. *Underline the text.* This makes review easier, and textbook authors will love you!

PREPARING FOR AND TAKING EXAMINATIONS

If you are looking for some way to pass examinations other than by thorough mastery of the material to be covered in the examination, you will be disappointed in what psychologists have to say about this subject. No one has yet come up with a magical shortcut or substitute for adequate preparation through study. Of course, mastery of the subject is sometimes not enough if the student is emotionally upset, fails to interpret questions properly, has his knowledge organized in such a way as to interfere with quick recall, or is overtired. If you follow the precepts of efficient study, you can avoid the factors which cause unsatisfactory test performance, despite adequate preparation. Get enough rest; do not engage in a last-minute *hurried* review instead of a planned, systematic one; and adopt a relaxed, almost fatalistic, attitude at examination time.

Essay and Objective Examinations

The examinations given in most schools divide themselves roughly into two main classes, the *essay* and the *objective.* Although there are exceptions, these types are likely to have different purposes. You should therefore prepare for them and take them differently.

Essay examinations emphasize the ability to understand, organize, and *recall* information. The student has latitude in which to discuss and qualify his answers. Essay questions let the student show the depth and breadth of his knowledge. And they also demonstrate his ability to set down his thoughts in good English and to communicate his ideas to others. Keep these points in mind as you prepare for and take an essay examination. When you begin the examination, don't just start writing on the assumption that if you write enough the teacher can find the correct point somewhere in the hodgepodge. Take time to organize your thinking before you begin to write. Remember that the teacher will think better of a paper if the information in it is well organized and to the point, rather than full of rambling and irrelevant discussion. Survey the examination as a whole before you write, and estimate the amount of time you will spend on each question. Try to leave time at the end for rereading your answers so that you can correct mistakes or add missing points.

Remember that most teachers generally think of grading papers as a chore. You can help "sell" your answers through good organization. Also keep in mind that your paper is compared with all the others in the class. Examinations are competitive. It is fair to say that they are graded fairly, although subjectively. You should outline answers, indent, and number points.

Objective examinations are usually *recognition* tests. The right answer is before you, as well as wrong answers. Your task is to pick out the right answer when you see it. Be on guard against careless reading of objective test items. All the answers usually have some degree of plausibility; otherwise they would serve no useful purpose as a testing device. Sometimes the correct answer may hang on such statements as "never" or "always" or "rarely," and you may miss the point if you do not read the questions carefully.

In objective-type examinations it is well to skip items temporarily on which the answer is uncertain, rather than to puzzle about them for an undue amount of time which might otherwise be spent on easier items. When you are finished with the easier items, go back to the harder ones. In objective examinations one question usually counts as much as another, so do not concentrate too much on difficult questions. Doing this will cause you to run out of time or make you rush through the remaining items and make needless mistakes. There is another good reason for perusing an objective examination and answering first those questions that you are sure about: To start with responses that you feel sure are right gives you confidence, facilitates your thinking, and helps you in seeing the relationship to other questions.

When your examination has been graded and returned, use the evaluation wisely for the future. Don't be content with a "Well, that's that" attitude. Learn from the results of the examination. Where should you have placed more emphasis in your study? Was your organization good? Do you have the proper technical vocabulary? What were the errors? Carefully work out the answers to these questions and profit from them in preparation for the next examination.

Steps in Taking a Multiple-Choice Exam

First, pay attention to the instructions. Let us assume that you are asked to choose the *best* answer of four or five possibilities. This means, of course, that perhaps two answers may be correct. Hence, do not waste time arguing with yourself that there may be more than one answer.

Second, the student taking a multiple-choice exam is in part like the accomplished poker player who is trying to get himself into a position where he is betting on a sure thing. In poker, one is in a stronger position if he knows pretty well what is in the other fellow's hand. In the exam situation, *knowing the material* is a first step. There is no substitute for study. It is also unlikely that you will be certain about *all* the answers. Our suggestions also assume that you are not penalized for guessing.

What are the next steps? Let us summarize from a study:

1. *Go through the exam a first time and answer all the items of which you are fairly certain.* This helps get certain items out of the way without wasting time on single, difficult items. There is sometimes another advantage in doing this. Having gone through the exam once will suggest the answers to questions that might have been difficult had they been answered in serial order.

2. *Go through the exam a second time, answering any other questions that now seem obvious.* There are usually a number of questions which were left unanswered from the first time through. It is in connection with these that the test-wise student knows what to do.

3. *Do not guess at this stage of the game. See what choices on any given question can be eliminated.* In a four-choice question, pure guess will give the student one chance in four of being correct. If one alternative can be eliminated as incorrect, the odds are reduced to one in three. If two can be eliminated, chances become fifty-fifty.

4. *Having eliminated some alternatives, choose the answer which you first thought of as right.* Studies show that this procedure is better than pure guesswork.

5. *If you have no choice at all as to the right answer, take choice "2."* Again, from studies come this suggested rule of thumb based on how teachers select items. When the instructor makes up a multiple-choice item, he usually has only a vague notion of what he wants to test. There is a tendency to make the first choice incorrect, the second choice the right answer, and the remaining ones anything that isn't too far afield. Of course, some instructors are conscious of this bit of behavior and correct for it. Remember, this suggestion is in the last-resort category!

6. *When finished, check your answers.* Clerical errors on exams are common for some people. Again, studies show that changing answers is in the direction of making them right. Yes, we are aware of the common misconception on this point. In a group of 100 papers (for example) it was discovered that two-thirds of the changes made in them resulted in the selection of a correct choice rather than a wrong one.

Besides studying *for the exam* and studying the *behavior of the instructor,* the above suggestions may help eliminate some of the anxiety one builds up about taking an exam.

Do we have any good suggestions for taking a true-false test? None except that one should study and look for give-away words such as "always," "never," etc. Remember, there is no substitute for learning the material in the first place, and for the time spent in overlearning.

READING

All that has been said about efficient study is based on the assumption that the student has normal reading, writing, and arithmetical skills. However, many studies, surveys, and reports from those who counsel students show that high school and college students have deficiencies in these basic skills. Probably the most common deficiency is in reading ability. Some college students read no better than seventh-grade pupils, and at least one-third of college freshmen read too slowly to do their most effective work.

Reading Is Complex Behavior

It is not surprising that reading deficiencies are so common because the reading act is complex. This complexity creates many opportunities for error to occur. Examining the behavior of the eyes during reading makes one wonder how reading is possible at all. If we stand directly behind a reader and carefully observe one of his eyeballs by reflection in a small mirror held just below it, we see that the eye moves from left to right, not with a steady sweep but with jerks and pauses. Then it swings back from the extreme right to the extreme left to start the next line. Experimental studies have shown that during the movement of the eyes, perception of letters and words is impossible. How, then, can one ever learn to read? We now know that the eye as a receiver of information from the printed page works during the *stops* or *fixation pauses.*

During fixation pauses the reader attends to the stimulus material not in a piecemeal fashion but as a pattern or whole. He does this because he has learned that it is not necessary to perceive every letter and every word in order to obtain the essential information. All languages contain letters and sounds that are redundant, and the languages themselves are redundant, i.e., they contain more words than are necessary for conveying information. When you perceive the letter *q,* you know it will be followed by *u.* When you see *informati,* you know it will be followed by *on.* When you see *ps ch l y,* you fill in the missing letters easily. When you see

The land   the free   home   brave

you fill in the missing words without difficulty. In reading, certain cue letters or words are all that is necessary for ordinary comprehension.

Slow and Fast Readers

What, then, is the difference between slow and fast readers? Both, of course, take advantage of redundancy in language, but the fast reader does so to a greater extent. He pauses just often enough to get the sense of what he reads and thereby reduces the number of glances per line. The *poor reader spends too much time looking at words* that carry irrelevant or repeated information. To improve his reading speed, he should therefore decrease the number of pauses per line. And to accomplish this it is necessary to expand the number of words perceived in a single glance. The trick is to force oneself to take in more territory during the information-gathering process when the eyes are at rest.

Another common fault of poor readers is to make *regressive eye movements.* Such movements are back tracks, or returns, to a word or phrase which did not clearly register. These movements usually defeat the reader's purpose, which is to gather information from the material before him. Regressive movements may impede the information-gathering process by interfering with the train of thought, so that ideas become jumbled and unrelated. If you are a backtracking reader, make every effort to break the habit.

Don't vocalize as you read. You have no doubt seen children whisper to themselves when they are beginning to read. As they gain reading skill, the whispering becomes inaudible, but their lips, tongue, and throat muscles still move as if they were talking. Some college students have not progressed beyond this stage. This kind of vocalizing lowers the rate of reading and acts as a distraction, preventing you from grasping the full significance of what is read. The purpose of reading is to perceive not words, in themselves, but significant cues, which are the raw material or vehicles of ideas. Phrases and sentences are the units which convey the ideas on the printed page, and they are the units which must be comprehended. Reading without vocal activity allows one to grasp the phrases, and hence the thought, quickly, in a minimum of time.

Efficient reading is, of course, impeded by a *deficient vocabulary.* You should not attempt to read with speed at all costs. Some students do this by skipping over new words, hoping to get their meaning from some later sentence or paragraph. Occasionally these deduced meanings are correct, but frequently they are not. The safe procedure is to get into the habit of checking definitions of all unfamiliar words. Underline new words when they are first encountered and look up their meaning in a good dictionary before leaving the assignment. After a dictionary has been consulted, return to the context in which the word was seen and reread it so that you can see how it fits into the total setting. This adds meaning to what you are reading and helps to establish the meaning of the word for future use.

What about *speed reading* courses? Studies have been inconclusive as to the value of speed reading programs. On the positive side (besides those who have commercial interest in speed reading programs, along with some of their customers), there are those who say that reading speed can be increased to between 1,000 and 2,000 words per minute. These proponents include some independent researchers who believe that comprehension at these levels is adequate for some types of material. On the negative side, there are those who say that high reading speed cuts down comprehension. Let us relate one study on the controversy.

College students who enrolled in a university speed-reading program were tested for immediate and basic comprehension. Four *different* types of literature was used. These included "heavy fiction" *(Doctor Zhivago),* "light nonfiction" *(Playboy),* "light fiction" *(Redbook),* and "heavy nonfiction" (a textbook in experimental psychology). The selections were about equally long. They were presented in the same format, double-spaced typing.

Each student read two kinds of literature and was immediately tested for comprehension. Weeks later, each student was tested again. Other tests were conducted, with the usual experimental and control groups involved. Three generalizations emerged. First, it is believed that the average speed reader cannot triple his reading speed (as often claimed), or even double it, without missing large chunks of the message. Second, there is some evidence of better comprehension at faster speeds. This suggests that some speed reading techniques can be valuable for some people and for certain purposes. For example, to skim literature intelligently may be a very useful skill. Most of us, after all, have only a limited amount of time for general reading. Third, the claim that most of us, most of the time, can increase our reading speed dramatically without loss of comprehension remains yet to be proven. Each of us should ask: "What do I wish to get from. what I read? How much time and effort will it take *for me*?"

Individual reading habits vary greatly. In general, those people who read widely—the subject matter ranging from newspapers and magazines to technical material and pleasure reading—read well. Availability of reading material is important, and so is convenience. Most people will not go out of their way to read a conventional bulletin board, but they may habitually read single daily items placed in the elevator or short items handed out at the plant gate.

Answers to Questions on the Study Habit Inventory

The good student answers as follows: (1) Yes; (2) Yes; (3) No; (4) Yes; (5) Yes; (6) No; (7) Yes; (8) Yes; (9) No; (10) No; (11) No;

(12) No; (13) Yes; (14) Yes; (15) No; (16) Yes; (17) Yes; (18) Yes; (19) Yes; (20) No.

SUMMARY

Too often we tend to evaluate ourselves not by our abilities and accomplishments but by our limitations and mistakes. We often forget that beyond a given level of general intelligence, personality, motivation, opportunities, education, and training contribute more to our occupational success and failure. Specific jobs require specific skills—psychomotor, athletic, mechanical, musical, artistic, and creative abilities.

Training relates to the teaching of specific skills. Education is broader and less specific; it refers to learning things in order to gain proficiency in future situations. Many college programs combine training and education. Self-confidence comes through self-understanding and relates closely to what we do with our abilities and how we learn to work around our limitations.

Acquiring efficiency in study hinges on "learning how to learn." It relates to motivation and study time habits; knowing how to prepare and take exams; and knowing how to read and check on one's progress. Learning will not take place unless there is an underlying motive to learn. Preparing a flexible study schedule can be helpful in budgeting time and effort. Both motivation and scheduling prepare the student for studying. The choice of a physical setting for study is also important.

Study assignments are made meaningful in four ways. First, skim the assignment to get a bird's-eye view of what is to come. Second, use a dictionary to learn the meaning of specific words. Third, make the study period meaningful by relating new facts to old problems. Fourth, summarize material in your own words. This helps to identify essential material to be remembered. Recitation is necessary in helping to stamp in what is to be learned. The advantage of recitation over passive reading is that one is forced to maintain an active attitude so essential to memory storage. Good note taking is an art whereby one evaluates the material that will be useful in the future.

Essay exams emphasize the recall of information. Objective exams emphasize recognition of material. Preparing for and taking exams is an art that can be acquired by following step-by-step procedures. There is no substitute for knowing the material in the first place, and here overlearning is important. Taking an exam is a skill which is to be learned much as any other skill.

The most common study handicap is deficiency in reading.

Reading is a complex behavior. Poor readers show four basic habits. First, they spend too much time looking at words that carry irrelevant or repeated information. Second, they make regressive eye movements which impede the information-gathering process. Third, they vocalize, which slows down reading. Fourth, they often have a deficient vocabulary.

Research on speed reading courses shows three things. First, the average speed reader cannot triple reading speed, or even double it, without missing large chunks of material. Second, there are some case evidences of better comprehension at faster speeds, but we need to ask what our purpose in reading is. Third, the claim that most of us, most of the time, can increase our reading speed dramatically without loss of comprehension remains to be proven. We need to ask: "What do I wish to get from what I read, and how much time and effort will it take for me?" Individual reading habits vary greatly.

PERCEPTION, COMMUNICATION, AND PROBLEM SOLVING **10**

As we face a variety of situations day-by-day, three things are essential if we are to handle them efficiently. First, we must know about the situation in a meaningful way. This involves *perception.* Getting an accurate view of a situation is quite complex, not nearly so simple as it first appears. Thus, many persons mistakenly assume that we simply see or hear what is "out there" and that is all there is to it. Actually, the world as we see it is not necessarily the world as it is. Second, most situations require that we *communicate* with others about the situation in one way or another. Third, many of the perceptions we make, and many of the communications we have, lead toward doing something about the situation. Here *problem solving* comes into the picture. In this chapter we shall examine various aspects of perceiving, ranging from interpreting what we experience to such influence structures as advertising. We shall talk about communication in terms of how we relate to others. We shall conclude with a discussion of what goes on during problem solving and outline a practical way of solving problems in human relations.

We shall have numerous occasions throughout this book to use the basic principles of perception in dealing with psychology applied to life and work. Even at this early point the importance of functioning sense organs is apparent in connection with the practical problems of architectural design, television and radio advertising, camouflage, and accident prevention. This conclusion has been reached through a comparison of the accident experience of workers whose visual skills were superior with the experience of those workers having inferior vision. The findings show that employees whose vision is adequate for the job have fewer accidents than do employees with less-adequate vision.

PERCEPTUAL ORGANIZATION

Perceiving takes place when stimuli activate the sense organs. But at that point the perceptual story is not nearly complete. When we ask about the nature of what is perceived, we observe at the very outset the distinguishing feature of *organization.* The sensory information from the eyes, ears, nose, and skin is arranged in an orderly and meaningful manner. The problem of perception is also semantic in nature; even simple words become involved. A color may be "blue" in English and "bleu" in French, but it is just another shade of what we call "gray" to the color-blind person.

Figure and Ground

One of the most elemental organizing principles in perception is the tendency to pattern stimuli in terms of a *figure-ground* relationship. Not all parts of a stimulating situation reach one's awareness with equal clarity. That which we focus on at any given moment with any of the sense organs is the *figure.* That which is experienced at the same time but is out of focus is known as the *ground.* At this very moment your perceptions are organized in terms of figure and ground as you read this page. The printed words represent figure and the white spaces are ground. In every perceptual act the figure-ground principle is operating when a selected part of the stimulating situation is perceived as standing out from the background: roses stand out against the green leaves of the bush, peach blossoms against the leaves and branches of the tree, mountains stand out against the sky, soloists against the background of the chorus, the melody lines of a trumpet against a background of harmonies. The factors that determine what will be figure appear to be distinctiveness of shape and contour, familiarity, novelty, grouping, and meaningfulness. In short, the things that make "sense" and are important to the perceiver stand out as figure, and the unimportant and less meaningful things form the ground.

Camouflage

Sometimes we want to make a deliberate confusion of figure and ground. The aim of camouflaging is to destroy the enemy's perception of the figure—to conceal things that are familiar, meaningful, and important. Thus sharp contours which make an airplane hangar stand out as figure are removed by the use of roof netting; a soldier's uniform is made to blend with the jungle; a field gun located on the edge of the jungle is painted to resemble trees. In the protective coloration of birds, animals, and insects, we see many examples of camouflage in nature.

Similarity

The organized nature of perception is strikingly apparent when we notice that we tend to group stimuli in certain ways. According to one grouping principle, stimuli that are more *similar* to one another will have a greater tendency to be grouped. In Figure 10-1*a* the rows are perceived as horizontal, owing to grouping by similarity. Similarity may, of course, manifest itself through a variety of characteristics—shape, size, color, expression, or any other distinguishable property of the stimulus. And the similarity must always be "seen" in a psychological sense, i.e., as perceived by the observer. To you, the similarity between a kangaroo and an opossum may simply be that both are animals; to a zoologist the similarity may be that both are marsupials.

Proximity

Another grouping principle has to do with how *near* in time or space stimuli are to each other. Stimuli that are in closer proximity have a

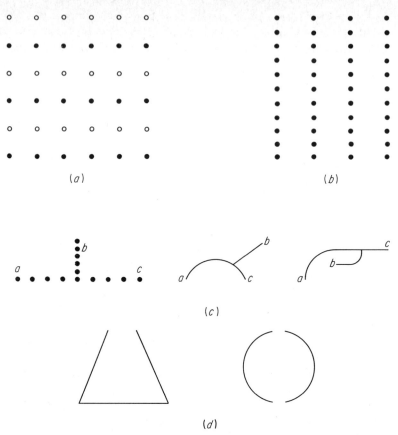

FIG. 10-1 Some stimulus organizational principles. In (a) the rows appear to be put together horizontally, rather than vertically, because of the complete similarity between elements. In (b) the dots are seen in vertical columns because the vertical columns are in closer proximity than the horizontal columns. In (c) the dots or the lines continue (ac), leaving the dots or lines of b going off alone. In (d) the figure at the left looks more like an enclosed triangle than a set of three lines. The figure to the right looks more like a broken circle than a pair of arcs.

greater tendency to be grouped. In Figure 10-1b the dots are seen in vertical columns because the dots are nearer to one another in the vertical arrays than they are in the horizontal direction. Grouping on the basis of nearness in time is apparent when, in a series of light flashes, the flashes occurring close together in time tend to be grouped.

Togetherness of Stimuli

Stimuli are also organized according to the *continuity* principle, which states that there is a tendency for elements to go with others so as to permit the continuation of a line, curve, or movement in the direction already established. The dots or lines in Figure 10-1*c* group themselves as *ac/b* rather than as *ab/c,* for it seems that with the *a* segment, the *c* segment is more continuous than the *b* segment. Because of the continuity principle, two crossing lines are perceived as two crossing lines instead of as four lines. The tops of the buildings in New York are perceived as a skyline, instead of as isolated units, because of the continuity principle.

Desire for Completion

A final grouping principle that shapes one's perceptions is called *closure.* This refers to the tendency to complete or close figures with missing parts. In Figure 10-1*d* the observer tends to treat the configuration to the left, not as a set of three lines forming two angles, but as an enclosed triangle. Similarly, in the other figure the perceiver is more likely to see a broken circle than a pair of arcs. There is a need, it seems, for one to complete a configuration. The closure tendency operates in other sensory areas, too. In hearing, for example, there is a strong tendency to bring about closure by completing the rhythm.

You now see not only that perception is a process of stimulating the senses, but also that the messages from the sense organs are arranged or ordered so that the world as we come to know it is organized. But there is more to perception. Still to be reckoned with are a variety of personal factors such as prior experience, mental sets, needs, and emotion, and the ways in which they influence one's perception of the world.

Perceiving Things Differently

The apparent size of people can be influenced by placing them in rooms of distorted shape. This is illustrated in Figure 10-2. Here we see three students of about the same height in a distorted room. They appear to be of three different heights.

Perception is certainly not a simple process. We see things in relation to our own needs, past experience, and feelings. In one experiment, a woman observed in a window the face of her husband to whom she had been married for twenty-five years. When compared with the face of another man in a nearby window, her husband's face seemed to her to remain unchanged as he moved around. The other man appeared to grow or shrink as he moved to and fro.

Suspecting that there might be some special emotional relationship between this woman and her husband, the investigator repeated this experiment with other married couples. A stranger acted as the control in each experiment.

Most of the individuals saw their partner grow and shrink in the usual manner, and to the same apparent degree as the control stranger. However, six viewers reported that their partners altered

FIG. 10-2 Three students of the same size in a distorted room. The man on the left is actually nearly twice as far from the camera as the one on the right, but the distorted perspective of the room conceals this fact. The floor of this room slopes upward to the right of the viewer. The rear wall recedes from right to left. A clue as to the construction of the floor may be noted by the way in which the men's shoes contact the floor.

less than the stranger or did not change at all. These couples turned out to be only recently married.

In another study, involving the use of distorted lenses, some interesting observations were made. When an enlisted man looked through the lenses, his immediate superior, an officer, appeared less distorted than enlisted men in the room. Later twenty-four navy recruits viewed two different men through the lenses. One man wore the insignia of the recruits' immediate petty-officer superiors. The other man wore the insignia and canvas leggings of a recruit. The results showed that twenty-two of the twenty-four subjects *required lenses of higher distortion power* to perceive the "officer" as distorted. Measurements showed that the increase in lens power averaged about 50 percent.

Is some emotional anxiety involved in these phenomena? Is some feeling of identification playing a part? We do not have good answers to these types of questions. Even children who view themselves in a mirror through distorted lenses report different kinds of distortion at different ages. Girls, who are typically more anxious about their appearance than boys, *consistently* report less distortion than boys of the same age. Both children and adults report that their own mirror image is distorted in different ways from that of another person. One's own image changes mainly in detail. The other person's image appears to change in overall size and shape.

There is little doubt that in daily living we perceive the same things in different ways, and at different times. Some people characteristically view their world for only a moment in time; other people relate to the past. Perhaps·one student put a great deal of understanding in this statement, "When I was nineteen my dad didn't know anything. When I was twenty-one I was surprised to see how much he had learned in two years."

PAST EXPERIENCE

The part played by prior experience in perceiving things is nicely demonstrated when a person localizes sounds. When you hear a sound, you try to locate it some place "out there." We are so used to doing this that anything which interferes with it upsets our localizing ability. Such an upset was experimentally studied by a psychologist who had people wear a device called a "pseudophone." The pseudophone consists of a pair of ear trumpets so arranged that each receiving trumpet carries sound to the opposite side of the head. Wearing this instrument was at first disturbing, since there was a reversal of sounds, right and left. If the person was spoken to at the dinner table by someone at his right, he would turn to the left in answering. On the street the wearer of the pseudophone would often bump into people, because upon hearing their approach, he would move in the wrong direction. In time the subjects learned to get used to the new locations and made appropriate responses. The experiment is an interesting example of the effect of past experience on perception.

Interpretations

Suppose that a man wearing a white shirt is standing in bright light holding a piece of coal. By physical measurements it could be easily shown that the amount of light reflected from the shirt is many times greater than that reflected from the coal. Now if the man goes into a shadowed area or a dimly illuminated cellar and physical measurements are again made, the amount of light reflected from shirt and coal would be proportionately the same. But a comparative measure of the total amount of reflected light in sunlight and shadow would show actually more light is coming from the coal in the sunlight than from the shirt in the cellar. Yet under all conditions of illumination, the coal looks black and the shirt looks white. We have learned these color properties from past experience, and this experience determines our perceptions, despite the physics of the situation. This discrepancy between perception and physics also occurs when, from past experience, you know the color of a dress or the upholstering of a piece of furniture. These familiar objects "keep their color," regardless of the conditions of illumination.

The ability to see objects in depth or at a distance provides a number of illustrations of the effect of past experience on perception. From experience we know that objects near us are seen in clearer detail than faraway objects; hence vagueness in detail means depth or distance from the observer. If you live in an industrial section of the country where there are smoke and fog, try sometime to guess distances in a part of the country where the atmosphere is clear; you will find that your estimates are quite inaccurate. From experience we know the approximate size of a man and also that a man looks smaller the farther away he is from the observer; hence, knowing the size of objects, we perceive them at various distances from us, depending on how big they appear.

The way one is reared in a particular culture often shows how past experience influences perception. For example, a loud belch from the mouth of a dinner guest in some places of the Orient is perceived as a compliment by his host. It goes without saying that an American without knowledge of Oriental customs would perceive this behavior quite differently. Another example is the case of a group of African visitors in London who perceived the London bobbies as especially friendly because they raised their right hand, palm forward, to approaching traffic. Instead of perceiving this behavior as a signal for stopping traffic, the Africans perceived it in terms of what this gesture meant in their own country.

To ignore a person's past experience is to ignore a major determinant of perception. The world is perceived in terms of experience formerly associated with it. Keep this in mind and you will stop making the common, and incorrect, assumption that everyone perceives the world in the same way.

MENTAL SET

Set is the term applied to the tendency of a person to pay attention to certain features of a situation. The sprinter is set when he is waiting for the race to begin at the crack of the starter's gun. A tie salesman is set to notice his customer's neckwear; a shoe salesman, his shoes. Some sets are habitual; others are determined by the immediate aspects of a situation, including instructions as to what we are to observe. Right now you are set to learn about the role of set as a perceptual determinant.

Consider the following facts, keeping in mind that you will later be questioned about them. At the first floor of a building an elevator starts with six occupants; it stops at the second floor where two people get off and four get on; four persons get on and one gets off at the sixth floor; on the eighth floor, two people get off and three get on. How many stops did the elevator make? Many people cannot give the right answer, because, instead of counting stops, they were counting the number of persons getting on and off at each stop.

Influence by Set

Here is a laboratory experiment which demonstrates the effect of set on perception. In Figure 10-3 the object in the center is exposed very briefly. After the exposure, the subjects of the experiment are asked to make a reproduction of what they have seen. When the subjects are told ahead of time that the exposed figure will be like a pair of eyeglasses, they perceive glasses, as indicated by reproductions such as those on the left. When other subjects are shown the same figure under the same conditions but are told to expect a dumbbell, they draw reproductions like that on the right.

Another experiment on set and perception was carried out by briefly exposing to groups of subjects a series of words, some in their normal printed form and some reversed. Without definite instructions as to what to expect, the subjects were slower to recognize the reversed words than those presented in their normal way. When, however, they were told beforehand that some of the words would be reversed, this induced set greatly increased their accuracy of perception.

Everyday living is full of examples of set as an important determinant of what one perceives. After hearing the words "ham

FIG. 10-3 The phenomenon of set. When subjects are told that they will be shown something that looks like a pair of eyeglasses and are very briefly shown the figure in the center, they make a drawing like the one on the left. When other subjects are told that they will see a dumbbell, they make drawings similar to the one on the right. In each case they are set to see a particular object.

and," you are set to hear "eggs." You are set to hear "beans" if you hear "pork and" first. And you will be likely to hear "beans" even if the word actually spoken is "greens." Some persons say that they cannot sleep because their hearts pound in their ears or because of the ticking of a bedside clock. Most of us are scarcely aware of this pounding and ticking. The insomniac, however, is looking for explanations for his sleeplessness and so is set for many types of stimulation which are disregarded by most people. Everyone will hear the ticking clock and beating heart if he sets himself to listen for them. The doctor generally hears the telephone ring in the night, but not the baby's crying. His wife, however, will sleep through the ringing telephone but waken to the stirring and crying of the baby.

NEEDS

Perceptions are largely determined by needs and desires. In other words, we see what we want to see. Like the mirrors at amusement parks, we distort the world; the distortion is in relation to our needs and desires. In the last chapter you saw the importance of needs in governing man's behavior. Perceptual behavior is no exception to the all-pervasive influence of needs.

The influence of need in shaping perception has frequently been studied in the experimental laboratory. An example is a study in which subjects in various stages of hunger were asked to report what they saw in ambiguous black and white drawings flashed before them for very short periods of time. The results of the experiment showed that as hunger increased up to a certain point, the subjects saw more and more of the ambiguous figures as articles of food. Thus the hungry subjects "saw" more steaks, salads, and ham sandwiches than subjects who had just eaten.

For an everyday example of the effects of needs on perception, consider two men looking through a store window at a display of automobile accessories. One man needs a tire and the other some antifreeze. Both men are exposed to the same objects in the window display. The first will notice the brand, tread, and price of the tires and generally neglect the other objects. The second will be able to tell you all about the antifreeze preparations and will have little information about anything else. What was clearly perceived by each of these men was determined by his particular need. If you need to buy a car, you will see structural characteristics, colors, and styling of automobiles that are missed completely by a person who has no interest in buying a car.

EMOTIONS AND PERCEPTION

A person's emotional state—whether he is angry, happy, sad, or excited—has a lot to do with his perceptions. A strong emotion, such as fear, can make a person perceive danger on all sides. People have been known to shoot bushes, trees, and fense posts when they anticipated danger. Such common expressions as "blind rage," "love is blind," and "paralyzing fear" describe the influence which emotion may have on a person's perception of a situation and his reaction to it.

Influence Without Awareness

In a study on emotion and perception, children at a summer camp judged the characteristics of faces in photographs before and after playing a "scary" game of "murder." The amount of maliciousness or evil seen by the children in the faces was much greater after the game than before. The emotional state aroused by the game caused the youngsters to perceive the faces differently than before.

Emotional states may even operate at a level so primitive that they influence perception before the individual is aware of the stimulus. This is indicated by an experiment in which subjects studied a list of nonsense syllables. Certain of these syllables were always accompanied by an electric shock on the subject's hand. Shock normally induces an electrical skin response which can be accurately recorded. After a number of pairings of syllable and shock it was possible to omit the shock and get the electrical skin response by presenting only the syllable. Now the experimenter presented the syllables in an exposure device for extremely short periods of time. The subjects gave the electrical skin response *before* they recognized the syllable. For syllables that were not accompanied originally by shock, the effect was not nearly so pronounced. It would seem that the shock syllables came to be threatening syllables, and their general fearful character was perceived before the detailed makeup of the syllables themselves.

ATTENTION

At this point in your reading about perception, it should be clear that in getting to know the world one selects or filters out stimuli from the sense organs and organizes them in a meaningful way. We use certain stimuli and reject others or else relegate them to minor roles. The fact that the perceiver picks out certain kinds of stimuli is another way of saying that he attends to only a few at a time. When you pay attention, you focus your attention on something. What, now, are the conditions which cause us to focus on what is going on in the outside world? You should have some ready answers. One's past experience, sets, needs, and emotions play important roles. And so does the way the world is organized in terms of figure and ground, similarity, nearness, and other principles of organization. But certain additional causes of attention warrant specific mention, especially in view of their use in applied psychology.

Factors in Attention

The changing quality of a stimulating situation makes us focus on it. *Change attracts attention:* change from one color to another; change from present to absent; change from one intensity to another; change from moving to stationary; change from big to small. Your cat ignores the stationary ball of yarn but pounces on it when it moves. You scarcely notice the traffic noises on a busy street, but if the volume of traffic decreases, the "quiet" attracts your attention.

Repetitiveness is another determinant of attention. "Help, help, help!" will attract attention when a single "Help!" would pass unnoticed. Repeated taps on the shoulder attract attention more surely than a single signal. A weak stimulus frequently repeated may be more effective than a strong one presented only once. But there are limits to the effectiveness of repetition. If a stimulus is repeated many times, it ceases to hold attention, because of its monotony, or yields to some other stimulus that has the advantage of novelty and change.

Intensity, of course, is a powerful determiner of attention. When we are not focusing on anything in particular, we are likely to notice the loudest noise, a bright flash over a faint twinkle, the most pungent perfume. With visible objects, size has the same effect as intensity. Small details are less likely to catch the attention than large objects.

Some stimuli are more potent than others in attracting attention because of their *novelty* or unusual quality. Recall how attention-demanding is a dog who runs onto the football field during a game. A new suit or hat, the smell of smoke where usually there is none—all these are examples of attention arrest by unusual or novel stimuli.

Difference or *contrast,* somewhat like change, contributes to the focusing of perception. Anything that is different from its general surroundings stands out and catches the eye: a hole in the carpet, a smudge on a smooth wall, a dark spot in a bright landscape, a small pebble inside one's shoe.

Social suggestions may cause people to attend to a particular stimulus. You probably know the old stunt in which several students gazing intently at an ordinary notice on a bulletin board soon attract a crowd. And perhaps you have tried the prank of looking intently at the sky, moving your head slowly in a wide arc, and having other people do the same thing even when there is nothing of interest to see. People respond to social suggestions by paying close attention to something which other persons are apparently observing.

DISTRACTION

It is appropriate to discuss in this chapter the influence of distracting stimuli on behavior because distraction simply means changing the focus of perception or attending to something else. Everyone has had difficulty in directing his attention because of flashing lights, loud noises, odors, gossip, or other kinds of distracting stimuli.

When the stimulus causing the distraction acts upon the same sense organ that is concerned with attention, we run into trouble. Thus outside noises interfere greatly when one is talking over the telephone, but flashing lights may have little distracting effect.

Of course not all distraction comes from the outside. It is difficult to attend to what you are doing if you are worried, afraid, or excited. In this connection it has been found that taxicab drivers who had family worries were more likely to have accidents than those who did not. The accidents occurred because the worried drivers were unable to meet the attention requirements of safe driving.

From a practical standpoint, the control of distraction is important because a person's efficiency may be reduced by stimuli that take attention away from his job. The accident incurred by the taxi driver is a case in point. In one study, the actual cost of distraction was determined in terms of the energy required to perform a unit of work. Typists worked under two conditions: some days surrounded by soundproof walls; other days in the same place except that the partitions were removed, allowing the usual noises to prevail. The energy cost was measured by having the typists breathe into a bag so constructed as to capture the expired air. The air was then analyzed for the amount of carbon dioxide, and from this, oxygen consumption was determined. The amount of typing accomplished under the quiet and noisy conditions was the same, but the energy cost was much greater under the noisy condition.

ILLUSIONS

When something goes wrong in either the physical or the mental world, the underlying reasons for the mishap may be more easily seen than when everything is running smoothly. For this reason we can learn something regarding the process of perception from a study of illusions. An *illusion* is a surprising error of perception. We experience illusions when a stimulus is so misleading that we fall into a trap and get a false meaning from the signs received by our sense organs.

You can easily demonstrate one of the oldest of illusions by shutting your eyes, crossing two fingers, and running a pencil between the fingers, as shown in Figure 10-4. Your perception will be such that you are aware of two pencils being run over your fingers instead of one. This occurs because, in the past, when adjoining fingers were stimulated on their outside edges, the stimuli always came from two objects, not from one. In other words, this illusion is due to habit and familiarity derived from prior experience. You should be reminded at this point of our earlier discussion about the importance of past experience in shaping all our perceptions.

Familiarity and habit give rise to what is known as the "proofreader's illusion." In learning to read, we respond to larger and larger patterns—words, sentences, paragraphs. Once these habits are established, they persist in the face of error. This means that a word will be perceived as such even when it is spelled incorrectly. The reader, set for the meaning, responds to a few cues and reads on, not noticing the printer's error. If the word as printed has enough resemblance to the right word, it arouses the same response. In the effort to print books perfectly, proofreaders are employed whose job is to look specifically for printer's errors. This means that the proofreader must ignore the tendency to perceive whole units and must concentrate on the elements. But so deeply ingrained is the old habit that even the profes-

FIG. 10-4 A tactual illusion.

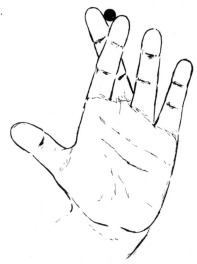

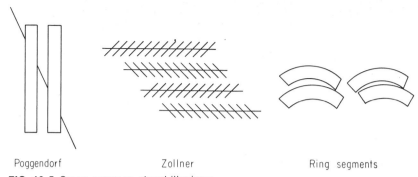

Poggendorf   Zollner   Ring segments

FIG. 10-5 Some common visual illusions.

sional falls into the trap of the proofreader's illusion and makes errors.

An illusion familiar to everyone is experienced at the movies. Actually, not pictures in motion but extended series of still pictures are projected on the screen. The seen or apparent motion must be in the viewer; in other words it must be the product of perception. You can readily demonstrate apparent motion by holding your forefinger about 3 inches in front of your nose and looking at it while blinking first one eye and then the other. To the left eye, the finger appears to one side and to the right eye, more to the other side. When you blink by closing one eye and simultaneously opening the other, the finger seems to move across your field of vision. Apparent movement is an illustration of the general tendency to perceive wholes or patterns. In trying to combine successive stationary objects into a perceptual whole, the observer creates a sense of movement between the stimulated unmoving points.

A variety of common visual illusions is shown in Figure 10-5. In the Poggendorf illusion the continuity of a line is interrupted by narrow strips laid across it at an angle. You can easily see what effect is given to the character of the line. In the Zollner figure, lines as indicators of direction are made misleading by the introduction of cross-hatching; the lines were originally drawn parallel. An interesting error occurs in the ring segments illusion: The two arcs are drawn with lines of the same length, but the misleading effect of the spatial separation of one from the other is clearly apparent.

Illusions are extreme instances of the difference between what *is* "out there" and what we *perceive* to be "out there." Illusions dramatically illustrate that perception can play tricks on us. The point to be remembered is that the world as people see it is not necessarily the world as it really is. We must be concerned with what people see in addition to what we show them; with what they hear besides what we say to them. Whether we feel hot or cold depends largely on us, not on the thermometer.

PERCEPTION IN ADVERTISING

Nowhere are the basic principles of perception applied more forcefully than in advertising. Printed advertisements, regardless of media, involve the eye exclusively. Radio advertising, in contrast, depends on the ear, and television involves both the eye and the ear. Let us illustrate with some studies showing how advertising and selling are related to some of the principles of perception described in this chapter.

Two investigators measured the relevance of illustration to copy in thirty-nine advertisements appearing in *House Beautiful* and *House and Garden.* The pictures were cut from the copy and mounted on a white-cardboard background. College student subjects were asked to indicate whether they had or had not seen each of the pictures before. They were asked what product was featured in the picture and what caught their attention. The product judged correct most often was the conspicuous, and in most cases the centermost, object; judged correctly next most often was the trademark. The product and its trademark stood out and were remembered best when there were fewer distracting objects in the picture. Plain, clear representation of the product was characteristic. Further, these pictures contained within their borders printed words which tersely spelled out the desirable features of the product. The human subjects in the illustrations reflected happiness and contentment in their faces. The investigators concluded that not only must an advertisement be perceived, its message must be understood. Word choice and sentence structure are vital to understanding. (Note how this is featured in the advertisements you remember.)

In a *spot-advertising* study, a packaged-drugs firm was interested in determining the effectiveness of its spots. Key words were taken from sample advertisements, and subjects were asked to free-associate with each. The final question posed was, "What product or service does this remind you of?" For example, when male and female subjects were asked to free-associate with the word "membrane," 42 percent responded with "form of skin or tissue." Also a mixed *emotional* attitude was found; 57 percent of the subjects expressed like and 42 percent dislike. The most frequent response to the phrase "shrinks swollen nasal membranes" was "colds." Further, the word had a high brand-associative value for the company.

The research indicated that very favorable feelings existed toward such words and phrases as "penetrating ingredient," "stimulates," and "gives you a lift." Such words as "antiseptic" and "medicates" aroused favorable responses, whereas unfavorable reactions were elicited by "bacteria," "congestion," and "inflamed." The researchers noted that when negative emotions are involved, the advertisement should provide a way out. The results of studies of radio spot ads are in effect similar. The "voice" of the announcer means much with regard to what feelings will be aroused.

In a very real way perception relates to many aspects of consumer behavior. Let us take a look at the role of psychology in this area.

PSYCHOLOGY IN THE MARKETING MIX

All of us as consumers are influenced directly and indirectly by advertising and selling. We react in varying ways to the radio jingle and the television cartoon. But we also are concerned with problems in buying and customer service, and with those other factors that make up psychology in the *marketing mix.*

Ingredients of the Mix

At the heart of the marketing mix is *advertising.* It is defined as any paid form of nonpersonal presentation and promotion of ideas, goods, or services by some identified sponsor. The media of advertising include magazine and newspaper space, trade papers, billboards, throwaways, programs and menus, car cards, catalogs, and local and national radio and television.

Advertising is designed to *influence* people and the decisions they make in a world of competition. Because Americans use some 20 tons of aspirins daily, firms pursue this market. There are 1,500 ads per day assaulting the eyes and ears of the American consumer. He shuts out more than 1,400 of these daily pitches, reacting to only 13. The psychologist is interested in which ones and why.

The power of *habit* dominates all of us, and advertising attempts to control the ways in which we change our behavior through learning. The bases of changing behavior through learning are described in Chapter 11.

The American consumer is peeped at, shadowed, grilled, and even analyzed in terms of his personal habits during the hourly and half-hourly station breaks on TV. Researchers use mathematics and high-speed computers to help manufacturers understand why people buy, or do not buy, a particular brand or product. And the housewife is surveyed over and over about her peeves. Sometimes she is more concerned with *little* frustrations than with big problems. In one survey of 1,100 women, some one-third complained about difficulty in opening packages, another 10 percent found fault with reclosing, and 10 percent complained of deterioration of packages. Less than 1 percent complained about false label information.

In one study, canned soups were arranged in alphabetic order by the type of soup—asparagus, bean, chicken, etc.—with the original amount of display space retained for each brand and type. Previously, canned soups had been grouped together by brand rather than by type. Although several signs were placed at the soup section telling the customers that the cans had been rearranged alphabetically, 60 percent of the customers were foiled by the new arrangement *and by their own habits.*

The power of habit was noted in another way. Under the original shelf arrangement there was no indication that consumers switched brands when the leading brand of tomato soup went out of stock. When the soup display was rearranged and the leading brand was out of stock, sales indicated that the next leading brand picked up from 50 to 80 percent of the sales which normally went to the leader.

Advertisers not only want to reinforce habits, they at times want to change them. (Note this type of battle among beer brands.) The success of a new product depends on whether customers can be induced to shift away from their former brands ("new low cost" or "new standard of performance"). The continued success of an established leading brand depends on the ability to strengthen existing habits ("the taste to stay with").

Selling involves both sales promotion and personal selling. In most companies, it involves the largest part of the marketing mix. As in advertising, the psychological factors in selling involve the sequence of perceiving, understanding, and feeling. The sales interview involves interaction between the salesman and the customer. Each provides a continuing stimulus for the other. What the salesman says and does must be perceived by the customer and responded to favorably if a sale is to take place. Thus, the focus of the salesman's attention is the customer. He must catch the small cues in the customer's behavior which indicate what to stress and what to gloss over. And good selling is *planned in advance.* One experienced Detroit car salesman put it this way: "I have found that most men who bring their car in for service are mad at the car. They are also mad at the manufacturer. This is particularly true if they have broken down on the expressway. They start taking out their anger on the service manager. He calls me in to take the beating. After the potential customer simmers down I let the mechanic tell him the car can be fixed. This turns his thinking from complaints to listening. I give him a cold Coke and take him over to a new car. He starts the new car conversation and then I make my sales pitch."

The thinking processes induced by the salesman must be considered. Concreteness of language and aptness of illustration, for example, often spell the difference between success or failure in selling. The mind works somewhat like a motion picture camera. It doesn't take in abstractions easily. When the stimulus word or phrase is abstract, the individual hearing it translates it according to his own ways of perceiving, feeling, and thinking. For example, if a salesman says of his product that it is of high quality, the associations aroused in any given customer may vary. One may conclude, "It is too expensive for me"; another may think, "It is overengineered for my simple use"; still another may think, "It's trouble free, just what I have been looking for."

The salesman may also base part of his strategy on rationalization. Here the customer is eased into believing what he wants to believe. It is just human nature to justify our behavior in our own eyes. The advertiser or salesman can help this along: "Order some now before the supply is exhausted." "These coats cost twice as much in the regular season." "The amount you save will pay your youngster's tuition for a whole year."

Customer service is a growing part of the marketing mix. "I don't mind buying it if I can just get it fixed" is a common remark. The selling of services in one form or another has grown until money now paid out for services exceeds that paid out for things. Service activities include maintenance and repair of products, technical and professional assistance in problem solving, help in training the customer's personnel in operating equipment, and marketing research on the customer's products.

In theory sales and service are supposed to complement each other. In practice the two are often in conflict. "Sales" makes commitments that "service" has difficulty in supplying. The car salesman promises one thing, and the service man says it cannot be done. The warranty on a new car, for example, may be honored without question by one dealer and virtually ignored by another. The sophisticated buyer studies service before determining where to buy.

One homeowner who maintained a contract with an exterminating company expressed the importance of service (feelings for the lack of it) this way: "When I originally signed the $700 contract to rid my house of beetles the company adhered to my every wish. The house was gassed, but to be on the safe side I took out their insurance policy against failure. Two years later bugs reappeared. It took me three visits, two long distance calls, and threat of a law suit to get the company to even come and look at the house."

Another part of the mix includes *public relations.* All employees informally contribute (for good or bad) to the public relations of a business. The larger organizations employ a specialized staff or outside agency to coordinate this aspect of the marketing mix.

Credit is involved in buying and selling as a part of the mix. It becomes important as the value of the purchase increases. And for most of us *pricing* is important in the mix. It has not only an economic base but involves psychological values as well, when status becomes important: "It costs a little more when you serve the best." And no small part of the mix involves *delivery* ("Do I get the product when the salesman says it should arrive?").

Purchase behavior by the consumer is related to psychological and sociological factors as well as to economic ones. Age of the buyer is important. From the "six-year-old purchasing agent" to "middle-age impulse buying," the psychologist is taking a look at the behavior of people of specific ages. This is why cereal commercials appear on children's shows and automobile commercials on late-night variety shows.

Beliefs are important in purchasing. In one study on consumer preferences for beef, two different displays were put on the counter. One was an economical product from cattle fed on grass. The other display was from cattle that had been more expensively grain-fed. The fat from the grass-fed cattle was slightly off-white in color, in contrast to the fat on the grain-fed beef. When the more expensive grain-fed beef was identified as such, it outsold the cheaper brand, but when neither was identified, and both were marked at the same price, each sold equally well.

In a follow-up study, customers said there was no difference in taste in the beef bought from the unidentified racks. But when identified, the customers said there was a difference—favoring grain-fed beef. Perhaps it pays to *tell people what they like!* With this thought let us take an extended look at various aspects of communication.

COMMUNICATION

Communication means different things at different times to all of us.

"I don't want to go to the dance. It's a real drag having to get dressed up."

"With my ability, I could have a much better job, but they need me here in the secretarial pool."

"It's raining in the whole rotten world, and you're an unfair mother to break your promise about going to the park."

Do you think each of these people meant exactly what he or she said? Or should the old saw be changed to read, "Listen to what I *mean*, not to what I *say*"? Perhaps the first girl felt she wasn't pretty enough to be asked to the dance. Was the secretary afraid to try out for a more demanding job? Was the little boy too disappointed at not going to the park to think about the effect of rain on the sandbox? To avoid the quick, sarcastic, communication-breaking remark, these people must be listened to. That's right, *really* listened to. True communication has to be a two-way street.

In this era of public opinion polls, dialogues, and rap sessions, students are probably bombarded with more pressure to communicate than almost any other group. One might say, "There must be something wrong with me, or my parents, if I can't get a simple idea across. With the way things are now, I should be able to make myself really understood just by *wanting* to badly enough. It seems like every time I try to talk to my folks about the race issue, or politics, or even if I can have the car Saturday night, we just end up shouting at each other. What's the matter?"

This failure in communication certainly isn't limited to the student. A worker may feel he can't tell his supervisor about how much his assembly-line neighbor's whistling annoys him. It might seem silly, even though it is hurting his efficiency. A preschooler may rush to his mother to have her come see his beautiful tower, but, finding her nursing the new baby, viciously kicks over the blocks. The child is in anguish over his inability to explain how he feels. He *wanted* to communicate as badly as the student, but couldn't do it either. At the foundation of many a troubled marriage is an almost total breakdown in communication, the partners having drifted along, relying on habit to hold them together, rather than honest understanding and an open discussion of the issues that divide them.

Communication and Language Usage

On the level of vocabulary and language usage, Bergen Evans has made some valuable comments. He stresses the importance of the nuts and bolts of vocabulary to a person in fully expressing himself. Unless it is suppressed, the colorful (if sometimes inaccurate) speech of children comes naturally. At suppertime, a four-year-old was heard to say, "I'm as hungry as a car without gas." By taking the time to listen, a parent can help a child stretch his imagination and his vocabulary at the same time. This leads to one of Evans' major points: An increased vocabulary makes learning easier. This statement makes a lot of sense, since you can neither understand what you are reading, nor reproduce what you have learned, if you lack the vocabulary. The use of a dictionary shouldn't be a shameful sign of *not* knowing something, but a positive sign of wanting to improve. The mature person will admit he doesn't know an answer, but then looks until he finds it. Teachers would much rather be given a paper using specific terms than vague generalities.

Evans emphasizes that a good vocabulary goes a long way toward avoiding misunderstandings, besides adding clarity and variety to speech or writing. He even states that in addition to the simple pleasure of using a well-chosen word, vocabulary largely shapes the decisions we make. The cliché "Words fail me," is sadly often true. Most people admire the person with a good vocabulary, if it isn't accompanied by a superior attitude. Further, Evans says that the ability to increase vocabulary throughout life is a "sure reflection of intellectual progress." And, most important for our purpose, "The better control we have over words, the more successful our adjustment is likely to be."

Artistic Communication

On a less obvious level, communication does not need to involve speech or conversation at all. It may be the passing along of one man's ideas and perceptions on an emotional level through his art. On this level, the cliché "A picture is worth a thousand words" is certainly true. A newspaper photo of a man's hand dripping with oil sludge after being dipped in Lake Michigan sparked the "Save the Lake" campaign in that area, leading to multimillion dollar antipollution proposals. No words were needed to arouse public interest in the situation.

The music of today's youth, probably more than that of other eras, serves as an outlet for their feelings on life, and should not be too lightly dismissed as "noise." Despite a number of banalities, and some works recorded for the sheer pleasure of rhythm, there are others which carry a serious message. "The Sounds of Silence" by Simon and Garfunkel and "Blowin' in the Wind" by Bob Dylan are examples from past years, and more appear all the time. The quasi-religious revival in some sectors could be seen in the rock opera *Jesus Christ Superstar* of 1970. The phenomenal success of such songs or hymns as "Amazing Grace" and "Put Your Hand in the Hand of the Man" are further evidence of this. Songs openly or indirectly referring to the drug scene can be heard, as well as many questioning establishment values. A parent truly concerned with communication with his teenager could do worse than listen. The titles and emphasis will change, but the effectiveness of their communication probably will not.

Literature, movies, painting, and sculpture as media of expression are also genuine communication, whether anyone agrees with the "message" or not. Andy Warhol's faithfully copied painting of a soup can and his elaborately tongue-in-cheek movies show a philosophy of a different sort. The paintings of Norman Rockwell are seen hopelessly saccharine to some and appealingly true to life to others, but they are the communication of his views. The "minimal" sculpture and "junk" sculpture of recent years could also be seen as communication of a sort without overly stretching the imagination. The man who covered the whole side of a cliff with plastic wrap had a message for some.

Communication in Marriage

It has been said that happiness in marriage centers on sharing common interests, friendships, and levels of aspiration. However, true communication may be the most important ingredient of all. And it should be clear by now that communication isn't just talking. It may consist of some things *not* said, if these would break down the exchange of ideas. Insulting one's in-laws would certainly be an example of this. Marriage partners need not completely "bare their souls" to one another, but the thought that is not expressed verbally or nonverbally, cannot be understood. One couple spent almost three months in an unhappy "battle-ready" state, until the meticulous husband revealed that the wife's neglecting to clean the cat hairs off the couch was terribly annoying to him. (Her instant remark "But that's crazy!" didn't do much for communication either.)

While the old saws about "getting things off your chest," and "not going to sleep mad" may hold a lot of truth, there are certain instances when arguments are unnecessary and a scene should be avoided. If a problem has been building for weeks or months, by all means get it out in the open. If the sharp retort is simply the result of a bad mood, or of being sick or overtired, it is best left unexpressed. And remember, fighting or bickering can become a destructive habit, the cutting remark automatic. Since love, and the expression of love, breeds more love, isn't that the best possible thing to communicate?

LEVELS OF COMMUNICATION

It is useful, particularly within a group situation, to think of communication as functioning at the verbal level, the feeling level, the understanding level, and, if one so chooses, at the levels of behavior and interaction. Much of our communication, of course, may involve all these levels: people to people, computers to computers, people to files, files to people. Even protest is a form of communication in which people respond with knee-jerk reaction.

At the *verbal* level we use words with different sets of meaning. We speak of denotative meaning which identifies the thing referred to, for example, the language of science or mathematics. However, outside of technical and professional fields most words conjure up *feelings* that may lead toward action. These connotative meanings constitute much of our spoken language and the letters and memos we write. A large part of the communication between a supervisor and his subordinates involves feelings. At the *understanding* level we are dealing with perception of not only the obvious but also the subtle and the emotional. Age is a key factor in understanding and relates to the so-called communication gap. The *behavior* level is characterized by the roles we play; at the *interaction* level the person relates to his organizational climate. One problem in vertical communication from the top down concerns degrees of sophistication. On the upper level, decisions must be made on enormously complex calculations. On the lower level, they have to be simplified, indeed oversimplified, to make them meaningful and acceptable. Sometimes perceptions of the problem become distorted in the process. All of us, of course, tend not to listen when there is information overload.

Language is more than just the use of words; it reflects both the personality and the environment of the person speaking or writing. It is in effect the mirror of the subculture we function in; hence we have the colorful language of the military man, the expressive words of the ghetto, and the jargon of the scientist. A verbal communication is rarely, if ever, perceived in isolation; we respond to communication in line with our predispositions. Language reinforces our ways of feeling, thinking, and behaving. The upward-mobile person uses "in" words, aggressive words, and influence words. The indifferent person may express himself with noncompetitive words, while the ambivalent person uses anxious words. Further, words not only mean different things to different people, but often also carry different degrees of meaning. A concept may, for example, be rated along a scale from "fair" to "unfair." This attitude-measuring device of securing ratings on a number of bipolar adjectives we call the *semantic differential.* It is, in effect, a test designed to get first impressions, immediate "feelings" about the items.

Some Examples

We all have our pet phrases, some of which are difficult to pin down in meaning—"a good day's work," "a dog's life," the "cat's meow." One labor-management dispute was taken to court for a definition of "a night's sleep" (a good eight hours of uninterrupted slumber). A linguist studying redundancy in language concluded that one reason a bank robber got caught was that he had a sixty-eight-word note that took too long to read. The linguist found that twelve words were enough to communicate a stick-up message. We tend to reject certain words. In a preliminary study of the wording of the 1970 U.S. census questions, it was found that people objected to the question: Do you "share" a bathroom or shower with someone else? The words "also use" were preferred. No doubt, most of us are sympathetic with the plumber who wrote the Bureau of Standards in Washington to say he had found that hydrochloric acid opened clogged drains in a hurry and asked if it was a good thing to use. The reply came back: "The efficacy of hydrochloric acid is indisputable, but the corrosive residue is incompatible with metallic permanence." The plumber replied that he was glad to know it was all right to use acid. The scientist showed the letter to his boss, who replied to the plumber: "We cannot assume responsibility for the production of toxic and noxious residue with hydrochloric acid and suggest you use an alternative procedure." The plumber thanked the Bureau and reported he was glad they approved of his use of acid. Finally, correspondence from Washington got through to the plumber: "Don't use hydrochloric acid. It eats the hell out of the pipes."

GENERALIZATIONS ABOUT COMMUNICATION

As we know, words will not always change behavior and neither will facts. We change behavior through searching for meaning. We may use phrases with an "engraved quality" and still not communicate. Studies indicate that:

1. People tend to favor communications which are congenial or satisfying over neutral or hostile ones. They are selective in what they see or hear.
2. We seek out communication situations which tend to boost our own ego.
3. If the audience for our communication is large enough, it is virtually impossible to get everybody in it to agree.
4. The higher the educational level of a group, the greater the reliance on print. The lower the educational level, the more people depend on spoken words and pictures.
5. Communications are more likely to reinforce existing positions than to change them.
6. Communication has more effect on changing minor issues than major issues.
7. After making a questionable decision, we tend to communicate with someone who will reinforce the wisdom of our decision.
8. The more personally involved we become with a subject, the more we wish to share it with other people.
9. People are limited in the amount of information they can absorb in any given period of time.
10. The more information a word carries, the less likely we are to guess its meaning in context (and the more we need a dictionary).
11. Man communicates even when he is alone, in the sense that he is thinking about what someone said to him or about him, or what he plans to say.
12. Good communication means the opposite of being ignored.
13. Self-awareness is important in communication and is a product of social interaction.
14. A person functioning in a group setting spends about two-thirds of his time talking and listening.
15. Many people do not have good listening habits.
16. Communication is a complex process involving stimuli, interpretations, and reactions with a feedback system.

PROBLEM SOLVING

The human being is very efficient in processing information. Yes, some people are poor problem solvers, but most of us can learn to solve problems more effectively. Here we shall consider two aspects of problems. First, we shall talk about theories of "problem spaces" based on research. Second, we shall present an outline of how to go about solving problems, based on much practical experience of people who have found it useful.

Problem Spaces

The newborn infant begins life with a complex set of inherited mechanisms. However, he or she also begins life relatively "content free," like a computer which has yet to be programmed. But as development occurs, information gets stored away, to be used later in helping to solve problems. Since different contents relate to different *kinds* of problems they are stored in different "problem spaces" (see page 283), presumably in the brain. Accordingly, information-processing theory says that problem solving takes place by search within a given problem space. When a problem comes up, we must first perceive the nature of it. Previous experience is helpful in both recognizing and understanding the problem. Next, we must search for a similar problem with its given problem space or, if one does not exist, we must construct one. Much of our intellectual activity consists of searching, changing, and modifying stored information in the course of seeking a solution.

Quite often, in our daily activities, stored information is ready for our use. For example, we enter a department store and ask: "Where do I find the sports department?" "Second floor, down the center aisle and to the left." "Thank you," and off we go with confidence because all the information is relevant to us. Progress in problem solving comes as the new gets integrated with the old, and for human beings this is a very rapid process. In as little as 100 milliseconds symbols can be stored. Thus, the possibilities for storage of new information in the brain are enormous, while searching through a problem space, selecting, and executing some solution can take place rapidly. Thus, we can make a split-second decision to head for the side of the road when we see a skidding car coming toward us. Of course, problem solving can be long and drawn out as we put more and more information into the various problem spaces; the long time spent in career decision making is an example.

Over a period of time, with each week or year of life, we are informationally richer than we were before. We have built into our problem-solving system a multitude of problem spaces that enable us to deal with decisions, to work math problems, or to plan our strategies for a campus dance. To repeat, problem solving is a very *orderly* process, even when we are dealing with a very complex problem in human relations.

PROBLEM SOLVING IN HUMAN RELATIONS

The old adage that the best way to handle a problem is to prevent it has merit. We, of course, cannot prevent many problems from coming up, but we often lessen them in degree and in frequency of occurrence. This can be accomplished by more self-understanding, by understanding why other people react to us as they do, and by familiarity with and skill at human problem solving.

Let us assume that we are aware of the *understandings* of human behavior. How can we handle the human relations problem when it does come up? There is nothing new or unique about the outline below on problem solving. An examination of it offers one systematic method of working out solutions in human relations problems and often in personal problems as well.

1. Defining the problem
   a. First indication that problem exists
      (1) What is bothering you?
      (2) Is it a real problem?
      (3) Is it a problem of your concern?
      Objective: To recognize a problem
   b. Selecting the problem
      (1) Does the problem need to be solved?
      (2) Is the problem made of a number of problems?
      (3) Is the problem within your capacity and knowledge?
      Objective: To differentiate main problem from subproblems
   c. Stating the problem: Can you write the problem out clearly and accurately?
      Objective: To state the problem
   d. Setting up tentative solutions
      (1) What possible solutions can you think of?
      (2) Why did you include these tentative solutions?
      (3) What outcomes might be anticipated?
      Objective: To see several ways of solving the problem with possible consequences of each
2. Working on the problem
   a. Recalling what you know: What do you already know that is vital to the problem?
      Objective: To see what information is available

b. Getting more information
- (1) What additional information is needed?
- (2) Where do you get it?
- (3) How can you get it?

Objective: To get all the facts

c. Organizing the information
- (1) In what kind of order could you write down the information?
- (2) Is any of the information irrelevant?

Objective: To have only pertinent information for use

d. Interpreting the information
- (1) How does the information relate to principles that may be involved?
- (2) Does an examination of the information lead to other problems?
- (3) If so, what problem should be solved first?

Objective: To see relationships

3. Coming to a conclusion

a. Stating possible conclusions
- (1) What are the possible conclusions?
- (2) How do these conclusions stack up with your tentative solutions in 1,*d*?

Objective: To clarify the alternatives

b. Determining the best conclusions
- (1) What conclusions can you eliminate?
- (2) What conclusions do you want to draw?
- (3) What conclusions seem most logical?
- (4) What conclusions can you draw?
- (5) What do you think will happen if you put the first-choice conclusion into effect?

Objective: To draw a logical and reasonable conclusion

4. Carrying out the conclusion

a. Doing something about the conclusion
- (1) What *action*, if any, does the conclusion call for?
- (2) If action is indicated, how and when can it be put into effect?
- (3) If no action is indicated—what then?

Objective: To act on the conclusion

5. Learning from above activity

a. Reviewing your behavior
- (1) Did the problem solving work?
- (2) If so, what do you think made it work?
- (3) If not, what made it not work?
- (4) What would you do, or not do, the next time you have a problem similar to this one?

Objective: To learn from experience

SUMMARY

Three things are essential in adjusting to day-by-day situations. First, perception involves the view of the situation. Second, communication relates to interaction with others. Third, problem solving means doing something about the situation.

Perception means organizing sensory information in an orderly and meaningful manner. We perceive the same things in different ways, at different times. Past experience influences perception. To ignore a person's past experience is to ignore a major determinant of perception, and to make the unwarranted assumption that everyone perceives the world in the same way. Through set we pay attention to certain features of a situation. We see and hear what we want to see and hear because much of perception is determined by needs and desires.

Emotional states are related to perception; they may even influence perception before the individual is aware of the stimulus. In getting to know the world, one selects stimuli to react to, a process we call "attention." Attention is gained through change and through repetition; intensity of the stimulus, as well as the novelty of it, is a powerful determinant of attention. Differences or contrasts help focus attention; social suggestions may cause people to attend to a particular stimulus. Control of distraction is important to the perceptual process because efficiency may be hampered by taking attention away from a task at hand. Illusions are errors in perception. They are misleading in that we may get a false meaning from the signs received from our sense organs. Illusions dramatically illustrate the fact that perception can play tricks on us.

The basic principles of perception are often brought to our attention by advertising and supported through other ingredients of the marketing mix. Decisions are influenced by advertising attempts to control the ways in which we build up buying habits. The mix also involves selling and customer service, credit and pricing. Beliefs, which influence buying, are important in the mix.

Communication means different things at different times to all of us, but it is always a two-way street of giving and receiving. Language is at the center of communication, but we also communicate through the visual arts and through music and literature. There is communication in marriage through sharing common interests, friendships, and levels of aspiration.

We communicate at different levels. At the verbal level we use words, with demonstrative meaning, and we communicate at the level of feelings. At the level of understanding we deal with perception. The behavior level is characterized by the roles we play. At the interaction level we relate to the organizational climate.

Language is more than just the use of words; it reflects both the personality and the environment of the person speaking or writing. Language reinforces our ways of feeling, thinking, and behaving. We tend to favor communications which are positive and boost our ego. Communication also relates to the size and education of audience and to individual beliefs. We can get an information overload. Good communication means the opposite of being ignored; it is a product of social interaction. Communication is a complex process involving stimuli, interpretations, and reactions with a feedback system.

The human being is basically an efficient information processor who, over time, builds up problem spaces that relate to different kinds of problems. Progress in problem solving comes as the new gets integrated with the old. Problem solving is an orderly process, whether we are dealing with something technical or with human relationships.

THE PRACTICAL ASPECTS OF LEARNING AND MEMORY 11

Learning is a universal human experience. A child learns to feed himself, to talk, to play, and in general to regulate his behavior toward people and things. He learns what is taught in school. He learns the social habits and customs of the community in which he lives. Later in life he learns how to do a job and how to meet the responsibilities of family life. Playing tennis, driving an automobile, getting along with one's spouse, handling the boss—all these kinds of behavior are possible because people are able to learn. An examination of learning leads to the simple but important conclusion that its chief feature is a *modification* or *change* in behavior that *lasts* for some period of time. It is helpful to remember that the learning process requires patience. It may be relevant to add that picking up information about the learning process can sometimes turn us off—we hate to be reminded of what we have to do the next day.

CHARACTERISTICS OF LEARNING

Let us now examine an everyday learning situation in order to see what happens when we learn. Consider the case of a person learning to drive an automobile. Despite his desire to drive, he does not have the necessary skill, so he sets out to change his behavior. At first his efforts are only partially successful. He starts with a violent jerk or stalls the engine. Once he is under way, steering becomes a problem as he cuts the corners too sharply or is unable to stay on the right side of the road. Abrupt stopping may occur because of inappropriate braking action. The driver displays many responses, some right and some wrong. Those which he perceives as wrong are gradually eliminated in favor of the responses which are right in that they lead him toward the goal of driving the car in the proper way. He repeats the right responses over and over again and they become smoother, more precise, and better timed. Eventually, driving an automobile is added to his repertoire of behavior. And in one way, at least, the individual is a *different* person from his former self. He is now an automobile driver, whereas before he was not.

The Learning Goal

Certain elements common to most learning situations are present in the driving task. In the first place there is a *goal*. This means that the learner wants something. He has a need or desire to learn. If such an urge is not present, he will never get under way. Before a man can be taught to operate a lathe, he must want to learn to be a lathe operator. You won't learn about psychology or tennis or calculus or typing unless you want to acquire this knowledge or learn these skills. Why a person would want to drive an automobile is perhaps obvious, but in this analysis the reason is of no consequence. The point to be remembered is that he did have the desire.

Often we fail to appreciate the importance of the learner's goal in teaching or training because the goal as the teacher perceives it may be different from the learner's perception of the goal. If the teacher's goal is to get the student to learn as much as possible about the subject matter in the available length of time, he may be disappointed when the student's performance falls far below the teacher's expectations. The reason for the mediocre performance may lie in the student's goal. Perhaps his goal was to learn just enough to get by or just enough to make a C grade. There will be a difference in what is learned in an industrial training program if the trainer's goal is to get the employee to learn to produce the maximum number of units of a given quality in a given time and the employee's goal is to produce just enough to keep the foreman off his back and the time-study man from cutting his rate.

Responses Are Necessary

After the individual has a desire or need to learn, so that there is a clear-cut goal in his own mind, what else is necessary if learning is to take place? The old adage that "we learn by doing" provides the answer. Thus, the second factor common to all learning is some kind of activity, or *response*. The learner himself must do something— make responses. This activity may be overt, e.g., arm, leg, or hand activity in playing tennis, or it may be internal, as when he manipulates ideas in solving a problem. Trying to teach a person anything by giving him a verbal description of what you want him to do, or demonstrating to him how the task should be done, or showing him by means of a film the nature of the skilled performance, is of little use unless it leads to active doing by the learner himself. The person who learned to drive the automobile not only had the desire to learn but he did something about it by resorting to many responses—arm, leg, finger, reading, judging responses—all of which were a part of his natural equipment.

Of course, the necessary responses for attaining a goal must be *potentially available* to the would-be learner. A feebleminded person cannot get through school because the intellectual responses necessary for schoolwork are not available to him. The very young child cannot learn to write until his nervous and muscular system are sufficiently developed to enable him to make the fine coordinations necessary for handwriting. The responses necessary for learning a new task may also be limited by *previous learning*. Learning may be slow or impossible in an advanced course in mathematics if a prerequisite is a basic course in algebra and the learner has never taken such a course. In the automobile driving situation the necessary responses are available to most people. In some cases, however, poor coordination, slow reaction speed, faulty vision, or some physical or mental defect may make it impossible to learn to drive.

Reinforcement

How now do we account for the fact that the learner with a goal, and making many responses, *selects* certain of these responses—the right ones—and eliminates the wrong ones? This question brings us to the third basic characteristic of learning: *reinforcement*. The learner selects from all the responses he is making those that are reinforced. The responses that are not reinforced are eliminated or not learned.

You can easily understand the nature of reinforcement if you keep in mind that the person trying to learn is, in a sense, out of balance with his environment. He sets out to restore himself to a balanced state by learning some adjustive act. The consequences of any act—reduction of pain, avoidance of distress or punishment, recognition, success, reward, pleasure—which lead the learner toward his goal are reinforcing. The satisfaction which accompanies a successful outcome reinforces the success-getting response, so the learner tends to repeat such responses. The unreinforced responses, since they are not successful in leading to the goal, are weakened. Our automobile driver resorted to many responses, some of which he eventually discovered were successful; others were unsuccessful. The former were repeated over and over again, each time receiving added reinforcement; the latter were not repeated because of lack of reinforcement, and hence were not learned.

The effect of knowing how one is doing—whether his reponses are right or wrong—provides the clearest and simplest illustration of reinforcement as a learning principle. In learning situations like playing tennis, bowling, casting for trout, or typewriting, the correct or successful response is usually apparent to the learner. When one makes a strike in bowling, the visual cues from the falling pins tell him immediately that the way he rolled the ball was the right way, and the ensuing reinforcement causes him to try to roll the ball the same way the next time. But suppose the learner has no way of knowing whether his response is correct. In a situation like this, reinforcement cannot occur, or is minimized, and hence learning should at least be retarded.

Lack of Reinforcement

A striking illustration of how the lack of reinforcement impedes learning progress is a wartime study in which men were being trained to track airplanes with a tracking apparatus. Two groups of equal tracking ability, as determined by previous performance, were observed. One group was given knowledge of results in the form of a buzzer which was sounded by the trainer whenever the trainee was off the tracking point by more than 2 miles. In other words, reinforcement was present in the form of feedback to the learner as to the correct and incorrect tracking responses. The other training group received no information at all and hence no reinforcement. After only sixty-eight minutes of practice, the group trained with the buzzer was found to be off target only 32 percent of the time, whereas the group trained without the buzzer was off 58 percent of the time. Reinforcement really works!

Classes of Reinforcers

Because of earlier discussions of perceptual principles you should not be surprised to know that the effect of reinforcement will depend on the *perception* of the individual who is learning. An outcome that is reinforcing to one person may not be reinforcing to another. What one person regards as a rewarding experience may be regarded as a neutral or even as a punishing experience by another. However, in general, one can count on an almost universal acceptance of certain classes of reinforcers such as money, food, status recognition, and companionship.

Reinforcement often occurs automatically, without the learner's being aware of the effect at the moment. Suppose that you have been playing mediocre golf for a couple of years and decide to improve your game with the help of a professional instructor. The instructor watches you play and criticizes your habit of gripping the club like a baseball bat. He says, "That is no way to hold a golf club. How on earth did you pick up that habit? You will probably reply that when you first took up golf, you simply picked up the club and tried to hit the ball. But why did you learn to grip the club in the wrong way? The wrong way must have been reinforced, otherwise it would not have been learned. The important point is that you did not perceive it to be the wrong way. Very likely you gave little thought to the grip, but concentrated on hitting the ball. The reinforcement that was responsible for your bad habit was probably the natural or comfortable feel of the baseball grip. You failed to grip the club the proper way because, to the novice, this way feels awkward and strained. Much human learning occurs and persists under conditions of reinforcement which were never specifically identified by the learner, or if once identified, were later forgotten. Since so much of our learning comes about through association, let us look briefly at this process, which we call "conditioning."

Conditioning

Day-by-day we run into many ways of associating things. For example, the normal stimulus to start a flow of saliva is the taste of food.

But how often our mouth waters at the mere sight of some favorite food. This happens because the sight of food has been associated in the past with its actual taste. This involves what we call *conditioning:* a given response (salivating) comes to be evoked by a previously neutral stimulus (sight) when this stimulus is combined several times with the stimulus which naturally elicits the response. In this illustration the flow of saliva is an unlearned response; that is, an *unconditional response* is a *conditioned* response. Thus sight has been substituted for taste in eliciting the response of mouth watering.

The more nearly alike a new stimulus is to the original stimulus, the better it will substitute for it. Sometimes we become conditioned to avoid things. A very unpleasant tasting medicine may be taken in a solution of orange juice. Weeks later the mere sight of an orange may make us shudder.

Through conditioning we often learn to attach value to things that have no intrinsic value. Let us illustrate by a study. In one experiment, secondary rewards ("poker chips") of certain colors were given to chimpanzees. Primary reward values (food, water, and play privileges) were assigned to different chips. The animals were placed in different cages that contained food and water vending machines, and a work apparatus requiring them to lift weights in order to get chips that would "buy" food, water, and play privileges. The chimps readily learned to operate the work apparatus, but they would not work for chips that would not buy them anything. They learned not only to manipulate the chips in obtaining rewards but to discriminate between chips (by color) that would buy food, water, or activity. And they learned to weed out working for chips that would not buy anything. If the animals had a large number of chips, they would not work very hard to secure additional ones. Some the animals even learned to trade "food chips" for "play chips."

Sometimes the "chimp-o-mat," as the vending machine was called, did not work. Yes, you guessed it—the animals banged it on the side! Both animals and humans behave in accord with many ways we have been conditioned. Here is where motivation becomes so important to us in our learning.

MOTIVATION AND LEARNING

Needs, wants, desires, interests, ambitions, and similar terms may all be subsumed under the more general term *motive,* as indicated in Chapter 2. Most students of human behavior agree that the human being is a goal-directed organism. This is another way of saying that man is motivated. You have no doubt used the word "motive" many times and think of it as something that moves a person to some kind of action. This is a conventional dictionary definition and, as a start, is acceptable from a psychological standpoint. A little reflection on your part about the conditions or bodily states or objects or events that arouse man to act in certain ways will bring to mind the need for food, the desire for recognition, the need for companionship, and the need for education. The interesting psychological question is: How does man come to have these many and varied motives? The practical answer to this question is that he is born with some of them and acquires others. We do not learn to be hungry or thirsty or to need sleep. We come into the world endowed with these needs. But we do learn to want or need a new TV set, a new car, a trip abroad, or an education.

We have mentioned hunger, thirst, and the need for sleep and designated them as unlearned. But the ways in which they are satisfied make it necessary to bring *learning* into the picture. You do not learn to be hungry, but you do learn to go to a restaurant or dining room or other food source to satisfy your hunger. The man who wants to go to Delmonico's for dinner is exhibiting two kinds of motivated behavior: the desire to eat, the primary motive, and the desire to go to a specific eating place, the learned motive. We do not learn the primary sex drive, but we do learn how to satisfy it. The primary motives, even though unlearned, energize or arouse the individual to learn ways of satisfying them.

Learned motives, although based on primary motives, may become motivating forces *in their own right.* By this we mean that a learned motive may call forth a specific kind of activity in the *absence of the primary motive* on which it was originally based. For example, a soldier learns to shoot a rifle in order to save his life. Handling the rifle skillfully is learned at first because of the primary need for self-preservation. But skilled rifle shooting, in itself, without any need to protect oneself, may become a motive that prompts the soldier to spend many hours on a rifle range long after the war is over. Now there is a motive in the form of a desire to use the rifle not to kill the enemy but to demonstrate to oneself and others how good one is at rifle shooting. What was once a means to an end has become an end in itself.

After a motive is learned, it may serve to induce still further learning. The rifle shooter may find it necessary to seek out certain influential people who can get him membership in a shooting club so that he can use the club's rifle range. Finding out who the influential persons are and persuading them to sponsor an outsider is quite a different kind of behavior from shooting at a rifle range. The learned desire for a college education induces some young men and women to take a job so that they can earn enough money to pay tuition. Learning to work as a steelworker or as a secretary is an altogether different kind of behavior from that which will be displayed in the classroom. Notice how the goal becomes complicated in a situation like this. To become a worker is not the ultimate goal; it is a means for attaining the ultimate goal of a college education. Learned motives may give rise to a wide variety of behavior, just as do unlearned motives.

HABITS

The story of how we learn would not be complete without an analysis of habits. When a way of behaving is so well learned as to be *highly automatic,* it is given the term *habit.* Much of our day-to-day living consists of habits: speaking habits, eating habits, dressing habits, habits of punctuality, of geniality, of shyness, smoking habits, and hundreds of other routine ways of behaving. All learning involves some degree of habit formation. Indeed, one of the ways we can view learned behavior is in terms of the accumulation of habits of varying degrees of strength. In discussing habits we do not need to introduce any new principles, since habits are simply well-learned acts.

Force of Habit

A good way to appreciate the characteristics of a habit is to inquire into the meaning of the phrase "force of habit." Why do we so often behave through force of habit when some other way would be more beneficial? The reason is that once we have learned to act in a certain way and that way has become automatic, requiring little attention, it provides us with the most comfortable way, the easiest response. It has proved satisfying or reinforcing in the past. Why try a new pattern when the old has worked for so long? There may be better ways, but can one be sure? The worker's reluctance to use a new tool, the businessman's hesitancy about installing a new time-saving method, the parents' tendency to raise their children in the old-fashioned way—all these are illustrations of adherence to habitual acts which have worked in the past and which are preferred to some new ways, the learning of which would require time and effort. In short, habits dominate much of our behavior because we are strongly motivated to behave now and in the future as we have behaved in the past.

Bad Habits

Why is it so difficult to break bad habits? If one feels that a habit is bad, it must have undesirable effects which would not be reinforcing, and reinforcement is necessary in order for learning to occur and persist in the form of a habit. The catch arises from the failure to recognize the *complex nature* of most habits. Take, for example, the habit of smoking cigarettes. What started it in the first place? Probably a number of factors, including curiosity about the taste, the desire to feel grown-up and sophisticated, and the desire to be socially acceptable. Therefore, although the smoker may no longer enjoy the taste of a cigarette or may feel that cigarettes are bad for his health, he continues to smoke because other components of the smoking habit are reinforced. When a bad habit is broken, some strong countermotivation must be present to overcome all the reinforcing effects which originally led to the establishment of the habit. If, for example, a smoker is convinced that continued smoking will cause lung cancer, fear may override all the positive reinforcing conditions which accompanied the act of smoking, and the habit will be broken.

HABIT HIERARCHIES

What is usually called a habit is often a combination of related habit sequences referred to by psychologists as "habit hierarchies." In typing, for example, one first learns to strike the correct keys. These responses are called "letter habits." When letter habits approach the point of acceptable proficiency, word habits are developed. Letters like T, H, E arouse a single word response instead of perceptibly separate letter responses. The typist perceives the word "THE," and the separate responses take care of themselves. Word habits are built upon letter habits, so to speak. After a while, phrase habits appear. Common phrases like "Very truly yours" are typed without the operator's paying any attention to the separate letters or separate words. This analysis of habit formation may lead you to conclude that different levels of habit are learned and organized one after the other, with, for example, letters learned first, then words, then phrases. This appears not to be true. The entire habit of typing has a psychological unity, consisting of separate elements which blend with one another as the final habit develops. Modern methods of teaching reading in the elementary school recognize that the learning of a complex skill consists of the simultaneous development of simpler and more complex habits. No longer does the child learn first all his letters one by one, then isolated words like "man," "cat," "girl," etc., then short phrases; rather, from the beginning he practices reading as a total, meaningful process.

A CASE STUDY

With the material on learning, motivation, and habits freshly in mind, let us postpone further elaboration of these topics and take a look at a case study, the understanding of which calls for practical application of what we have so far studied.

Five supervisors were employed during the Vietnam war in the Methods Engineering Department of the Sundale Paper Company. During the early days of the war the five supervisors applied for officers' commissions in the Armed Forces. All but one, Bill Miller, were commissioned. Bill was turned down because of a diabetic condition which, however, never interfered with his work. The four men who left were replaced with temporary employees of very limited experience and little or no familiarity with Sundale's practices and procedures. In effect, Bill, who before this had been merely one of the supervisors, now became Chief of the Methods Engineering Department with greatly increased responsibilities. He had some misgivings about his new job, but decided to give it all he had in order to help the company and do his bit in the war effort on the home front. He made a good start and continued to make progress in his overall supervisory work. He was pleased with himself, and the company was pleased with him. Throughout the war years Bill did an excellent job.

This state of affairs continued until about four months after the end of the war, at which time the four former supervisors returned to take up their old duties. In effect, the wartime job ended and Bill once more shared responsibilities with his former partners. Shortly after the return to prewar operation Bill became dissatisfied with his job. Indeed he became somewhat of a problem child in the department because of his refusal to cooperate. Finally, Bill appeared before the works manager and announced that he was quitting his job at Sundale and taking a new job with a competing company at no increase in salary, but where, in Bill's words, "his ability would be recognized."

In terms of the principles of motivation, learning, and habit formation, what was the basis for Bill's decision to change jobs? The works manager felt that Bill was very unreasonable because it had been thoroughly understood by all parties that the wartime assignment was of an emergency and temporary character, and that there would be a return to the status quo when the war ended. The works manager repeatedly stated that he could not understand what had come over Bill. Before and during the war he was hard-working and cooperative and suddenly his behavior was completely reversed.

In analyzing this case it should be clear to anyone with psychological know-how that Bill before the war and Bill after the war were in some ways different persons. Bill's behavior patterns had changed because of something he had learned. Recall the conditions necessary for learning; it will be apparent that all of them prevailed during Bill's wartime job. He was willing to take the job and the company wanted him to do so. In other words there was a need or desire to undertake the supervisory task. Not only was there motivation to learn, but there was response making—active participation by Bill. He set to work. He tried out various responses which he perceived as necessary in supervising people. And he selected and continued to perform those that were successful, i.e., the responses were reinforced. The evidence for reinforcement is that everybody concerned, including Bill, felt that he did a good job. We need not mention here the specific responses that Bill made. The point to be remembered is that they were made. Behavior that is repeatedly reinforced is learned. Since it was practiced over many months, it became highly habitual. Bill had learned in no uncertain terms that he alone could handle a supervisory position that he did not have before the war. He is now a changed man. With a full-fledged learned or secondary motive as a part of his behavioral repertoire, he has a desire to be the kind of supervisor that he learned to be. With this analysis it should be clear why he decided to quit his job. The return to his old status required him to give up a job which he was motivated to do and which he could do with facility.

The lesson from this study is that we should expect different behavior from a person if he is placed in a situation where new motives and new skills are added to his behavioral makeup. An individual who has with all honesty and good intention made predictions about what he will do in the future will behave as he claims if his perceptions remain the same. But his perceptions will change if his behavior is modified through learning. This is precisely what happened to Bill and what caused him to quit his job.

LEARNING CURVES

Let us return to the analysis of learning by inquiring into the nature and significance of learning curves. The precise changes in performance that occur when a person learns can be measured and presented in the form of a learning curve. Learning curves tell us not only that behavior has changed, but also to what degree and whether the change has been smooth or irregular.

Figure 11-1 shows some of the ways in which changes in behavior resulting from learning can be depicted by means of learning curves. One common type of learning curve (graph A) shows that production, as measured by the number of work units produced, perhaps refrigerator doors, or food mixers, or automobile wheels manufactured or utility bills processed, increases with practice until it levels off. The learning shown in this curve was that of learning to be efficient production workers. What practical information does the learning curve provide? Suppose that graph A was made by averaging the daily production of a large group of trainees. The graph would answer a number of important questions about the progress the trainees were making. It tells us that on the first day the average

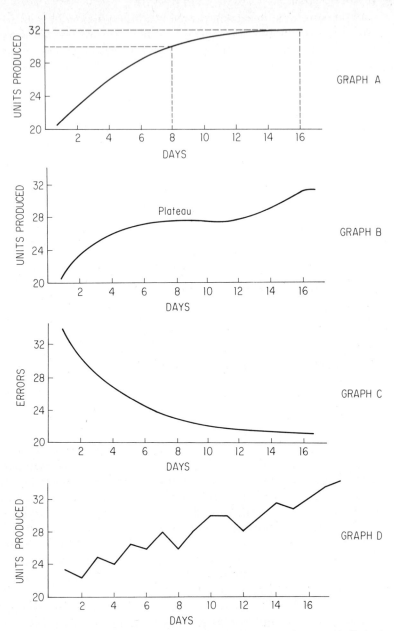

FIG. 11-1 (A) A common type of hypothetical learning curve. Output increases until production levels off as practice has its effects. (B) The plateau, where learning is temporarily halted. (C) Another way of showing learning through decrease in number of errors or in waste. (D) A graph that is rather typical of learning most anything, characterized by ups and downs which show that the progress of learning is not smooth. The important thing is that overall the trend is upward.

learner would produce about twenty units and that after eight days he should be producing about thirty units. After sixteen days he should have reached a peak efficiency of thirty-two units. Considerably more progress would be expected during the first days of practice than during later days. Indeed, between the eighth and sixteenth days, an increase of only two units could be expected, whereas between the first day and the eighth day there is an increase of ten units. If thirty-two units represents standard production, one would be justified in assuming that further practice would not bring about any increase in the production rate. Under the prevailing conditions the worker has reached his final plateau.

The Learning Plateau

Reaching a plateau does not mean that the learner is necessarily at the limit of his learning efficiency. Motivation may be increased by increasing incentive pay, for example. Or the worker may be given a new method of work or a job shortcut of which he was previously unaware. If such a change in conditions occurs, it might lead to further increases in production after the leveling off that was previously considered to be the maximum.

In some cases plateaus seem to be a necessary part of the learning process. We need time to pull together previously learned elements before overall learning can occur. In learning to receive telegraphic code one shows improvement while he is learning the individual letters, but having learned them he must practice some time without further apparent improvement, while he masters word and phrase or sentence units. The situation just described is represented in graph B. Most often plateaus occur in prolonged learning processes such as learning a foreign language, learning to read, to operate a complicated machine, to play golf, or to typewrite.

Where plateaus appear normally in learning, it is important for a teacher or trainer to know of their existence. The ordinary learner does not realize what is going on as he learns and is likely to be discouraged and let down when he hits a plateau. The teacher or trainer can counteract this by explaining that the plateau is temporary and that with continued application it will pass. Knowing that the plateau is a characteristic not of himself but of the learning process is often enough to prevent the learner from giving up. In one industrial concern, workers are given a card showing a typical learning curve for their job, with the plateau plainly marked. With the aid of the card the foreman in charge of training shows the workers who hit the plateau that if they stick to their jobs they should expect to meet the standard rate even though they seem to be stalled for the time being.

Learning Is Seldom Smooth

Another way of showing learning is pictured in graph C. This curve shows that with continued practice the time needed to do a single job decreases. Or it shows that fewer errors are made or that less material is scrapped as skill develops.

Curve D shows what the learning curve of an individual is likely to be. An individual's learning progress is seldom smooth, but the upward trend is unmistakable.

TRANSFER OF LEARNING

So far we have been examining learning as it occurs in a specific situation. But people move from one place to another in everyday life. They learn in school and then move to a job outside of school. The soldier learns in the training camp and then moves on to the field of actual war operations. The child learns in the home and then moves to the homes of his friends. Does the learning that occurs in one place transfer to another? Most of us are inclined to answer, yes. The right answer is that there is indeed transfer of learning but only under certain conditions.

Similarity of Stimuli

Let us analyze an instance in which transfer of learning is known to take place in order to clarify and specify the necessary conditions. Consider once more the case of the person who learned to drive an automobile, and let us say that he learned to drive a Ford. If now he moves to a Chevrolet, will he be able to drive it? Of course he will. He will have little or no difficulty transferring his driving skill from one make of car to another. There may be minor differences between the two cars; the dashboards may not be exactly alike, or the windshield may be a little higher on one than on the other. But in general, the stimulus conditions of the two cars are similar. If one studies Latin, the learning of Spanish is made faster because of transfer. Again, the reason transfer occurs is that some of the stimuli in learning Latin are similar to the stimuli encountered in learning Spanish. In general, the degree of transfer will increase the more similar the stimuli are in the two situations.

Similarity of Response

Transfer depends not only on similarity of stimuli but also on similarity of response. In the two car-driving situations the driver uses his right foot to accelerate, his left hand to release the emergency brake, his hands to steer, and so on. In summary, then, we may say that the greater the similarity of stimuli and response in two situations the more transfer will take place.

Keep in mind that similarity exists for the learner only if he perceives the similarity. This would certainly be the case in driving automobiles. But in intellectual tasks the similarity may not be so obvious. To the expert mathematician it may be clear that a principle of the calculus is applicable to two different problems. To point this out to the student is important, but in the long run it will do little good unless the student himself perceives the transferability of the principle.

Negative Transfer

Transfer of learning is not just a matter of considerable benefit, slight benefit, or no benefit at all. In some cases there is negative transfer. This occurs when something previously learned hinders learning in a new situation. A simple illustration is provided by the story told by a famous psychologist many years ago involving a change in the place where he carried his watch. He observed that if he changed his watch from the left vest pocket, where it was usually carried, to the right trouser pocket, he generally made a number of false movements when he wished to know the time. He eventually corrected these movements, but after the watch was returned to its original place, false movements again occurred. Old habits kept interfering or transferring to new situations, because opposite or competing responses were involved.

Negative transfer may have serious consequences. A pertinent example comes from a study of airplane accidents conducted during World War II. In one incident a pilot was undershooting the field in attempting to land. He perceived his mistake and attempted to make a correction by pulling back on the throttle and pushing forward the stick. The plane nosed into the ground because the throttle and stick responses were just the reverse from what they should have been. When questioned later, the pilot reported that he was accustomed to flying planes in which he operated the stick with his left hand and the throttle with his right. In the plane in which he had the accident the positions of the controls were different so that he used his left hand on the throttle and his right hand on the stick. The old habits interfered and resulted in a near fatality. The key principle to keep in mind regarding negative transfer is that situations requiring dissimilar responses, i.e., opposite or competing responses, account for negative transfer.

PUNISHMENT IN LEARNING

An old question that is pertinent to learning and applying principles has to do with the role of punishment in learning. Everyday observation would indicate that people learn things through punishment or threat of punishment. The young child who pulls the dishes from the table learns to leave them alone if the act is followed by punishment. If one is tinkering with an electrically activated device and receives a shock, he quickly learns to stay away from that part of the circuit that caused the shock. These examples point out what has been said about reinforcement as an essential condition for learning. The child who pulls at the dishes and is punished may continue to be attracted by the dishes, but fearing that he will be punished, he learns the response of not reaching. In not reaching, his fear of punishment is reduced or eliminated, and this relief is rewarding or reinforcing. In other words, *punishment is not reinforcing, but the avoidance of punishment is.* The use of punishment is generally not advocated as a reinforcer. Studies have shown that the wrong or erratic or undesirable response that is punished is suppressed and may appear again if the source of punishment is not present. Furthermore if punishment comes from another person—a teacher, a boss, a parent—the learner may develop strong negative attitudes toward the punishing individual so that the effectiveness of that individual is lost in situations where he does not resort to punishment.

What about learning situations where one actually performs a sequence of acts and learns them even though the act is always accompanied by punishment or unpleasantness? Soldiers, for example, learn different kinds of military maneuvers under extremely unpleasant conditions. What can possibly be reinforcing in such situations? Any soldier can tell you if you ask him. He learns these unpleasant tasks because not to learn them may mean future guard duty or KP duty, or even his life on the battlefield. The realization that not to learn may be embarrassing, uncomfortable, or diastrous sets up tension or anxiety states that are relieved by learning. Thus it frequently happens that punishment or unpleasantness may facilitate learning if what is being learned will enable the individual to avoid punishing or less-pleasant circumstances.

ORGANIZING WHAT IS TO BE LEARNED

In applying learning principles to the problem of changing one's behavior in the home or school and on a job, we must consider how material to be learned should be organized. Suppose one is setting up a training program for apprentices in a workshop and their task is to learn how to operate a lathe. How should practice be organized throughout the day so as to yield the fastest and most efficient learning? Should the apprentice be given a continuous session until he becomes proficient, or should practice be spaced throughout the day? A logical approach to this problem would seem to indicate that if the practice sessions are too far apart, what the trainee learned in the first part would be forgotten by the time he got to the second. On the other hand, if the practice sessions are too close together or if there is a single continuous session, the employee's learning would be slowed down because of fatigue and boredom.

Spaced Practice

There is considerable evidence to show that spaced or distributed practice is preferable to concentrated or massed practice. For example, in a typical experiment students read a passage of over four thousand words, either four times at one sitting or once a day for four days. Then they were given an examination on this material. It was found that the distributed method gave better results than the concentrated readings. In learning manual skills and memorizing verbal material, generally a subject finds that distributed practice is superior to massed practice. Further research is necessary, however, before a sweeping generalization is in order. We must keep in mind the *length* of material to be learned. Distributed practice may be all right for short bits of material, but when we have to learn a five- or six-step list of instructions for starting a machine, for example, it is wise to mass the practice (read the list over and without pausing) rather than to distribute it.

The ideal way to distribute learning time depends on the nature and difficulty of the material to be learned. Distributed practice is best when the learning situation is such that continuous practice causes fatigue; when motivation wanes (the learner may work more intensely if he knows that a rest is soon to come); or when the task is so complex that responses interfere with each other.

An Old Problem

A question closely allied to the spacing of time in learning concerns learning by *parts* or *wholes.* Should the student deal with separate, or detached, pieces of an assignment, or should the material be dealt with as a whole? If a salesman wants to memorize his sales talk, should he learn one paragraph, then the next paragraph, and then another until the talk is learned, or should he read the entire talk over and over again? Studies of this problem indicate that the best first approach to most learning tasks is to deal with the task as a whole. When this has been done, the more difficult elements in the total task may be attacked by the part method. This makes good sense in terms of the principle of reinforcement. A total appraisal enables the learner to see the relationship among the parts, and this is more satisfying than trying to learn something that makes little sense. Concentrating on difficult items later saves time and effort on the easy items and allows the learner to see the difficult items in their proper meaning context.

LEARNING AND REMEMBERING

One of the most interesting topics related to the analysis of learning is *remembering.* How much of what we learn do we remember? Why is it so hard to remember certain common things? Why do we forget? What can be done to prevent forgetting? Answers to most of these questions will become apparent as you proceed through the next few pages.

In taking up the topic of remembering we are not leaving the field of learning for the study of a new psychological process. Remembering is simply one way of viewing learning. It is the mark or criterion of learning. It is a present knowledge of some fact or event that has occurred before. If your behavior now shows the effects of previous learning, you have remembered. Indeed, the only acceptable evidence that one has learned anything is a demonstration that he has remembered or retained the effects of some prior mental or physical activity.

Sometimes the term "remembering" is applied to the maintenance of learned acts over relatively long periods of time—weeks, months, or years. The term is equally applicable for as short a period as ten seconds. If you learn a person's name, can repeat it one minute later, and then forget it, you have remembered for one minute. Some previously learned acts are remembered for a few minutes, some for months, others for years. What are the conditions that make it possible for us to maintain learned responses for varying intervals of time? Let us seek an answer by examining the nature of *forgetting.*

FORGETTING

If you were to ask a person what caused forgetting, you might get the offhand reply, "I guess it happens because of the passage of time. As time passes I seem to remember less and less." And everyday observation seems to support this belief. Do you not remember more of Monday's lesson on Tuesday than on Friday? Very likely you do, but not primarily because of the difference in time. Many experiments have demonstrated that it is not just the passage of time that determines how much we forget, but also *what happens during that time.* One of the most striking demonstrations of this comes from a famous experiment on the ability to remember after a period of sleep and a comparable period of waking. In this experiment two students learned lists of nonsense syllables like BAF, LUM, and SEV at about 11 P.M., and soon thereafter went to sleep. After intervals of one, two, four, or eight hours, their retention was tested. For controlled comparison, the same students learned similar material at 9 A.M., and retention was measured after one to eight hours of normal waking activity. The results are shown in Figure 11-2. The curve of remembering during sleep shows superiority, or less forgetting, at all but the one-hour interval. Interestingly enough, there is practically no forgetting during the period between the second and eighth hours of sleep. Since comparable subjects, learning comparable material, showed differences in forgetting over the same period of time, we could conclude that forgetting was caused by the interfering effects of other activity, not by the mere passage of time. True, some forgetting did occur even when the students were sleeping, but in general activity rather than time itself causes forgetting. Although one is not learning while sleeping, dreaming and other bodily activities might intefere with the recall of what was originally learned.

FIG. 11-2 A graph showing that we forget less when asleep than when awake, because there is not so much interference with what has been learned.

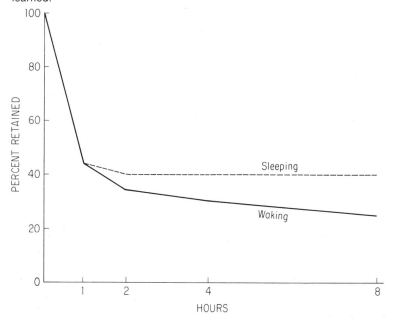

What Happens Between Learning and Tests for Retention?

Experiments on *retroactive inhibition* support the view that forgetting is due to what happens between original learning and tests for retention. Retroactive inhibition simply means the influence of other material on previously learned material. A simple demonstration of retroactive inhibition is set up in the following table.

ORDER OF PROCEDURE	EXPERIMENTAL GROUP	CONTROL GROUP
First:	Learns material A	Learns material A
Second:	Learns material B	Rests or engages in conversation
Third:	Recalls material A	Recalls material A

As the table indicates, two equivalent groups of subjects learn the same kind of material, perhaps nonsense syllables or words. One group (experimental) then learns another list of nonsense syllables or words. The control group rests or engages in conversation or some activity not related to the learning material while the experimental group is learning the nonsense syllables or words. Finally, both groups are called together and tested on how well they can remember what they originally learned. Under these conditions, the retention score for the experimental group is always much lower than that for the control group. A wide variety of experiments shows that the degree of forgetting resulting from retroactive inhibition is directly linked with the similarity of materials designated as A and B. A highly similar intervening task, like learning a second list of nonsense syllables right after the learning of an original list, causes much interference; a very different type of intervening task has less effect.

The sleeping experiments, and those on retroactive inhibition, point to the conclusion that forgetting is a matter not so much of a fading away or weakening of learned activities as of the interference or obliteration of previously learned responses by recently learned ones.

OVERLEARNING AND RETENTION

You will recall from earlier discussion that practice makes perfect if the practiced response is repeatedly reinforced. Repetition under the proper conditions leads to degrees of overlearning, depending on the

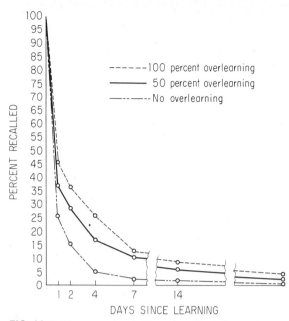

FIG. 11-3 We remember better when there is overlearning, as shown originally in this early study. Other studies emphasize the same principle.

amount of practice. It follows, then, that the degree of overlearning determines how fast and how much the individual will remember, i.e., *overlearning should aid in remembering.* This has been amply demonstrated in numerous experiments. In one study the subjects learned lists of nouns with different amounts of repetition beyond that required for the first perfect recall. A list was considered just learned (with no overlearning) when the subject could go through it once without error. A criterion of 50 percent overlearning was determined by having the subjects repeat the list of nouns half again as many times as they did in the no-overlearning situation. That is, if twelve repetitions were required to meet the no-overlearning criterion, then eighteen repetitions were used for the 50 percent overlearning criterion. One hundred percent overlearning was induced by having the subjects repeat the lists of nouns with 0, 50, and 100 percent overlearning; remembering tests at intervals of one, two, four, seven, fourteen, and twenty-eight days gave the results shown in Figure 11-3. These data were gathered in 1929. In Figure 11-4 we see a study reported in 1962 with more preciseness of control. This and other recent studies support the view that for efficiency in recall you should study material until you have learned it and then continue studying awhile longer. This is just as true for text material as for words.

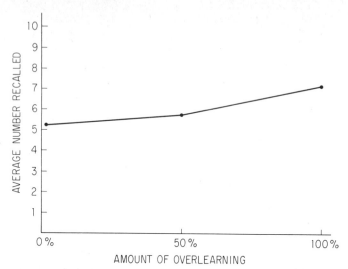

FIG. 11-4 Another demonstration that overlearning increases recall. In this experiment the subjects learned both frequently and infrequently used words. Overlearning by 100 percent is better than by 50 percent in helping the subject retain what he has learned.

Retention is increased, or forgetting is reduced, by overlearning. Other experiments show that we retain much more when we overlearn even more than described above. There are limits however, to this process; improvement does not increase infinitely with the amount of extra practice. Diminishing returns show themselves sooner or later.

Overlearning helps us make satisfactory adjustments in everyday living. You can certainly recall times when you have been frustrated because of your inability to remember a name, an address, or what you had studied in yesterday's lesson. The obvious way to avoid such predicaments in the future is to resort to overlearning. Overlearning is, in effect, habit formation. When you overlearn something, you are increasing its habit strength. Well-learned acts are, of course, less likely to be affected by other activities than are acts learned less well.

REPRESSION

Clinical psychologists and psychiatrists often find that certain kinds of experience, even though well learned, are difficult to remember. Such findings would seem to contradict what has been said about the effect of overlearning on retention. A case in point is a study of the legal testimony given by two young girls who had been placed by their parents in a house of prostitution. When the girls' plight became known to the police authorities and the girls were called in for questioning, they gave highly detailed information sufficient to incriminate their parents. However, some months later, when the girls were again questioned, they were unable to remember much of the factual detail that they had previously reported, even including the more lurid parts of their experiences in the house of prostitution. Even when some of their earlier testimony was summarized for them, they denied that such things could have happened. And there was every reason to believe that they were sincere in their denials. In a case like this, where experiences are intense and vivid, it would seem logical to assume that they would be well remembered. Apparently, some psychological process is at work that causes the individual to "forget" such experiences.

Learning to Forget

The tendency to forget the painful or unpleasant is called *repression.* The person who represses develops the habit of not recalling those experiences that are distasteful. All of us, at one time or another, engage in a mild form of repression when we refuse to talk or think about some unpleasant experience that has occurred in the past. In extreme cases, where one has undergone some terrible emotionalizing experience, he may even inhibit the recall of this past life. This condition is called *amnesia.*

How can repression be accounted for in terms of learning principles? A reasonable answer is in terms of *learning to forget.* The response of remembering acts is a stimulus. Every time this stimulus appears, the result or effect is distasteful. The reward or reinforcement comes from avoiding the stimulus, and so the person practices this avoidance response, with the result that he learns to forget the stimulating situation that made him unhappy.

SELECTION AND ORGANIZATION IN REMEMBERING

You have already had a hint in the discussion of repression that remembering is a selective and organizing process. This should not be surprising, since perception and learning have been shown to have these characteristics.

Remembering Unfinished Tasks

An experiment on the influence of failure to complete an assigned task illustrates how certain responses are selected for retention. Subjects were asked to do a group of twenty tasks such as stringing beads, modeling animals, naming twelve cities beginning with K, and solving puzzles and arithmetic problems. Most of these tasks required three to five minutes for completion. In half of the tasks, the experimenter permitted the job to be finished; in the other half the subjects were interrupted and required to go to a new task. As soon as the series of problems was completed, retention was tested.

The results of the experiment were striking. It was found that the *incompleted tasks were remembered about twice as frequently as* the completed ones, and this was true even though the subjects had actually spent more time on the completed tasks. The experimenter concluded that the unfinished tasks were remembered more vividly because the subjects were tense or anxious about them. Apparently we desire to complete a job once it is started.

Many experiences of everyday life illustrate the selecting of incomplete tasks for retention. Take, for example, a man who has to deliver an important speech. He will compile material and remember it well when he delivers the speech. But several days later he will have forgotten much of it. The task as he perceived it was delivering a speech, and until this was done the man was anxious because the goal had not been attained. He was motivated to remember those experiences that would eventually be reinforced. He forgot the material after the speech because there was no longer any need to remember. You practice the same kind of selective remembering when you gather information solely for the purpose of passing an examination. Under such motivation you generally forget most of the material after the examination is over.

Details Are Rapidly Forgotten

Part of the selective and organizing nature of remembering is our tendency to forget certain details but remember the general idea of an experience that has occurred in the past. Suppose that I am asked if I remember a vacation cruise I made twenty years ago. Of course, I say—it was the most interesting and exciting vacation that I ever had and I remember it vividly. Actually I am unable to remember most of the details of the trip. I do remember the ship, the time of the year when the trip was taken, the various ports of call, and that I had a fine time. If you ask me for details I provide them but not really from memory. My remembering of the details is hazy, so I reconstruct them in accordance with what I think they were. Thus if you ask me to describe the street in Kingston, Jamaica, which runs from the ship's wharf to the post office, I would describe it as a very narrow street, because I remember that many of Kingston's streets are narrow. Actually I do not remember enough of this particular street to be sure that it is narrow. The point of all this is that in remembering we recall *organized patterns of events* that have been learned in the past. We select certain key experiences and organize them into a meaningful scheme. When forced to fill in details, we tend to reconstruct items that are in harmony with the overall pattern, and often these items are false.

The tendency to remember a general plan, order, or arrangement and to fill in this plan with logical but false details has been studied by many psychologists. One investigator had English university students read a story taken from the folklore of a culture that was foreign to them. The story dealt with ghosts, war parties, seal hunting, and canoes. After reading the story twice the subjects were asked to reproduce it in writing as accurately as possible. The reproductions, although maintaining the general trend of the story, showed many errors in detail, all of which, however, made good sense and in no way destroyed the story's theme. Thus the more familiar word "boat" replaced the original "canoe," and instead of "hunting seals" the subjects used the word "fishing." There is no doubt that in telling our favorite stories we sometimes change some of the details a bit. As has been said: "The story wouldn't be as interesting if it contained only what really happened." Some of us make a habit of telling a good story!

Forgetting details and remembering the overall scheme sometimes gets us into trouble, but in terms of one's total life adjustments it works well. We are exposed to so many different experiences that it is impossible to remember all of them. So we select and organize related experiences, and these take the form of a meaningful frame of reference on which to base adjustive acts that call for remembering.

MEASURING RETENTION

There are a number of ways for measuring how well we remember. One way is by recalling previously learned material. Look at the digits 3, 6, 9, 2, 8, 1. Now cover them up and try to repeat them. If you can do this, you have *recalled* these numbers. Suppose you go to a party and are introduced to a dozen people. If you can give the names of all these people the next day, you have recalled these names perfectly. If you can repeat only six of them, your recall score is 50 percent. Essay examinations illustrate the recall method of measuring retention. Recall is one index of remembering, but not the only one. Strictly speaking, recall and remembering are not the same, because it is possible to obtain evidence of remembering even though the recall score is zero. In order to do this it is necessary to resort to more sensitive ways of measuring retention—by recognition, for example.

Recognition Easier Than Recall

The chief difference between recognition and recall is that in the former, the stimulus is present for your perception, whereas in the latter it is not. The difference is shown in connection with the average person's vocabulary. The number of words that an individual can recognize in reading is much greater than the number he or she can write out, even with plenty of time. Multiple-choice examinations test retention through recognition, i.e., following the question is a number of alternative answers, only one of which is correct. The correct answer is before you; all you need do is recognize it. Recognition is easier than recall because identification and familiarity rather than exact reproductions are called for. We often recognize names, dates, and objects when we see them in print or pictures, or hear them mentioned or described. We recognize tunes when they are sung or whistled which, for the life of us, could not be recalled.

Existence of Traces of Learning

Even though you cannot recall or recognize, there is still the possibility of obtaining evidence that you have retained some previous learning. This can be demonstrated through *relearning,* the third method of measuring retention. You might, for example, completely fail a recall or recognition test on some school subject. If, however, you study the lesson a second time, relearning it to the point of being able to pass a test, and if it takes less time to learn the lesson the second time than it did the first, then you have retained the effects of the first learning. Traces of the original learning were present, even though they could not be detected through recall or recognition.

SHORT- AND LONG-TERM MEMORY

What is our purpose in attempting to remember something? In making a telephone call, we may need only short-term or immediate use memory. Unless we have reason to call a given number again and again, why put the memory of the number in long-term storage? On the other hand, much of our learning is for a period of time—hours, days, or even years. We would classify the learning of some basic principle as long-term memory.

According to the theory of *two-stage memory storage,* immediately after every learning trial a short-lived electrochemical process is established in the brain. Within a few seconds or minutes, this process decays and disappears. However, before it fades out, a second series of events is triggered in the brain which is chemical in nature. New proteins are produced and higher enzymatic activity levels are induced in the brain cells. Theoretically, this process provides the more enduring long-term memory. Whether short- or long-term memory is involved, "bringing it back" can be important. Fortunately, most of our memories have order to them. They are related in time and space and often are associated with other events. These memories tend to recur with our individual interpretation, often including any emotional associations (see page 62).

There is more efficiency in remembering when the trains of associations, thoughts, and expectancies occur in context, i.e., in some meaningful framework. As events occur in context, they are stored in context. Somewhere there are cues that help reestablish the context order in retrieval, but when these cues are lacking, we cannot remember. We all know the vague and rather frustrating experience of having something on "the tip of our tongue" but being unable to express it. Often we may get a cue by asking someone to ask another question, since questions seem to have a way of unlocking memory.

Dialing a number or remembering the amount of gas pumped into the car involves short-term memory until the number is called or the amount of gas is recorded or money asked for. Long-term memory, on the other hand, involves two kinds of storage. First, we have long-term memory for stored *facts* useful to us in some way or another. Second, we have long-term memory for stored *rules.* In problem solving, for example, we call up the ways in which we should proceed. In theory, memory for solving problems for making decisions involves storage in "memory regions" of the brain, also called "problem spaces." Once we find a critical cue, we "unlock" the "space" and whole things become clear. The cue may come from outside or from within us when our search behavior makes us look for something relevant. On the practical side, one of the assets we need is learning *what we do* when we learn. This helps us in the process of bringing memories out of storage. It is also of value to become aware of *why* we were learning something in the first place.

SUMMARY

Learning, the modification in behavior that lasts for some period of time, is a process that requires patience. Characteristically, it involves goals and is an active process; we "learn by doing." The necessary responses for attaining a goal must be available to the would-be learner. Responses necessary for learning a new task may also be limited by previous learning. Learning involves selection of responses, and here reinforcement plays a major role. The satisfaction which accompanies a successful outcome reinforces the success-getting response, so the learner tends to repeat such responses. Unreinforced responses are weakened.

Much of our learning comes about through the association process of conditioning. A given response comes to be evoked by a previously neutral stimulus when this stimulus is combined several times with the stimulus which normally elicits the response. The more nearly alike a new stimulus is to the original stimulus, the better it will substitute for it.

The human is a goal-directed organism. Hence, motivation plays a large role in learning; learned motives may become motivating forces in their own right. After a motive is learned, it may serve to induce still further learning. Much of what we learn becomes habitual through repetition. Habits may be good or bad in terms of the adjustments we are called upon to make. Over time we build up habit hierarchies, or sequences of behavior. Learning curves give us a graphic way of measuring progress; learning plateaus relate to the fact that learning is seldom smooth. Plateau analysis is useful in getting an overall picture of the learning and teaching processes.

Transfer in learning is related to both similarity of stimuli and similarity of response. Negative transfer disrupts behavior; this occurs when something previously learned hinders learning in a new situation. Opposite or competing responses account for negative transfer.

Punishment in learning is not reinforcing, but the avoidance of punishment is. Although not advocated generally as a teaching method, punishment may facilitate learning if what is being learned will enable the individual to avoid unpleasant alternatives.

In organizing what is to be learned, we find that spaced practice is generally preferable to massed practice. In terms of the principle of reinforcement studies indicate that the best first approach to most learning tasks is to deal with the task as a whole. When this has been done, the more difficult elements in the total task may be attacked by the part method.

Overlearning is beneficial not only in academic situations, to counteract forgetting, but also in making satisfactory adjustments in everyday living. It is, in effect, habit formation. For practical reasons, it is important to distinguish between short- and long-term memory. Some things are needed only for immediate processing, whereas other things must go into long-term storage. Retrieving information from storage is helped when we are aware of why we learned something in the first place.

FOUR

TOWARD CAREER PLANNING

COUNSELING AND GUIDANCE

On the college campus one will usually find the office for counseling and guidance. It may be called "Personnel Counseling" or "Bureau of Measurement and Guidance," or it may have one of several other titles. It may be located in a temporary wooden structure or in the former living suite of an old mansion. Regardless of title or location, here one finds the "psychological center" of the campus. It is here that most students, at one time or another, come face to face with those all-too-familiar questions of their personal identity crisis:

Who am I?
Where am I going?
What will be the costs in getting there?
What questions should I learn to ask, and when should I ask them?

We may conclude that there is some chance that all of us will be less lonesome when we come to know ourselves.

THE SEARCH FOR IDENTITY

Discovering our individual identity involves knowing not only where we plan to go but where we come from. Some of us enjoy competition and others do not. One follow-up study of 440,000 high school students across the nation concluded that most young people do not make an appropriate choice of career while attending high school. This often becomes clear during the early months of college, and professional help is sought. Several factors enter the picture. First, in career planning, abilities, interests, and attitudes are important. In counseling we learn that we do not have to be good in everything in order to succeed in a few chosen areas. Second, we need to discover our assets and build upon them rather than to overemphasize our liabilities. Third, we need to learn how to "put it all together"— abilities, desires, personality, and opportunities. We all need help in learning to adjust to problems. Everyone, at times, needs someone to talk to, particularly the person facing something new. The "something new" may be the college environment, the world of work, or a creative idea looking for a sympathetic ear.

Much of what we call counseling is very informal—that brief chat with the classroom teacher or with a friend. More formally we have educational counseling dealing with problems of study skills, reading disabilities, and other academic difficulties. Closely related is career counseling, or guidance, which attempts to identify the particular line of work for which a person is best suited. In counseling, intelligence tests may be employed to determine the students' general level of ability. Achievement tests are particularly valuable for reading and certain quantitative skills. Personality tests are sometimes useful, and special aptitude tests may help provide some practical answers in counseling. A person may, for example, show considerable interest in music but not sufficient aptitude to become a professional. He may therefore come to satisfy his interest in music through listening or playing in the band, while pursuing a career in something else. But there is still another aspect to counseling that is vitally important to the search for identity—the questions that are raised for one to ponder.

Studies show that well-adjusted people perceive themselves accurately and are open to experience. They ask questions (not always expecting answers) and tend to recognize threatening experiences. Poorly adjusted people, on the other hand, tend to avoid questions and experiences. Well-adjusted students, many of whom seek counseling, tend to show four things in common. First, when faced with problems, they are sustained by remembering past occasions of having coped successfully. Second, they make an effort to learn about new situations. Third, they tend to identify with well-adjusted students. Fourth, they see the search for identity as a help in maintaining perspective and in preparing for the future.

The college student who seeks out counseling is trying to do more than get a quick answer to some problem of the moment. He thinks of counseling as a broadening experience, part of his search for identity, which is basically a continuing process. It is as though we go from "identity" to "placement" in life and work.

COUNSELING INTERVIEWS

In the college setting, counseling may involve talking problems over with family and friends, particularly with classmates. More or less formal counseling frequently begins with the classroom instructor.

The Classroom Teacher

Some of the most effective teaching (and counseling) may occur when a student comes to his instructor. "I don't think these objective tests really measure what I know." "I study harder for this course than any other, but I can't seem to get the hang of it." Such statements often mean: "I have a problem I want to talk over and you seem to be an understanding person."

Students often want to get to know their instructor better. Some students are really lonely. Others have strong dependency needs. But in the main, students want to talk over problems, perhaps about their parents, or about not being accepted in the group, or they are looking for tips on study habits (see Chapter 9). If professional counseling services are available on campus, the teacher usually encourages the student to use them. The classroom teacher is a good person to recommend services.

Empathy in the Interview

Interestingly, there are some sex differences related to counseling. Female clients express more emotion in counseling than male clients, regardless of the sex of the counselor, but male clients do not differ in expression of feeling with male and female counselors. This is true whether the counseling is educational or vocational.

Studies also show that clients who prefer counselors for their warmth and friendliness tend to focus on discussion of personal problems in the first interview. Clients preferring logic and efficiency in their interview tend to focus on the practical job aspects of educational or vocational problems.

Clients prefer a counselor who shows *empathy* in the first interview. Such a counselor seems to put himself in the position of the client. Empathy literally means "feeling into." One person "feels himself into" the action or attitude of another. Watch the stands at a football game. As the home team rushes the line, the supporters of the home team also lean forward and push with it. At a track meet, persons viewing a high jump or pole vault will often lift one foot from the ground and strain with the athlete.

The professional counselor, of course, knows when and where to show empathy or to be hard-boiled. Rapport may start with empathy and then move in the direction of objectivity.

The Disciplinary Interview

Both in the educational setting and in industry some counseling involves the sometimes unpleasant task of discipline. Discipline may or may not strain relations between the client and counselor. Some of the most respected people on the campus are deans, and they often gain respect by invoking discipline. The same may be said for the executive who must discipline the subordinate.

The discipline interview offers one opportunity not always present in the more voluntary situation. When discussing the discipline, the counselor has the opportunity to note attitudes, emotions, habits, and other behavior patterns.

One of the big problems for the supervisor, as well as for the dean, is to be able deftly to play the different roles of disciplinarian and, at the same time, of friendly confidant. In a later chapter we shall talk about industrail counseling in relation to supervision and leadership (see page 421).

Atmosphere of the Interview

Counseling on personal problems must be conducted in an atmosphere of confidence. Only in exceptional cases, such as the case of a seriously maladjusted person, are confidences revealed.

The establishment and maintenance of *rapport* is essential. Three elements are involved: (1) the understanding attitude of the counselor, (2) the physical and psychological climate underlying the interview, and (3) the attitude of the client.

In most instances one wishes to establish a *permissive* counseling interview. Here the client is encouraged to speak out—and without fear of reprisal. This situation is helped when the counselor listens attentively without being critical (certainly at the beginning of the interview). He knows that some things do not make logical sense, that they are only felt emotionally.

Good listening is not only an art, it is a trying experience as well. To be able to sit through talk, and often illogical reasoning, takes patience.

The interview opens with ordinary courtesy—a friendly and courteous greeting by the counselor. "How can I *help* you?" may be a better opening than "You are the young man the dean sent down here."

Phrasing questions is important. Questions that call for a yes or no answer tend to cut down the flow of conversation. "Maybe you would like to tell me why you came in?" or "Would you like to discuss your problem?" are questions which encourage expression. Any impression of cross-examination from the counselor inhibits, or at least delays, the process of getting problems out in the open.

Many clients have difficulty in verbalizing their problems. Even people with high verbal skill hit roadblocks in expressing emotional problems. The counselor must avoid putting words into the client's mouth. The *nondirective* approach of "I see" or "I understand," can help the client come to point after point. Even "Yes" may serve to bridge the conversational gap or keep the client talking so that the counselor can pick up *nonverbal cues.*

Silence in the interview is to be expected. This is particularly true after the frustrations have been expressed and the client begins to think. Such silences seem to the client (and to the inexperienced listener) to be endless. Actually they are short. They may be broken by such remarks as "Tell me more."

Experienced counselors know the importance of keeping their *vocabulary understandable.* The old pro knows the advantages of keeping the *number of ideas* per interview to a minimum. "Telling all" sometimes is just that and is very time-consuming. And the counselor is also adept at telling the difference between the sympathy seeker and the person with a specific problem. It should be remembered that he too has had an occasional ache in the back of his throat.

How to end an interview is important. Said one counselor: "I keep the clock in full view. Many clients have the tendency to just talk and talk as though time is free. Seeing how time is passing brings them more quickly to the problem." Quite often the counselor must be the one to bring the interview to a close: "Do you think we have done all we can for today?" "Is there *one* more thing we should discuss before we close?"

USEFUL GENERALIZATIONS ABOUT COUNSELING

Experienced counselors have expressed several generalizations about counseling. Let us present them here to pull together some of the things we have implied before. We hope that in addition to providing general information, they may be helpful to the reader when he next goes for counseling.

1. *The problem volunteered by the client may be only a small part of the actual problem.* Complete frankness in the beginning of an interview is often embarrassing. The employee who asks for a transfer has to give reasons, and these may be embarrassing, even threatening. The same is true of the student who may be having difficulty with a teacher or even with "the system." Sometimes the counselor can sense the client's unvoiced questions and discuss them without becoming too specific. He or she knows when the client has paid his obligations to the system and he is ready to move on to his real problem.

2. *Personalities of client and counselor sometimes clash.* Most counselors ask themselves, "What does this person think of me as a counselor?" With time, conflict may be resolved. Where there is more than one counselor available, a switch may be the best way out.

3. *Much is conveyed by nonverbal behavior.* The professional soon learns to read signs. "What you fail to say tells me much." "Your facial expressions give me cues." These thoughts help to guide the counseling interview.

4. *Recurring ideas and statements are important.* One counselor added up the times that one company was mentioned in an interview about job selection. Company ABC was mentioned more than twice as often as all others combined. Was this favorable or unfavorable? At least it was a clue to be followed.

5. *Measuring instruments often are not called for.* Often clients

come in and "want to take a test." The trained counselor knows when and when not to use measurement and diagnostic devices. After all, testing is expensive and often unnecessary. And when tests are given, they need to be interpreted.

6. *Some clients take their aggression out on the counselor.* The old pro can soon sense this and does not become disturbed.

7. *Some clients get helped without knowing it.* One counselor tells of a client who came in three times and was handled in a completely nondirective manner. He later told the dean that he didn't get any advice so he stopped going to the counseling center. "Did you get your problem solved?" asked the dean. "Yes, but I did it myself—the counselor never did anything but puff on his pipe and say occasionally, 'I understand,' or ask, 'What do you think?'"

8. *The good counselor gets the client to see his or her strong points.* "They come in with their weaknesses," is the way one guidance person put it, "but in time they begin to concentrate on what they *can* do rather than what they can't do."

9. *Whatever the action planned, the client should feel it is "his" plan.* One of the difficult jobs the counselor has is getting reinforcement himself. He knows the client must feel that *he* solved the problem himself. Little wonder counselors sometimes become discouraged. If the counseling is effective, an emotional relationship may develop. The counselor must avoid giving the impression that he has gained some special advantage over the client.

10. *The professional counselor has no formulas.* Even the most sophisticated of us want a magic remedy for our problems. The counselor must make it clear that he can provide an appropriate climate for thinking but only *the client* can solve his own problem. The guidance counselor has the particularly difficult task of helping the client to see that goals are reached step by step, not in one massive leap. A beginning is made when the client first realizes that there is no script to solve his problems, that counseling involves more than just trying to find a psychological waterhole.

SOME PRECOUNSELING THINKING

It is probably reasonable to assume that the reader will from time to time find himself or herself *as a client* in a counseling session. Let us here give some working statements about human behavior that may help provide a background for at least some of the problems the reader may encounter. Here we are making suggestions relative to personal problems.

1. *Know what you "bring to" the situation.* How an individual responds to a counseling situation (or any other situation) depends on what he *brings to* it. This includes at least a vague knowledge of one's abilities, attitudes, skills, habits, and specific problems. Of course, one of the reasons for seeking counseling in the first place is to find out about such things. But even thinking about these things provides a start.

2. *Know how someone else besides you may perceive your problems.* This may be possible only if you know your counselor well, but at least you can make some guesses about how he or she will look at things. In any human relationship, particularly in a problem-solving situation, one must consider the interrelationships between the parties involved. The old expression is apt here: "Consider the other person's angle."

3. *Find out something about the background of the counselor.* The experienced counselor is usually a person of considerable experience and wisdom, having "been there before." Just as we suggested above that you be aware of your background, it is helpful to know what the counselor "brings to" the situation.

4. *Learn the early signs of a problem.* When an individual fails to make a suitable adjustment to a situation, he or she becomes stirred up, disorganized, and confused. Each person has characteristic ways of showing emotional upset. The ways are often recognizable in the beginning stages. What are the typical ways in which *you* react?

5. *Be able to recognize the behavior sequences when frustration leads to aggression.* Emotional upsets vary in degree, but they all involve a build-up in tensions. The individual seeks release from these tensions by doing something. What he does may be beneficial to himself or harmful. It is helpful to know what to expect in your own behavior when you are stimulated emotionally.

6. *Accentuate the positive as well as the negative.* If everything goes well, there is no need to seek counseling on emotional problems. However, since much counseling involves problems that are not disturbing, one should pay some attention to planning ahead. It is wise to review our accomplishments. Too often we think of counseling only in negative terms; we think of going for guidance only when we have a problem. Guidance often is understood best when it is free of emotional content.

7. *Be aware that stimulation without effective outlet induces tension.* When we are stimulated and have built up effective habits to deal with the stimulation, little or no tension results. On the other hand, stimulation which does not operate within the patterns of the individual's habit structures induces excessive

emotion and conflict. Knowing how we let off steam or bottle up our troubles is important.

8. *Know what your dominant wants are.* Some people find it helpful to list their needs and wants and put them in a one-two-three order. Failure to understand need satisfaction can lead to defensive behavior, as discussed in Chapter 4 (see page 80).

9. *Recognize the relations between your level of aspiration and your level of ability.* When these levels are separated too far, we encounter difficulty. If, in some area, we have too much ambition and too little aptitude, then feelings of inferiority are generated. If, on the other hand, we have far more ability to do something than we have the desire to do it, we may be establishing lazy habits.

10. *Expect occasional failure.* What we are saying in effect is that if you have never been thrown from a horse, you haven't ridden enough—at least you haven't tried enough spirited horses. The person who tries inevitably fails in some things.

11. *Know something about your creative experiences.* The thrill of discovery is stimulating. And the reverse is true. When we no longer discover something new now and then, we are getting away from seeking things to create.

12. *Understand the nature of problem solving.* One of the main reasons in going for counseling is to practice problem solving under guidance. It takes a long time to learn how to solve problems. Trying to understand what we are doing when we work on a problem is helpful (see page 254).

GUIDELINES RELATING PEOPLE AND JOBS

Vocational guidance demands that we not be naïve about people and jobs. From experience and research, we have found many helpful generalizations to consider in vocational guidance. Several of them are listed below. These generalizations help form a base for dealing with such questions as: What kind of job do I want? What kind of job can I do? Where do I find this job? How do I get it? How do I move ahead? We are going to devote the next chapter to such questions, but before facing them, the following guidelines may well be in order.

1. *People differ; they differ in abilities, interests, personality, and ambition.* Where do I stand concerning each of these? Here one begins to analyze himself or herself as an individual—a first step in answering the question, "Who am I?"

2. *Organizations differ; they differ in the opportunities they*

provide for taking care of individual differences. One person is better suited to a military organization than to business. Another may get along better working in industry. The person who likes show business may find working in a bank less stimulating although it may offer more job security.

3. *Companies, even local plants or offices, differ in their psychological climates.* A climate that may provide stimulation and satisfaction for the aggressive person may arouse fear in the introvert. It is important for the individual to ask, "What kind of climate is most suitable for *me?*"

4. *Selection of the career job cannot readily be undone.* True, a person can usually change jobs, but he or she is a different person by virtue of previous job experience. When we invest time, money, and *ego* in a career, it produces changes in us. These changes may, of course, be for better or for worse. That first full-time job after leaving school should be chosen most carefully.

5. *The perfect job does not exist.* Somewhere compromise has to be made between abilities, interests, values, and opportunities. The person who starts out to look for everything in a job is unrealistic.

6. *Each person has the potential for success in a large number of different occupations.* This generalization, on first thought, makes us feel that career planning is easy. True, many potentials provide for more alternatives in choice. But at the same time they produce more possibilities for conflict in making job choices.

7. *Childhood and adolescent experiences play some role in the interests we develop.* To be sure, the fantasy stage of childhood and the dreamy stage of adolescence are unrealistic in many ways; nevertheless, here is where some interests begin, provided that the required abilities and opportunities are present.

8. *Possibilities for job changes will always face most of us.* The person who is "on the way up" will face changing jobs more often than the indifferent person. He or she should study the decision-making process—study the "whys" of failure and of success. Such experience gives guides for the future.

9. *Life-styles are determined in large measure by vocational choices.* Prethinking in this area can be helpful in giving direction to one's goal orientation.

10. *Work is a way of life.* When we are busy or tired, it is not uncommon to think of the pleasures of retirement: "I would stop work if I had enough money to live on." This thought overlooks what we know about boredom. To be sure, some people could be satisfied just sitting and rocking—even having an automatic rocker. But for most of us, satisfaction comes through activity. Ask the man who has been out of work for some time, or the

energetic woman who was forced into retirement. The most effective personal adjustment comes when the nature of the work itself and the way of life that goes with it—community, home, leisure-time activities, friends—are congenial to the aptitudes, interests, and values of the person in question.

11. *No job provides for complete satisfaction. No person completely fits the job.* The interaction of the individual and his environment is very complicated. Vocational guidance can help by making us realize this. It may also cushion some of the blows.

12. *Tradition has established that some areas are male-dominated while others are female-dominated.* For example, most doctors are males and most nurses are females. This can influence one's thinking before he or she arrives for the counseling interview.

VOCATIONAL SELECTION—A TWO-WAY STREET

Each person *selects.* We select our friends and the activities in which we engage. Each individual also is *selected*—for the band, the football team, the dance committee, the job. Selection is a continuing process, lasting from childhood to old age. At certain times we are in the role of selectee, and at other times in the role of selector.

Selection may be made haphazardly, or with thought and preparation. As far as getting a job is concerned, most people unfortunately use a method somewhere between worry and luck. This is an area in which guidance and planning are especially important.

Personnel selection is one of the traditional areas of industrial psychology, an area increasing in importance as technology adds to the complexity of jobs at all levels of industry. It takes place not only when the individual is first hired by a company, but also each time he or she is promoted, transferred, or reassigned. Recently, selection has become related to problems of retraining workers whose old jobs have been made obsolete by technological changes. By its very nature, the selection system involves figuring the odds. It is a safe bet that the rancher will make some mistakes in selecting his future breeding herd because of the many factors he must consider. The same holds true in personnel selection. The industrial psychologist recognizes these problems. He is also aware that more and more companies are using psychological techniques in their prediction because few, if any, other procedures have worked out as well over the long haul. The psychologist is also aware of his or her obligations to society and to the dignity and welfare of the individuals involved. Further, he or she must follow government guidelines on hiring and firing practices.

THE EMPLOYER'S SELECTION PROBLEMS

Suppose we have three positions to fill and thirty applicants for them. Within that group of thirty there are probably three persons whose combined job performance would be superior to that of any other group of three candidates. Of course, we cannot know just who those three are unless we put all of them to work and see who does the best job. Short of that, what could we do? We might choose three applicants at random, or perhaps the three most attractive, the three tallest, or the three most articulate. We probably would make mistakes using any of these approaches, since no method can perfectly predict future events. Our problem, then, is to use an approach that would identify the three individuals whose performance would be superior to that of any other candidates selected by any other approach.

The Assignment Process

There are advantages to using a selection model in which we either select or reject each applicant, but many situations are more complicated, as we shall see. When we are selecting for a number of jobs simultaneously, we must often work with the aim of making the company as effective as possible. In other words, rather than attend to the performance on one job, we must consider performances over many jobs. For example, one individual may be adequate for several jobs. Rather than assign that individual to the job which would be optimal for him or her, we must consider the other people who are available for the several jobs. The efficiency of the company as a whole may require us to assign the person to some job other than the one for which he or she is best suited. This *classification* or *assignment* problem is difficult to handle.

Another complication of the simple select-or-reject model occurs when we consider *placement.* This is a special case of classification, in which we have to make assignments by rank—ordering personnel; one example is the placement of college students in advanced, regular, or remedial classes of freshman mathematics. Here again, the selector has several decisions to make other than "reject." Often an organization may have special reasons for keeping an employee at a certain level on the payroll. In practice, things are seldom either-or.

Most employment situations are mixed; they are neither pure selection nor pure classification, and they involve at least three aspects of the selection process. First, to evaluate the effectiveness of any selection procedure, we must first agree on an index of job

success which will permit at least a crude ordering of job performance. Second, we must measure the job success of those individuals
who are not selected as well as the success of those who are. Third, we
must determine the *standards* of success and failure in our selection procedures. Once we have set these standards, we must test
various types of selection procedures to see how well they work out in
practice.

Projected Manpower Needs

One part of the problem of selection which is becoming increasingly
acute is that we find ourselves in an age of technology, with a
shortage of those able and willing to do the nitty-gritty work of the
engineer and the technician. Figure 12-1 is a projection of industrial
manpower needs made in 1968 and running through the late 1970s.
Note that with an increase of 26 percent for all groups an increase of
54 percent is projected for professional and technical workers. It is
anticipated that the rapidly growing two-year colleges will supply
much of this trained manpower. At what point in the individual's
career will selection be made—before, in, or after college? Will
selection become a continuing problem? Will less attention be given to
selection and more to training as fair-employment practices are
implemented? When pretraining has to be given before a person can
even fill out an application form and take a test, will the under-
privileged have a fair chance? These questions relate to the employer's side of the picture. Let us close this chapter with a brief look
at where the job seeker fits in the two-way selection process.

FIG. 12-1 Projected manpower increases by selected U.S. occupational groups for
the late 1970s.

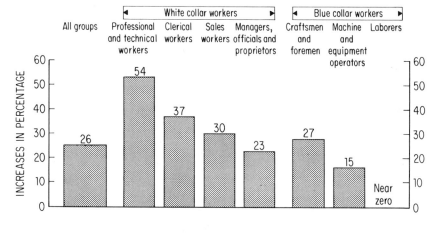

THE EMPLOYEE'S SELECTION PROBLEMS

There are several ways of getting a job. At the worker level, getting a job is largely in the hands of someone else. A union-member friend may recommend a job, or it may come from a visit to one of some four thousand employment offices in the United States. Abilities and interests may or may not be measured. Supply and demand largely determine the placement of unskilled and semiskilled workers. Above this level the job applicant is more on his own both in making decisions and in getting vocational guidance.

At the level of technical skills, in prosperous times employers often recruit on campus. The visit of the personnel recruiter has become as much of a two-sided sales pitch as a selection process. Both recruiter and job seeker are under enormous pressure, with the recruiter seeing dozens of applicants in a few days. In slack hiring periods campus visits decline or are eliminated altogether.

For the person who plans a career with care, getting a job is more involved. Recent research has emphasized that upward mobility depends not only on aspiration or opportunity, but also on long-range planning. Many people do not get, or perceive, the chances of mobility. Most recruitment is for one job only; advancement plays no part in selection. There are exceptions, of course. In some managerial and professional recruiting, people are chosen with development in mind. Many people at these levels have confidence that they can get ahead through their own efforts anyway.

Workers often feel that pull and luck are necessary for advancement. Few have aspirations beyond the level of foreman. In contrast, for the person who wants to move up, getting ahead is a part of the game. It is a game in which education and guidance, formal or otherwise, are essential for the understanding of alternatives in aspiration. It is a game in which the requirements for career survival are planned. The aggressive person must weigh both sides, giving careful thought to the psychological as well as the physical costs involved in moving ahead.

Education is being upgraded and is becoming more work-oriented. As technology has grown, specialization has become commonplace. Technical school graduates are sought after, and so are those in the health fields. The person in sales or in management may be welcomed with open arms, but how long will this attention last? For the few, of course, it may become a way of life. For the many, however, technological and professional obsolescence come fast. In a technological world rocking with change, vocational guidance attempts to project beyond the reef of security. And many people need help. Some are models of tranquility while others collapse in neurosis. Some are locked in by never having had an opportunity. These and other things become important to us when we come face to face with making career decisions.

Recruitment and Promotion Patterns

Regardless of public relations efforts to the contrary, many recruitment and promotion procedures for men and women differ. Women may find that although getting a job initially may be relatively easy, they must "break in" to the organization if they wish to work their way up, often at a point at which many newly hired male employees are starting. Men are frequently hired with promotion in mind; women often are not. Studies show that proportionately more men than women are put on the fast track to promotion and are encouraged to be generalists. Women are encouraged to specialize; specialization acts as a built-in brake on career aspiration.

The Civil Rights Act of 1964, which includes guidelines on hiring or firing discrimination on the basis of ethnic background or sex, has had a noticeable influence on personnel practices. In general, surveys show that whereas hiring of minority groups is generally increasing, promotional opportunities are not. There are regional differences, and differences from industry to industry. Even at local, state, and federal service levels, hiring and firing have shown varying patterns, related to both local customs and bureaucratic practices. For the job seeker, search for opportunities may well be planned as a part of one's evaluation of organizational climates (see page 407). In local areas, counseling and guidance can be most helpful in matching the individual to the proper work environment.

SUMMARY

On the college campus the search for identity often relates to formal or informal counseling and guidance. Well-adjusted students, many of whom seek out counseling, tend to show four traits in common. First, when faced with problems, they are sustained by remembering past occasions of having coped successfully. Second, they make an effort to learn about new situations. Third, they tend to identify with other well-adjusted students. Fourth, they see the search for identity as a help in keeping down overconfidence and in preparing for the future.

Counseling centers on interview situations. To ensure a successful interview, the student will find that precounseling thinking can be helpful. Many suggestions are offered: knowing oneself and how the counselor may perceive the problem; knowing the signs of a problem and the sequences of problem-solving behavior involved; knowing

COUNSELING
AND
GUIDANCE

301

wants and aspirations and about failure; knowing something about creative experience and the nature of problem solving.

Guidelines relating people and jobs are important to vocational guidance. They include knowing how both individuals and organizations differ; knowing about psychological climates and where experience, abilities, interests, values, and opportunities fit into the picture; knowing that the perfect job does not exist, that each person has potential for a variety of occupations, that childhood and adolescent experiences play a role in interests; knowing that job changes will face most of us; and realizing that traditions relate to opportunities and that life-styles are determined largely by vocational choices.

Vocational selection is a two-way process whereby each person selects and is selected. Selection models involve classification and placement, and they change with manpower needs. At the center of the "select" or "reject" model of recruiting and selection are the legal complications related to the Civil Rights Act of 1964. In general, surveys show that whereas employment selection of minority groups is increasing, promotional opportunities have not followed a similar pattern.

MAKING CAREER DECISIONS

13

The individual who goes through the long process of career planning gradually comes to realize that it is difficult to plan for a career in which he or she has had little or no experience. This problem relates to a growing trend whereby colleges are instituting programs of "education-work-more education-more work." Getting work experience can be helpful in career decision making if the work is sandwiched in between semesters of education. But for many, this is not possible, and for some probably not desirable. In either case, projecting ahead relates to career decision making. In this chapter we raise some points to consider in the decision-making process and talk about available alternatives. The person who works and goes to school part-time is often in a favorable position to make wise choices, having learned what he or she likes and does not like. For many people, moving ahead on a job is even more important than getting a job. We shall talk about what is involved here.

Let us remember that the problems one faces in middle age, at the reevaluation point of "no return," can be lessened by planning one's career carefully (see page 184). Too often we tend to drift into work; we may pay for it later. "Job hunting should never be hit or miss. Such a method produces nothing but weariness, discouragement, and loss of self-confidence. It is a sales campaign and it requires careful planning and intelligent development. Most people do their poorest job of selling with the most important product they will ever have to sell—themselves." These are the words of a successful personnel man. And a psychologist adds: "Decision making is one of the most involved processes which engages the human. It sets him in a position out in front of animals."

DECISION MAKING

It is estimated that because of rapidly advancing technology each person now twenty years of age may have as many as six careers during his or her lifetime. Yes, we mean careers, not just jobs. This means, for all practical purposes, that the individual who learns to make decisions appropriately early in life will have advantages over the person who moves along deciding matters by trial and error. More than ever, the student of today must be future-oriented. This may be helpful in keeping one from becoming emotionally unhinged in facing questions which have no built-in answers.

We all recognize that decisions cause problems as well as solve them. Getting ready to make a decision is in reality a part of the process of making a decision. Further, the human being is limited in the ability to sort out information. One must also evaluate the source of information; this is very important in career planning.

Information, Attitudes, and the Sleeper Effect

What is the source of the information? Can I believe it? These are questions we have to face in making many decisions. They are particularly important when the decision making involves career planning. Let us look at a study of the "sleeper effect" in getting and changing attitudes and then return to the two questions above.

Communication has most influence when the information appears to be true and complete, and when it is transmitted by a source of high credibility. Two psychologists presented college students with information about selling drugs, the future of movie theaters, and similar questions of public interest. Each communication was presented to some of the subjects as coming from a source of high credibility. For example, the information about the future of movie theaters was attributed to *Fortune* magazine as a high-credibility source. For a low-credibility source the information was attributed to a female Hollywood gossip columnist. The actual communications attributed to the two sources were identical.

The subjects tended to judge the communication from the reliable magazine source as fairer, and 23 percent of them changed their opinions in the suggested direction. Only 6.6 percent of the subjects in the low-credibility group changed opinions. However, when attitudes were measured four weeks later, there was a *decrease* in the favorability of the attitudes of subjects who had received the information from the high-credibility source. There was an *increase* in the favorability of the attitudes of subjects who had received the information from the low-credibility source. Here we find the sleeper effect operating. That is, the subjects tended with time to forget the source of the information but to remember the content. They were influenced by this remembered content. These data are shown graphically in Figure 13-1.

Now let us return to the question of evaluating sources of information about careers and jobs. In this chapter we shall talk about sources, but one point we wish to emphasize. In career decision making we should allow some time for the sleeper effect to operate. Fortunately, in most instances career planning lasts over a long period of time. Emotions associated with attitudes sometimes lessen with time. This allows for thinking, and in thinking the intellectual components of attitudes become more important. Time allows us to line up and evaluate alternatives. After weighing many factors, we begin to eliminate those which are irrelevant in solving our problem.

Eliminating Alternatives

It cannot be assumed that having more information makes a decision easier or better. Taking more and more characteristics into account in

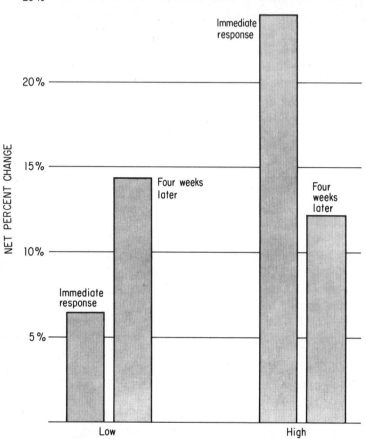

FIG. 13-1 The "sleeper effect" in changing attitudes on the basis of whether the source of information has low or high credibility. At first a source of low credibility influenced attitudes in only 6.6 percent of the subjects. Four weeks later this figure increased to 14 percent. In the high-credibility situation, 23 percent of the subjects were initially influenced by the information given. Later this figure dropped to 12 percent. The subjects tended with time to forget the source of the information but to remember the content.

comparing alternatives brings about more opportunity for confusion. This is one reason why it is helpful to *eliminate* some alternatives as soon as one can. One way to do this is to make a list of questions, eliminate some from consideration, and combine others into a few alternatives from which a choice can be made. This, of course, is a difficult process, but all the more reason why we should start early in asking questions about career possibilities. Let us see what is involved in asking *one* such question.

What Kind of Job Do I Want?

This question brings in a number of alternatives. Let us list these alternatives in terms of questions.

1. *Do you want to work with people or with things?* Some students answer "with people" because this seems to them to be the "right" answer. Not so by any means. Some people do not have the human relations skills or potentials for working effectively with people. Do not list ability to get along with people as an asset unless you really have such ability. Some of us are just not "calibrated" to people.

2. *What studies have you enjoyed most? What studies did you have to force yourself to work on?* Such questions bring out some indicators of interest and aptitude.

3. *Which of your abilities do your friends comment on most frequently? Can you make a living at it?* Our associates usually know something about us, and we should not ignore their views. Having ability and interest in something, however, is not enough when we are considering career alternatives. We need to look at opportunities as well. No doubt there are people trying to make a living at some activity that might better have been considered a hobby.

4. *What things do people criticize you for?* Although we may not agree with the criticism, nor with the critics, they are at least "critical incidents" that should be considered in self-evaluation.

5. *There are some twenty thousand ways in which people can earn a living in the United States. If you had to choose five, what would they be? Which would you list first? Why?* In this series of questions we are going through a process of narrowing down alternatives.

6. *Do you want to work for yourself or for an employer?* This question relates to motivation and personality variables.

7. *Do you want to work for a large organization or a small one?* This question opens up an array of problems centering on organizational climates, which we shall discuss in Chapter 18.

8. *Do you prefer to work at home or away?* This opens up problems related to opportunities and to possible restraints.

9. *What pay level do you have in mind to attain?* Involved here is thinking about work and pay in relation to both the present and the future.

10. *What status level do you hope to attain?* This question is related to identification of needs and to personality.

11. *What price are you willing to pay to reach your goals?* Here we are relating ambition to the real conditions involved in goal seeking.

12. *What kind of job would your spouse like to see you in?* For married people career decision making involves family considerations.
13. *What are the requirements of the kind of job you would prefer most?* This is a question of selection of a job in terms of reality rather than through fantasy.
14. *When do you wish to arrive at your goals?* Being aware of time as a decision dimension is important in setting up alternatives.
15. *Have you time, money, and desire for additional education that may be needed?* Obsolescence hits everybody in a changing organization. This question relates to the quest for knowledge, for both its own sake and for vocational reasons.

Answers to the above types of questions offer a good starting place in thinking about job opportunities in relation to what *you* have to offer an employer.

Beginning of Self-Analysis

Where do I start? We suggest that you sit down and carefully consider the above questions. Make a list of your capabilities and shortcomings under the headings "Assets" and "Liabilities." You may wish to check this analysis with someone on the faculty, with friends, or with your counselor. This is a test of your self-analysis, not a substitute for it.

PEOPLE AND OCCUPATIONS

Only in a general way can we take an overall look at the pattern of occupations. Effective occupational adjustment involves more than just matching individual aptitudes to job requirements. Listed below are occupational groups with a very brief statement about people who go into jobs in these groups. The reader should keep in mind that these descriptions have their limitations and exceptions, and that some persons would place themselves under more than one grouping.

> *Group I: Service.* People who work for the "common good" or who "render service," such as educational and vocational counselors, social workers, FBI agents, hairdressers, ushers, and watchmen. Persons in this group tend to be high in social values. High verbal skill is found at the upper levels of these jobs.
> *Group II: Business Contact.* Salesmen, buyers, agents, interviewers, and peddlers. These people score rather high on tests of influence.
> *Group III: Organization.* Industrial executives, personnel man-

agers, postmasters, foremen, and file clerks have a high interest in personal relationships. Economic and status values rate high with those in the upper levels.

Group IV: Technology. Engineers, factory managers, contractors, mechanics, and truck drivers. In the upper levels of these jobs one finds persons with intellectual interests, of a quantitative nature. Mechanical aptitudes and interests are high. This group is "object-oriented."

Group V: Outdoor. Landowners, farmers, oil drillers, teamsters, and laborers tend to come from family backgrounds of the same sort. Intellectual and artistic interests range widely. Mechanical interests are often high.

Group VI: Science. Mathematicians, scientists, nurses, medical technicians, and embalmers have strong intellectual interests.

Group VII: General Culture. Teachers, clergymen, news commentators, librarians, and reporters. This group is verbally oriented and usually interested in people.

Group VIII: Arts and Entertainment. Artists, professional athletes, showmen, race drivers, and stagehands. Special artistic or physical abilities play an important role. These people do not shy away from being in the public eye.

The person who "likes people" will generally move toward occupations in which friendly, frequent contact with others is a part of the job. Working "with things" does not necessarily mean dislike for people. Those who like to work with things tend toward production-oriented enterprises. The person who wants to manage finds himself in the organizational setting which prizes practical decision making. The artistic types tend to group together and seek occupations which do not demand clock punching.

SOME QUESTIONS IN CHOOSING GOALS

You probably know someone who works behind a desk all day and likes it. And you no doubt know someone else who would be most unhappy in the same job. He would much prefer to be on the road selling. All of us have a certain amount of choice in the way we spend our time *before* we settle into a job. Some people face a permanent desk job with horror. Others want just such a position. And, of course, there are those who want it both ways. Many jobs allow both desk work and some moving around. Teaching is one example.

Here are a few questions you may wish to think through before finding yourself in a position of choosing goals.

1. *Do you want to schedule your own time and activities?* The salesman is relatively independent in how and when he spends his time. He usually determines the appointments he keeps. His effectiveness is determined by his selling results. To a lesser extent the physician in private practice sets his own time schedule—but physicians, as well as ministers, are in some respects at the command of others.

Some people say that they must have a fairly rigid work schedule or they won't get much done. Having independence may be good, but not for the irresponsible person. Textbook writers, for example, know that it takes effort to keep going during periods of discouragement, and so do college students. It requires much in the way of self-discipline and good work habits to live the independent life. The free life is not so easy as it is sometimes described to be. It is often laced with one procrastination after another.

2. *Do you want to be relieved of self-prodding?* Having to work certain specified hours is some relief from making continuous choices of what to do and when.

3. *How do you want to be evaluated?* Some people like to be judged on what they accomplish each hour or each day. Others would rather be judged at the end of a month or even a year. Many of us, of course, may do better if our work is evaluated over short periods of time—this provides a cushion against laziness!

4. *What kinds of activity do you engage in that bring on feelings of accomplishment?* One person gets a kick out of promoting something. Another tries to avoid promotion at all costs. Let us rephrase this question to read, "From what do you get your kicks?"

5. *What types of enterprise do you take initiative in?* Take a look at yourself as a student. Are you an organizer? Do you read beyond the assignments? Do you know in what areas you have influence? Do you start money-making schemes and carry them beyond the requirements of necessity? Answers to questions such as these help one in planning goals by giving indicators as to what to stay away from and what possibly to follow up.

6. *Are you an idea person?* The urge to discover, to know the answer, and to come up with something new characterizes this individual.

7. *Do you want to manage?* Among the several known qualities of leadership (see page 421), the desire to manage is very important.

8. *Do you enjoy a good fight?* Success in many conflicting situations entails fighting for one's ideas and principles. Do you have the psychological resources to stand both prosperity and losses?

9. *Do you want to be on your own?* This question covers a wide range. It may be related to whether a person goes into business for himself or seeks the protective umbrella of some organization. It

may also be more subtle in dealing with how independent you really are.

10. *Do you like to negotiate and bargain?* These skills are basic to working effectively within organizations. Some people like such "gamesmanship," while others try to avoid it.

11. *Are you rules-oriented?* Some people like well-planned rules to follow; for example, this is characteristic of many persons who have engineering interests. Other people, for example, writers, are less structured.

12. *What factors do you feel will influence you in choosing a job?* Answers to this question are somewhat individual. Studies show, however, that most college students include eight factors near the top of the list: (1) type of job; (2) opportunity for advancement; (3) location of the job; (4) starting salary; (5) organization reputation; (6) training program; (7) educational benefits; (8) size of organization.

SOURCES OF JOB POSSIBILITIES

Each region may have a particular type of employment service, but in the main there are six different sources of information on jobs other than direct application to an organization. One place to start is the *college placement bureau* or its equivalent. Not only will you find company brochures, but the bureau staff sometimes can give opinions that may be useful; for example, "Our graduates in the ABC Company have received favorable promotional opportunities." *Counselors, professors,* and *college administrators* sometimes can pass along information about jobs. *Friends, relatives,* and *alumni* sometimes know about job openings. *Employment agencies,* both government and commercial, know something of the larger picture of job opportunities. But remember, some of the better jobs do not get listed with such agencies.

Business connections may lead to job information. Bankers, for example, usually know much about local community situations. Other ways of getting a line on jobs include *advertising* and *personal solicitation.* Letters offer one way to establish contact with an organization.

LETTERS OF APPLICATION

Once you have narrowed down the companies and kinds of job you are looking for, you should plan to talk over job situations with the right people. The purpose of a letter of application is to *get a personal interview.* There are a number of do's and a host of don't's connected with writing such a letter. One personnel manager, after analyzing thousands of letters, concluded that most letters of application are bad. "Our company handles around 15,000 letters of application a year," said one executive. "What would you look for in such a letter?" One study shows that people have a tendency to concentrate on a few large, well-known companies, flooding them with applications. They often overlook the smaller companies where their applications not only would stand less competition but might turn up an even better job.

To be effective a letter of application should reveal that you are courteous, able to express yourself clearly, and qualified for the position for which you are looking. There is no one way to write such a letter. The author has reviewed many articles on the subject; they all agree that a good letter of application should be brief and factual, should show interest, and should, where possible, be typed. The letter should be addressed to a specific individual.

One important aspect of letter writing is to get attention in the opening paragraph. Just how to get this attention may be a matter of concern. Using an unorthodox method, as in show business, may not be the best way to approach a conservative steel company. The middle paragraph of your letter of application may well include age, education, training, qualifications, and experience. The last paragraph may well be designed to elicit the desired response; namely, the interview. One way to keep the letter itself short is to accompany it with a one-page résumé that gives a full, but brief, outline about you. It may be well also to ask yourself *what behavior* your letter may be likely to evoke in the reader.

In one study, made by a company which wishes to remain anonymous, all letters of the following types were classified as "bad": mimeographed letters, letters revealing defensive or egotistical behavior, and letters giving the impression that the writer is desperate for a job. The study concluded with the warning that one should not expect all favorable replies. Even the best letter may not evoke the desired response.

INTERVIEWS

Let us begin our discussion with the *campus interview,* although only about 1 percent of employers send repersentatives to visit colleges, and less than one-third of most graduating classes secure employment through college recruiting. Although company recruiters have in the past looked for men only, equal opportunity employers often go out of their way to recruit minority people, especially women.

The Recruiting Interviewer

What are some of the general facts we can estimate about the recruiting interviewer although we know there is no typical interviewer? Chances are that he (now often she) is a member of the company's personnel department, a person of some experience in interviewing, and one who is somewhat on the spot to pick the right individual. The medium-sized company looking for sixty graduates may canvass forty colleges, by no more than two or three interviewers. The interviewing season is short. The interviewer must pack in as many twenty-minute interviews as possible (the usual time limit) and move on to the next college, often traveling most of the night. He or she frequently is physically tired, but must keep up good public relations appearances.

In the twenty-minute interview one must put the applicant at ease, determine interests, and try to get a line on abilities. The interviewer must evaluate personality, observe dress and deportment, probe for weaknesses, and pick out the applicant's strong points. In addition, the interviewer must describe the company's training program and opportunities for advancement, explain and sell the company's pay scale, and have you leave the interview feeling that you have been treated fairly. All this he or she must do in twenty minutes, and repeat, and repeat, and repeat!

Your Part in the Interview

As a job applicant, you can help make the interviewer's job a little easier and possibly sell yourself at the same time. How?

First of all, have a ready answer to the request, "Tell me about yourself," or "What can I do for you?" *Preparation for the interview* not only shows that you have done your homework, it helps put you at ease, and composure is one quality the interviewer may be looking for. A well-adjusted person knows how to stand properly and control one's body movements. The suggestion is frequently made that you wear conservative, clean clothing, but be sure you feel comfortable in it. Since you have probably spent most of your school days in informal attire, it may take a while for you to get used to more formal wear.

You may think it out of place to remind you of good manners, but one study indicates that many students are negligent in manners. Chewing gum during the interview, for instance, may be taken as indicating that you are not socially perceptive about the right and wrong things to do.

Take your cues from the interviewer about whether to shake hands and when to sit down. Tell about yourself only what is relevant to the situation. Certainly the interviewer does not want to listen to your troubles unless they are relevant. By all means know something about the company being represented.

Interviews Away From Home

Being interviewed away from your home campus is in some ways a little more leisurely process, but it is at the same time more difficult for you. Most likely you will be looked over by several persons, whether you visit the company's headquarters, plant, or educational center. Aside from the more formal aspects of being interviewed, you may well be evaluated by the secretary as you report for the interview. If you are courteous, perhaps the secretary will not mention this fact to the boss because courtesy is expected of you. On the other hand, let us say that your behavior was somewhat brash; there is a good chance that the secretary would mention this to the interviewer, and you would have a strike against you from the beginning.

When you are trying for a job, your behavior is observed in many subtle ways, just as it is on the job. The following case may illustrate the point.

The senior class of Blank University was visiting a company during the fall as a scheduled part of the class work. James M. and a friend arrived at the plant twenty minutes late and found that the tour for the students had started on time. Somewhat disappointed, James spoke to the public relations secretary in the office about his problem. She went to the trouble of making arrangements to have the two students catch up with the party. Instead of showing his appreciation for her efforts, as did the other student, he bawled her out for not holding the tour up for his convenience. She continued to be polite, however, asking James for his name and address so that he could be put on the mailing list.

Springtime came and James M. had decided to apply for a job at the company which he had visited in the fall. He was asked in for an interview. All seemed to be going well with the interview until a secretary handed the interviewer a note. He was soon politely dismissed and told that the company had no job for him. Later he found that the secretary to whom he had been impolite a few months earlier had recognized his name on the interview roster and had informed the interviewer of her previous observation of his behavior.

To be sure, getting a job and being promoted on a job depend on several kinds of abilities. How one *behaves* may be just as important as how much one knows, or even more important.

Anticipating Questions

There are no hard-and-fast rules as to how to handle all questions in an interview. Some questions are loaded. Try to anticipate some of these questions and do some "prethinking" about them. Let us take a question that may sound innocent enough, but may well be a part of the interview technique: *What salary do you expect?* Your answer could be interpreted variously as possibly indicating modesty, conceit, wishful thinking, pride, or true value. Your employer knows within a range what he is going to pay. Most beginning positions normally have a set starting salary. A little scouting around in your preparation for the interview can give you a picture of the going rate for different kinds of jobs. In filling out an interview form in answer to the question, "What salary do you expect?" you may insert what you have learned to be about average. If you are totally in the dark, you might better write in "open." During the interview itself, some writers advise delaying until the end of the interview any questions about salary; show interest in the job first!

MOVING AHEAD ON THE JOB

During peak years of employment getting a job is not nearly so hard as getting promoted on the job. In many companies, both those with and those without a formal training program, the first year in the job is in itself a selection process. This is when the company can take a close look at abilities, personality, and ambitions. This is when they can find out if the person has patience and can handle responsibility.

Getting Acceptance

It is always difficult to get started well on a new job. Men, and more particularly women, must sell themselves not only with the type of work they turn out but also by the attitudes they evoke. The new person meets with some resistance from the old-timers, not only because he or she is entering their territory (see page 36), but because new people are sometimes seen as threats. The new person, with complete enthusiasm, may push the boss too hard or even violate some accepted custom of the work climate. It is particularly important not to criticize before coming to understand how criticism will be received. Frankness, accepted by the old-timer, may not be tolerated in the newcomer.

For women, getting acceptance in traditional "men's" jobs is noticeably difficult in higher level positions. For example, in the home offices of insurance companies women hold only about 20 percent of the supervisory positions. Interestingly, two-thirds of all insurance company employees are women.

One analysis of women holding positions of responsibility in business and industry indicated that the way women *behave* on the job, rather than the way they *perform* on the job, chiefly determines how they will be accepted as administrators.

Prejudices

The concept of an "ingroup" and an "outgroup" can provide a natural base for the institution of prejudice. By definition, one cannot be "in" and "out" at the same time. Prejudices are found literally everywhere. They extend beyond the usual associations with groups that are characterized by words like "racial," "religious," "national," or "cultural." Prejudices are, of course, irrational negative attitudes. With women and other minorities, on-the-job prejudice may be subtle or out in the open. Many persons who feel they have been discriminated against may not make a legal appeal, as provided by the Equal Employment Practices Act, even if they understand the act and realize that an employer is forbidden to fire an employee while an investigation is being conducted. They may hesitate for various reasons, such as fear of being fired at a later time.

Women, for example, may be treated differently from men in a number of small ways. Bibliographies often list men by initials, but women are given space for their first name; one computer dating service charges female registrants less money. Few women hold high positions in church organizations. One study concluded that our society is becoming more and more aware of its tendency to link opportunity with sex. This tendency often shows up in the pigeonholing of women on the job.

Studying the Organization

The person who takes a good look at the company before applying for a job may see more clearly how good the chances for promotion are. What he or she discovers may help decide whether to accept a job. Once on the job, knowing the psychological climate of the organization may well give one the cue as to whether to speak up or bide one's time before criticizing procedures or asking for a promotion or raise. In some companies, aggressiveness is respected. In others, the new person who bucks established practices or customs is in for a hard time unless he or she has some other factor going.

Learning the language of the plant or office is a help to the new employee, as is a strong willingness to learn. Doing a good job is important in moving up, but you may ask, "Good in relation to what?" One person may do an adequate job but operate below his or her level of ability, while another attempts to close the gap between ability and effort. It is the latter individual who attracts favorable notice.

Again, study the history of promotions in the organization. Some people no doubt fail to get promoted because they are potentially better than the boss. The boss may be protecting himself or herself by keeping a subordinate down. In some organizations, even the "system" works against promotion. For example, the United States Postal Service affords limited opportunities for promotion. Even for the most dedicated of the 700,000 employees some 60 percent of all postal workers retire at the same grade at which they entered.

Whether one works for a promotion is, of course, an individual matter. Not everyone can get to the top, as we all know, and possibly some should not try. The setting of goals is individual. One needs to make a rational evaluation of potentialities and set aspiration level accordingly. For those who plan to move upward it is important to consider many factors. The large elements in decision making are usually prominent. Consideration should also be given to how one spends one's time and to the smaller elements.

Managing Time Effectively

"I have seldom found an executive who controls as much as 25 percent of his time," says one management consultant, "and the housewife has a similar problem of managing her time." Interestingly, working couples often seem to manage time well. Getting ahead includes using time effectively. How do you spend your time?

The sales manager cannot tell the customer "I'm busy"; the hospital administrator cannot know what is going on unless he or she attends meetings with staff, doctors, nurses, and technicians. The student always has more problems than time to solve them, and often teachers find their time expenditure directed by students and deans. In terms of consuming time we are all *other-directed* in one way or another. Mostly, however, we fail to manage our time effectively because we do not realize that time has much the same value as money.

Let us list some suggestions for learning to better utilize our time:

1. Keep a daily time log for several weeks and then critically examine it.
2. Make a list of those things you do that do not have to be done.
3. Note those instances in which you interfere in another's business.
4. Note those things you do that waste the time of others.
5. How often do you do the work of someone else?
6. Plan warm-up time for creative work and problem solving.
7. Plan your energy expenditure. If you are most efficient in the early morning, then use this time for your more difficult tasks.
8. How much time do you waste in negative thinking?
9. Do you overplan your day?
10. Do you oversocialize?

Small Factors in Decision

Two persons were being considered for one job promotion. They were about equal in background and abilities. The promotion went to the one who perceived work as an opportunity rather than to the one who somewhat exaggerated the amount of work and the importance of the job. Small attitudinal matters to be sure, but the combination of these "small" matters often determines promotional notice. It may well be that promotional consideration might be held back from the employee who has displayed that a change of status would require considerable change in life-style. Or again, it may be better to use an indirect approach in finding out about a job opening than to rush in and apply for it. The job may not even exist, or, for some valid reason, you might not quite fit the opening. Sometimes one can avoid embarrassment by finding out indirectly what the chances are for the promotion.

Drifting vs. Planning

Since this chapter is written primarily for the student planning a vocational career, let us emphasize that promotional opportunities in a specific sense are hard to anticipate. Before taking a job in the first place one should know in a general way what the future holds as we indicated (see page 307). Contrast the person who drifts into a job with the person who plans his career.

A young man starts out casually enough and takes a job of average pay and with fair working conditions. It is his first job, his first real money, and the job is not too unrewarding because he hasn't given much thought to this as a problem. The years pass, he marries and takes on family responsibilities. By now he may well have discovered that his job is distasteful to him. He wants to quit, but he now has responsibilities; he cannot quit for he would most likely have to start over elsewhere, and this he cannot afford. One may feel this is a situation where he is walking through vocational quicksand. At best, it is a nervous way of making a living.

A young woman takes what she considers to be a part-time job while her husband is in school. As time passes, promotions come steadily, and later she hesitates to give it up in order to go with her husband, who has the opportunity of a good out-of-town job. What can she do?

Although it may not be advisable to try to select a job with promotional possibilities spelled out in detail, the person who asks the question "What do I want to do one, five, ten years from now?" is at least meeting the future with some degree of realism. Of course, one may say that if a person doesn't like a job, one should change. This may be true, but the change should be based on planning. Frequent changes of jobs, unless each change is clearly an advancement for the individual, may be harmful to a career. Once the person gets labeled as a "floater" or "job hopper," he, and sometimes she, has this stigma to buck in addition to everything else. One common complaint against college graduates is that they are impatient with slow, steady progress. On the other hand, patience may be a virtue at times, providing a link to security, but it can also entrap a person.

Time With an Organization

There are *advantages* to sticking with the same employer over a long time. It helps the person to learn the business and become identified with the organization. Since most organizations promote from within, stability in the job may help self-development.

There are also *disadvantages,* mostly psychological, to sticking with the same company for a long time. The person may be lulled into a false sense of security and fail to broaden experience. He or she may become too well satisfied and lose drive, get lost, or hit a dead-end job without realizing it until too late.

There is some evidence of a positive correlation between length of service and technical ability. However, studies show that promotion supposedly based on superior ability is often made for other reasons, often for personality reasons.

Promotional paths do get clogged, and the ambitious young person may be held back by unpromotable oldsters ahead. The individual picking a company for job security reasons where turnover is low may find promotional opportunities lessened. These kinds of "contradictions" make it important to analyze a job from every angle.

Changing Jobs

Changing jobs, whether or not for reasons of advancement, requires subtlety. Chances are that every student reading this chapter will change companies several times and will change jobs many times during his or her working life. How one leaves a job may be just as important as how one performs on the job. Companies have been known to blackball people with other companies because of the manner in which they quit their job. In moving from one company to another, one should follow the protocol of submitting the resignation in person to one's immediate superior. Sufficient notice should be given, of course, but the main thing is to leave a job with good will on both sides. Your former company may be asked about you sometime in the future. One might give planned attention to how to leave the job. One negative case may illustrate just how important this can be.

Robert S. had been a successful engineer for the ABC Company for six years. He had done a good job, had received promotions, and was on his way up. He was offered what was apparently a better job with another company. In great glee he informed his boss that he was changing jobs.

He even went to the trouble to put in his letter of resignation some three pages of negative comments about the whole structure of the organization, and concluded by stating how glad he was to leave the "sinking ship." Five years later Robert decided to try to get back with his old company; he was being given serious consideration by the management for the job until his negative letter of resignation was discovered in the files!

OCCUPATIONAL CHOICE AND CONFLICT

In a nationwide survey of 4,585 college students some interesting information emerged on what students look for in their "ideal" jobs. The investigator found that, by and large, students enter occupations willingly. Actually 78 percent of the students desired to enter the occupations they expected to enter. At least they come to "want" what they realistically expect to get. Most students want a job in which they can use their special abilities, or in which they will have an opportunity to be creative and original.

How well the student can anticipate the role he or she must play after college is important in making the transition from college to work. Students in this study placed a strong emphasis on the chance to work with people. Many were convinced that having a pleasant personality is an essential ingredient for occupational success. Not only do people choose a given occupation to satisfy a value, they may also choose a value because they consider it appropriate for the occupational status they expect to fill in the future. The person who "moves toward people," "who wants to be helpful," will be guided toward a general area of occupations in which friendly, frequent contact with others is inherent in the structure of the occupation. A person who needs to express control, mastery, or domination will move toward those occupations in which this need can find expression. Some people will choose occupations negatively; we find the person, for example, who wants to have as little as possible to do with people or who wishes to avoid problems. This individual will be likely to seek out an occupation that makes few demands.

One conclusion from this study which may reinforce the reader's own experience is that *making a choice of an occupation involves a great deal of conflict.* This is particularly true among those planning to enter some phase of business. Another conclusion is that in terms of motivation, some people have gifts but are too lazy to unwrap them. This may be just as true for some who are born into cultural comfort as for those so deprived.

SUMMARY

Projecting ahead relates to career decision making. The individual who learns to make appropriate decisions early in life will have advantages over the person who drifts along, deciding matters by trial and error. Getting ready to make a decision is itself part of the decision-making process. Evaluation of sources of information is relevant to career planning.

Studies show that subjects tend with time to forget the source of information but to remember the content. In career decision making, we should allow time for the sleeper effect to operate. This allows for thinking. Time allows us to line up and evaluate alternatives, and eliminate those which are irrelevant in solving our problem.

Career planning can well begin with asking questions about what kind of job one wants, what one likes and dislikes; asking questions about abilities and about status levels, and about the price one is willing to pay to reach individual goals. Self-analysis of our assets and liabilities is important. Effective occupational adjustment involves more than just matching individual aptitudes to job requirements. The person who likes people will generally move toward occupations in which friendly, frequent contact with others is part of the organizational climate. People who like to work with things tend toward production-oriented enterprises.

Pre–decision-making questions may well include those centering on how one likes to spend time, motivational problems, and how one prefers to be evaluated. Important questions are related to feelings of accomplishment and individual initiative, to personality variables, and to education. The job seeker should know about sources of job possibilities, about letters of application, and about the general purposes and techniques of interviewing. How one behaves may be just as important as how much one knows.

Moving ahead on the job is often more involved and difficult than getting a job. Getting acceptance on a new job has always been important. To this problem have been added problems of tradition and of prejudices, with the concept of "ingroup" and "outgroup" providing a base for the institution of prejudice. Job prejudices may be subtle or out in the open, and organizations differ widely in terms of their history of promotions. In some organizations, even the system works against promotional opportunities. Promotion, after all, is an individual problem. One must not only study a given organizational climate, but evaluate potentialities and set individual aspiration level accordingly.

Moving ahead involves consideration of how one spends work

time and a host of other factors related to choosing a career and getting a job. For the student planning a career, two things should be emphasized: First, promotional opportunities in a specific sense are hard to anticipate, but planning is still more productive than drifting; second, making a choice of occupation involves a great deal of conflict.

BUSINESS AND INDUSTRY 14

Most people work and most people work for somebody else. Most students begin their work experience not too far from home. Many students have had work experience before entering college and some work while attending college. From the hour the college student starts on a job in the small company or enters the training program of the large corporation, he or she moves into an environment swarming with human problems. It will help the student's career if he or she can relate work experience to plans for the future. Although we talk from time to time about "humanizing work" and fostering the "dignity of man," few organizations function with a primary purpose of satisfying human needs; these come more as by-products of our individual efforts. Learning how to get satisfaction from work can begin by looking at the many human variables that relate to the places in which we work.

Business enterprises are usually called "firms" or "companies," as they may differ in size as much as the family grocery store on Main Street differs from the United States Steel Corporation, with offices and mills in many cities and small towns, iron and coal mines in several countries, and hundreds of ore ships sailing the lakes and high seas. The company, large or small, is owned and controlled as a unit, however scattered its parts may be. It is thus a business unit under some form of coordinated management. The independently owned grocery store is managed by the proprietor; the automobile service station has home management, although it may be owned by an oil company. We generally refer to these many relatively independent organizations as "business." What then is "industry"? Economists use the term to denote the producing of any commodity and the rendering of services. Farmer Ted Streff is a part of the beef industry if he raises cattle; his brothers Ken and Fritz may be contractors, and therefore a part of the construction industry. Sister Nancy may be a fashion buyer in the clothing industry.

Most business enterprises used to be small and communication between the owner and employees was comparatively easy. The workman was skilled in all the jobs required for the manufacture of the product. The owner was frequently the president, manager, and superintendent of the company all rolled into one; the worker reported directly to him. Many firms of this type still exist, and in rural areas it is not uncommon to find a single business enterprise influencing the entire community. Even in an urban area many businesses function as local enterprises. It is here that the young person starts work in the local store or dentist's office. Local work places can also be parts of a broader "system" that includes a number of human variables. Let us use an automobile service station as our illustration, since most readers are familiar with the nature of this business.

WORK WITHIN A SYSTEM—AN EXAMPLE

"Systems thinking" is a way of stating problems and seeing how changing one part of a problem may affect the whole. A systems analysis involves studying the interrelationships of *inputs, controls,* and *outputs.* Thus, the systems concept of work involves "putting it all together." Psychology is related to this since so much of "the whole" involves human behavior.

The purpose of the service-station system is to provide gasoline, water, oil, and other things for the motorist with a minimum average waiting time. *Output* from the system includes a variety of things besides putting gas into tanks and oil into crankcases; it includes putting air in tires and water in batteries and—not altogether incidentally—satisfying customers. Output relates to both quality and quantity of product and also to tolerance of the customer. Studies show that the average customer will tolerate a three-minute wait for service but is unlikely to return if required to wait more than seven minutes. Waste is a form of output for which there is no customer. Even young loafers who congregate around the station are waste if they keep the customers from driving into the station.

An *input* is anything that comes into the system, ranging from customers to items to be sold. It may include the heavy snowstorm that brings people in or emergencies that have to be coped with. It may also include the passing motorists who stops in to get route directions or ask for a map.

At the center of the system is *control,* which includes (1) people who vary in aptitude and knowledge, in skill and motivation, and in their attitudes, (2) the routine procedures and rules that govern the operation of the station, and (3) decisions which must be made. A systems analysis includes giving service at peak hours and studying competition. These, and many more things, are involved in running a service station. Larger organizations are, of course, much more complicated. Although there is no really typical industry, most such enterprises are organized in similar ways. Let us take a look at the structure of a modern company, where so many students go to work after they leave college.

THE ANATOMY OF THE MODERN COMPANY

The administrative anatomy of a company is designed for the purpose of making decisions most effectively. Only in the smallest of firms are decisions made by a single individual. Ordinarily, even though the final responsibility for taking an action may rest on one particular person, there are usually formal and informal preparations made by a number of people which lead to the decision situation.

The decision-making process of converting policy into practice necessitates an administrative setup in which each division of a company is headed by someone who has both authority and responsibility for its supervision and control. Similarly each division may be broken down into a framework of departments with an operating head for each.

No two companies are identical. Company organizations vary not only in size but also in the character of the people making up the company. However, there are five principle types of administrative organizations into which most firms can be placed.

Line Organization. This is a very simple structure. Responsibility and control stem directly from general manager to superintendent to foreman to workers.

Line and Staff Organization. As companies get larger, they become more complex, and top executives can no longer be personally responsible for such different functions as research, engineering, testing, planning, distribution, public relations, and other activities requiring special training and experience. In this type of organization executives and supervisors retain authority and control over activities in their particular departments. But this *line* function is aided by *staff* assistance from engineers, budget officers, and other specialists.

Functional Organization. This structure is an extension of the line and staff organization; here more attention is given to specialized skills, mainly at the supervisory or foreman level. One foreman may serve as the production boss to meet quotas, another as inspector, and a third may be responsible for maintenance. In this system the clear-cut lines of responsibility and authority of the line organization have been lost, but gains have been made in terms of getting more specialized work supervision.

Line and Functional Staff Organization. This type of organization gives the functional staff more responsibility and authority in consultation with the line organization in such specialized functions as inspection, purchasing, and shipping.

Line, Functional Staff, and Committee Organization. In order to facilitate communication involving decision making, some large companies construct a network of committees to work with the line and staff organization. In certain companies these committees are permanent and meet regularly. In others they are organized to serve a temporary function only.

THE ORGANIZATION CHART

The organization flow chart of a large corporation is presented in Figure 14-1. Here we see in the top-management section that the

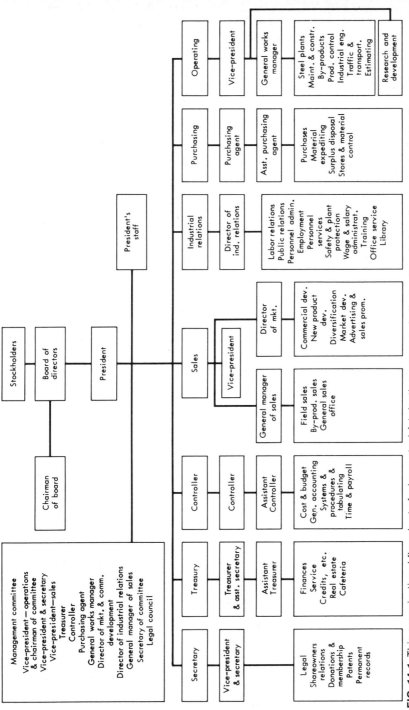

FIG. 14-1 This organizational flowchart of a large steel-fabricating company indicates the chains of command and the lines of responsibility within the organization.

stockholders are represented by a board of directors under a chairman. Responsible to the board is the president, who is charged with the formation and supervision of the policies of the corporation. In some companies the rank of the board chairman and the president is the same; in others the chairman is superior in authority to the president. Most frequently, however, the president is the ranking working officer of the company. He in turn delegates to the treasurer responsibility for carrying out the financial policies of the company and to the secretary the responsibility for corporate records. As can be seen from Figure 14-1, the president may have staff officers, such as the legal counsel and the director of industrial relations, reporting directly to him.

Lines of Responsibility. In theory at least, organizational structure demands that not too many men are required to report directly to one man. In large organizations, industrial psychologists employed by the company often operate in the department of industrial relations. Their duties may range from those of human-factors specialist to those of consumer researcher. Consulting (outside) psychologists may work at any level within the organization. Consulting organizations are often brought in to advise the president and other officers.

In the company of moderate size, employing some two thousand or fewer persons, the organizational structure is less spread out. For example, a works manager rather than a vice-president may be in control of such staff functions as industrial relations, product development, and purchasing.

Size of Company. As one comes to understand business organizations of different sizes it soon becomes clear that each size has characteristic strengths and weaknesses. Since no one man in the large company can have the personal knowledge of what is going on and personal contact with his workers which an owner-manager has, the large company is forced more in the direction of coordination and group action. Personal interests, though always present in the so-called company man, may be placed more in the background in the larger organization.

The organizational structure of most companies of medium or large size has a built-in problem. There is not enough flexibility to meet emergencies when perfect coordination fails. Supervision at the foreman level finds itself in a myriad of what appear to be impossible demands coming down from the top. There is insufficient flexibility to overcome the gremlins of distribution, material shortage, and machine breakdowns. However, modern management is attacking such problems with systems analysis, mathematical programming, automation, communication control, or what has recently been called "information technology." Yet the biggest problem of the entire industrial scene involves the human element. Asks one observer,

"What will happen to the individual? Most every organization in the world is getting larger while the world itself is getting smaller. . . . We will grow bigger and alas for all of us, not just for the young, facelessness will follow bigness, as the night, the day."

Some Pros and Cons of Size

On the pro side the *small* company offers the employee more of a chance to be an individual and often for those who like to get involved a chance to participate more directly in the decision-making process. Communication can be more personal, sometimes on a one-to-one basis. The company can move faster in adjusting to change or meeting some crisis situation. The employee also is able to get the overall picture in the small organization. On the con side, small companies may not have enough financial resources to meet emergencies or to grow in order to meet competition. In the small company the individual may have limited advancement possibilities; even health and retirement benefits may be more limited or more costly for fewer employees.

The *moderate* size company offers more local control than large organizations. Often within a favorable economic structure, the aggressive person may still be able to find individual attention and influence without the problem of remote leadership. However, moderate size companies sometimes get swallowed up in mergers, and the long-time employee could well find his or her status, or even job, in jeopardy.

The *large* company often offers status, security (not always!), and benefits on an expanded scale, but the individual, even at a high rank, finds that he or she is a small part of a big system, rather than an individual. It bears repeating that size is a big variable in making organizational climates differ (see page 413). Size of the company helps to determine the individual's status within the organization.

When we think in terms of size of an organization, it is important at times to distinguish between the overall size of the corporation and its subunits, such as divisions or departments. In terms of overall size we can say that large companies have many technical and financial-resource advantages, more community and international prestige, and offer self-fulfillment opportunities for a small number of people in the middle and upper levels of management. Bigness also has disadvantages—delay in decisions, ego-satisfaction problems for a large majority of people, and problems of bureaucratic power for the subordinate. There is evidence that productivity and profitability are lower in the large divisions of a company than in the small divisions and that workers in small work groups or departments are better satisfied than workers in large groups or departments. More absences and turnover are found among large work groups, but the general belief that communication is better in the smaller organization is not necessarily true. Size is a variable in identifying and handling personnel problems, but it is important to specify whether we are talking about company size or the size of subunits.

STATUS

Individual status—who outranks whom—has long been a part of our culture. The tenet that all men are equal does not apply in business or industry. As a matter of fact, it does not apply in the home, in the school, or in the community.

Within many business organizations, status is not only defined by the person's administrative rank, but also is symbolized by rugs, pen sets, and other trappings. The visitor to the headquarters of a large modern corporation might well judge the relative importance of his vice-president acquaintance by whether he is taken to lunch in the executive dining room on the sixteenth floor or in the thirty-second floor. For some people and some situations, status involves "dressing up"; for others, "dressing down."

One large corporation changed job titles and then studied the effects on the people involved. It was found, for example, that changing a title from "staff engineer" to "plant engineering associate" enhanced the status of the person involved. Other changes in a positive direction included changing the title "clerk" to "confidential clerk," "motor vehicle inspector" to "motor vehicle supervisor," and "general plant employment supervisor" to "general plant personnel supervisor." When a title was changed from "draftsman" to "tracer," the study showed a loss rather than a gain in status. It was also found that even changing the name of the place where people worked was important. For example, employees preferred to say that they worked "on the lower level" rather than "in the basement." Some workers prefer "incentive pay" to "piece rate." Even the word "company" often evokes a friendlier association than that of "corporation." However, some executives prefer to say that they work for a "corporation" because it sounds more prestigious. The word "corporation" sounds harder and more powerful than "company," an association made by high-level leaders. It has been experimentally demonstrated in laboratory studies that people tend to match sounds with particular persons, places, or things.

One kind of status in business comes as a result of the administrative structure in which one person is boss and the other is subordinate. This status relationship establishes differences in rank and designates the right (and often the obligation) to give orders. In another kind of status relationship the executive is deferred to by the worker, but has no right to command the worker. The worker may step back and hold the door open for the manager, but the latter, as a general rule, has no right to demand such service unless the worker's job involves opening doors. A third kind of status relationship is found among people of equal rank. Here conflict often arises as the people compete for subtle indications of status dominance. One may observe this by watching two foremen vie for the attention of the super-intendent; the one who gets told things first may feel himself more in the know and therefore in a more prestigious position.

We all struggle for status, whether we are high or low in any given hierarchy. One observer found that many more people will cross illegally against the light at a busy traffic corner when a prosperous-looking man leads the way than when the same man repeats the performance dressed like a bum. Status seeking appears to be a universal form of behavior which we must consider in trying to understand human relations in industry and to cope with the many signs of status anxiety. One writer, commenting on hierarchy struc-tures in colleges, concluded that even in such an intellectually oriented environment, such as a college, it is impossible to escape the implications of status. Consider the differences between academic vice-president, dean, chairman of the department, and instructor.

Some aspects of status differences within a company make sense, and others do not. Most people would agree that the seniority of the older worker entitles him to higher status than a young worker even though the younger person may be more skilled. However, it can hardly be considered logical that the office boy who works in the research department has a higher status than the office boy who works in the engineering testing department. But in many instances he is made to feel superior. An even more illogical status difference has grown up in some industries where women doing the same work as men are regarded as inferior to them. In one plant a strike was called when women were placed beside men on an assembly line, doing the same kind of work. The men maintained that this lowered the status of the job.

STATUS AT DIFFERENT RANKS

One way to portray status hierarchy in industry is to describe in detail the work situation of people in different ranks. For comparative purposes we shall describe the job of the foreman, the department head, the superintendent, the vice-president, and the president of a mythical manufacturing company. This will be followed by a discus-sion of women at work and by a description of the status differences in the labor-union structure, where the worker finds what little status he or she possesses.

In the following descriptions we shall intentionally speak of "he," for in reality most production industries are led by men.

The Foreman. The foreman is the first-line supervisor of the workers. In some companies he is definitely accepted as a part of management; in others he feels he is a part of labor. In still other companies the foreman is in the awkward position of not being quite accepted by either management or labor. He spends a good part of the day on the floor, carrying out orders from above and seeing that work gets done. Though technically considered the first level of management, the foreman often feels that he really isn't in the know. At the same time, the foreman is not accepted as a worker. Rarely does he belong to the workers' union, and he must maintain a status position above those whom he supervises. His ability to maintain a distance from the workers and an identification with them at the same time is an indication of his success as a foreman.

The foreman usually starts the day at his desk looking over the work orders. After he has done his turn around the shop, getting work started, he sometimes talks with neighboring foremen and with his department head about plans for the day and about yesterday's difficulties. Much of the foreman's time is taken up listening to problems and making decisions as he circulates among the workers. To the workers, the foreman is the boss. He judges their work, maintains discipline, enforces the rules, gives orders, listens to their troubles, and tries to maintain smooth relations with the shop steward (the workers' union spokesman).

The foreman often finds himself in a position so close to the work and the workers that he fails to get an overall view and becomes impatient with those in the hierarchies above him. He feels that many of the orders which come down from above are unreasonable, while at the same time believing that the workers do not understand the company's problems. The foreman is usually as impatient with paper work as is the enlisted man in the army.

Of course, foremen differ widely in their personalities and attitudes. Some of them try to cover up for their men and their mistakes and resist putting in changes that upset established routine. Other foremen play the company-man role and are critical of the workers.

Management often claims that the forman needs more training, particularly in the area of human relations. (The foreman's superiors often fail to tell him that what they mean by "human relations" is that he is to follow orders, get the work done, and keep the problems at a minimum.)

As the workers see him, the foreman is to represent their views to management and to protect them from excessive pressures from above. He is viewed as the vital first link in labor-management relations and is expected to know all the answers.

And what does the foreman think about his status? There seems to be one universal attitude: He feels that he never has enough authority to carry out his responsibilities.

The Department Head. The department head, or chief, as he is sometimes called, is unquestionably a part of management. His relationship to the workers is quite different from that of the foreman. Whereas the foreman deals directly with the workers in getting the job done, the department head uses the foreman as the buffer for his demands. In problems of discipline of the workers, failure to meet production quotas, or worker complaints, the department head centers his attention on the foreman. He thus avoids becoming involved in many energy-sapping frictions with the men, while at the same time he can play the role of the big boss.

The department head spends much of his time at his desk away from the work location. He reads reports, screens the type of information that should be passed up the line, and filters out the communications coming down which he feels should be passed along to the foreman. The head is in a position to know what is going on, since he spends a great deal of time in conferences with other department heads, with design and test engineers, with inspectors, and with other staff people. He has his ego boosted by showing VIPs through the department and by having his advice sought as a line officer.

The department head is actually too busy to find out firsthand what is going on in the shop. Hence he is quite dependent upon the foreman to keep him informed. This dependency is a club which the foreman may hold over the chief in order to get his cooperation when it is most needed. It is through the department head that foremen indirectly have a voice in the lower-level decision making.

The workers see just enough of the department head to know that he exists; hence they often let the foreman know that he, too, has a boss. The head can overrule the foreman, or he can make a decision without having to cope with its consequences. If the chief is friendly, the workers feel he is a last resort to hear serious complaints. If he is unfriendly, then the workmen feel that no one will listen to them directly, and they turn their complaints into formal channels through their union steward.

Psychologically, the department head is in an awkward position. He frequently does not possess as much formal education as the engineers with whom he works, but he is above the level of the foremen, the group from which he was most likely chosen for his present job. He is the last visible authority for the workers. He is consulted in some decisions and left out of others. Though primarily management-minded and officially a part of management, the department head is nevertheless in the quandary of not quite knowing where he stands. The brass decide at any given time whether or not he is to be included in making policy or procedural changes.

The Superintendent. The superintendent, or works manager, is in the top-management bracket. Psychologically, at least, he is quite far away from the actual work of the plant. He keeps in touch with its activities through conferences, reports from department heads, memos, and data sheets. In the larger companies the superintendent often functions under the vice-president in charge of manufacturing and so is the eyes and the ears for his boss, helping to make policy recommendations above the level of everyday details. He is in a status position which allows him to disagree with the ideas of vice-presidents (up to a point!) as he upholds the importance of getting the work turned out. The manufacturing superintendent is often a case-hardened old-timer who has risen through the ranks from foreman. He may or may not have much formal education, but he knows the plant and as a consequence has good cause for feeling secure in his job. At the same time the superintendent shows defensive behavior in resisting changes suggested by the top brass. In some respects the superintendent holds a status position, at least in the plant, above that of vice-presidents, even though they outrank him.

The Vice-President. Vice-presidents are frequently in an awkward status position. They have often come into the company from outside or have come up through staff positions in sales, engineering, accounting, or some other speciality, and hence do not have a detailed knowledge of the operations of the company as a whole. Vice-presidents sometimes hold the rank for public relations reasons (this is particularly true at the assistant-vice-president level) and attend meetings and luncheons. They are often active in community affairs. Vice-presidents, except for those who merely hold the title for prestige reasons, are in policy-making positions and hence have much power. By the time a man has reached the level of vice-president, he "is high enough to be shot at," as one observer put it. He has status, but he has to continue the competition game to hold his power. It is at the vice-president level, as well as at certain lower executive levels, that we find the man's industrial status carrying over into the community. He is named to important civic committees and to boards of directors, and he usually expends much energy in playing the role of the important man around town.

The President. "The most lonesome man in the organization" is one way this man has been described. He has status, and he possesses so many status symbols that he can afford not to flourish his rank for prestige purposes. Most presidents are professional managers and have attained their position because they have real ability and a strong constitution. The president is a lonely man for several reasons.

In the first place, he faces certain problems that only he can deal with. Not only does he have to steer his organization so that it will meet the ever-present problems of competition, he must also keep abreast of the social, economic, and political changes that affect business. Second, the president has virtually no one of his own status who can listen to his complaints or share his frustrations. He cannot become too confidential with other people in the organization for fear of revealing some of his own weaknesses. He must be very cautious of his statements because his every word may be interpreted as a commitment or policy indication. The new president soon finds that his old vice-presidential acquaintances gradually begin seeing less and less of him as he expands outward, as he attends more and more dinners and business meetings. These outside contacts, which make it possible for him to get to know other top executives in other companies, mean that he has less time for his old friends.

Although the president's attention is focused outward, he still must keep informed about how things are going within the company. Although he receives information prepared especially for him and is given advice by his staff, much of the problem solving is still his. With all that he has to do to keep up with his many jobs and the demands placed on him by his status as well as by the company shareholders, the president soon finds his time and energy taxed to the limit.

One psychologist asked 200 company presidents to look at themselves, and they came up with many common problems, likes, and dislikes. Problems centered on having to make that final decision, having to play a role as a model for the rest of management, and being unable to afford the luxury of competing with anyone else in the firm. In general, almost every man, regardless of the size of his company, reported that he did not know what it was to be president until after he had settled down into the job. On the positive side, the job of president carries with it the satisfaction of self-realization; on the negative side, it brings the distaste of being treated as an office instead of a person, and often as the symbolic whipping boy. Opportunity to build, innovate, and receive the rewards of prestige and income help to offset the intangibles of accomplishment.

As one president remarked, "When I was further down in the hierarchy I wanted more status. Now that I have it, I do not have time to recognize it or the energy to enjoy it."

WOMEN AT WORK

Attitudes about women and work range widely, and the pressures of the women's liberation movement are changing some of the prejudices against women at work.

When equal pay for women was made law in 1963 in the United

States after two decades of legislative debate, reactions ranged from "It's about time" to "It's truly revolutionary." An article in a technical journal concluded: "Women are a minority group, in the social sense of the term, regardless of what percentages of the population they may actually make up." And one spokeswoman of the National Organization of Women said: "The only jobs for which no man is qualified are human incubator and wet nurse. The only job for which no woman is qualified is sperm donor."

Women constitute over one-third of all workers in the United States, whether as production workers in a plant, as office managers or clerks, or in professional jobs. During World War II women in steel mills broke tradition and gave to their sex a power status never before experienced in heavy industry. At the professional level, teaching and nursing are still the most obvious choices of careers for women, although business, engineering, and the sciences are increasing in popularity as women's status changes.

Several things are affecting the better utilization of woman-power in our economy. Both attitudes toward women working and attitudes of working women are becoming a little more favorable. Sex labels attached to jobs are beginning to disappear as women are given the opportunity to show what they are capable of doing. Nonindustrial jobs in government and education are opening up for women. Continuing education programs especially designed for women in their middle years who want to complete or update their education are now receiving support in many quarters. The number of middle-income families continues to grow and women in these income groups have been going to work part-time in increasing numbers. Women, although still restricted, are finding greater freedom to choose the pattern of employment which best satisfies their needs.

Opportunities for women in middle-management brackets are expanding, but higher level positions, with few exceptions, are hard to reach. Women officers in industry are about only 5 percent of the total. Only a handful hold board directorships, and very few in any field occupy top-level executive jobs. Equal pay legislation, and voting power potentials in expanding union organizations, are having its effects on improving the lot of the woman from worker to professional. Slow in coming, womanpower appears to be moving from the future to the now.

THE STRUCTURES OF LABOR UNIONS

Some people believe that a labor union is extraneous to the structure of industry. In actuality the labor union can be and, with all but the smaller industries, is as much a part of the total industrial structure as are engineering, accounting, or any of the other functions organized within a framework of management.

Importance of Labor Unions. Labor unions are important in our economy, in industry, in politics, and socially. Most of us become aware of the economic part played by organized labor when we see it exercising vast pressures on wages, hours, and working conditions. Within industry, the labor union is the power behind the worker in his daily grievances with the foreman. This important contact between labor and management rarely gains public attention except for publicized strikes. On the political front, organized labor is becoming more and more of a force in the selection of officeholders, both local and national. As lobbyists, its representatives are most effective. Socially, labor unions satisfy the need for belongingness of millions of industrial workers. Union organizations vary in size; very small unions may have only a dozen or so members, whereas the AFL–CIO has several million. The number of local unions in the United States approximates sixty thousand.

Structure of the AFL–CIO Union. The organizational structure of a large union does not differ very much from the company flow chart. A close look at Figure 14-2 reveals that the AFL–CIO union is in some ways larger than the mammoth General Motors empire. The large national and international unions are primarily concerned with such broad policies as membership qualifications, area and trade jurisdiction, national politics, and the sort of industrywide bargaining which makes for a very complex structure, as we shall describe below.

Local Unions. It is the locals of the larger unions and the small company unions which function on the important day-to-day basis with management. The local in any one plant or department usually has a fairly simple structure. It has a chairman, an executive board, stewards, and general members.

The offices of the local are held by regular plant employees who are elected by the members. Depending on the particular practices of any given local, complaints or grievances may be taken to the steward, the executive committee, or its chairman. Since all the officers are working in the shops, they have direct contact with their fellow workers and often have a feel for the problems.

The Shop Steward. As a general rule the shop steward, or "committeeman," as the union's representative in each shop or department of the plant is called, acts as the contact point between the members and the higher union leadership as well as the intermediary on complaints with the foreman. When complaints or grievances cannot be ironed out at this level, the steward may take them to the next level of management supervision directly. If the problem has to be carried to a higher level, the union executive board usually takes over.

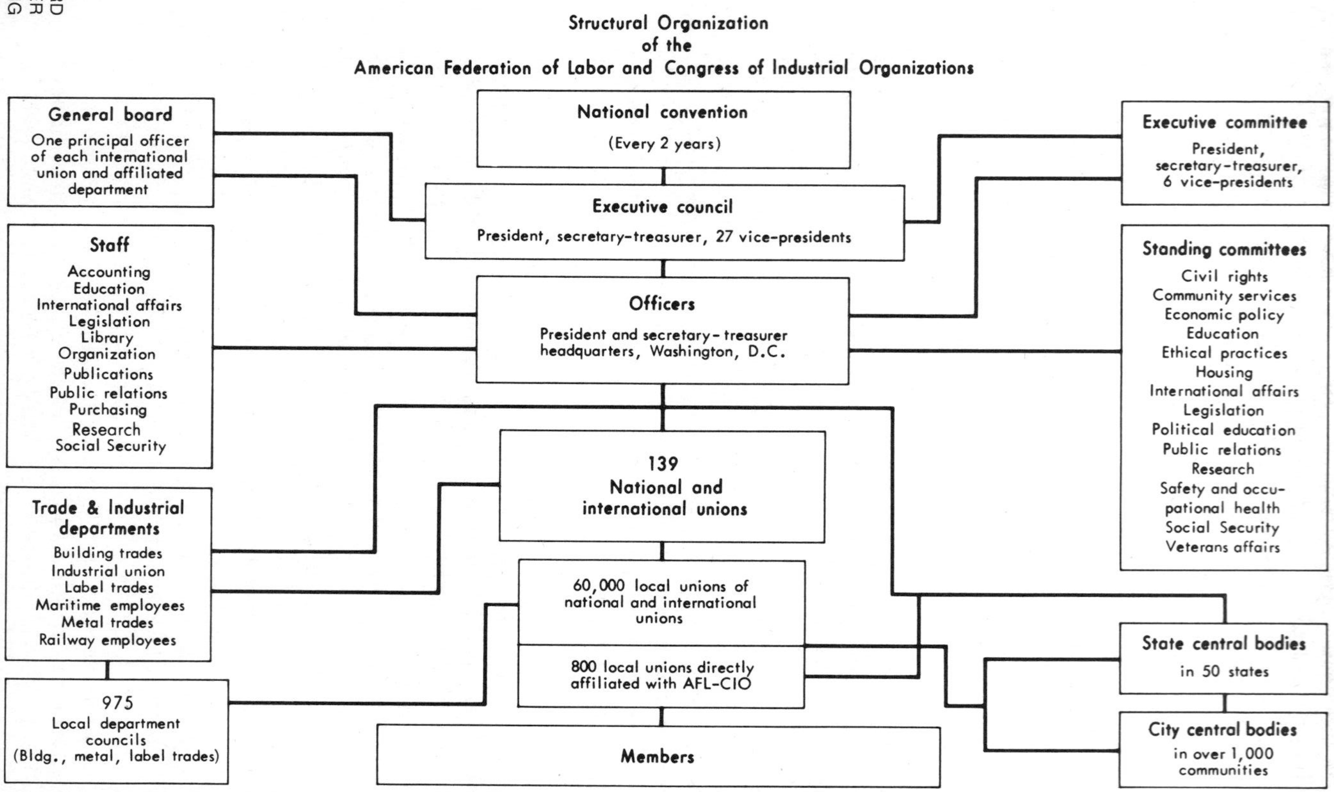

Structural Organization of the American Federation of Labor and Congress of Industrial Organizations

National convention
(Every 2 years)

Executive council
President, secretary–treasurer, 27 vice-presidents

Officers
President and secretary–treasurer headquarters, Washington, D.C.

139 National and international unions

60,000 local unions of national and international unions

800 local unions directly affiliated with AFL-CIO

Members

Executive committee
President, secretary–treasurer, 6 vice-presidents

Standing committees
Civil rights
Community services
Economic policy
Education
Ethical practices
Housing
International affairs
Legislation
Political education
Public relations
Research
Safety and occupational health
Social Security
Veterans affairs

State central bodies
in 50 states

City central bodies
in over 1,000 communities

General board
One principal officer of each international union and affiliated department

Staff
Accounting
Education
International affairs
Legislation
Library
Organization
Publications
Public relations
Purchasing
Research
Social Security

Trade & Industrial departments
Building trades
Industrial union
Label trades
Maritime employees
Metal trades
Railway employees

975
Local department councils
(Bldg., metal, label trades)

FIG. 14-2 The organizational structure of the AFL-CIO is similar to the company flow chart. This vast union is, however, much larger than any one corporation. It also operates differently in some respects from the company organization.

STATUS WITHIN THE UNION

One mistake commonly made by the outsider is to believe that unions are organized along the same lines as management. To be sure, the usual structure of a union local is a hierarchy made up of members, stewards, executive board, and a chairman of the board; the organizational chart of the large international union may look like that of any sizable corporation. But the union functions quite differently.

Power-Status Paradox. In the local union the hierarchy is not one of authority where the steward is over the members, and the chairman is boss. The chairman does not give orders or make decisions which can be forced on those below him. Although the chairman of the local may have status in one way, he does not have power status as does the foreman, the department head, or the superintendent in management. The workers do not have to take orders from the officials of their local unions, and locals do not have to follow the dictates of any higher headquarters. The president of a large union, such as the AFL–CIO, and his executive board may have the official right to negotiate contracts and to function in many ways in collective bargaining. They may agree to a new contract with a company, and they may use all the prestige of their office to get the locals to agree to it; but they cannot guarantee that the union membership will accept it.

One of the frustrating situations facing management in negotiating with a union is that it must work out agreements which not only satisfy the union officials but are also acceptable to the union membership. Although unions are becoming better organized, they still are rather loosely coordinated. It is not just window dressing when we hear that the larger international unions at times refer problems down to the lowest levels for decision. They have to.

Worker Status. It is through his identification with the union that the worker has status. It is through the union that he feels strength and has a means to fight power with power. Whereas the man in management possesses symbols of status represented by titles, executive dining rooms, and company airplanes, the union man identifies himself with the heroic figures of union movements and the folklore of struggle. He can express himself through such traditional songs as "I'm a Union Man." The union leader, regardless of his power and prestige, is never allowed to forget that he has risen to his position through his ability to get and maintain the support of his fellow union members. This is quite a contrast to the management executive who attains position through the approval of his superiors. In many respects, however, union executives function as do all executives.

Union Officers. When the union leader moves up from the local through regional and district offices into headquarters, he moves into a different world. While in the local, whether he was a steward or chairman of the executive board, he was still a worker, paid for his work. Union activities were extracurricular. As he moves up and his union activities demand full attention, the union officer goes entirely on the union payroll. In a psychological sense he has moved up above the rank and file and is no longer accepted as one of them. Consequently, even the most popular union leaders feel insecure when they lose touch with the men in overalls. If a union official becomes too friendly with management, he jeopardizes his leadership role, unless at the same time he continues to make gains for the workers. Herein lies at least one basic cause of so much industrial conflict.

UNIONS AT THE PROFESSIONAL LEVEL

The positive reasons for workers joining an industrial union include four things: (1) the desire for job security; (2) the desire to be a member of an organization; (3) the social pressures demanding that one join the union; and (4) the feeling of belongingness that comes with being a union member. The same reasons are today being given by others for joining unions. There is the angry middle manager who quits and others who "retire on the job," and there is a growing number who look toward union organizations to help them survive the anonymity of bigness. There is the government worker who resents being classed as just a timeserver; that is, there are some go-getter government employees who see the union as their best bet to operate within a system that discourages initiative. Some say that the bureaucracy of the nation's biggest employer, the federal government, will be subject to stronger unionization.

Engineers, physicians, and dentists are unionizing and there are many others seeking ways to be heard through joining unions. Toward the top of this growing list is the teacher. One of the new emphases on the scene is that of the teaching profession. Teacher unions have been growing rapidly, particularly in urban areas, where experience shows that success depends on functioning within the climate of a power structure. The old feeling that unions are for blue-collar workers only is passing. There are numerous examples of professional teachers in high school, college, and universities joining unions. Let us illustrate what they are after with one example.

A Community College Contract. A collective bargaining contract between teachers and sixteen New York community colleges was signed in 1972. This contract covered 106 different items ranging from recognition and pay scales to retirement provisions and class size. It included such things as sabbatical leave, tenure, merit increases, overtime compensation, and management rights. Teachers were given options to select their own textbooks and to participate in curriculum building. Said one teacher: "I became tired of being part of a crowd without being heard."

The collective approach in working toward economic goals has long been a part of our democratic society. Today we are extending efforts to pay more attention to the psychological needs of man and woman. The nature of the human problems we all face in one way or another at work will be covered in the following four chapters.

SUMMARY

Few organizations function with a primary purpose of satisfying human needs; these come more as by-products of our individual efforts. Most people work in business and industry. Work places can be small and relatively independent, but many are also parts of a broader system, which involves larger planning. Systems thinking can be viewed as a way of stating problems and seeing how changing one part of a problem may affect the whole. A systems analysis involves studying the interrelationships of inputs, control, and outputs.

The administrative anatomy of a company is designed for the purpose of making decisions. Only in the smallest firms are decisions made by a single individual. No two companies are identical, but all involve some kind of organizational structure for control and for setting up lines of responsibility. Size of a company is a crucial determiner of structure. Small, medium, and large companies all have characteristic strengths and weaknesses. Size of a company, or its subunits, is a basic variable in identifying and handling personnel problems.

The small company offers the employee more of a chance to be an individual, with communication on a one-to-one basis. It has the advantage of being able to adjust to change rather rapidly, but it may lack large resources. The moderate size company offers more local control and may have sufficient resources. The aggressive person may still be able to find individual attention and influence within its structure. These companies, however, can be swallowed up in mergers. The large company offers status, security, and benefits on an expanded basis, but the individual, even at a high rank, finds that he or she is part of a system, rather than an individual.

Size of the company helps to determine the individual's status. Status is defined not only by rank, but also by symbols and practices; and, regardless of rank, we all struggle for status. Some aspects of status differences within a company make sense, and others do not. In general, different ranks provide both some given status and some given expectances ranged in a fairly clear order from top to bottom.

For the most part, males in industry dominate in both rank and status, but in some ways this is changing. Attitudes about women and work range widely, and attitudes of many people are changing some practiced prejudices against women at work. Sex labels of many jobs are beginning to disappear. Slow in coming, womanpower appears to be moving from the future to the now.

Labor unions have long been an integral and accepted part of larger industrial enterprises. Workers join unions mostly for job security and the desire to be a member of an organization. Some join because of social pressures and for the feeling of belongingness that comes with being a union member. At the professional levels, unions are increasing their memberships among engineers, physicians, dentists, and teachers. Unions, which began in industry, are moving more and more into government and educational settings.

FIVE

HUMAN ASPECTS OF WORK

SOME PSYCHOLOGICAL VIEWS OF WORK 15

Work means many things to many people and for the same individual it may mean different things at different times. When we have more to do than can be done in an allotted period of time, we perceive work as an overload, maybe even as a burden. For the unemployed person work may be sought after; the person who is bored perceives that he has nothing to do. But for most of us, most of the time, work is a way of life. It may come at a time when we would rather be doing something else. Psychologically work is the way we *perceive* it individually.

We talk about work being heavy, light, strenuous, good, or poor. We think in terms of work being related to fatigue, boredom, and accidents. We associate work with pay or incentive, or we think of it as being hazardous or safe. Work is all these things; in particular, work is thought of in terms of satisfactions or dissatisfactions. We may be working when we lie in bed and plan our next day's activities or prepare to write an English theme. Work may be programming a computer or writing a lab report; it may be selling an insurance policy or deciding to pay a stock dividend. Work requires activity on the part of the individual. The utilization of the worker's skills or the supervisor's decisions means cost in terms of effort expended in reaching the goal. The stress involved in management decision making is very much an aspect of work, as is the give-and-take that goes on in the college classroom.

As we know so well, we can be faced with too much work at any given time. It is not unusual that workers often refuse overtime work for one reason or another. As a matter of fact some union contracts regulate the conditions of compulsory overtime work. Experience has shown that some people like the four-day work week, while others do not.

WORK AS A WAY OF LIFE

According to B. F. Skinner, "Men are happy in an environment in which active, productive, and creative behavior is reinforced in effective ways." Most people want psychological and economic rewards for their work, but they want work. One way to appreciate the place of work in all our lives is to look at it from the point of view of the person who is out of work. The psychological effects of unemployment on both men and women have been studied extensively. The course of unemployment goes through three stages.

First, there comes a feeling of *shock* at the loss of one's job even if all signs had warned that it would happen. In this stage the individual goes over and over the sequence of events leading to the unemployment. Rationalization (see page 83) sets in: "I should not have taken that job in the first place," "I can use a much-needed rest." Second, we have the stage of *job hunting* which is related to a self-appraisal of one's abilities. Most people first look for a better job than they had and then for a similar one. With time, they begin looking for any kind of job. Although unhappy, the individual is still hopeful of success; the spirit is still unbroken. Third comes the *breaking down* of the individual. Not being able to find a job at all, the person becomes anxious and pessimistic and begins to lose hope. The more successful the individual has been, the longer each stage lasts. During the final stage, personality deterioration becomes noticeable; new faults appear, along with irritability, breakdown of morale, and loss of emotional stability. Little events become big events.

For the unemployed man (somewhat less for the unemployed woman) time hangs heavy. Daily routines become interrupted and he becomes excessively depressed if his family, relatives, and friends change their attitude of sympathy and understanding to one of criticism.

Life-styles associated with work are beginning to change in some people. When both marriage partners work (which is happening increasingly), commuting and extensive travel in work often involve a change in role behaviors. Husband and wife may share housework; children are often given more tasks and forced to become more self-reliant. Hence, we see that work is more than devoting oneself to some task or job. Work helps to mold life-styles, and work differs from play primarily on a psychological level.

Why can't we define work and play the same way? Doesn't the golfer use his physiological and mental processes in an attempt to attain the goal of winning the game? Indeed he does. But the difference between work and play centers on *motivation.* For the professional golfer making a living is the motivation. The amateur wants to do a good job for self-satisfaction, for relaxation from his real work of being a student, teacher, mechanic, or executive. What is play to some people is work to others although the performance elements may be the same. Motivation makes the difference. We may think of the child engaging in play, but for him it may be work. For both boys and girls, toys often reflect the adult world.

COMMON CHARACTERISTICS OF WORK

A variety of changes takes place during the course of most work activities, both in physical and in mental work. Six common characteristics of work are shown in Figure 15-1 and are described below.

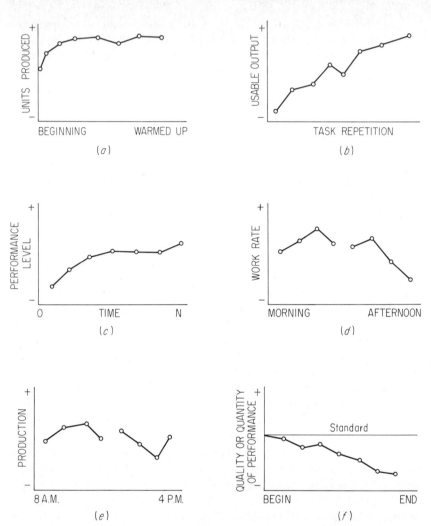

FIG. 15-1 These hypothetical curves show six common characteristics of work: (*a*) warm-up effect; (*b*) curve of acquisition, representing a person's output as he learns through repetition; (*c*) plateau of nonimprovement in performance, a common phenomenon in work; (*d*) variation in work output related to the time of day; (*e*) end spurt of increased production near the end of the workday; (*f*) work decrement, which, under certain conditions, occurs as a person continues to work.

Changes take place in work over a period of time. In Figure 15-1*a* we see the *warm-up effect*. Getting started on a job is a slow process. The baseball pitcher must "warm up" to get his muscles in appropriate condition for pitching, and so it is with the worker getting everything set to run a complicated machine. Not so noticeable may be the effort involved in mental activity, but even here warm-up is necessary. The committee member must warm up to the conference situation. And the student is well aware that study involves a process of getting "into the groove."

In Figure 15-1b we see a curve of *acquisition.* This type of work curve is characteristic of the person who is learning to perform a certain task. Motor skills, such as driving a car or running a crane, are usually acquired slowly. They may show improvement over a period of days, weeks, or even, if the task requires great skill, years. Note that the acquiring of the skill does not result in a smooth curve. There are always some ups and downs in improving one's performance. The important thing is for the general direction of the curve to be upward. Not only motor skill is involved in reaching the peak of one's perform-ance. Studies show that *attitudes* are important also. For example, in model changeover in the auto industry, or in the dressmaking indus-try, the physical skills involved may be essentially the same for the worker on a new model as they were on the old. But reaching peak performance seems to be related to an attitude that the new work is no longer new.

One of the most common phenomena in work is a leveling-off process in which performance stays the same. This period of nonim-provement is called a *plateau* and is shown in Figure 15-1c. It is usually temporary.

Time of day for work output is important for productivity, mental or physical. Some people seem to be alert and to function at their best in the early morning hours. Other people function at their best later in the day. For both types of workers, however, work output seems to fall off just before noon and just before quitting time, as is indicated in Figure 15-1d. This *variation* in work output related to the time of day, however, is associated with another phenomenon (noticed sometimes in the closing minutes of a football game), which we call *end spurt,* shown in Figure 15-1e.

Work decrement very often occurs when performance dimin-ishes over a period of time. This work decrement is seen in Figure 15-1f.

In Chapter 9 we discussed various aspects of improving study. Note how the common characteristics of work may be related to college work. It is not uncommon for class efficiency to be at a low ebb just before lunch or for fatigue to set in toward the end of the day. Scheduling study periods should include questions such as, "Am I the early-morning type or the late-evening type?" When asking these questions, however, the student should be aware that defensive behavior, such as rationalization, may come into the picture.

FATIGUE

No introduction to a chapter on work would be complete without a few words on feelings of tiredness or *fatigue.* One of the most perplexing problems to the student, worker, supervisor, and executive centers on the fact that different kinds of tiredness are related to different kinds of work. It is well for you to understand why you become tired, assuming that you wish to understand your condition and possibly do something about it.

An emotional upset may involve a kind of tiredness different from that resulting from a hard day of physical labor free from frustration. Physical tiredness of this sort may be relieved with rest. The person may even feel a certain amount of satisfaction from "an honest job well done." But fatigue related in whole or in part to frustration and conflict prolongs recovery. Although we have no really good measures to tiredness, we know that most people learn to adjust to physical fatigue by rest pauses or changing activities. "Psychological fatigue" may be different, characterized by feelings which extend over long periods of time.

One personnel manager reports the case of a female worker who frequently complained of feeling tired on the job. Following up on the suspicion that the woman was not being accepted in her particular work group, he had her transferred to a similar job with a different group of workers. Here she came to feel that she *belonged.* Complaints of fatigue lessened.

One college counselor tells of the case of a newly married male student who was having difficulty with his studies. Each night he came home determined to put in a good session of study. Although he fought the impulse, he would invariably fall asleep over his books. Unsuccessful in keeping awake he would retire with homework unprepared. Finally, he came to discuss his deteriorating scholastic performance with a counselor. Together they analyzed his past performances and changes in his living that may have been related to his worsening grades. Sometime later he and his wife moved out of his mother-in-law's home, and in two weeks the symptoms of fatigue were completely gone. Study efficiency improved. Weeks later he stopped the counselor on the campus and related the following: "I took my wife over to visit her mother last night, and minutes after we entered the house an overwhelming need for sleep came over me, the first time that has happened since we moved."

IMPROVING EFFICIENCY IN WORK

Much is being said these days about reducing the work week. Will a shorter day mean more efficiency, more production? Records show that when the work week was reduced from fifty-eight hours to fifty-one hours, hourly output increased. When the work week was reduced further, output again increased, but just how much of the improvement was due to cutting down on hours could not be determined because better equipment came in at about the same time. No one knows what the optimum work week really is. Factors enter the understanding of work that go beyond mere physical effort. Studies show, for example, that the modern bricklayer can lay 2,000 bricks per day without undue strain, but at the present time 300 is the maximum allowed by most union contracts. Complicating the problem still further are factors of boredom, wage incentives, and automation.

Rest Pauses

Numerous studies in the laboratory and in industry have shown that distributing work through the introduction of rest pauses results in increased output. In a typical laboratory study, subjects lifted weights until they were exhausted. After a five-minute rest they could lift the weights with about 80 percent of their previous ability. They returned to 95 percent of their best output after a rest of twenty minutes.

Work supervisors sometimes argue that most employees take unauthorized rests when there are no regularly scheduled rest periods. Are there any advantages of authorized rest periods over periods of unauthorized rest? A study of a group of comptometer operators in a government office provides one answer to this question. The operators were observed without their knowledge for a two-week period during which a record was kept of the number and length of their unauthorized rests. Later a rest schedule was formally introduced, consisting of an eight-minute pause in the morning and a seven-minute pause in the afternoon. Because of government regulations, the workday was lengthened by fifteen minutes to make up for the time spent in the regularly scheduled rest periods. Total working time thus remained unchanged. The changed system resulted in a significant decrease in the time spent in unauthorized rest and a 35 percent increase in work completed.

Authorized Rest Periods

One reason for the advantage of authorized over unauthorized rest periods is probably better placement of the rest interval during the work period. The best way to determine how rest periods should be scheduled is to plot production records throughout the work period and note drops in production. Consider, for example, the production

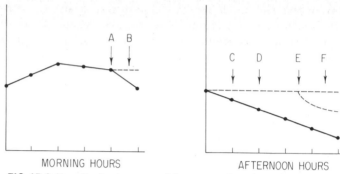

MORNING HOURS   AFTERNOON HOURS

FIG 15-2 Hypothetical curves of the proper location of rest pauses. Since production is beginning to fall off at point A, the pause is introduced at point B. If the worker knows when the pause is coming, the anticipatory effect is sufficient to keep him going during the interim. The dotted line show the effect on production of introducing the rest period. In the afternoon, the pause is introduced at C or D, and again at E or F if production falls during the late afternoon. Shortening the hours to be worked may change these curves, but rest pauses are still beneficial. They are often written into union contracts.

curves shown in Figure 15-2. Since production is beginning to fall off at point A, this is the logical place to introduce a rest pause. The pause may be introduced at point B if the worker knows when it is coming, because the anticipatory effect is sufficient to keep him going during the interim. The dotted line in the figure shows the effect on production of introducing the rest period. In the afternoon, the pause is introduced at C or D and again at E or F if production falls during the late afternoon.

How can we account for the beneficial effects of rest pauses on production? A number of plausible reasons come to mind, the most obvious being that rest provides the opportunity to recover from fatigue. The physiologist has demonstrated that work causes an accumulation of waste products within the organism which reduce work capacity. Rest provides a period during which the waste products are dissipated and bodily capacity is restored. In heavy muscular work, physiological fatigue is unquestionably a major factor contributing to work decrement.

Coffee Breaks

When work does not involve the expenditure of a great deal of physical energy, the beneficial effect of rest periods may be due to relief from a task that creates in the worker feelings of boredom. The worker is not physically tired—he is irritated, lacks interest, is fed up with his job.

He wants a change, a break from what seems to be interminable activity. Rest pauses provide an opportunity to talk and think about nonjob activities. When the worker returns to his job, he is psychologically refreshed, so to speak, and this is reflected in increased output.

The effectiveness of introducing rest pauses may be due to still another factor—a change in attitude toward the company, including, of course, the work supervisor. A worker with a favorable attitude toward his supervisor is much less likely to loaf on the job than the worker who dislikes his boss. The introduction of rest periods may be tangible evidence that management has an interest in the welfare of the worker, and he may respond with more efficient output. On the other hand, the worker may feel differently if the coffee break, for example, is gained through union negotiations. Like other authorized rest periods, the coffee break may lead to abuse, not only in extra time taken out but in psychological time lost in getting back into the full swing of work. It is a loss somewhat related to the unproductive minutes before quitting time. One insurance company, after a study in its nationwide offices, defined the time from 4 to 5 P.M. as "the most expensive hour in America."

Boredom

The introduction of rest periods is not the only way to alter the shape of the work curve in the direction of increased output. The nature of the job itself has to do with how long a person can maintain a high rate of production. We "stay with" interesting jobs longer than with uninteresting ones, and repetitive jobs appear to be least interesting. We reflect this lack of interest when we say that the job is boring. Actually, the job itself is not boring. *Boredom is the worker's reaction to the job.* More specifically, boredom arises from a conflict between the necessity for doing a dull job and wanting to turn to more interesting activities.

Attention requirements have much to do with the degree of boredom caused by repetitive tasks. A highly repetitive job to which the worker becomes habituated elicits relatively little boredom in some workers if they do not have to pay close attention to what they are doing. If the worker can do the job without thinking, he is free to talk to his fellow workers about yesterday's football game or next month's vacation. Or, if conversation is impossible, he can daydream. Boredom will be pronounced on a repetitive job like an assembly-line operation where the continuous work flow and the task requirements occur over and over again but permit few lapses or shifts in attention. Boredom is not a problem in a complex and varied task which because of its intrinsic nature tends to hold attention.

Eliminating Boredom

The problem of eliminating the effects of boredom is acute in present-day industry, where many repetitive tasks result from the fractioning of work into smaller and simpler units. An obvious but naive answer to the question of how to eliminate boredom is to do away with tasks of a repetitive nature. This is not only impractical but to a considerable extent unnecessary.

A promising lead on how to reduce boredom comes from the finding that repetitive tasks do not give rise to the same degree of boredom in all persons. For example, in an investigation of women sewing-machine operators, those reporting the strongest feelings of boredom disliked routine activity, more often preferred active leisure activities, and indicated lack of satisfaction with their home and personal life. Operators who were least susceptible to boredom were placid and generally contented with the existing state of affairs.

Another study of women preforming repetitive work in a chemical factory showed that those experiencing the most boredom tended to be more extroverted than introverted, desired opportunities to use their own ideas, and attached great importance to promotions. There is also evidence that persons of low normal intelligence are less bored by repetitive work than persons of higher intelligence. Additional study of the personality characteristics associated with feelings of boredom is necessary. The available evidence indicates that decreases in production resulting from boredom can be reduced by selecting persons who will not be bored with the jobs to which they are assigned.

Need for Change

Although rest periods tend to reduce the harmful effects on production resulting from boredom, the effect is due not so much to a need for rest as to a need for change. The bored worker is fed up with doing the same old thing. Rest periods provide an opportunity for change, of course, but boredom can frequently be relieved by giving the worker another kind of job. *Variety* is the spice which makes work interesting, and the interested worker is never bored. One observer reports a practical application of the principle of variation concerned with two types of maintenance jobs, dusters and solderers. The workers complained of overwork and were apparently bored with the tediousness of their routine tasks. They were eventually given the opportunity to exchange jobs, and all of them accepted. Half the workers dusted and half soldered, but every two hours they exchanged jobs. Feelings of boredom were reduced, and, significantly, the dusters now dusted as much on a half-time basis as they had previously on full time.

Exchanging jobs is not a general cure-all for boredom. The effectiveness of the practice depends at least in part on how similar the jobs are and how often the exchanges are made. If two jobs are perceived as highly similar, changing from one to the other will do little good. On the other hand, if they are so different that great versatility in skill is required, boredom may be reduced but at a great loss in efficiency. Where there is a moderate degree of similarity which allows the use of the same skills but the experience of doing something different, the beneficial effects will be maximized. Even in this situation operations may become confused if the jobs are alternated too often.

Stimulation and Boredom

What will *more* leisure do to people? Boredom, even fatigue, may increase with shorter work hours. Many workers are even now taking on second jobs, and for reasons in addition to bringing in more income. Such moonlighting is one way to deal with the problem of additional leisure time; for some persons it is perhaps a better way than developing new and more expensive tastes. Boredom is affected not only by individual personality but by job perception and even by mood. On the job, in addition to job rotation and job enlargement, introducing subgoals that allow the worker to complete a whole job, rather than a fraction of it, may sometimes help to lessen boredom.

One other factor should be considered. One worker may be easily bored but also easily stimulated. A second worker, also easily bored, may be hard to stimulate. In the second instance, boredom may become a serious psychological problem for the individual.

WAGE INCENTIVES

Some form of wage incentive is offered to about 60 percent of all industrial workers in the United States. Let us take a look at the broad outlines of a fairly typical incentive system that has been in operation at the Procter & Gamble Company since 1928. Consider the case of Frank Handy in his job of sealing boxes of soap in the packing room.

Frank's job requires him to put glue on the flaps of the boxes and push them into the sealing belt as they pass down the line. The job has been studied to find both the correct method of doing the work and the average time normally taken to do it. The standard time for this job has been set at thirty-six seconds, or 0.01 hour per box. The rate of 100 boxes an hour means 800 boxes per eight-hour day. However, since Frank can and does seal 125 boxes an hour, or a total of 1,000 boxes, he gets credit for two extra hours, for which he receives a bonus of two hours' pay. So much for the overall picture. The kind of job study on which the system is based is worthy of more detailed treatment in view of what we shall say later about some of the shortcomings of incentive systems.

Job Study

In an actual job study, an examination is made of the various ways or methods of performing the task; this is followed by the selection of the best method. This method is written out in terms of specific job elements, and the employees are trained in this correct method. Next, there is a determination of the average time it takes the employees to do the job. Thus as Frank Handy seals boxes, the job-study engineer records by stopwatch the time for each element of the job. The worker's performance is considered in terms of how *smooth* his operations are, how *quickly* he seals the boxes, how *accurate* he is in applying the glue, and how *careful* he is in lining up the flaps. How well he *plans ahead* in filling the gluepot is also considered. Is Frank physically fit to do the lifting required? Is he the right height to reach the machine? All these factors are critical in the job study.

After studying Frank's job performance, the engineer finds that Frank's skill and effort are above normal. On the basis of company skill and effort values, it is judged that 16 percent more time should be added to make Frank's actual time equal to a fair normal time. This addition amounts to 7.2 minutes per 100 boxes.

In addition to the time required to do the work, an allowance is made in the standard for personal needs and tiring. A fatigue allowance is added to compensate the worker for the effects of getting tired when he maintains a consistent work pace throughout the day. By comparing Frank's job with typical fatigue allowances based on company experiences, the job-study engineer determines that this allowance should be 15 percent of the normal time. This addition amounts to 7.8 minutes per 100 boxes.

When we add together the time for each step in the study of Frank's job, we get the final standard time that is allowed for doing the work:

	MINUTES PER 100 BOXES	HOURS PER BOX
1. Frank's actual average time	45.0	0.0075
2. Allowances for skills and efforts	7.2	0.0012
3. Personal needs and fatigue	7.8	0.0013
Final standard time	60.0	0.0100

The analysis described above shows the extent to which a job can be objectified. It sets up a standard and provides the worker an opportunity to earn extra money. The company benefits by employing what seem to be the most efficient work methods. At first glance, some kind of incentive system would seem to be an ideal way to step up production and make more money for both employee and employer. Yet despite the apparent objectivity of an incentive system based on a job analysis, important judgment and value questions enter the picture, which give rise to a variety of problems. What is normal job production? What is a fair rate of pay for achieving it? What about employees displaced by production increases?

Why Incentive Systems Sometimes Fail

When an incentive system fails, the reasons are sometimes psychological. The announcement of an incentive plan based on a job study such as that exemplified in the case of Frank Handy may be reacted to with distrust, much as the student may question some aspects of an evaluating system. The job analyst is often seen as a management man who sets arbitrary rates in order to compel the worker to produce more for the same amount of money. Many workers feel that the analyst will establish a standard production rate that is too tight. Hence even though a bonus is provided for exceeding the standard, the extra pay is not worth the effort. Or if the production rate is not too tight and many workers exceed it and thus make more money, the company will cut the rate. This suspiciousness may cause workers to hold back on production. In a nationwide poll of workers, nearly 75 percent said that a worker should hold back on production because his piece rate would be cut if he worked to full capacity. From a psychological standpoint, it is interesting to note that workers also hold down output in order to protect the less skillful members of their work group. Apparently their loyalties to fellow workers outweigh the desire for financial gain.

An overall appraisal of incentive systems in general would be that sometimes they work well and probably just as frequently they do not. The details of the various incentive systems now in operation are probably of minor importance in determining their success. The important thing is how the worker *perceives* the system in relation to *all* his needs, psychological and material. The value of incentive pay cannot be viewed in isolation. Work behavior cannot be manipulated solely by the manipulation of money. Financial rewards are part of a total picture. They are effective when other basic needs are also satisfied.

MERIT RATING

On so-called production jobs, proficiency is usually evaluated in quantitative terms. Quantity is often considered to be the only variable. If Frank produces 100 units per hour, he is viewed as being more proficient than John, who turns out 80 units per hour. But of course, in actual practice, most items vary in quality. Thus in measuring worker proficiency, it is necessary to set up a standard which requires that the product be of specifiable quality in order to be acceptable. If units produced are rejected because of qualitative deficiencies, they must be considered waste and subtracted from the output measure. Plotting a work curve is meaningful only if the counting of units produced is based on a consideration of both quality and quantity.

When we come to the problem of measuring proficiency on nonproduction jobs, difficulties arise. Nonproduction jobs are those in which quality plays a predominant role. On nonproduction jobs proficiency is usually measured through the use of judgment techniques, which, although subject to some degree of error, have proved useful. Evaluation of a worker's proficiency by a qualified second party familiar with the job is termed *merit rating.* A wide variety of merit-rating systems is used in industry, each with special features. Let us examine three of the most error-free systems.

Three Rating Methods

One of the most widely used methods of employee rating is the *employee-comparison* system. In this plan, each employee working under a given supervisor is compared with every other employee. The workers are arranged in pairs. Periodically the supervisor checks the person in each pair who is better in overall performance. The system, however, has limitations. It cannot be used for promotional purposes, counseling, employee improvement, transfer, or layoff, because it cannot show the reasons why an individual was rated low. However, in layoffs it may be enough to identify the lowest in the group.

Another system of rating, the *forced-choice* method, requires considerable preliminary work in developing the scale. Pairs of statements about job performance must be found, both of which express equally favorable or unfavorable things about a worker; but only one of the statements in each pair actually differentiates between the persons known to differ in job performance. The statements are then printed on the rating form in groups of four. Two of the four statements are favorable (and equally favorable), and the remaining two are unfavorable (and equally unfavorable). The rater is asked to check two of the four statements—the one which most accurately describes the person being rated and the one which least accurately describes him or her. The plan has not had widespread use in industry because of the preliminary work involved and the difficulty encountered in keeping scoring secret. It deserves greater consideration because it produces objective evaluations, yields a more nearly normal distribution than most rating methods, can be scored by machine, and yields ratings that are related to valid indices of good and poor performance.

An increasingly popular and useful method for evaluating proficiency is the *critical-incident* technique. In this method, superiors are interviewed to determine those types of behavior which workers exhibit or fail to exhibit that are critical to success or failure in a given job. Once such a list is compiled, supervisors are asked to watch for these kinds of behavior during work performance. If a considerable number of good critical incidents is noted about a worker over a given period of time and few negative critical incidents have been observed, the worker's rating will be high. Conversely, if most of the incidents observed are negative, the rating will be low. In this rating we are getting reports on actual behavior, not just opinions about behavior.

Merit Is More than Output

Although some system of merit rating must be resorted to in evaluating proficiency on nonproduction jobs, performance on production jobs should also be evaluated in terms of merit. Merit is a far more general aspect of proficiency than production in terms of items turned out per time unit. Merit includes a variety of characteristics which make a valuable employee, such as the worker's attitude toward other employees and the supervisor, observance of safety regulations, assumption of responsibility, and the like. Systematic merit rating brings to the supervisor's attention many aspects of the employee's performance that can be improved and often suggests the appropriate course of action.

In Figure 15-3 we see an employee report form somewhat typical

EMPLOYEE STATUS REPORT	Name			Badge number	Date
Location	Department			Job	

Instructions: Move down the items judging carefully on the basis of your observation of the man. If you think a problem _may_ exist but are uncertain, check the question mark column. Comment wherever you think it is indicated.

Items	Status			Comments
	No problem	?	A problem exists	
1. How is his attendance?				
2. Is he often late to work?				
3. Does he give a good day's work?				
4. Does he do good quality work?				
5. Does he work safely?				
6. Does he learn easily?				
7. Does he need close supervision?				
8. Is he hard to supervise?				
9. Does he take excessive breaks?				
10. Is he an agitator or a chronic complainer?				
11. How does he get along with other workers?				
12. How is his housekeeping?				
13. Is he a loyal employee?				
14. Does he observe company rules?				
15. Is he physically able to do any job in your department?				
16. Does he accept changes in work procedures?				
17. Has he the ability and outlook for bigger jobs?				

What are the two or three highest jobs on which this man is fully qualified?

Report submitted by _____ Position _____ Department _____

Industrial Relations Department

Reviewed by _____ Position _____

FIG. 15-3 Supervisor's Employee Report Form.

of those used in production-work industries. Note that a rating is made by one person *and reviewed by another.* This offers some safeguard against a supervisor "who is out to get someone." In addition this form has been found to be one way to make the initial rater feel more comfortable. This relates to the principle that most of us feel some discomfort, even threat, when we have to sign some document of record.

Glancing through the questions, we note that the rater does not have to be a behavior expert to fill it out. The form applies only to workaday life, where evaluation is based on actual *work behavior* and not on some feelings that may lie behind these behaviors.

The reader may find it of interest to redesign this form to make it applicable to a shop or office situation with which he or she is familiar. Often we learn a little more about our own behavior when we have before us those types of items that will be used in rating us. Before we shoot from the lip a little self-evaluation may be called for. At least it may remind us not to kick a leg out from under the table until we have something to prop it up with.

SUMMARY

Work means many things to many people and for the same individual it may mean different things at different times. For most of us, most of the time, work is a way of life. Psychologically, work is the way we perceive it individually. One way to appreciate the place of work in our lives is through the experiences of the unemployed. He or she encounters both economic and psychological problems. Time hangs heavy, and eventually boredom and depression set in.

Life-styles, in our present changing social patterns, associated with work are changing for some people. Work helps to mold life-styles, and for the individual it offers some common characteristics, ranging from warm-up effects to feelings of fatigue. And the ability to do efficient work at any given time may relate to emotional upset or even to the psychological climate of the work setting. Distribution of effort and rest pauses relate to efficiency in work, whether it be at the physical or the mental level.

Lack of interest in work relates to the common experience of boredom. Actually the job itself may not be boring; rather, boredom is the worker's reaction to the job. Boredom will be pronounced on a repetitive job which permits few shifts in attention, but it is not a problem in a complex and varied task which because of its intrinsic nature tends to hold attention. Research indicates that production slowdowns resulting from boredom can be reduced by selecting persons who will not be bored with the jobs to which they will be assigned. Change and variety in work help prevent boredom. One worker may be easily bored, but also easily stimulated. A second worker, also easily bored, may be hard to stimulate. In the second instance, boredom may become a serious psychological problem for the individual.

Wage-incentive systems and merit-rating procedures, necessary as they are, have never been perfected. The reason is that they each depend so much on how the worker perceives them. Financial rewards and ratings are only a part of a total system. Neither can be viewed in isolation. They are effective when other basic needs are also satisfied.

MAN AND MACHINES

16

One large manufacturer of home appliances has a human factors home-environment laboratory on a quiet suburban street. From the outside it looks like any other modestly priced home. Inside are kitchens of various design, filled with a variety of products. This is a home-making laboratory that looks like a home, but what goes on here is different in one respect. Not only are men, women, and children asked to tell what they think of the various designs, and to suggest improvements, but they come in to give adult dinner parties and birthday parties for children. Through unnoticed audio and video recording devices (all subjects are shown what is going on) the use of the kitchen is observed and recorded. Observations are made on the use of different refrigerator and stove designs, and on the placement of cupboards, working space, and the like. Changes in spatial arrangement of any given kitchen can be made on request. The conventional procedures for conducting a controlled experiment are followed (see page 7). Says the engineering psychologist associated with the project: "We are learning that people do know what they like and do not like, and what changes they would make that fit their life style. A user of a kitchen knows what a kitchen should be like, and we are finding out."

Engineering psychology, frequently called "human factors engineering," helped design the L-shaped desk for the secretary, to bring an enlarged work space within easy reach. The psychomotor behavior of cashiers and cash register design is being studied to make the check-out counter operation in grocery stores more efficient, less fatiguing for the cashier, and more comfortable for the customer. Designs of computer consoles for programming are being studied in relation to the abilities of people to process information quickly in short-term memory (see page 282). Such tasks require virtually *immediate* memory for one-time use, in contrast to long-term memory, where material is stored for minutes, hours, days, or longer. Research on the nature of immediate memory is not only raising theoretical issues about the functions of the nervous system in memory storage, but is giving us a new slant on improving human behavior in which speed, accuracy, and ease of operation are involved. The computer has introduced both complexity and "all-at-onceness" to which the human must adjust.

Psychology in engineering is interested in how people and machines can be made to work together more efficiently. This covers a wide range of problems, from the design of a household appliance to the design of a manned space vehicle. Much study has gone into the design of automobile seats, which must accommodate persons of various shapes and forms.

As a part of the noise elimination campaign, noise abatement has been one successful aspect of automobile design. But has so much noise elimination been for good? Can it be that cutting down on road noises has some dangers? Yes. The "silent one" is a great advance in motoring comfort, but this kind of car illustrates the reason for the existence of a field that combines the skills of both engineers and psychologists. The driver of an automobile, isolated and cushioned as he or she is, has little appreciation of the speed and power of the vehicle being driven. Direct sensory inputs in the modern automobile, large or small, are attenuated by windshields with tinted glass, by springs, and by foam rubber. As a result the operator depends in part upon instruments. Only indirectly does the speedometer tell him about his environment and his relation to it. He uses controls, such as power steering and power brakes, which cut out information. They buffer immediate responses so that the driver's reactions have only indirect effects on the automobile. The engineering improvements are highly desirable as such, but they give rise to psychological problems. These range from simple questions of the legibility of numbers on the speedometers and road signs to subtle issues of sleep induced by monotonous turnpike driving. Air conditioning allows noises and wind to be shut out, and the music that comes from the stereo radio helps to direct attention away from possible vital cues of safety. Comfort needs may have been satisfied in the modern car, but perhaps the "open," non-air-conditioned model is safer. As a matter of fact, statistics show proportionately more turnpike accidents for the "closed" car model. Sufficient inputs and feedback are lacking.

In this chapter we shall talk about equipment design, about sensory inputs and motor outputs, and about accidents and safety, all in relation to helping bring the human and his mechanical world into better harmony.

EQUIPMENT DESIGN

Almost everyone who has had experience in reading meters knows that some can be read rapidly while others are seen with difficulty. Engineering psychology is concerned with designing equipment which is *easy for the human operator to run.* This is just the reverse of designing a machine so complicated that it takes great ability and long training for the operator to learn to operate it.

With advancing automation it is essential that visual displays (speedometers, pressure gauges, thermometers) be designed so that the human operator can read them efficiently (Fig. 16-1). For the homemaker the engineering psychologist has made studies on the speed of reaction and the errors that people make in turning knobs.

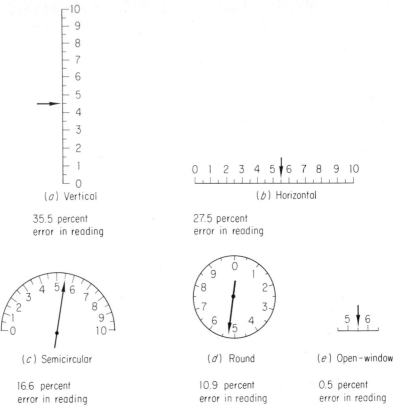

(a) Vertical

35.5 percent
error in reading

(b) Horizontal

27.5 percent
error in reading

(c) Semicircular

16.6 percent
error in reading

(d) Round

10.9 percent
error in reading

(e) Open-window

0.5 percent
error in reading

FIG. 16-1 The percentages of errors in reading five types of dial.

They have, for example, come up with a virtually error-free design for a four-burner cook stove on which each control knob is placed with its burner. This is shown in Figure 16-2.

The most common types of display involve dials. They range from simple scale markings on a yardstick to the more complex instrument panels of a modern spacecraft. Dials vary in size and shape, in length of scale units, and in the number of space markings. They also vary in the spacing of markers and in the size and style of letters and numbers. Some dials are designed for rapid reading; others are designed differently for very careful reading.

For *rapid* reading, greater accuracy is achieved with a dial having *few scale markers.* On the other hand, a dial with *individual markers* corresponding to each scale unit yields better results when there is plenty of *time for reading.* In Figure 16-1 we see the percentage of errors in reading five types of dial. Several conclusions have come from such studies:

1. The open-window type provides the most compact design.
2. The semicircular and horizontal scales require the eye to cover increasingly more ground.
3. On semicircular and horizontal scales, errors are more common at extreme positions.
4. Horizontal eye movements are easier and faster than vertical eye movements.
5. Reading habits tend to favor the horizontal type of scale.
6. In qualitative or check reading (to see whether equipment is functioning in a safe range) the dial and moving-pointer display is superior to the open-window type.
7. Time required to identify different dials increases with the number of dials in the panel. However, the increase in time is greater when the normal pointer positions are not aligned.

In Figure 16-2 we see the arrangements of a simulated stove used in the study of the speed and errors involved in turning on and off

FIG. 16-2 The control-burner arrangements of a simulated stove used in the study of human reactions. There were zero errors for design I in the upper left-hand corner. This design also had the shortest reaction time of the four models; it has better compatibility with the subject. The other three arrangements induced errors and long reaction times even after much practice.

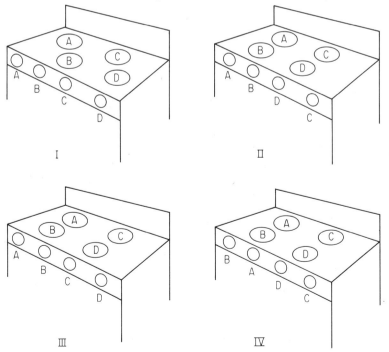

burners relative to the positions of the control knobs. There were zero errors for design I. Note the A-to-A, B-to-B, etc., spatial relations involved. This design also had the shortest reaction time of the four models studied. It has better compatability with the subject. The other three arrangements induced both errors and long reaction times even after much practice.

Getting man and machine together better involves a knowledge of what things man can do best and what things machines excel in. We see a summary of this in Table 16-1.

SENSORY INPUTS

From experimental psychology has come much information about the inputs through the human senses. Let us describe the senses in terms of practical rules for their efficient use.

The Eye

Visual fatigue is caused when the eyes are used too long or when they are strained to perceive near or beyond their limits of acuity. Change of focus back and forth for long periods causes the eyes to tire because the various muscles used become fatigued.

Work in very uneven illumination causes eyestrain. Looking from a bright instrument panel to outside darkness is fatiguing. Readers experience a similar strain when they look back and forth from a well-illuminated book to a darkened room. Looking at unclear objects, such as fine print, causes undue fatigue, as does glare.

Some practical rules for *day* vision are:

1. When possible, avoid looking at small objects.
2. Use good illumination without glare.
3. Do not look back and forth between far and near objects too often.
4. Blink when the eyes seem to need lubrication.
5. Avoid general fatigue. The small muscles of the eye are affected quickly by waste products.
6. Remember that an excessive amount of alcohol affects the visual nerve centers.
7. Avoid emotional upset (if possible!). The person in a "blind rage" can be just that.

Some practical rules for *night* vision are:

1. Have night vision tested. Some people are night-blind in varying degrees.
2. Stay in the dark for thirty minutes before night observation. Dark adaptation takes time.

TABLE 16-1 MAN VERSUS MACHINE

MAN EXCELS IN	MACHINES EXCEL IN
Detecting certain forms of very low energy levels	Monitoring (both men and machines)
Sensitivity to an extremely wide variety of stimuli	Performing routine, repetitive, or very precise operations
Perceiving patterns and making generalizations about them	Responding very quickly to control signals
Detecting signals in high noise levels	Exerting great force, smoothly and with precision
Storing large amounts of information for long periods—and recalling relevant facts at appropriate moments	Storing and recalling large amounts of information in short time periods
Exercising judgment where events cannot be completely defined	Performing complex and rapid computation with high accuracy
Improvising and adopting flexible procedures	Sensitivity to stimuli beyond the range of human sensitivity (infrared, radio waves, etc.)
Reacting to unexpected low-probability events	Doing many different things at one time
Applying originality in solving problems: i.e., alternate solutions	Deductive processes
Profiting from experience and altering course of action	Insensitivity to extraneous factors
Performing fine manipulation, especially where misalignment appears unexpectedly	Repeating operations very rapidly, continuously, and precisely the same way over a long period
Continuing to perform even when overloaded	Operating in environments which are hostile to man or beyond human tolerance
Reasoning inductively	

After Woodson and Conover

3. Try to avoid looking directly at a light.
4. Look to the side of what you want to observe. Seeing out of the corner of the eyes utilizes the rods (night receptors in the eye). Avoid the straight-ahead look because this stimulates the cones (daylight and color receptors).
5. When possible, choose a contrasting background for observing an object.
6. Practice recognition of targets. Familiarity helps with the "fill in" of what you observe.

The Ear

While the eye is primarily used to perceive space, the ear is a temporal sense. Space location by ear may be very inaccurate.

Some practical rules for good hearing are:

1. Colds cause dull hearing by producing unequal pressures in the ear.
2. When flying, keep swallowing to help equalize the pressure on the two sides of the eardrum.
3. Loud sounds mask out faint noises. Repeated loud sounds, such as one's own rifle fire, cause temporary deafness.
4. In the midst of loud noise sticking one's fingers in one's ears improves the hearing of shouted speech.
5. Become familiar with certain sounds. You will hear them better.
6. When a loud sound is expected, be on the ground if possible. Explosion vibrations generally go up from the ground.
7. Open the mouth when an explosion is coming. This helps equalize eardrum pressure.

The Nose

Smell is a "ground sense." Walking erect cuts down on the efficiency of smelling. When you think you may smell fire in a room, sniff at floor level. Smell adapts very rapidly particularly when we sniff hard. Smell stimuli comes to us as gases. There are about 60,000 odorous substances.

Some practical rules for good smelling are:

1. Note individual differences in sensitivity to smell; some people have very little.
2. Adaptation to smell is rapid. Colds may abolish it entirely.
3. Some fumes, particularly those from gasoline, dull the olfactory sense temporarily.
4. Tobacco smoke dulls olfactory sensitivity.
5. Do not try to test for gas on high ground. Gases tend to settle in low places.
6. Learn the odors of different gases from weak dilutions of the gases themselves.
7. One odor may mask out another. Learn which types dominate.
8. Odors are often mixed. Learn to detect such combinations.
9. Be aware that each person emits his or her own characteristic odor and is usually adapted to this odor; others, however, may sense it.
10. Perfume tends to mix with body chemicals over a period of time, producing a very unpleasant odor. Adding more perfume only increases the unpleasant effect.

Motion

Motion sickness is quite common. Nausea is caused not only by disturbances of the vestibular organs associated with the ear, but by visual disturbances as well. Odors may be nauseating; even imagination adds to the picture. *Suggestion* plays a big role in causing motion sickness. It is easier to be sick when other people are sick, when you think about it, or when you expect to get sick. It is possible to *learn* not to be sick.

Here are some rules for avoiding motion sickness:

1. Get used to motion. Sailors and flyers do.
2. Think about things that do not stimulate sickness.
3. Try to avoid associating sickness with specific situations.
4. Breathe fresh air.
5. Avoid overeating, hangovers, and fatigue.
6. Use only pills which have been prescribed.

Touch

The skin is our largest sense in terms of receiving sensory inputs related to feelings of pressure, pain, warmth, and cold. We are aware of these experiences, but possibly we do not think of the skin as a communication channel very often, unless, of course, we see a blind person reading Braille.

Military organizations, along with organizations devoted to the study of communication for the deaf-blind, have conducted research on "talking through the skin." Although such cutaneous communication has not as yet provided rules for improving perception through the sense of touch, we wish to describe briefly some of the research that has been going on in the military, in universities, and in other experimental laboratories.

We believe it important to point out that military organizations sponsor much research in both basic and applied psychology. We use the description below as one of many examples.

The practical needs for a tactile communication system have whetted the imagination of many persons. Research is now underway to find ways of communicating with frogmen by using mechanical vibratory codes sent to them from a distance. With vibrators attached to the body, secret transmissions are quite feasible. Studies are being made on efficient ways of communicating with tank drivers via coded electrical "pulses" tuned for reception through the skin. These can be felt when noise masks out speech. Work is being done to improve aircraft landings on carriers by supplementing the eyes and ears with information supplied through the skin.

Research is being conducted with astronauts for communication in space under conditions where sight and sound may be distorted. It has been found that *seven* classes of information can be conveyed through the skin using such signals as mechanical vibrations (similar to the feelings one gets from touching a tuning fork) and electrical pulses (very mild "taps" on the skin). Some research is going on in the use of small air jets as stimuli.

It has been found that *amounts* can be presented through the skin, providing quantitative information or giving quantitative instructions, such as, "add three more pounds of pressure." *Coordinates* can give relational information; e.g., "The target is located where coordinate A crosses coordinate B." In landing an aircraft both *directions* and *rates* can be transmitted through the skin.

Research is being carried out utilizing the attention-demanding qualities of vibration, or an "electrical nudge." Such stimuli can always break through noise or inattention, giving *warning* to the pilot that he is to be ejected from the spacecraft. The Navy has been using cutaneous vibrations in studying the *vigilance* of sailors on watch.

The primary demand for a cutaneous communication system has been for its use in transmitting *language.*

The skin as a sensory channel for communication has one unique advantage; it is rarely ever "busy." Even though there is a wide range of individual differences in skin sensitivity, for all practical purposes there is no such thing as complete "skin deafness." The skin, of course, has a long history of serving as a communication channel for the blind, Braille having been invented in 1826. Braille, however, even when thoroughly mastered, is still slow and cumbersome. Recent research indicates that much more efficient systems for communicating through the skin are not far off. This indicates once again that many research projects undertaken to find answers to practical military problems also give answers to peacetime problems.

ENVIRONMENTAL INPUTS

Both our working and living environments provide us with a variety of inputs. Let us look at a few of the common ones.

Noise

Noise is usually regarded as a distractor and therefore as interfering with work efficiency. "I can't do my job properly around this place because it's too noisy" is a common worker's complaint. Actually, clear-cut evidence that noise reduces work output is very scant. We do know, of course, that many people find different kinds of auditory stimulation irritating. Thus high tones and very low tones are judged almost universally to be more annoying or irritating than tones in the middle ranges. Unexpected noises, intermittent noises, and reverberating noises are also irritating to most people. Such knowledge as this has made it possible to sound-treat work areas in order to reduce the irritating effects of noise.

An interesting study of the effects of noise in a work situation was conducted in England in a film-processing plant. Different measures of efficiency were made in untreated workplaces and in the same places after the noise level was measurably reduced by acoustical treatment. The results of this study showed that rate of work was not improved by noise reduction, but that error was significantly less frequent when the noise level was less.

Another study had to do with the output of weavers over a period of twenty-six weeks during which the workers wore ear defenders on alternate weeks. The protective devices reduced the noise from 96 to 87 decibels. There was an increase of 12 percent in speed of production while they were wearing the ear defenders.

To one person rock 'n' roll music is enjoyable; to another it is noise. In some situations a background of noise may be helpful to us in getting a job done. For example, the student who is used to some background sound may find a really silent library disrupting—it becomes a "loud quiet." We may welcome noise when we are lonely. Noise takes on unpleasant meaning when it is unwanted. Some communities have legislation prohibiting noise pollution; for example, in New York State televisions and radios must be turned down after 11:00 P.M. Many apartment dwellers find noise control rules spelled out in the lease. But only to a point can noise be avoided, and habituation to noise makes the world tolerable. How well a person adapts depends not only on the conditions of the stimulus but on personality characteristics as well. Some people are better able to ignore unwanted noise than others. Some people even seek out noisy situations; for example, auto-race fans give, as one the the reasons for attending speed contests, "all the noise."

Music

Within recent years, the practice of introducing music in the workplace has become common. Music is alleged to improve attitudes and morale, and to increase production. Some of these claims have been subjected to experimental inquiry. In two investigations significant increases in production were associated with the use of music. In both of these studies the workers performed relatively simple tasks, so before it can be assumed that all productive effort will be enhanced by music, the effects of music on different kinds of tasks must be determined.

In one study of the effects of music on a complex industrial task, attitudes were revealed as important. This investigation was conducted in a rug-manufacturing factory and dealt with a task known as setting. Setting is a relatively complex job involving the preparation of material for rug looms. The work requires a high level of mental and manipulative skill and considerable physical endurance. Music was found to have no favorable or unfavorable effects upon the production of workers in the setting operations. Despite these findings, questionnaire results showed that the workers were favorably disposed toward music and, perhaps more significantly, that they believed that it increased their actual production.

It is not entirely clear why simple task performance is sometimes improved by music and complex task behavior is not. One possibility is that the workers in the setting operation, being highly skilled and experienced, had developed stable habits of production and adequate adjustments to the work environment and that music effects were not sufficiently strong to break these well-established habit patterns.

Illumination

Despite a vast literature on the effects of illumination on work efficiency, solidly established relationships are practically nonexistent. Studies have been conducted in actual work situations, and in some cases changes in illumination appear to be related to output, but so many variables have been left uncontrolled that it is impossible to assess the effect of illumination per se. There have been some well-controlled laboratory studies, but in these cases the tasks were often not of the kind that are performed in the industrial workshop. Where there does appear to be similarity between the laboratory tasks and workshop tasks, it is possible to make some educated guesses as to the probable effects of different illumination levels on industrial output. Tentatively, it has been concluded that the majority of industrial operations could be carried out with maximum efficiency in the neighborhood of 10 footcandles. In exacting visual tasks like drafting and typesetting, as high as 40 footcandles are required, and spectral qualities are often important.

The color dynamics of the workplace is often claimed to be important in work efficiency, but there is no supporting evidence. One of the few experiments related to the color problem deals with the effects of colored illumination upon perceived temperature. This study was prompted by the almost universal tendency to speak of green and blue as "cool" colors and red and orange as "warm." The experimental question was: Can a person's judgment of the temperature of the air around him be biased by the color of his surroundings?

Subjects performed a number of tasks illuminated by different spectral lights and were asked to indicate by a switch when the temperature rose to a point at which they began to feel uncomfortably warm. The findings showed no change in the levels of heat they would tolerate as a function of the colors of illumination, but nevertheless they persisted in believing that blue and green are cool colors when asked to rank the colors they had experienced. It appears, therefore, that despite color efficiency, any attempt to change the comfort of persons in a work environment through variations in colored illumination may be unsuccessful.

Atmospheric Effects

Every worker at one time or another has complained about the "heat" or the "cold" in terms which imply that his efficiency is being affected adversely by the temperature of the working environment. A determination of temperature effects on work effeciency would seem to be an easy matter. The problem actually is complicated because almost always when atmospheric temperature varies, other conditions such as humidity do not remain constant. A few studies exist which have been summarized by one investigator. He concludes that the desirable temperatures for sedentary work in winter are from 68 to 73°F and for the same kind of work in summer, 75 to 80°; for moderately hard work in all seasons, the desirable temperature is 65°, for strenuous work, 60°. Humidity effects are considered negligible because in the range of temperatures investigated relative humidity is an unimportant variable.

The role of humidity has been demonstrated in a number of studies, so that there is a factual basis for the common expression that "it's not the heat, but the humidity" which causes discomfort. In one of these studies workers were exposed for one hour to different combinations of humidity and temperature. Temperatures as high as 140°F were judged to be tolerable when the humidity was only 10 percent. On the other hand, when the humidity reached 80 percent, a temperature of 110° was judged to be intolerable. In the home, of course, we are becoming more aware of atmosphere effects as air conditioning becomes more common.

Besides temperature and humidity, air circulation is another atmospheric condition that is critical in a good work environment. An example is a study in which electric fans were operated on alternate days for a period of six summer weeks and the effects on a weaving operation were observed. For every hour of the working day, production with the fans stopped was less than when the fans were running. The beneficial effects of the fans were greater in the afternoon than in the morning, for the most part, although the third hour of the morning and the second hour of the afternoon showed the greatest production increases.

Altering atmospheric conditions in order to create a favorable working environment is nowadays frequently accomplished through the installation of air-conditioning systems. Indeed, these systems are now under such precise control that humidity, temperature, and air-circulation problems would appear to be amenable to ready solution. However, the problems are not as simple as they appear. The complicating factor is the worker's reaction or perception of the change brought about through the manipulation of physical variables. A case in point is the reaction of workers in a factory built in Texas during World War II blackouts. The building contained no windows or skylights but was conditioned to control temperature, humidity, and air circulation. Since the ceiling was 50 feet from the floor, most of the air vents were located near the top of the walls.

From the beginning employees complained about the bad air. It was too hot, too humid, and too close. A thorough check of the system was made, and it was found to be in excellent working order. Complaints persisted until it was recognized that the workers were rural people unaccustomed to industrial work and air conditioning. They felt cooped up in a windowless plant where they could not feel a breeze. Since the vents were too high for the workers to feel the moving air, they needed some visual indication of stirring air. When tissue streamers were fastened to the ventilators high on the walls, the workers could see that the air was moving, and the frequency of employee complaints soon became negligible.

OUTPUTS

In some ways we may think of human efficiency as the ratio of output to input. Input may be the number of man-hours spent, and output may be the number of airplanes serviced or potatoes peeled. But such inputs and outputs are difficult to measure.

A great deal of work has been devoted to *psychomotor* skills. The word "psychomotor" suggests that some thinking precedes the muscular, or motor, response. Measures of movements have been made, and it has been found useful to speak of several kinds of movement when we are talking about efficiency of muscular work.

First come the basic movements, called *simple positioning.* An illustration would be the hand moving from one location to another; e.g., twisting a knob from one setting to another.

A second class involves *tense* movements. In tense movements the arm, for example, is caused to shift in position, but finds opposing muscles operating. In driving a truck over smooth roads steering involves only "simple positioning" movements. However, driving over rough country of rocks and ruts causes forces to be applied that either add to or subtract from the force produced by the driver. This leads to a "tense" kind of movement pattern.

Third come *ballistic* movements, as in throwing a football or swinging a golf club. Here no opposing muscles are functioning. And here we find one disadvantage—the unpracticed amateur can "throw his arm out." Flipping a switch is an example of a "ballistic" movement.

Static movements are a fourth class. They are similar to positioning movements, but differ in being very small; e.g., pushing a brake pedal.

Fifth come *sequential* movements in which actions are repetitive. Wheel turning or tapping tasks are of this sort. While we are learning to make such responses, we must think about what we are doing. Once these habits have been established, they go on automatically without our having to think about them. This is one reason why we should learn such skill movements correctly from the beginning.

There are many motor-ability tests to find people with abilities in wrist-finger speed, aiming ability, manual dexterity, and some forty other skills involved in psychomotor coordination. A person may be very good in doing one kind of movement and poor in some other kind. Fortunately, different jobs demand different skills. What the instrument maker has to do and what the ballplayer has to be skilled in are different. There are some general suggestions, however, for increasing motor skill and efficiency.

Some of the rules for determining the best method of work are similar to points discussed about work in Chapter 15. They include:

1. Keep the number of movements to a minimum.
2. Arrange movements so that each ends in a position favorable for beginning the next.
3. Make sequence of movements in rhythm.
4. Minimize the number of body parts involved.
5. Arrange for the use of both hands as much as possible.
6. When possible, provide for intermittent use of different muscles.
7. Provide for symmetrical motions of both arms.
8. Arrange the work space efficiently.

We are all aware of the psychomotor involvements in driving an automobile. Coordinating the inputs-control-outputs without disruption is quite a feat at times. Failures to "put it all together" are common—accidents are a universal example of this. Let us conclude this chapter by talking about this problem in applied psychology, so common not only at work and on the highway but also in the home.

ACCIDENTS AND SAFETY

Any chain of events, however well planned, may include some unplanned event. It may be the result of some nonadjustive act on the part of an individual, some malfunction of a machine, or some situation in which we are unprepared for a contingency. There is evidence, both from common experience and from research, that certain physiological and psychological agents and conditions render the individual more likely to be involved in an accident; fatigue, emotional upset, attitudes, alcohol, drugs, experience, and training all may play a part in the total picture of accidents within a systems concept. Even the concept of "accident-proneness," if it exists, is a very complex matter. The factors which make an individual susceptible to accidents may differ from person to person, and there does not seem to be any simple shortcut to identifying the so-called accident-prone. A person's liability to accidents is rather specific; the fact that he or she is accident-prone under one set of circumstances does not mean that he or she is accident-prone under different circumstances. Accidents certainly bring about talk from all of us, and no doubt we all have our theories; we store personal experiences in long-term memory and we have statistics given us from many sources.

Faulty perception may cause accidents, as is illustrated by so-called deer blindness. Many hunters can look straight at a deer in the woods and not see it, and these same people can easily mistake a human target for a deer. Seeing deer, or other game, is an art acquired from experience. Distinguishing just what is moving is important. For this reason safety precautions include the hunter's wearing bright orange, to aid the fast-draw rifleman in his perception. Hence, we emphasize that accident prevention relates as much to inputs as to outputs.

DEFINITION OF AN ACCIDENT

If a workman falls off a ladder and is not injured and does not cause any damage to equipment, is this an accident? Frequently the answer is "no." Suppose he sprains his ankle in falling off the ladder. Is this an accident? What about the worker who falls off the ladder and rubs the skin from his elbows; shall we call this occurrence an accident? Indeed, in all three of these instances we have an act or instance of behavior which we must call an accident. There are of course differences. In one case the results are inconsequential, in another there is a skin abrasion, and in still another there is an incapacitating sprained ankle. However, common to each of these instances is the act of falling off the ladder. The differences lie in the *results* of falling off the ladder.

There are instances of behavior involving acts with common features and different results. There are other instances in which the acts are different but the results are similar. A complete understanding of the nature of accidents and their prevention requires that a careful distinction be made between acts and the results of these acts. The appropriate distinction is made in the following statement: An accident is *an unexpected, incorrect, but not necessarily injurious or damaging event that interrupts the completion of an activity.*

Some of the major classes of accident results can be enumerated without difficulty. First, there are results which do not involve injuries of any consequence. These are no-injury accidents. A workman bumps against a piece of moving machinery. Result: just grease on his overalls and a button ripped off his suspenders. Second, there are minor-injury accidents. A workman bumps against the same piece of machinery and suffers a slight laceration of the skin on his forearm. Third, there are accidents involving major injuries. Contact with moving machinery results in a mangled hand which has to be amputated. And of course there are accidents in which there is damage to equipment. A workman bumps into the moving machinery, and his recoil causes a nearby wrench to fall into revolving gears. There is a damaged machine although no bodily injury. Widely different results are apparent in each of these cases, but each result stems from the same or nearly the same happening.

Some Statistics. A report of the National Safety Council indicates that industrial accidents alone cost well over 3 billion dollars a year. The monetary cost is enormous, but in terms of life and limb the situation is tragic. No one really knows the cost of accidents in the home and on the highway. Even the causes of accidents may range from the simple case of a person walking through a glass door to a sequence of pilot errors that eventually result in an aircraft crash.

In the United States in any given year roughly 100,000 people are killed and around 10 million more injured through accidents. About half of all accidental deaths are related to motor vehicles, a fourth to the home, and some 15 percent to work. At work and at home, falls lead in causes, followed by handling objects, being struck by falling objects, and contacting harmful substances. Electricity, heat, explosives, and machinery account for most accidents. Hazards on the farm range widely, from handling anhydrous ammonia or operating a power-driven posthole digger to caring for a dairy bull or handling a sow with newborn young. Of the 1,000 lives lost each year in United States farm-tractor accidents, 600 are due to overturning.

Some 500,000 persons suffer serious eye injury at home and in school every year—and about 90 percent of these injuries could be prevented by using protective shatter-resistant eyewear.

Aware as we are about accidents at home or at work, we hear most often about highway accidents. Did you know cars have killed more Americans since 1900 than the death toll of all United States wars since 1775? About one-half the persons killed in auto accidents involve drivers between fifteen and thirty years of age. While only 2 of every 100 vehicles on the road are motorcycles, at least 3 of every 100 persons killed are cyclists. And the Stanford Research Institute has suggested that traffic fatalities could be reduced by 90 percent if sufficient drastic action were taken. A reduction of 20 percent in all speed limits would cut the number of traffic deaths in half, provided a network of computerized speed traps was set up to enforce this action. And did you know that there are more turnpike breakdowns between 1 and 3 in the afternoon, and that there is a step-up in accidents when the highway is wet because of the hydroplaning effect as a film of water puts the tire off the pavement? There are more pedestrian accidents during those months when there is the least amount of daylight. It is also true that accident rates on superhighways are lower than on regular roads, and that accident rates on exit ramps are nearly twice as high as on access ramps. Practically all studies of accidents have indicated that the human factors predominate in causing them.

Industrial Incidents. The following four unedited cases have in common the disregard of safety rules. They bring up some problems. What action does the company take? Should the worker be fired? Should he be given a disciplinary layoff? If so, should the flagrant violator be disciplined before an accident occurs? What is the union's point of view likely to be if the discipline were given after the accident? Could additional training in safety help? What really caused these accidents?

1. A glass storing gang, consisting of a craneman and two floormen, places packs of glass into and removes packs of glass from storage racks. As they were placing a buggy (wagon) of glass down, the first plate broke. A piece, approximately 79 inches long and about 24 inches wide at the top, tapering down to a point at the lower end, fell off. The glass struck one of the floormen at the very back edge of the safety toe of his safety shoe, went through the top of the soft part of his shoe, and severed his second right toe. Although this job required metatarsal guards, or "spats" (regardless of wearing safety shoes), the injured man was not wearing his spats.

2. A repairman was checking foot bearing inside a Zaremba Cooler which had been "boiled out," then drained before the vessel was entered. Wearing RX glasses and hard hat, the man turned his head sideways, horizontal to the floor of the tank, in making his exit.

Caustic-laden condensate from the roof of the tank dropped into the man's right eye, causing extensive third-degree burn of the cornea and conjunctiva. Monogoggles, or face shields, are required for this job, but had not been worn on this occasion. Probable total loss of vision in the right eye resulted.

3. A glass cutter suffered a puncture wound and severed tendons on the top of his right foot and ankle when a piece of glass he was trimming fell from the cutting table and struck his foot. The injured man was not wearing the required safety equipment (spats and leggings) at the time of the accident. Surgery was required to repair tendons; estimated time lost from work: three months.

4. A general maintenance repairman was removing a large bracket made of angle iron with channel iron gussets from a steel support in the side of a brick building. He was standing on about the fourth rung from the top of a 20-foot ladder using a cutting torch. The bracket fell, landing on a steel grating, bounced outward, striking the bottom of the ladder, kicking it outward onto some ice. The man had previously used the cutting torch to remove the snow and ice around the area where the ladder was placed. The bottom slid outward and the top slid straight down the side rail of the wall. His foot went through the ladder and the side rail came down across his leg four or five inches below the knee, breaking both bones. He attempted to get up about three times with the ladder side rail still across his leg, before he realized it was broken. It was a compound fracture of both bones. The single bone supporting the kneecap was fractured into three or four pieces.

The bones required pinning in three places. A cast was placed on the leg and the man was sent home from the hospital. Where the bones protruded through the flesh, there was considerable bleeding which soaked through the cast. He was returned to the hospital and when the cast was removed, considerable flesh had died. Extensive skin grafting was tried, but did not prove successful. So much of the flesh was removed that the bone was exposed and started to turn black, so it was decided, after five surgical operations, to amputate.

The injured man had been instructed twice (immediately before the accident) by his foreman not to use a ladder because of ice and snow on the ground, but rather to use a portable scaffold which was already set up only 50 to 60 feet from where the injury occurred.

Home Accident Behavior—A Study. Most accidents recorded as happening in the home are of little scientific value because they are reports, not experimentally designed studies. We wish to summarize one experiment which was well planned, controlled, and statistically evaluated. One psychologist made studies in a laboratory setting which did not appear either as a laboratory or as a study of safety practices. Studies were made in a mobile van into which were built a simulated home kitchen, two observation rooms with one-way screens, and a testing room. The 226 selected women subjects believed they came to the van to test a kitchen layout, but they were quite willing to be given tests and a lengthy interview following work in the kitchen. The selection of subjects included some whose state auto-accident reports and driving violations were available. Several generalizations relevant to the content of this chapter came from the study.

It was found that visual measures proved to be good predictors of accident criteria. Simple reaction time was related to only one criterion: personal injury. Those who were slower to react were somewhat more likely to have a personal injury. Subjects who appeared to the observers to be nervous had statistically more property-damage accidents. It is worth noting that these subjects had significantly more property-damage and personal-injury accidents than did average subjects. Heavy or obese subjects had more total accidents than did average subjects. Subjects who had more children had lower accident rates. It was also found that subjects who took tranquilizers had more property-damage accidents and auto violations. Those who took stimulants had more automobile accidents and traffic violations but no more kitchen accidents than those who did not.

Kitchen behaviors which predicted *high* kitchen accident rates could be classified as unsafe practices, unsanitary practices, and failure to follow directions. On the other hand, kitchen behaviors which predicted *low* accident rates included safe practices and making use of correct tools which were available. This study made two basic conclusions. First, there should be a broadening of the term "accident" to include all those human behaviors which are unplanned, unintentional, nonadjustive, inappropriate, or just plain "wrong" as well as the absence of those behaviors which would, in such circumstances, be adjustive, appropriate, or "right." Second, if accidents are to be prevented, human behavior must change. Just how and what behaviors should be changed were not suggested by the study. This study, along with others, suggests that minor accidents parallel major accidents to some undetermined but discernible extent.

THE CAUSES OF ACCIDENTS

A close examination of accident causes reveals two general categories—unsafe conditions and unsafe acts. *Unsafe conditions* involve some aspect of the physical environment which sets up or makes probable the occurrence of an accident. Cluttered arrangement of machinery, poor lighting, unguarded moving parts, and oily floors are examples of unsafe conditions. *Unsafe acts* are those kinds of behavior which lead to an accident or those failures in performance which result in an accident.

At work and at home, falls lead in accident causes. This chief cause is followed by handling objects, being struck by falling objects, and contacting harmful substances. Electricity, heat, explosives, and machinery account for most other accidents. Practically all studies in the field of accidents have indicated that *human factors rank number one in causing accidents.* Unsafe acts and unsafe conditions may interact in such a way that an accident may be caused by both.

Let us push our analysis of causes a little further and ask what causes the unsafe condition or the unsafe act. Since we are getting further and further removed from the actual accident, we may call these matters "indirect causes of accidents." The unsafe-act and unsafe-condition categories we may conveniently call the "direct causes of accidents."

What causes a person to perform an unsafe act? A number of possibilities are immediately apparent, such as faulty vision, illness, worry, intoxication, poor coordination, lack of job know-how, and the like.

All these states or conditions reside within the individual; they make up the so-called human element, and we may justifiably call them "human factors."

HUMAN FACTORS IN ACCIDENTS

Analyzing the nature of causes to the point where we are dealing with human factors is helpful in understanding accident causation because we are now dealing with something which can tell us why the unsafe act was performed. If we can isolate a human element responsible for the unsafe act, we can do something to correct it. Thus if one of the human elements responsible for the unsafe act is lack of job know-how, we may be able to eliminate this causative factor by training. If the cause is faulty vision, corrective glasses may remedy the situation. If the human factor is incorrectable, the offender can be removed from the job and placed in a less hazardous type of work. Usually, however, we are just a bit more cautious of safety when doing hazardous work. Statistics show, for example, that the accident record of professional window washers is low, much lower, in fact, than the accident rate found among housewives cleaning around the home.

Unsafe conditions usually stem from human factors. A worker overloads a conveyor belt and leaves the scene; later the belt breaks, and the result is an accident to someone in the immediate vicinity. The direct cause of the accident, the broken belt, is an unsafe condition caused by an unsafe act. But why did the worker commit the unsafe act of overloading the belt and walking away? Was he distracted by worry over unpaid bills or the illness of a member of his family? If we trace the accident back to its source, we find that the worker's state of mind was the indirect cause out of which the direct causes originated.

As a matter of fact it is not hard to present a strong case for the contention that all unsafe conditions have their origin in human factors. Worn-out machinery can create an unsafe condition which might cause an accident. But if the machine had been properly maintained and the wearing parts replaced soon enough, the wearing out would have been avoided, and the unsafe condition would never have occurred. Why did a worker fail to maintain the machine in proper working order? What human factor in him caused the neglect? A steampipe may burst and be the cause of an accident. This looks like an unsafe condition in which no human factor is involved. But steampipes are supposed to be tested periodically for stress potential, and failure to do this is an unsafe act by a human operator. Once again we may ask: Why was the operator negligent? Cases like these are frequently classified as unsafe conditions caused by nonhuman factors, but it is obvious that the classification is arbitrary. It is used where the causative human agent is not readily identifiable.

Risk Taking

One area of research has to do with the concept of risk as a basic human factor in accident causation. The term used to describe the performing of an act likely to *fail* is *risk acceptance.* Immediately we think of gamblers who range widely in how much risk they will take. At one end of the scale we find the calculated-risk taker (who may often succeed), and at the other end of the scale, the wild-chance taker who reacts as though he can beat all odds (he often fails).

In one study a simulated laboratory situation was used in which the subjects were classified into a "low-risk" group and a "high-risk" group on the basis of personality tests. Following this classification the subjects were put on jobs with the same possible accident hazards. After a period of time it was found that the subjects in the high-risk group had incurred more accidents, were less skillful, and varied more in performance than the low-risk group.

Fatigue

The critical point at which fatigue becomes an accident cause has not been determined. We do know, however, that extreme fatigue leads to increased accident frequency. For example, in a shell factory in England during World War II the accident rate among women workers was reduced by more than 60 percent when the factory changed from a twelve-hour to a ten-hour day.

We must be careful in attributing accidents to fatigue if there is an accompanying change in production rate. What may seem to be a fatigue factor may really be a tendency to overlook accident dangers because one is working faster. The way to separate these two factors may be illustrated by an analysis of accidents made by the United States Public Health Service in which the effect of production rate was held constant. The technique was to divide the accident index by the production index for a given work period; in other words, to report in terms of accidents per unit of output. Results showed that in the *earlier hours* of the day the index rises and falls with the output rate. Increases in production bring a corresponding increase in the number of accidents. However, this relation breaks down in the *closing hours* of the working day. Here the accident rate remains high relative to the production rate. Such an analysis makes it possible to show the importance of the fatigue factors. Formal studies have shown essentially the same thing as the experience many people report. On the highway, at work, and in the home fatigue interferes with our psychomotor coordination and lessens our alertness. One observer put it this way, "When I get very tired and keep going I'm just an accident looking for some place to happen."

Coordination

It would seem reasonable to suppose that slowness of response and clumsiness would contribute to accident frequency. Yet speed of reaction in itself has been found to have no significant relation to accident frequency in industry. However, more complex reaction tendencies are important.

One investigator used a battery of tests consisting of a dotting test, a device for measuring speed of reaction to a signal. Another test required the subject to change his muscular performance in accordance with changing signals. When 500 employees were divided into two groups on the basis of high and low test scores, the poorer performers had 51 percent more accidents than the better three-quarters. Other investigations support the conclusion that poor muscular coordination has a bearing on accident susceptibility.

Vision

How well a person can see would appear to be a factor contributing to accident susceptibility. Research supports this contention. For example, one investigator found that only 37 percent of a group of machine operators who passed visual tests had accidents during a given year. On the other hand, 67 percent of those who did not pass the vision test had accidents.

Personality Characteristics

There is mounting evidence that the personality and temperament of the individual have a great deal to do with the susceptibility to accidents.

A relationship between emotional cycles and frequency of accidents has been reported from a study which showed that the average worker is emotionally low about 20 percent of the time and that more than half of the 400 minor accidents studied occurred during these low periods. Another study showed that the high accident rates were found among the men most disliked by their fellow workers. Men well liked by their associates tended to be accident-free. Other studies show that when one is excessively elated he is subject to being in accidents more than when he is in a neutral emotional state. On jobs with high attention requirements introverts are less likely to have accidents than extroverts.

What about intelligence scores and accidents? The literature on this subject is not clear. Dull people do not seem to have any more accidents than bright people in some situations, but they do have more in other situations. Intelligence seems to be related to accidents involving errors of judgment, but not to accidents involving only manual skills. Very likely a minimum amount of mental ability is necessary for accident-free behavior in all occupations.

ACCIDENT REDUCTION

Accident reduction is achieved through training only if the worker learns to behave safely on the job. If a new worker who does not know the company safety regulations is given this knowledge and demonstrates that he or she knows it, has that person been trained in accident prevention? Not necessarily. Knowing will not always ensure doing. The problem of training clearly involves two phases: First, the worker must learn how to behave the safe way; second, he or she must be stimulated to do it. Thus the safety slogan of the United States Steel Corporation—"Knowing's not enough."

Basic accident-prevention strategy calls for:

1. A *cause analysis of accidents.* Speculation that an accident was the result of worry, lack of attention, or carelessness has no place in accident-prevention strategy. Strategy requires observation of people at work and, from these observations, an identification of unsafe acts and unsafe conditions.
2. *A distinction between accidents per se and their results.* To define an accident as "an act in which someone gets hurt" makes cause analysis difficult if not impossible. It is poor policy to wait for an injury before making a cause analysis. The same principle applies to cause analysis resulting in loss of time.

3. *Elimination of unsafe acts.* When the cause analysis points to an unsafe act, appropriate action must be taken to correct this factor. This may require training, and the nature of the training depends on the need. It may be that the trainee does not know what to do, or he or she may know and not put that knowledge into practice. If the unsafe act cannot be eliminated by training, the employee should be placed in a less hazardous job.
4. *Elimination of unsafe conditions.* If some factor in the physical environment is leading to accidents, it should be eliminated. Wearing safety equipment may be the right step. Proper maintenance of machinery is another possibility. A guard or other safety device on a piece of machinery is still another. Research on the design of equipment is always leading to the discovery of additional unsafe aspects of the physical environment.

Accidents now outrank diseases as a leading cause of death from age one to age thirty-four. Industry is now paying more attention to the off-the-job accident as a major step in preserving effectiveness on the job. Major strategies include the control of exposure to risk, the reduction of accidents during risks, the prevention of injury when accidents occur, and minimizing the effects of injury.

The Industrial Accident Report

Where shall we turn to obtain reliable data useful for an accident-prevention program? The basic source of such information is the accident report. A good accident report should include data on such items as the following:

1. *Date, hour of the day, shift, and location.* Working conditions often change, sometimes in a systematic manner from day to day, from hour to hour, and from shift to shift. For example, the day-shift worker usually comes to work after a full night's sleep and breakfast. The preceding activity of the night-shift worker is usually more varied. Fatigue effects are greater during the latter part of the working day. These and other factors under this category may influence accident behavior.
2. *Job classification, job operation, and job unit.* These data give specific information about the type of work in which the accident occurs. The hazard potential of different jobs and operations within jobs can thus be determined. Suppose that a painter fell from a ladder while descending with his back to the rungs of the ladder. His job classification would be painter; his job operation, using a ladder; his job-operation unit, descending the ladder.
3. *Accident type.* Information in this category should include an exact description of the nature of the accident, including a description of the contact agent. These descriptive data are not necessarily

extensive and detailed. For the painter who fell from the ladder, a statement such as "fell to the floor" would be sufficient. (The floor is the contact agent.)

4. *Immediate cause of the accident.* This information covers the cause of the accident in terms of specific unsafe acts or conditions or both. Among other findings, we get from this information an answer to the question: What violation of a commonly accepted safety procedure resulted in a particualr accident? We need to know what actually was done or was not done that contributed to the accident.

5. *Results of the accident.* Data under this heading cover bodily location of the injury, description of the injury, and extent of property damage. Frequently the person who fills out the accident report cannot immediately describe the injury or property damage precisely. Medical assistance and help from someone responsible for assessing property damage are needed.

6. *Experience.* How important experience on the job is in relation to type of accident can be determined only by a careful analysis of reliable data, the source of which must be the accident report. Data such as these can be of great help in planning a safety training program.

7. *Psychological data.* If available, scores on aptitude tests, personality inventories, and achievement tests should be included in the accident report. The analysis of such data may help in identifying some of the personal factors contributing to accident behavior.

The Automobile Accident Report

Many of us are familiar with accident reports as they involve us and our auto. All states and many local communities require accident reports when human injury occurs or when property damage exceeds some given amount. This varies across the country. Such reports are not as detailed as industrial reports which are organized within a fairly restricted situation, but they are very useful. They are used to improve safety regulations, to give leads toward better engineering designs of vehicles and highways, to satisfy certain legal and insurance requirements, and to provide data relevant to driver's license loss or renewal. Such reports have provided data leading to discussions of no-fault insurance. Once again we have the conclusion that unsafe human acts and unsafe conditions interact to produce most auto accidents. Whether in the home, on the job, or on the highway accidents are caused primarily by people. Since information processing is a perceptual problem (see page 228), some reports have shown that new road signs are needed for making driving easier and safer. How do you react to the signs in Figure 16-3? According to the U.S. Department of Transportation high-speed and clogged highways are

FIG. 16-3 Highway symbols are perceived better than words.

making it increasingly difficult for drivers to read words on road signs, especially on the interstate highway system. Tests have shown that symbols are perceived faster and more accurately than words. For example, "H" with an arrow gets through better than "HOSPITAL" with an arrow.

SUMMARY

Psychology in engineering deals with the principles of how man and machines can be made to work together more efficiently. Problems range widely, from the design of household appliances and work areas to that of automobiles and space vehicles. Engineering psychology aims at designing equipment to fit the person, rather than the reverse. Efficiency in machine operation relates to perceptual problems, such as reading dials, and to psychomotor behavior, such as driving a car or turning on a kitchen stove. There are those things that man excels in doing and those things in which the machine is better.

Engineering psychology pulls information from experimental psychology about the inputs from our senses and the outputs from our muscles. It offers us practical rules for day and night vision and for good hearing. Suggestions related to better utilizing our senses of smell, motion, and touch are given.

Noise and noise pollution have been studied in relation to both work and living. Many kinds of auditory stimulations are irritating. High and very low tones are judged almost universally to be more annoying than tones in the middle ranges. Unexpected, intermittent, and reverberating noises are irritating to most people. Noise is also perceptually defined; music enjoyed by one person may be noise to another. And noise may be welcome when we are lonely. How well one adapts to noise depends not only on the stimulating conditions but also on personality.

Engineering psychology is interested in the effects of music on behavior, and in how illumination and atmosphere affect morale and productivity. Much research has been devoted to the study of psychomotor skills and to the efficient methods of coordinating inputs-control-outputs.

As a common psychomotor function, safety has been studied extensively, relating accidents in the home, at work, and on the highway to such factors as fatigue, emotional upset, attitudes, alcohol, drugs, experience, and training. An accident is defined as an unexpected, incorrect, but necessarily injurious or damaging event that interrupts the completion of an activity. There are two basic causes of accidents—unsafe conditions and unsafe acts. Studies indicate that human factors rank first in causing accidents. Unsafe acts and unsafe conditions may interact in causing accidents.

Human factors in accidents center primarily on risk taking, fatigue, coordination, and personality. Accident reduction strategy centers on information and training and on analyses of accident reports. At the individual level, doing the right thing is important— "Knowing's not enough."

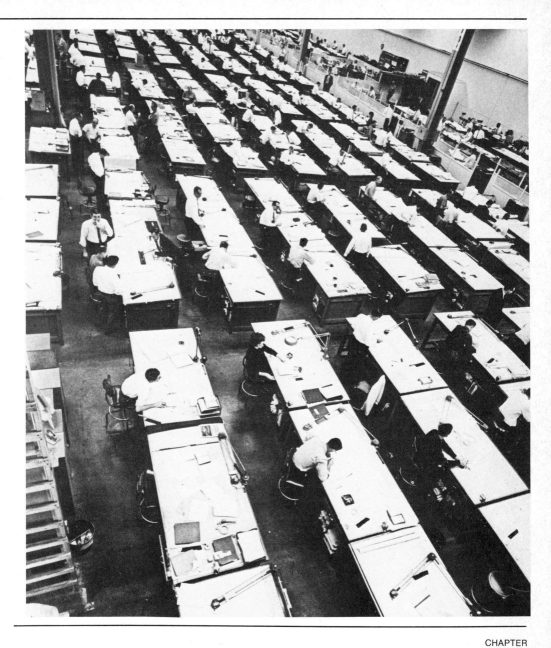

GETTING
SATISFACTION FROM WORK
17

What does the worker want from the job? What does the manager want from the job? What do the teacher and the student want from the job? How do personal attitudes affect what we do? These questions are related to job attitudes, job satisfactions, and morale. They are important to each of us regardless of what we do. And what is even more important, we know some practical answers to the question, *How can I prepare myself for liking my job?*

There have been some four thousand research studies about what people think about their jobs in terms of the *feelings* they have. From these studies came the conclusion that there is urgent need to better understand how people feel about their jobs and *how education and expectancy are related to job satisfaction.*

There is considerable evidence that job dissatisfaction is often associated with generalized maladjustment of some kind. People who are dissatisfied with their jobs are less outgoing and friendly, are more emotionally unbalanced and show more boredom, daydreaming, and general discontent than do their satisfied coworkers. One observer put the problem in a nutshell: "The dissatisfied person is the one who has come up with the wrong answers."

On the average, persons dissatisfied with their jobs in various industries total about 13 percent. Age as a factor has been shown from twenty-three studies. In general, job satisfaction is high among young workers, but tends to go down during the first few years of employment. The low point is reached when workers are in their middle and late twenties or early thirties. Then it increases steadily until a temporary middle-age revolt sets in. Initial enthusiasm for work is apparent among the younger group, but any failure to get ahead lowers job satisfaction for a period. Gradually, really dissatisfied workers are weeded out, and the rest struggle to survive and move ahead. In late middle age, positive attitudes toward the job are found in the person with seniority. For most of us, there is the realization that life is not a neat package. For some, dissatisfaction results from the frustration of being ignored.

One study conducted on a large national sample showed that 25 percent of unskilled workers were dissatisfied with their jobs compared with near 0 percent of businessmen. Sustained job-interest studies have shown that professional people lead the list in degree of job satisfaction, that salaried workers are next, and that factory workers rank lowest.

Let us take a look at things which affect attitudes and morale, discuss factors related to liking and disliking one's job, and conclude with the point that after all, satisfaction on-the-job is highly individual regardless of any efforts to create a favorable environment.

ATTITUDES AND MORALE

Do attitudes affect the amount and quality of work production? This is an involved question. What are the facts? In one report twenty-six studies were cited in which some quantitative relationship between productivity and job attitudes in a variety of jobs had been measured. Fourteen of these studies found that workers with positive job attitudes showed higher productivity than those with negative attitudes; for nine studies, there was no relationship; and in three studies, workers with positive job attitudes actually showed poorer production records than those with negative attitudes. The contradictions in these studies may be due in part to differences in the research methods involved, or in the workers surveyed, or in their work situations. One basic consideration is that high productivity accompanies high morale only when the attitudes of the work group favor maximum output. This is particularly true when the work group is very cohesive, when the atmosphere is friendly, and when belonging to that specific work group is highly desirable to its members. A group of this kind can either restrict or raise output regardless of how its members are satisfied with their jobs.

The findings of studies relating attitudes to job turnover and absenteeism are generally in agreement. Twenty-one of twenty-four studies cited in the literature report that workers with positive job attitudes have less turnover and absenteeism than workers with negative attitudes. Two studies report no effects, and one study showed workers with positive job attitudes as having more turnover. One investigator has shed some light on the problem in his study of telephone company employees. He found that those who quit felt that they were less personally involved in their jobs than those who stayed; they left, in part, because they had had no chance to help make decisions, and they felt they had not contributed to the success of the company. Another investigator found virtually the same situation with bricklayers and carpenters, who were less likely to leave their jobs when given some say in the composition of their work groups.

It has been found that the critical employee is not always a poorer producer than the uncritical one. However, most evidence concludes that workers with positive job attitudes outproduce workers with negative job attitudes when the psychological climates favor high production, where there is good supervision, and where the employee really wants to produce and get ahead.

Aspiration and Productivity

One researcher has made the point that employee satisfaction depends not only on how much a person receives from the job situation but also on where he stands with respect to his level of aspiration. When the environment provides little possibility for need satisfaction, those people with the strongest desires, or highest aspirations, will be the least happy. Or as this researcher has put it, "The greater the amount the individual gets, the greater his satisfaction, and, at the same time, the more the individual still desires, the less his satisfaction." From her interview studies of white-collar clerical workers and supervisors, she makes the point that if an employee is in a situation where he is not making any decisions, *and does not want to make any,* he will tend to be highly or moderately satisfied with his work, but if he is not making any decisions, *and would like to make some,* he will tend to derive little satisfaction from his job.

With satisfaction seen then as a function of both the strength of needs in a particular area and the amount of "environmental return," we can see how *education increases the strength of need for pay and for job status.* This factor is of vital consideration to the college student in planning his or her career. As the person grows older, the need for pay and job status increases. This can lead to job dissatisfaction when the discrepancy between levels of aspiration and possibilities of attainment becomes too great.

Kinds of Informal Organizations

Both the formal and the informal structures of an organization may be described by the *roles that people play,* by the ways in which they communicate, and by the final decisions that are made. Formal structures are, of course, the official way in which a company is organized. Informal organizations, on the other hand, result from friendships, car pools, nearness of workplaces, community interests, union associations, and the like.

One scientist, writing on the social psychology of industry, describes three kinds of informal organizations. First, we find the formation of groups based on some *issue.* For example, a revolt in the ranks of the United Steel Workers lined up people for and against existing policy-making groups. Later when issues had been cleared, the union became stronger than before. Second, we have the clique, which, for example, may be based on a common workplace or on the sharing of some common task. The group consisting of *intimate friends* constitutes a third kind of informal organization. How these groups interact determines the morale of an organization to a large extent and often serves as the key element in productivity. Many informal groups have leaders who may actually set production norms. The real power of these informal groups was first adequately observed in the Hawthorne Studies. These studies pointed out that such devices as trading jobs, helping one another, talking, engaging in horseplay, and teasing were all prohibited by management rules; but the foremen did little more than wink at them. As a matter of fact, some studies have shown a high degree of labor turnover in jobs where there was little opportunity for conversation among workers.

On mass-production jobs in the automobile industry, one investigator has explained low job satisfaction among the workers on the basis of the lack of social contact due to the impersonal pressure of the assembly line. A number of findings have revealed that work situations that inhibit the formation of informal work groups are not conducive to good employee morale.

The Sociogram

The sociogram was developed in the early thirties to describe relations among people. This unique instrument offers a graphic way to look at communication. One can see how these "who works with whom" structures can have a bearing on morale, either at the worker level or at the management level. Let us illustrate some patterns which these relationships may take.

Figure 17-1 shows kinds of sociograms found among workers. A diagram of a cohesive group without a strong leader (indicated by 1) is shown in *a*. The sociogram of a group with a strong leader is represented in *b*. An unstructured group with cliques, isolates, and mutual-admiration societies is shown in *c*.

Laboratory Studies

The manipulation of the variables affecting morale in an actual business organization has certain limitations as to experimental control. Hence, why not build a miniature organization in the laboratory? True, such laboratory experimentation has limitations when it comes to relating results to real organizations. But the laboratory situation holds the advantage that one variable at a time may be

FIG. 17-1 Sociograms representing one graphic way to portray communication among people: (*a*) a cohesive group without a strong leader, contrasted with (*b*), one with a strong leader, and (*c*), an unstructured group with cliques, isolates, and mutual-admiration societies.

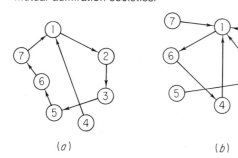

(*a*)   (*b*)

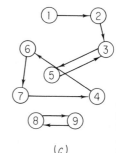

(*c*)

GETTING
SATISFACTION
FROM WORK

manipulated and it is possible to get at some of the relatively isolated factors operating in job satisfaction.

In a series of laboratory experiments, answers were sought to such questions as:

1. What difference does it make in an organization if communication is limited to certain channels?
2. How will the morale and performance of an individual member be affected by the centrality of the position he occupies?
3. What is it about a central position in an organization that is so satisfying?
4. Does the position of "autonomy" affect job satisfaction in the individual?

Communication networks were established in which subjects in any one group were seated around a circular table separated from one another by radial partitions which extended so that the subjects could not see one another. They communicated by means of written notes passed through slots in the partitions. The communication network of any group was controlled by having some slots open and others closed. Problems were provided by the experimenter. The groups developed their own system of pooling information and working out answers.

The drawings in Figure 17-2 represent the "organizations," or different groups. In the "star" group all information is sent to a central person, who then transmits the answer back to each individual member. In the "chain" network, the information is sent by the end men, the men on the periphery (P), to the middle men (M), and then in turn to the man in the center (C). The "Y" network is a combination of the star and the chain. The "circle" network lacks centralized organization; thus problem solving is made more difficult. In such a network, pieces of information could bounce around for some time before someone accumulated all of them and took the lead in sending out answers.

Results of the experimentation showed, first, that for efficiency

FIG. 17-2 Four communication networks showing how the group is hung together. In the "star" the men on the periphery send information to the central person, who then transmits answers back. In the "chain," middlemen are interposed between the center and the periphery. The "Y" network combines the star and the chain. Problem solving is more difficult in the noncentralized "circle" network.

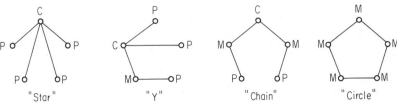

"Star"   "Y"   "Chain"   "Circle"

in problem solving the star and Y networks did better than the chain and the circle. Second, the members differed both within and across networks in the amount of satisfaction derived from their jobs in the group, and in the amount of status accorded them by other group members, as measured later by questionnaire. Even in these experimental situations, devoid of much reality, the persons occupying central positions expressed greater job satisfaction and were seen as having higher status than the occupants of the peripheral positions.

Satisfaction of Individual Needs

The descriptions above represent only a few of the experiments on this problem. As far as job satisfaction is concerned, they add up to the following conclusions:

1. A central position in a communication network usually has associated with it a larger amount of autonomy. Its occupant can personally decide what to do next. The person on the periphery has to be *told* what to do. In our culture, at least, being able to decide for oneself is more satisfying than having to be told.
2. Being autonomous has more effect on satisfaction than does merely being central.
3. In positions in which the person is in a position of being both central and autonomous, satisfaction is highest.
4. Members of the groups whose personalities (measured before the experiment) showed strong psychological needs to be independent were more dissatisfied with positions of low autonomy than were members who had weaker independence needs.

Why do people get together in certain groupings, derive satisfaction from belonging to a particular group, and leave it only with reluctance? It is here that the *individual* finds a climate suitable to his needs and one where other members of the group help him satisfy his desires for recognition and status, his feelings of being wanted, and most of all, his feelings of security. When these needs *in the individual members* of the group are satisfied, group cohesiveness produces high morale, and, in turn, high productivity, especially where leadership and company loyalty are also a positive part of the psychological climate. When there is good reason for suspicion, the group can sometimes limit production *and* get by with doing so.

Resistance to Change

There is some tendency, both within and without industry, for people to resist change, even though the change may be best for the individual or for the group. As simple a situation as introducing safety devices on machines to prevent accidents has even caused strikes among workers when the devices necessitated changes in work habits.

One investigator describes how a wage-incentive system was

introduced into an automobile factory without any explanation of the reasons for it, or of the results it was supposed to produce. The plan was a failure. Others tell of the failure to increase production in coal mines by changing to the use of modern machinery which had been shown to be effective in other mines. The workers not only resisted verbally, but they failed to produce with any appreciable change in output. The modern machinery caused the men to lose identification with their jobs. They had not been consulted about the change, and therefore, they were not conditioned to accept it.

In a somewhat similar situation in a textile plant, a proposed change in production operations was put to the workers *as a problem.* The workers themselves, thus being involved in a solution affecting them, accepted the change. The workers also increased their productivity during the course of the problem solving.

FACTORS AFFECTING JOB ATTRACTIVENESS

Follow-up studies of college graduates show that dissatisfaction is directly related to income. Often it is a matter of comparative incomes, rather than the absolute rate of pay, that affects attitudes. It has been discovered that among executives in the middle-pay bracket, the best morale is found in small companies. This apparently is because middle-management executives in the small company are not isolated either from the workers or from decision-making top management.

It is not at all uncommon to find low job satisfaction among workers in the lower social strata where family ties are weak, housing is substandard, and the opportunites for achieving stable work habits are limited. Such habits as shiftlessness, irresponsibility, and lack of ambition are normal responses which the worker has learned from his physical and social environment. The well-educated girl from a professional family may scorn a job as a waitress, whereas someone from a lower social class may be happy with it. There is considerable evidence that the attitude people have toward their jobs is more than just an individual matter; it is related to both the value system of the class and what we expect to find. Just before we choose some work situation, we look upon a potential organization favorably (see Figure 17-3). Just after we make a choice, organizational attractiveness is higher. One year later it is much lower and studies show that three and one-half years later attractiveness is no better. One reason for this loss in satisfaction with the work situation is our overestimation of the organization in the first place. This is very true of the college graduate on whom the data for 17-3 were obtained.

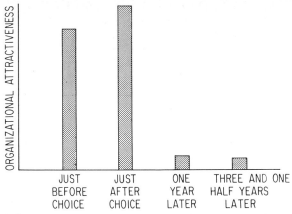

FIG. 17-3 Attractiveness for the organization and the job at four points in time.

WHY DO THEY LEAVE?

Professor Marvin Dunnette and his colleagues at the University of Minnesota surveyed over 1,000 men and women who had attended college and gone to work in a variety of jobs. A random sample who had left one company during a two-year period with a tenure of four years or less were studied as to why they quit. These represented people in production, purchasing, traffic, industrial relations, finance and marketing, and technical jobs.

Five areas out of a total of fifteen reasons for disenchantment were highlighted in the study and are starred in Figure 17-4. These areas included pay, interesting work, opportunity to advance, accomplishment, and use of abilities. The three sets of curves represent first job in company, job held at time of leaving company, and present job in *new* company. On the vertical axis we see how these curves relate to "experience better than expected," "experience as expected," "experience worse than expected," and "experience markedly worse than expected."

The disenchantment with the first job with the company was seen as one that severely frustrated the graduates' high hopes and expectations of opportunities to use their abilities. This finding was interpreted as reflecting a supervisory practice (see page 421) that is apparently prevalent in many large companies—namely, the practice of "breaking the new person in" by assigning tasks that are so trivial that they convey the idea that the newcomer is not yet capable of doing anything important. Often this type of communication (see page 249) shows the newcomer that "he [or she] really isn't so smart even though he [or she] has been to college." This person feels

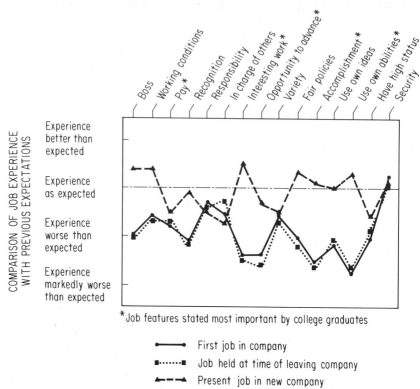

*Job features stated most important by college graduates

●——● First job in company

■·······■ Job held at time of leaving company

▲——▲ Present job in new company

FIG. 17-4 Discrepancies Between Job Expectations and Job Experiences of Terminated Employees in First and Final Jobs with First Company and Present Job in New Company.

strongly that his or her college-gained knowledge and skills are not fully used or appreciated.

Studies of the two types represented in Figures 17-3 and 17-4 stress that career planning should take into account a conflict between expectancy and reality on the job. This may help lessen the psychological blow and at the same time not require one to become quite so dependent on seeking satisfaction only from a new job. Knowing what to expect and what not to expect relates closely to the development of our attitudes. And we do know that attitudes have an influence on productivity.

FACTORS RELATED TO LIKING THE JOB

"What do you want most from your job?" "What things give you satisfaction in your work?" "What causes the most dissatisfaction for you?" Studies show that when thousands of persons were asked many questions such as these, some ten factors emerged, and these are listed below. The data were summarized by using computers.

Individual Differences

The studies showed that most people like and dislike much the same things about their work and their jobs. However, when a person is asked what factor is the most important *to him* or *her,* the next most important, and so on, some individual differences are found. For example, for a newly married man wages may be of primary importance. At some other time, or under other conditions, it is quite possible for wages to be placed low in any comparisons. Opportunity for advancement or some other factor may well take first place.

Where, for example, does money fit into the picture? Do we each value it differently? Probably each of us could say something like the following:

> Money is a way of rewarding behavior.
> Money is an anxiety reducer in making one feel more secure.
> Money is an instrument for gaining certain things.
> Money is important but not what I most want.
> Money isn't everything.

All these things may be true, yet we often behave as though money is primary with us. Says one psychologist: "We talk about money more than anything else and behave as though it comes first—executives sacrifice health for it; entertainers work toward more and more lucrative arrangements; bankers embezzle; robbers rob; employees strike; and professors publish to earn increased salary and enjoy royalty checks. Yet we must not conclude that bankers embezzle *only* for money and professors publish *only* for financial return."

We know that money can be lowered in value by what we have to do to get it. We know also that people tend to exaggerate what someone else may make. Studies show, for example, that secret pay policies contribute to job dissatisfaction because we usually overestimate the pay of others and we don't like it.

Money acts as a symbol in different ways for different individuals. A person's desire for money, or choice not to struggle for it, tells something about his personality, past history, and how well certain nonmoney needs are being satisfied. Let us look at satisfaction and dissatisfaction of pay in relation to the nine other job factors when we consider the list below.

Some Typical Rankings

Although individual differences are important in how people react to work and express how they feel about their job, we can still give some "typical rankings." We shall present such ranks below. It is possible, of course, that you, or any other single individual, would not rank these factors in the order in which they are presented. It is also possible that a person would shift these rankings from time to time. Nevertheless, average ranks are useful in seeing how one compares with other people.

1. *Security.* This factor deals with the steadiness of employment, with the feeling of the manager or worker that he has a reasonable chance of working under conditions of company stability. The man with security feels that he is valued by the firm and that he has the abilities and the opportunity to keep his job. Security is a strong reason for liking a job and is generally mentioned first by men and women as contributing to job satisfaction. The lower one gets in the occupational scale, the greater the importance attached to the security factor. The greater skill and responsibility demanded in higher-level jobs give more "salability" and hence create a demand for one's services, both within one's own company and in others.

   Security is a job-attitudes factor which increases slightly in importance with an increase in age. There is evidence that security is less important to employees with more education. It seems to be equally important to employees regardless of their dependents, with the possible exception of the single man who is entirely on his own.

2. *Opportunity for Advancement.* What are the chances of getting ahead? This factor ranks high in importance, particularly to the person striving for upward mobility. Opportunity for advancement is quite a different problem for persons at opposite ends of the socioeconomic scale. The professional man and the corporation executive have this factor primarily within their own individual control. To the man in middle management, however, the problem of opportunity is of greater concern, for his future is tied in largely with what happens to and within his company. To the woman, being accepted adds another dimension (see page 335). To the worker, advancement is related to merit, to be sure, but seniority plays a big role where union contracts are in effect. The young, ambitious, good worker may find advancement held back because of seniority agreements.

   Once a person has reached his or her "opportunity level" and becomes adjusted to the situation, other factors become more important—length of service in a stable company, for example. Intelligence and education are substantially related to the opportunities factor.

3. *Company and Management.* What constitutes a good company and management? To one employee it may mean how well the company gets along with the union. Another may rate the company on its sponsorship of athletic teams. Whether we are dealing with the size of the organization, reputation, earnings, or public

relations, the employee believes that a good company is one which creates the feeling of stability in the job. Like security, this job factor is seldom a strong reason for dissatisfaction, but it contributes substantially to the employee's satisfaction.

In terms of occupational level there is some evidence that the higher the skill level, the greater the satisfaction with the company. Older workers show a slightly greater concern for the rating and reputation of the company than young workers do. Perhaps their years of service to the company have made them a little more ego-involved with it.

4. *Wages.* When this factor is ranked with the nine other job factors, employees give it fourth place. It is interesting that employers generally rank this factor near the top when they are asked what the employee wants. Although there is some indication that wages and opportunity for advancement are related through the element of money, employees consistently have rated wages as much less important than either opportunity for advancement or security.

Studies show that the factor of wages contributes more to the dissatisfaction than to the satisfaction of the worker. Rarely ever does a worker express satisfaction with the amount of money he or she is making.

Wages are more important to men than to women workers, and are generally more important to factory workers than to office workers.

5. *Intrinsic Aspects of the Job.* There are many reasons why people like their job simply for the sake of the job. One person may like what he or she is doing because of having the right ability and training for it. Another may like the job per se because it brings recognition; a third person may like the job because it is easy, provides opportunity to travel, or is free of tension and pressure. Whatever the reason, the nature of the job contributes to both satisfaction and dissatisfaction.

There is an important relationship between a person's skill and education and the requirements of a job. It has been found, for example, that a reduction in the skill requirements of a job increases the dissatisfaction of the more skilled worker, whereas it would not affect the less skilled worker. The higher the occupational and skill level of the person and the higher his or her education, the more important the challenge of the job becomes. Most people in executive or supervisory positions say that they like their job because intrinsically it challenges and stimulates them. One difficult thing for successful leaders to realize is that employees in lower-status jobs often do not like jobs with challenge. For them, other factors must be involved if the job is to lead to satisfaction.

6. *Supervision.* To the worker, the supervisor is both a father figure

and an irritating boss who is an equally strong contributor to both satisfaction and dissatisfaction. Women seem more sensitive to supervision than do men, but for both, bad supervision may be a primary reason for absenteeism and labor turnover.

Supervision seems less important at the high levels, even though people in high positions have a greater tendency to verbalize what is wrong with their particular supervisory structure.

7. *Social Aspects of the Job.* This is one of the most difficult of the job-attitudes factors to describe. It involves such needs as belonging and social approval. This factor contributes to both satisfaction and dissatisfaction of the employee. A man who feels himself a member of a productive, cohesive group is happier with his job than is someone who finds himself a misfit. The social factor appears only slightly more important to women than to men; it is relatively independent of age and occupational level.

8. *Communication.* An old military expression, "There is always someone who does not get the word," is expressive but hardly a complete definition of the factor of communication. The lack of good communication may be a reason for disliking a job, but it is never a specific reason for liking a job. What, then, is really meant by communication? To be sure, it means the formalities of conveying information, giving orders, turning out annual reports. But to the employee it also means being listened to, receiving recognition, and "knowing why." Good communication, as far as feelings go, means the opposite of being ignored. The factor of communication seems to be more important at the higher educational levels.

First-line supervisors list the lack of good communication as one of their chief annoyances. Perhaps this is because they feel that they are "told" by higher management, rather than "conferred with." In one company an atitude survey was made among 120 foremen. When asked to describe their biggest problem, most of these supervisors listed communication. In a few months these men were brought together to discuss company policies and problems. After a one-day session they returned to their jobs. One year later when they were asked to identify problems, communication was far down the list. A follow-up study showed that merely being brought together and asked for views on company problems had made the men feel that communication was now good. Recognition that he or she is a part of management may well be what the supervisor wants when he or she asks for improved communication.

9. *Working Conditions.* Temperature, lighting, ventilation, parking facilities, cafeteria, toilets, and the like always afford a chance for criticism when the employee wishes to let off steam. Actually working conditions have been found to make an equally low

contribution to both satisfaction and dissatisfaction. They are substantially more important to women than to men. Hours are more important to men than any other specific aspect of working conditions; but among women, especially married women, this aspect has even more significance. To the more educated and higher-level employee, hours are almost negligible in importance. Few, if any, executives work the limited hours of the union man! To workers in hazardous jobs, safety conditions are most important; but when they are ranked with the nine other job factors, working conditions come in next to last.

10. *Benefits.* Retirement provisions, hospitalization, leaves, vacations, and holidays are now somewhat standard features of most jobs; there is greater uniformity throughout industry in these factors than in any of the other major factors. Benefits have not been mentioned as a real contributor either to satisfaction or to dissatisfaction in the many studies of job attitudes. It is interesting to note, however, how much attention is paid by union representatives to fringe benefits at the time of contract negotiations.

The Individual. The person giving serious consideration to his or her career may find the factors described above useful in helping establish an individual need hierarchy. The individual will no doubt find that he or she wants all these factors in a job, but will want them in different degrees. As time goes on, one will find attitudes shifting, but it is important that the person have a base of understanding from which to operate in making decisions about work and life-style. We wish to emphasize that the environment can contribute only so much to satisfaction; basically satisfaction comes from within the individual. The key, of course, is discovering one's own personality.

SUMMARY

Job satisfactions are measured in terms of feelings, and relate to the individual, to age, and to education. Job dissatisfaction is often associated with generalized maladjustment of some kind. People who are dissatisfied with their jobs are less outgoing and friendly, are more emotionally unbalanced, and show more boredom, daydreaming, and general discontent than do their satisfied coworkers. Professional people lead the list in degree of job satisfaction, with salaried workers next. Factory workers are least interested in their jobs.

High productivity accompanies high morale only when the attitudes of the work group are cohesive. Workers with positive job attitudes outproduce workers with negative job attitudes when the psychological climates favor high production, where there is good supervision, and where the employee wants to produce and get ahead. Job dissatisfaction results when the discrepancy between levels of aspiration and possibilities of attainment becomes too great. Morale relates to both formal and informal organizations. Work situations that inhibit the formation of informal work groups are not conducive to good employee morale.

In a communication network, the person in a central position usually has a larger amount of autonomy; the person on the periphery has to be told what to do. In our culture, being able to decide for oneself what to do is more satisfying than having to be told. People like stability; in general they resist change. Being involved in the decisions related to change can lessen this resistance.

Factors affecting job attractiveness relate to five areas: pay, interesting work, opportunity to advance, accomplishment, and use of abilities. Studies show that career planning should include an understanding of the possibility of conflict between expectancy and reality on the job. Studies show that the newly hired college-trained person feels strongly that his or her college-gained knowledge and skills are not fully used or appreciated. Knowing what to expect and what not to expect relates closely to the development of attitudes; and attitudes have an influence on productivity.

Most people like and dislike much the same things about their work and their jobs. Rankings of job satisfaction factors are individual and they change with time and with circumstances. *Security* is a job attitude which increases slightly in importance with age; it is less important to employees with more education. *Opportunity for advancement* ranks high with the upward-mobile person. Minority group individuals may be handicapped in this beyond a given level, as are those with minimal skills. *Company and management,* like security, is seldom a strong reason for dissatisfaction, but it contributes substantially to the employee's satisfaction. In general, the higher the skill level, the greater the satisfaction with the company.

Wages is a factor that contributes more to the dissatisfaction than to the satisfaction of the worker. Rarely ever does one express satisfaction with the amount of money made. *Intrinsic aspects of the job* are individual. What a person does on a particular job contributes to both satisfaction and dissatisfaction. The higher the level of education, the more important the challenge of the job becomes. *Supervision* contributes to both satisfaction and dissatisfaction. Women seem more sensitive to supervision than do men, but for both, bad supervision may be a primary reason for absenteeism and turnover.

Most people rank *communication, physical working conditions,* and *benefits* relatively low in the hierarchy order. In the end, the key to getting satisfaction from work lies in personality.

THE INDIVIDUAL AND THE ORGANIZATIONAL CLIMATE 18

Personalities and job requirements interact to produce a *climate* that can be significant to both the individual and the organization. We encounter another climate when we enter a place of worship and still another in the college we attend. Students are aware that the size of a class helps to determine the amount of interaction; so does the personality of the teacher. Whereas one instructor encourages discussion, another, equally competent, having the same size class, may prefer to teach by the lecture method, with little or no questioning involved. One class may be more formal than another. The personality makeup of a class helps to set the climate also. Generally, technical students are more reserved than liberal arts students. We can even describe some aspects of the overall college climate in terms of student subcultures. The student may well ask: "Which is the right group for me?"

In many respects, campus life has changed considerably, although there are a few residuals. This world of athletic heroes, fraternities, sororities, dates, cars, and campus fun has for the most part been modified as colleges have become more open. The athlete is still there, but he too has joined a prevocational group. Those fraternities and sororities that still exist function more as housing arrangement organizations than as social clubs. Cars have become modes of transportation rather than status symbols. Dates of course are still dates, although a little more out in the open, where behaviors may be inhibited by the presence of others. A changing society, part-time work, more vocational interests, and urban and rural locations where students live at home all contribute to a changing scene in higher education.

College climates are very real and vary with a wide variety of student and faculty inputs. They can even be measured along such scales as scholarship, awareness of community problems, propriety, and practicality. Other dimensions involved include intellectual orientation of students and faculty, grades, self-expression, artistic orientation, student camaraderie, press for status, friendliness, social orientation, conformity, age, and tradition.

The student who takes a close look at the psychological or organizational climate of his particular institution can learn much about some of the things to look for on the job. Many people, most of us in fact, experience feelings of uncertainty upon going into a new environment, and there is a good reason to believe that the failure of many people to adjust to the industrial scene is due to the fact that they do not know the nature of the climate they are getting into. On the other hand, many people who find success in industry and other organizations attribute it, in part, to an early discovery of what a specific environment consists of.

ORGANIZATIONAL CLIMATES

By climate we mean *those characteristics that distinguish the organization from other organizations and that influence the behavior of people in the organization.* It is in effect what we react to—the whole context of stimulation and confusion where we work, where we live, or where we go to college. Let us look at the makeup of organizational climates in more detail.

Home environments have their physical descriptions in terms of houses or apartments, split-level homes or those without basements. They also have their psychological environments, described in such terms as friendly or formal; permissive or tense; or as being a nice place to come to or a place to avoid as long as possible. Colleges have their environments in terms of different climates, as we mentioned.

For the salesman, who must do much of his work on the road, hotel climates become important, and different people may have quite different reactions to the same hotel. One person may like a hotel because it is sophisticated; another may dislike it for the same reason. Tour agencies have long been aware of the importance of matching individuals with appropriate accommodations suitable to their status, demands, and pocketbooks. One person may like the small friendly hotel where he is called by name and known individually. Another person may prefer the large hotel where he can get lost.

In much the same way that we can describe the atmosphere of the place we live in, we can describe work environments on the job. We are interested in the psychological atmosphere or "climate" of these places because it is related to problems of satisfaction and dissatisfaction, to problems related to success and failure.

"What kind of climate is best for *me* to work in?" If the individual is an outgoing person who is full of ideas and likes to participate, he may be better satisfied working in a democratic or permissive climate. On the other hand, if he prefers to be told what to do and does not relish taking part in decision-making conferences, he may be better off in an autocratic climate.

Some organizations seem to be permeated with fear, and some function in an atmosphere of permissiveness. Psychologists who have worked with different industries believe that companies fall into psychological patterns. One young computer programmer says, "In my company I am well paid, but I have the feeling that I never know where I stand." A secretary says, "I dislike being made to feel just like another piece of furniture." There are those who, in seeking a good climate, find that the balance between chaos and order is easy to tilt, and some of us find it difficult to regain our position in a climate that has left us behind.

The personality of a company, in many respects, is a composite of the varied ways of behaving of the people within it. Let us take a look at this picture.

PERSONALITY TYPES

Some people may be described as "tender-minded" and others as "tough-minded." Some people are very practical, others are idealistic. The practical individual accepts rules and customs *as they are.* The idealist is concerned with how things *ought to be.* We can see these different types of people on any campus or in any large work situation. Such disparities of personality often make for stimulating classroom discussions. At work they sometimes are related to conflict.

Studies show that there are three general types of personality in any organization of an appreciable size. Found at or near the top of the organization pyramid are the "upward mobiles," who react positively to the large bureaucratic situation and succeed in it. The uncommitted majority in the organization are the "indifferents," who see their jobs as mere instruments toward obtaining off-work satisfactions. Then there is a small, perpetually disturbed minority composed of persons who can neither renounce their claims for status and power nor play the disciplined role to get them. These descriptions are oversimplified and idealized, but useful in better understanding organizations and people.

Though one may not wish to place people rigidly in pigeonholes, their types of behavior do *point in directions* leading to the assumption that the large organization provides a more sympathetic workplace for the upward-mobile person (who is less critical of some of those values that lead to success) than for the person who wishes to escape through indifference or the one who wishes to contest the *status quo.* We shall give some generalized descriptions of these three general personality types, which will possibly not give an adequate picture of any one individual. Most individuals combine some of the characteristics of all three types. One person may play an upward-mobile role to reach a position of relative security where he can afford to be indifferent to the job and yet induce change by indirect means.

Many researchers say that both upward mobility and indifference are functions of class and education as well as of personality. It is also true that attitudes toward "pyramid climbing" are complex and contradictory. Within this frame of reference we give the following brief descriptions.

Upward Mobiles

These people have tendencies toward high job satisfaction and identify strongly with the organization. Typically they get a disproportionately large share of the organization's rewards in power, income, and ego reinforcement. A lack of success is more likely to be interpreted by them as personal failure than as system failure. The upward mobile is an organization man (and increasingly, woman). He is a conformist who can act without much self-analysis. He plays at human relations as a career utility, is sensitive to feedback, and behaves accordingly. This driving type thinks in stragetic terms and will use ritualistic behavior to conceal resentments. He realizes that power is potential influence.

The upward mobile is rule- and procedure-oriented and often views individuals in detached terms. He places personal advancement before group acceptance, feels little sense of conflict, and goes in heavily for the paraphernalia of organizations. His interests and aspirations are tied to the organization so much that he finds little difficulty in rationalizing organizational claims. He seeks out the sights and sounds of power. Often he lacks broad or national perspective on problems. Upward-mobile people generally are not hampered by any desire for obscurity. Sometimes when they fall, they go down hard.

Indifferents

The great mass of wage and salary employees come within the category of the indifferents. These are the people who withdraw from system participation when possible. In one sense they sometimes regard organizations, especially large ones, as "planned systems of frustration." Compared with the upward mobiles, they do not compete strongly for rewards. Since this is a typical pattern of the majority in an organization, the upward mobiles get more chance to operate. In effect, then, the indifferent shares in neither the ownership and profits nor the ego involvements of the organization. He or she must therefore seek off-the-job satisfaction. They reject the values of success and power, paying lip service to the system only when they have to. Nevertheless, the indifferent person still wants to be treated as an individual. He or she does not want to be analyzed or computerized; they want to be recognized.

Many indifferents, both blue-collar and white-collar, pay lip service to getting ahead, but transfer their expectations to their children. They "expect less" and therefore may be "less disappointed." Status anxiety, success striving, and self-discipline, which are characteristic of the upward mobile, are rejected by the indifferent. After putting in the required hours of work, he or she jealously guards the remaining time, having separated work from personal life. On the job, anything that is not routine worries the indifferent person.

It is noticeable that in the mass-production type of industry the indifferent person may depreciate the things he or she makes. ("If people only knew how shabby those things are, they would't buy them"). This person has become conditioned not to expect much from the organization and not to identify strongly with it. This may be related to the fact that he or she gradually becomes immune to discipline and seeks to identify with work companions. Labor economists say that this attitude allows the small group to play a protective role and thus, through the union, shields this person from real or imaginary threats from management.

Sometimes, as his organization changes, the formally upward-mobile person shifts to a role of indifference. This is related in some respects to the "middle-age revolt" which was described in Chapter 8. Advancement may be rejected because of the added responsibility it entails. The indifferent person frequently has generally satisfactory interpersonal relations, since he or she is not perceived as a threat by colleagues. Even in the large union, the indifferent worker only helps provide numerical support for decisions made by others. For indifferent persons, blue-collar or white-collar, people, jobs, and organizations are not much different; *they tend to adjust to each.*

Ambivalents

These people are described as both creative and anxious. They usually find themselves in a marginal position, with somewhat limited career chances. They can neither reject the organization's promise of success and power nor play the varied roles required to compete for them. While upward-mobile anxiety is usually adaptive, the ambivalent attitude tends toward the neurotic. While the upward mobile likes the status quo and the indifferent person accepts it, the ambivalent person wants to change it.

Intellectual interests of the ambivalent person tend to run high. He or she is frequently found with limited interpersonal facility, not knowing how to get along with people. This person is often subjective, withdrawn, or introverted, but may attack "the system" when sufficiently aroused. He or she honors theory and knowledge and has a high verbal skill, but is in no way system-oriented, even resisting bureaucratic rules and procedures. Career expectations are idealistic, often unrealistic, which frequently puts the ambivalent person in a poor bargaining position. Repeated frustration on the job tends to increase the *psychological distance* between the ambivalent individual and the organization.

The ambivalent person rejects authority and cannot believe that those who reach authoritative positions merit them in terms of talent, wisdom, and morality. This attitude may be related to the finding that in a number of companies studied, there was no relationship between intelligence and aptitude, on the one hand, and rank and salary, on the other.

Instead of playing a role, the ambivalent person plays himself or herself and consequently may be out of step with the system. He or she cannot conform to folkways, often rejects work-group values, and cannot condone the compromise that people make in status seeking. Whereas the upward mobile is sustained by status rewards and expectations and the indifferent person adjusts by limiting his or her aspirations, the ambivalent individual becomes disturbed. He or she may develop a compulsive interest in work, not primarily for its intrinsic value but as a means of obtaining sufficient recognition to set him or her off from the rank and file. The ambivalent is not good in practical decision making and in a sense is unsuited for the large organization in all but one respect—his or her critical function as an agent of change.

DETERMINERS OF CLIMATE

Five dimensions are important in determining the psychological climate of an organization: (1) goal directions; (2) size and shape; (3) leadership patterns; (4) communication networks; and (5) decision-making procedures.

Goal Directions

One of the main differences between a college, a military organization, and a company are the differences in their reason for being— respectively, education, fighting and keeping the peace, and making a profit.

Among companies, climate descriptions are related to the answers to a variety of questions: What does the company make? What underlies a company's approach to human relations? What are the ways in which the organization seeks change? Does the company actually help the individual to grow? Who sets the goals in the organization?

These are some of the questions important to determining climate. Questions and answers vary with other dimensions, but particularly with size. The small company may be able to specify its goals more clearly and, in effecting change, may be able to relate cause and effect more closely.

Size and Shape

One may easily appreciate the difference in size between the 160-acre farm and the vast million-acre spread of the King cattle ranch in

Texas. But it may be more difficult to get the full impact of the fact that the federal government employs more people in engineering than in typing jobs and that more and more persons are going to work for the larger industries. In the past two decades the number of self-employed declined; during the same period the number of private wage and salary workers almost doubled, and the number of government workers increased more than twofold. The chief merit of the large organization, whether an industrial, governmental, or research bureaucracy, is its technical efficiency, with a premium on precision, speed, and control. Today, big corporations and the federal government account for 70 percent of all patents issued.

As a business grows, the old face-to-face techniques are no longer adequate; new and different ones are required. Such factors as the kinds of skill and the location of pools of skill within the organization, the decentralization of authority, and the development of new kinds of communication networks may change radically as the company grows. Often there is a tendency to perpetuate solutions that were successful in the past, trying to solve tomorrow's problems with the techniques that worked yesterday. Size, of itself, is not necessarily harmful; however, size has a seductive quality in that it may lead to the belief that the organization is strong and powerful just because it is big. Whereas the smaller organization may be able to maintain agility and flexibility in adapting to changed conditions, the larger one may be handicapped in this respect, thus hindering some individuals within the organization (see page 329).

The shape of the organization in some companies is changing from *pyramidal,* with workers in the majority at the base, to *hexagonal,* with the blue-collar workers at the base about equaling the number of men in the management teams at the top, and the majority portion including large numbers of professional staff persons. Figure 18-1 represents the pyramid type of organization, typical of most companies, on the left. On the right is the hexagonal figure representative of the newer type of research and development organization.

The vertical communication system of the old up-and-down pyramid is in for changes, and no small part of the problem involves effective supervision and coordination of these highly individualistic staff professionals. When bureaucracy is the end product of increased size and complexity, and when the personality pattern of the bureaucrat is often centered on impersonality, one can easily see the likelihood of conflict within the organization as well as with customers and the public.

Psychologically, the size of the organization may be thought of as one dimension of organizational climate, and one may picture the

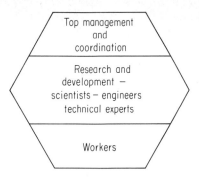

PYRAMIDAL STRUCTURE   HEXAGONAL STRUCTURE

FIG. 18-1 The pyramid-structure type of organization on the left, with the majority of people being the workers at the bottom. On the right is the six-sided structure hypothetically representative of the growing research and development organization, where the number of workers at the bottom about equals the number of persons in the top management-coordination team shown at the top. The majority of people are in the middle. They are the scientists, engineers, technical experts, and a host of specially trained people who support them.

individual being treated more and more impersonally the larger the organization becomes. Yet, as we have noted, size alone, important as it may be, does not determine job satisfactions. The level at which a person finds himself in the organizational structure, whether the organization is large or small, is a most important variable, as is the size of the subunit in which the individual finds himself.

Leadership Patterns

After years of research, psychologists have concluded that there is no simple relationship between morale and productivity in the office, the plant, or the laboratory. High job satisfaction does not necessarily mean high productivity. Much depends on other variables—types of incentives, supervision, hierarchy status, personal-need achievement, occupational levels, and a host of other factors. We know well that good supervisory practices must be the concern of all levels of the organization. A local foreman will have some difficulty trying to exert a democratic type of leadership pattern when his bosses and the structure above him are autocratic. One plant superintendent, speaking before an assembly of lower supervisors gathered to take a course in human relations, passed out a set of specific rules telling the men how they were to become more permissive in their leadership roles. He concluded, with emphasis, "We will have good human relations in this plant even if I have to demote each of you." Certainly in such a situation a democratically oriented instructor may experience difficulty, to say the least.

In a study of four managerial levels it was concluded that the leadership hierarchy, like any other social structure, has role differentiation. Each role player, whether a foreman or a top manager, contributes only a segment of the necessary conditions that will lead to organizational effectiveness. We seem to be heading toward a condition in which leaders will be judged more on how well each performs his personal obligations and less on how well the organization as a whole performs. This may be one reason why industries are now laying so much emphasis on individual performance appraisal. It must be recognized that not every promising recruit is a potential member of top management. Some persons will become outstanding leaders as foremen, as plant superintendents, or as professional specialists, but not necessarily in top management. People at all levels should try to develop to the fullest their potentialities in the role they can fill best. It must also be recognized that in an era of computers, expert teams, and government consensus, leadership patterns are changing in ways that put demands on the individual.

There is some evidence to support a situational approach to leadership. In one study, for example, employees in small work groups, where there was a great deal of interaction among workers and between workers and their supervisor and much interdependence, favored equalitarian leaders. On the other hand, employees in large work groups, in which opportunities for interaction among workers and between workers and their supervisor were greatly restricted and in which individual employees were highly independent, favored authoritarian leadership.

At one extreme, the leadership pattern may be very rule-centered and bureaucratic. At the other extreme, it may be very group-centered and democratic. In between are found authority-centered or autocratic patterns of leadership and individual-centered or idiocratic leadership patterns. There is growing evidence that organizations may be described largely in terms of typical leadership practices.

Communication Networks

The consultant frequently asks the department head, "What do *you* think is the main problem here in the plant?" Quite often he gets the reply, "Communications." One writer points up the problem by concluding that what we call "communication problems" are often only symptoms of other difficulties which exist among persons and groups in an organization; communication, other than the most formal kinds, flows along friendship channels. When trust exists, content is more freely communicated and more accurately perceived by the recipient. When individuals have different goals and value systems, it is important to create understanding about needs and motives. Often the free flow of ideas and information is restricted by the feeling that one may not receive credit for the contribution or by fear that his idea will be stolen. Basic to free (and accurate) communication in an organization are questions of task assignments, authority and responsibility, status relationships, and the question, "Where do *I* stand?" One observer reports the instance in a university of a professor with high status who, though for years he had been a good source of information, a good sounding board, and a champion of unpopular causes, literally stopped communicating. Later he explained that he wanted to see where he fitted into a yet ill-defined climate. He had a new department head, a new dean, and the president had just announced his own retirement.

Basically the firm, as a communication system, may be defined in terms of four elements. First, there is the information taken into the firm from the outside in a wide variety of ways, ranging from sales orders and reports of salesmen about competitors to a family problem told to a foreman. Second, there are the firm's rules for doing something about the information. What happens to the sales order? What will be done about the word concerning the competitors? What will be done, if anything, about the worker's family problem? Third, there are rules about handling information generated inside the organization. What parts of the organization make decisions, issue orders? How does the information move through the firm? Fourth, there is the information leaving the firm, through orders to suppliers, deliveries to customers, and public relations releases. It makes a difference who gathers the information, who filters it and for what purpose, and how various people perceive and interpret the information.

Getting accurate information upward through the organization is particularly difficult. The foreman may sense the feelings of a group of workers, filter out that which makes him look at fault, and pass the information to his boss, who in turn follows a similar screening procedure. The use of the problem-solving approach not only stimulates less-filtered upward communication, but also helps to create a climate more favorable to decision making and helps remove sources of resistance to change. When people near the bottom of the pyramid feel that their views are getting to the top unaltered, they are more receptive to the orders coming down through channels.

An important question to ask about the best way of communica-

THE
INDIVIDUAL
AND THE
ORGANIZATION-
AL CLIMATE

417

tion is "Communication for what?" One experimenter set up a laboratory situation in which A talked to B without return talk, which he termed one-way communication. Two-way communication was set up similarly; this time there was conversation, that is, communication from A to B and from B back to A. Later the same format was followed involving more people. Several practical findings emerged from the studies. One-way communication was much *faster,* but two-way communication was *more accurate,* and the receivers felt more sure of themselves in the two-way system. The sender found himself more vulnerable in the two-way condition because the receiver picked up his mistakes and oversights and told him about them. The two-way system, in some college classrooms, for example, is more noisy and disorderly; there are interruptions, expression of feelings, demands for clarification, and so on. The one-way method, on the other hand, appears neat and efficient to the outside observer, but communication is less accurate. The same patterns have been found in nonacademic situations. If speed alone is of primary importance, for example, in a military situation, then one-way communication has the edge. If appearance is important, when one wishes to look orderly and businesslike, the one-way system is preferable. The same is true if the sender wishes to keep his mistakes from being recognized or wants to protect his own power by blaming the receiver for not getting the message. In a two-way system the sender may be criticized, but he will also get his message across. Said one observer, "It's easier to give a speech than to induce appropriate behavior in others." No doubt feedback types of communication are sometimes avoided because of the psychological risks that may become involved. Communication is in part what the speaker says, but it is more what the listener hears. There are those people who hear only what they want to hear.

Decision-Making Procedures

Centralization of decision-making power, long established on the management side of single organizations, seems to be increasingly characteristic of industrial unions. And more recently companies have united, to some extent, in industrywide bargaining. University scholars are giving more attention to the basic problems of the nature of decision making, and some industrial organizations are studying their own structures to determine the levels of influence in both policy and operating decisions. For example, a study in one large corporation led to the conclusion that decision influence is multidimensional; no single individual actually makes a companywide decision.

Psychologists have long been interested in problems about the impersonal quality of a decision, on the one hand, and its degree of acceptance, on the other hand. Many studies have been conducted on leader behavior and the amount of influence which various persons have in decision making and on both systems and personalities involved. Hundreds of studies have dealt with such problems as group participation in problem solving, authoritarianism of supervisors, concepts of autocratic, democratic, and laissez-faire leaders, source of organization control, decision rules, individual adjustment patterns, and a host of other problems about decisions and what they do to people. Top management recognizes the need for large hierarchic structures, and sometimes it recognizes the problems that such structures impose on individuals. Recently there has been some concern about the place of the computer in decision making. "It is of great value *below my level,*" is not an uncommon reaction. Some people use the computer as an excuse for not making decisions themselves.

In contrast to the 1960s when top management made or influenced virtually all the higher level decisions, the 1970s are showing some changes. The Ralph Nader type of influence is having an effect ranging from product recall to membership additions to a few corporate boards of people from consumer groups; here and there minority groups are being represented on boards of directors. Further, rank-and-file influence on decisions in some large organizations is being felt at the highest levels, particularly in those climates where unions are strong. Decisions on compulsory overtime, the shorter work week, and various "humanization" efforts (e.g., more freedom in rotating assembly line tasks) are being influenced from outside the corporate structure. There is more participative management at different organizational levels. Even a few colleges and universities now have student and faculty representation on their boards of trustees.

EFFECTS OF CLIMATE ON PEOPLE

Every student knows how accurately a sophisticated upperclassman can describe the diverse environments between the authoritarian class and the permissive one where the instructor encourages class argument. The worker's reaction to a new supervisor and the speculation that goes on in middle management when a vice-president has a heart attack both show that people react to climates and climate changes. It is not uncommon at any level to hear words to this effect: "I did not object so much to *what* was done, but I did object to *how* it was done." Organizations sometimes change because individuals change. A modification of climate also offers one good way to observe the effects that climate has on the people in the organization.

How Psychological Climates Can Change

The psychological climates of organizations change sometimes for good and sometimes for bad. A change may happen even where there is no turnover in company personnel. Let us illustrate how the character of one organization became different as the president modified his behavior over a period of some five years. The president initially worked cooperatively with his executives, often taking their advice and sharing in the give-and-take of conference behavior. The business expanded, profits increased markedly, and so did problems. Then gradually the climate of the organization began to change from permissive to autocratic. Fewer and fewer conferences were held, and the president made more and more decisions without consultation. One observer described the process as "decision by desperation." Both staff and line officers, who had previously been free and open with constructive criticisms, now found that criticisms not only were not wanted, they were in effect forbidden.

What had happened? When the president began his term of office, he never considered suggestions and criticism to be a reflection on his ability. A few years later, however, he was taking all such comments personally. He read into them an implication that he personally had failed for not having foreseen and forestalled the situation which was being criticized. Whether he also suffered from the ego inflation that goes with prolonged occupancy of a top administrative post is not so clear. It may be that he just grew tired of facing new disruptive problems.

The effect on the organization all the way down the line was one of clamming up. People began to censor what they would say and consider to whom they would talk. A few of the top people resigned, but on the whole the organization became adapted to the new climate.

Some recent studies aimed at determining the main variables which differentiate the activities of organization have shown that individual labor-union locals show differences in character. Sometimes a clash in personalities between the company and the union may be a precipitating cause for strikes. Sometimes such clashes may change the climates of both organizations. There is evidence that certain industries are consistently strike-proof, while others are consistently strike-happy. Keen observers of the labor-management scene report that some regions of the United States are known to be strike-happy, while others are relatively strike-free. Often these strike-happy communities are the cities or towns where industry has not been very progressive in research on human relations.

The Influence of Climate

Conflict between individuals and organizations is inevitable. People with strong needs to be independent find that most organizations do not provide a proper setting. Learning theorists and training directors have long known that in general rewards are better motivators than punishments, yet most industrial organizations provide for much punishment. One training program may succeed because it is operating in a climate of rigid and formal rules with people who are rules-oriented. In the same climate the program may fail if the trainees involved are unstructured and ambivalent. With some people conflict increases with the number and concreteness of regulations; with others it may decrease. The training director who receives the assignment to help develop a future executive might well ask, "For what kind of climate?"

Two kinds of climate influence on individuals may be distinguished. First, there is a *direct influence* that affects all or almost all members of a company or subunit. The second kind of effect, termed *interactive influence,* exists when a climate has a certain effect on some people, a different effect on others, and possibly no effect at all on still others.

Some types of behavior never occur because the stimuli that would elicit them are never presented. Organizations themselves place constraints on people through rules and regulations, routine practices, and taboos. It is not uncommon for the ambitious person to find himself or herself in a climate that puts restraints upon freedom, thus narrowing his or her alternatives of action. One psychologist has emphasized that in any organization there accumulates through time a common fund of experience. Out of it develop ways of behaving, ways of working, ways of loafing, ways of cooperating, and ways of resisting. A newcomer to an established subculture may rebuke the old-timers as being cynical about the system, apparently unaware that there is at times a thin line between cynicism and wisdom. He may find to his embarrassment that hasty evaluation of people and established practices can backfire.

THE CLIMATE OF SUPERVISION AND MANAGEMENT

Everyone who works has a boss. The man on the assembly line relates directly to his supervisor; the president of the corporation works for the board of directors who in turn represent the stockholders. The woman who owns and operates a dress shop in reality works for the customer, and many of us have several bosses. As we know, all bosses have bosses. For the student who comes out of college becoming a boss in a period of time is common. He or she will become a supervisor and some later move on to higher management levels. From supervisor to executive, leadership is the key concept which affects the organizational climate.

Studies involving over six thousand people have led to some very practical understandings about supervisor-worker relationships. When employees were asked about the most irritating factor in their work situation, 75 percent of them responded, "The boss." The response was strongest where the boss was closest to the worker in distributing work, supervising training, handling grievances, and enforcing discipline. But to these same people, the boss was also something of a father figure who meant much in their daily lives.

A great deal has been said about the worker's need to get a feeling of accomplishment from his work. The importance of this need has long been recognized, but how can the person in the low-level unskilled job or the person who has reached his limits of job accomplishment feel that he is making progress? Studies of workers in such categories show that feelings of accomplishment do not have to be directly associated with the job itself. If the job helps the man to feel that he can buy a car or build a cabin, then some degree of satisfaction may be present. A good foreman looks for these signs of progress as well as for the feelings of satisfaction that may come from the act of work itself, the intrinsic aspect of work. Study has brought out another aspect of the supervisor-worker relationship not often voiced. It was found that over a period of time workers build up an emotional resistance against the driving foreman which hinders production. However, emotional pressures brought on by unavoidable events are quite different in their long-range emotional impact on the worker. Since these events are impersonal, they are unlikely to arouse antagonism and a desire to fight back.

One experienced supervisor up from the ranks put the problem of supervisor-worker relationships thus: "It seems the lower a person is on the chain of command, the harder he is to supervise and the harder he is to motivate. It's hard for the supervisor to provide drive that isn't there."

Tensions of Workers, Supervisors, and Managers

To fully understand the adjustment problems of the supervisor or manager, we must look at the tensions of their climate. One must live with the worries of the worker, frequently a person with a limited range of abilities who is often on a highly repetitive, fast-paced job and for whom job safety hazards sometimes create special adjustment problems. The production employee has little control over what he or she does or how it is done, or when, and turns to the foreman for help. In a sense the boss is put in a similar position to the parent.

The supervisor has tensions also, a fact sometimes overlooked by the subordinate. A large number of people create problems for the first-line foreman as a matter of routine—inspectors, dispatchers, engineers, stockroom clerks, cost-control analysts, labor relations people, and a host of others. The production-line foreman's job also involves many decisions, ranging from "Throw it out" to "I'll see that you get it by noon." In one study of foremen on the assembly line in automobile factories it was found that the number of their activities ranged from 237 to 1,073 for an eight-hour day. The average number of activities was 583 per day, or *1 every forty-eight seconds.* And many of these activities involved decisions. Yes, the foreman has his tensions also. He knows that some decisions he has to make will cause difficulty. For example, it is recognized in the auto industry that cars made on Mondays are more prone to defects. This is the day when plant absenteeism runs high and supervisors are obliged to put second-string men on the line who are less proficient.

The supervisor also faces another type of problem—the line worker may make more money than he and enjoy security and fringe benefits through the union. Some good foreman material is lost to industry when workers do not want to turn in their blue-collar jobs for white-collar ones; some people are quite content to serve in the ranks. The supervisor also knows that the longer he is on the job, the more enemies he is likely to have.

Defining the term "manager" or "executive" is difficult, as anyone who has ever tried to write a formal description for the job will recognize. One popular conception is given by the wife of a newly promoted man: "more money, more status, new clothes." Another, just about as useless, is that of the employee who identifies executives as "the ones who are allowed to use the private company parking lot." Likewise, though having a key to the private washroom may indicate status in the organization, it is hardly a workable description of the executive's job. What do people think executives do? What do they actually do?

What Executives Do

There are those who picture the executive as a person who sits at a great walnut desk surrounded by telephones, masterminding the fate of his company and its employees. This mythical executive spends his day making split-second decisions and issuing directives, like a master puppeteer who decides what each act shall be and who shall do the performing.

Then there is the conception of the executive, probably equally hypothetical, as the master expediter who is always on the go, never in the office. He has few, if any, scheduled routine responsibilities. If he were suddenly to leave for a six months' tour of Europe, his absence would scarcely be noticed, except by those members of the organization who were perceptive enough to observe that things were not running quite so smoothly as usual and that morale was suffering a little. In general, we might say that in the absence of this executive, communication was more difficult and objectives were not so clearly defined. In other words, the primary function of this second mythical person is to maintain a favorable environment for effective work by other people in the organization. This role requires that the executive be an expert in an almost impossible degree in the motivation of human behavior.

What executives actually do is a little less romantic than the picture given above. He or she actually spends most of the time in planning and preparing procedures and methods for getting things done; supervising technical operations; personnel activities; and public relations. The executive must provide inspiration and create an organizational climate in which the followers willingly accept the leader as their agent in cooperative endeavor. The executive must spend time in keeping up with, or ahead of, the competition. He or she stands not only as a leader but also as a symbol—almost everything the executive does and says counts in some way.

The attributes of successful executives have been studied by hundreds of researchers. Here we shall list ten characteristics found important:

1. High drive to get ahead.
2. Willingness to move if it means promotion.
3. Respect for superiors.
4. Ability to organize.
5. Ability and willingness to make decisions.
6. A lot of self-confidence, but willingness to listen to other people.
7. Some fear of failing. This attribute makes the executive plan in ways that will prevent failures.
8. A strong reality orientation.
9. Loyalty to the overall goals of the organization.
10. Ability to handle people. Good executives are high in human relations skills, in working with both groups and individuals.

One price of executive leadership is that the leader bears a heavy part of the burden. In one person, leadership may be manifested by aggressive actions, while in another leader, influence may come through a quality of stillness. Effective leadership means generating participation as well as obedience. How this is done influences the organizational climate all the way down the line.

SUMMARY

Individual personalities and job requirements interact to produce a climate significant to both the individual and the organization. By climate we mean those characteristics that distinguish the organization from other organizations and that influence the behavior of people in the organization. One question is important to each of us—what kind of climate is best *for me?*

The personality of a company, or other organization, is in many respects a composite of the varied ways of behaving of the people within it. There are the upward-mobile personalities who identify strongly with the organization and get a disproportionate share of the organization's rewards in power, income, and ego reinforcement. This driving type thinks in stragetic terms; they are rule- and procedure-oriented, and are usually found at or near the top of the organization.

Most wage and salary employees fall within the category of the indifferents. They do not compete strongly for rewards. They expect less; they reject success striving. And in most organizations we find a smaller group of creative and anxious ambivalents. While the upward-mobile person is usually adaptive in anxiety, the ambivalent person tends toward the neurotic. While the upward mobile likes the status quo and the indifferent person accepts it, the ambivalent person wants to change it.

Determiners of climate include goal directions, size and shape, leadership patterns, communication networks, and decision-making procedures. Organizational climates change, sometimes for good and sometimes for bad.

Conflict between individuals and organizations is inevitable. People with strong needs to be independent find most organizations do not provide a proper setting. Organizational climate directly affects all or almost all members of the company or subunit. There is also an interactive influence which exists when a climate has a certain effect on some people, a different effect on others, and possibly no effect at all on still others. Climates are influenced strongly by supervision and management creating tensions for workers. But supervisors and executives likewise have tensions centering on responsibility and decision making. The supervisor must live with the worries of the worker and is under pressures from above. The executive often finds himself required to be an expert to an almost impossible degree in the motivation of human behavior. The executive must provide inspiration and create an organizational climate in which the followers willingly accept the leader as their agent in cooperative endeavor. He stands not only as a leader but also as a symbol. Effective leadership means generating participation as well as obedience.

Adelson, D., & Kalis, B. L. (Eds.), *Community psychology and mental health perspectives and challenges*. San Francisco: Chandler, 1970.

Ardrey, R. *The territorial imperative*. New York: Atheneum, 1966.

Astin, H. S., et al. *Women: A bibliography on their education and careers*. Washington: Human Service Press, 1971.

Baer, D. M., & Wright, J. C. Developmental psychology. *Annu. Rev. Psychol.*, 1974, 1–82.

Baldwin, A. L. *Theories of child development*. New York: Wiley, 1967.

Bandler, R., Jr., & Moyer, K. E. Animals spontaneously attacked by rats. *Comm. Beh. Biol.*, 1970, **5**, 177–182.

Bandura, A. *Principles of behavior modification*. New York: Holt, 1969.

Bardwick, J. M. *Psychology of women*. New York: Harper & Row, 1971.

Bergler, E. *The revolt of the middle-aged man*. New York: Wyn, 1954.

Berkowitz, L. *Aggression: A social psychological analysis*. New York: McGraw-Hill, 1962.

Bischof, L. J. *Interpreting personality theory*. New York: Harper & Row, 1970.

Blanchard, E. B., & Young, L. D. Self-control of cardiac functioning: A promise as yet unfulfilled. *Psychol. Bull.*, 1973, **79**, 145–163.

Bradford, L. P. et al. (Eds.), *T-group theory and laboratory method*. New York: Wiley, 1964.

Brady, J. V. Ulcers in "executive" monkeys. *Scientific Amer.*, 1958, **199**, 95–99.

Buckhout, R. (Ed.), Violence. In Buckhout, R. (Ed.), *Toward social change*. New York: Harper & Row, 1971.

Burtt, H. E. An experimental study of early childhood memory. *J. Genet. Psychol.*, 1941, **58**, 435–439.

Calhoun, J. B. Population density and social pathology. *Scientific Amer.*, 1962, **206**, 139–150.

Campbell, B. S., & Misanin, J. R. Basic drives. *Annu. Rev. Psychol.*, 1969, **20**, 57–84.

Campbell, D. P. *The results of counseling: Twenty-five years later*. Philadelphia: Saunders, 1965.

Campbell, J. P. Personnel training and development. *Annu. Rev. Psychol.*, 1971, **22**, 565–602.

Carter, C. O. *Human heredity*. Baltimore: Penguin, 1970.

Chapanis, A., & Lindenbaum, L. A reaction time study of four control-display linkages. *Human Factors*, 1959, **1**, 1–7.

Chapanis, A., Garner, W. R., & Morgan, C. T. *Applied experimental psychology*. New York: Wiley, 1949.

Clark, K. B. *Dark ghetto*. New York: Harper & Row, 1965.

Coleman, J. C. *Psychology and effective behavior*. Glenview, Ill.: Scott, Foresman, 1969.

Coleman, J. C. *Abnormal psychology and modern life*. Glenview, Ill.: Scott, Foresman, 1964.

Cook, L. A. An experimental sociographic study of a stratified 10th grade class. *Amer. Sociol. Rev.*, 1945, **10**, 250–261.

Cronbach, L. J. *Essentials of psychological testing*. New York: Harper & Row, 1970.

Crosby, T. *Architecture: City sense*. New York: Reinhold, 1965.

Darley, J. M., & Latane, B. Bystander intervention in emergencies: A diffusion of responsibility. *J. Pers. & Soc. Psychol.*, 1968, **8**, 377–383.

Deci, E. L. Intrinsic motivation, extrinsic reinforcement, and inequity. *J. Pers. & Soc. Psychol.*, 1972, **22**, 113–120.

Dunnette, M. D., et al. Why do they leave? *Personnel*, May-June 1973, 25–39.

DuPont, R. L., & Greene, M. H. The dynamics of a heroin addiction epidemic. *Science*, 1973, **181**, 716–722.

Erikson, E. H. *Identity: Youth and crisis*. New York: Norton, 1968.

Evans, B. *Word-a-day vocabulary builder*. New York: Random House, 1963.

Farnham-Diggory, S. *Cognitive processes in education*. New York: Harper & Row, 1972.

BIBLIOGRAPHY

Fetter, J. R., & Gilmer, B. v. H. A study of bank officer and teller attitudes. Pittsburgh: American Institutes for Research, AIR-F-52-167 FR, 1967.

Finger, F. W., & Mook, D. G. Basic drives. *Annu. Rev. Psychol.,* 1971, **22**, 1–38.

Flanagan, J. C. Education: How and for what. *Amer. Psychologist,* 1973, **28**, 551–556.

Flanagan, J. C., et al. *The career data book: Project TALENT'S follow-up study.* Palo Alto, Calif.: American Institutes for Research, 1974.

Forehand, G. A., & Gilmer, B. v. H. Environmental variation in studies of organizational behavior. *Psychol. Bull.,* 1964, **62**, 361–382.

Freud, S. *New introductory lectures on psychoanalysis.* New York: Norton, 1933.

Galle, O. R., et al. Population density and pathology: What are the relations for man? *Science,* 1972, **176**, 23–30.

Geldard, F. A. *The human senses.* New York: Wiley, 1972.

Ghiselli, E. E. Some perspectives for industrial psychology. *Amer. Psychologist,* 1974, **29**, 80–87.

Gilmer, B. v. H. *Industrial and organizational psychology.* New York: McGraw-Hill, 1971.

Gilmer, B. v. H. Problems in cutaneous communication from psychophysics to information processing. *Amer. Foundation for the Blind,* March 1966, 1–40.

Gilmer, B. v. H. An analysis of the spontaneous responses of the newborn infant. *J. Genet. Psychol.,* 1933, **42**, 392–405.

Goldstein, J. W. On the explanation of student drug use. In Good, E. (Ed.), *Marijuana.* Chicago: Aldine-Atherton, 1972.

Graf, R. G. Speed reading. *Psychology Today,* December 1973, 112–113.

Gregg, L. W. Human factors engineering. In Gilmer, B. v. H. (Ed.), *Industrial and organizational psychology.* New York: McGraw-Hill, 1971.

Grier, W. H., & Cobbs, P. M. *Black rage.* New York: Basic Books, 1968.

Guilford, J. P., & Zimmerman, W. S. *The Guilford-Zimmerman temperament survey.* Beverly Hills, Calif.: Sheridan Supply Co., 1949.

Guilford, J. S., et al. *An experimental study of home accident behavior.* AIR-D85-12165-TR, December 1965, 1–159.

Hall, E. T. *The hidden dimension.* New York: Doubleday, 1966.

Harlow, H. F., et al. From thought to therapy: Lessons from a primate laboratory. *Amer. Scientist,* 1971, **59**, 538–549.

Harlow, H. F., & Harlow, M. K. Learning to love. *Amer. Scientist,* 1966, **54**, 244–272.

Heath, D. H. *Growing up in college.* San Francisco: Jossey-Bass, 1968.

Heron, W. The pathology of boredom. *Scientific Amer.,* 1957, **196**, 52–56.

Heston, L. L. The genetics of schizophrenia and schizoid disease. *Science,* 1970, **167**, 249–256.

Holzman, P. S. Personality. *Annu. Rev. Psychol.,* 1974, 247–276.

Hovland, C. I., & Weiss, W. The influence of source credibility on communication effectiveness. *Publ. Opin. Quart.,* 1951, **15**, 635–650.

Howard, K. I., & Orlinsky, D. E. Psychotherapeutic processes. *Annu. Rev. Psychol.,* 1972, **23**, 615–668.

Hylton, J. On my own. *Stock Car Racing,* November 1966, 36–39.

Izard, C. E. *Patterns of emotion.* New York: Academic, 1972.

Jacoby, N. H. The environmental crisis. *The Center Magazine,* 1970, **3**, 37–48.

Jarvik, M. E. Effects of chemical and physical treatments on learning and memory. *Annu. Rev. Psychol.,* 1972, **23**, 457–486.

Jenkins, R. L., & Bayer, A. Types of delinquent behavior and background factors. *International J. Social Psychiatry,* 1968, **14**, 65–76.

Jones, R. L. (Ed.), *Black psychology.* New York: Harper & Row, 1972.

Jourard, S. M. *The transparent self.* Princeton, N. J.: Van Nostrand, 1964.

Kagan, J., & Moss, H. A. *Birth to maturity: A study in psychological development.* New York: Wiley, 1962.

Kamiya, J. Operant control of the EEG alpha rhythm and some of its effects on consciousness. In Tart, C. (Ed.), *Altered states of consciousness.* New York: Wiley, 1969.

Kanfer, F. H., & Phillips, J. *Learning foundations of behavior therapy.* New York: Wiley, 1969.

Kaplan, B. *The inner world of mental illness.* New York: Harper & Row, 1964.

Kewin, K., et al. Levels of aspiration. In

Hunt, J. McV. (Ed.), *Personality and behavior disorders,* Vol. I. New York: Ronald, 1944.

Kieren, D., & Tallman, I. Spousal adaptability. *J. Marriage and Family,* 1972, **34,** 247–255.

Kinsey, A. C., et al. *Sexual behavior in the human female.* Philadelphia: Saunders, 1953.

Kinsey, A. C., Pomeroy, W. B., & Martin, C. E. *Sexual behavior in the human male.* Philadelphia: Saunders, 1948.

Kira, A. *The bathroom: Criteria for design.* Ithaca, N.Y.: Center for Housing and Environmental Studies, Cornell University, 1966.

Kirkendall, L. A., & Whitehurst, R. N. (Eds.), *The new sexual revolution.* New York: Scribner, 1971.

Kleinmuntz, B. *Essentials of abnormal psychology.* New York: Harper & Row, 1974.

Krech, D. Brain research, intelligence and society. Walter Vandyke Bingham Memorial Lecture, Carnegie-Mellon University, March 30, 1967.

Kroll, A. M., et al. *Career development: Growth and crisis.* New York: Wiley, 1970.

Krueger, W. C. F. The effect of overlearning on retention. *J. Exper. Psychol.,* 1929, **12,** 74.

Lancaster, E., & Poling, J. *The final face of Eve.* New York: McGraw-Hill, 1958.

Latane, B., & Darley, J. Bystander "apathy." *Amer. Scientist, 1969,* **57,** 244–268.

Layton, W. L., et al. Student development and counseling. *Annu. Rev. Psychol.,* 1971, **22,** 533–564.

Lazarus, R. S. *Patterns of adjustment and human effectiveness.* New York: New York: McGraw-Hill, 1969.

Lepper, R. L., & Moorhead, R. Ride on. *Industrial Design,* 1971, **18,** 26–27.

Lewis, M. F. (Ed.), *Current research in marijuana.* New York: Academic, 1972.

Lieberman, M. A., et al. *Encounter groups: First facts.* New York: Basic Books, 1973.

Looft, W. R. The psychology of more. *Amer. Psychologist,* 1971, **26,** 561–565.

Lynch, K. *The image of the city.* Cambridge, Mass.: M.I.T., 1960.

McClelland, D. C. *The achieving society.* Princeton, N. J.: Van Nostrand, 1961.

McCormick, E. J. *Human factors engineering.* New York: McGraw-Hill, 1970.

McDonald, F. J., & Forehand, G. A. A design for accountability in education. *New York University Edu. Quart.,* 1973, **4,** 7–16.

MacKinnon, D. W. Creativity in architects. In *The creative person.* Berkeley: Institute of Personality Assessment and Research, University of California, 1961.

Maier, N. R. F. *Principles of human relations.* New York: Wiley, 1952.

Maslow, A. H. *Motivation and personality.* New York: Harper & Row, 1970.

Masters, W. H., & Johnson, V. E. *Human sexual response.* Boston: Little, Brown, 1966.

Max, L. W. An experimental study of the motor theory of consciousness. III. Action-current responses in deaf-mutes during sleep, sensory stimulation and dreams. *J. Comp. Psychol.,* 1935, **19,** 469–486.

May, R. *Love and will.* New York: Norton, 1969.

Megargee, E. I., & Hokanson, J. E. (Eds.), *The dynamics of aggression.* New York: Harper & Row, 1970.

Milgram, S. The experience of living in cities. *Science,* 1970, **167,** 1461–1468.

Milgram, S. Behavioral study of obedience. *J. Abnorm. Soc. Psychol.,* 1963, **67,** 371–378.

Miller, N. E. *Selected papers.* Chicago: Aldine-Atherton, 1970.

Moos, R. H. Conceptualization of human environments. *Amer. Psychologist,* 1973, **28,** 652–665.

Mosby, D. P. Toward a theory of the unique personality of blacks: A psychocultural assessment. In Jones, R. L. (Ed.), *Black psychology.* New York: Harper & Row, 1972.

Moyer, K. E., & Gilmer, B. v. H. Attention spans of children for experimentally designed toys. *J. Genet. Psychol.,* 1955, **87,** 187–201.

Murray, J. P. Television and violence. *Amer. Psychologist,* 1973, **28,** 472–478.

Newell, A., & Simon, H. A. *Human problem solving.* Englewood Cliffs, N. J.: Prentice-Hall, 1972.

Newman, O. *Defensible space.* New York: Macmillan, 1972.

Oates, W. E. *Confessions of a workaholic.* Cleveland: World Publishing, 1971.

Patrick, C. Creative thought in artists. *J. Psychol.,* 1937, **4**, 35–73.

Pearce, W. B., & Sharp, S. M. *Self-disclosing communication: A critical review.* Grand Forks, N.D.: University of North Dakota Press, 1972.

Pedersen, D. M., & Shears, L. M. A review of personal space research in the framework of general system theory. *Psychol. Bull.,* 1973, **80**, 367–388.

Postman, L. Retention as a function of degree of overlearning. *Science,* 1962, **135**, 666–667.

Pressey, S. L. Viewpoint: Not all decline. *Gerontologist,* 1966, **6**, 1–2.

Pressey, S. L., & Robinson, F. P. *Psychology and the new education.* New York: Harper & Row, 1944.

Proshansky, H. M., et al. (Eds.), *Environmental psychology.* New York: Holt, 1970.

Ramsay, R. S. *Supervisor's employee report form.* Personal communication, 1972.

Ray, O. S. *Drugs, society, and human behavior.* St. Louis: Mosby, 1972.

Riesman, D., et al. *The lonely crowd.* New Haven, Conn.: Yale University Press, 1950.

Roethlisberger, F. J., & Dickson, W. J. *Management and the worker.* Cambridge, Mass.: Harvard University Press, 1939.

Rogers, C. R. *On becoming a person.* Boston: Houghton Mifflin, 1961.

Rosen, E., et al. *Abnormal psychology.* Philadelphia: Saunders, 1972.

Rubin, Z. *Liking and loving.* New York: Holt, 1973.

Sales, S. M. Organizational role as a risk factor in coronary disease. *Admin. Sci. Quart.,* 1969, **14**, 325–336.

Schachter, S. *Emotion, obesity, and crime.* New York: Academic, 1971.

Schein, E. H. *Organizational psychology.* Englewood Cliffs, N.J.: Prentice-Hall, 1965.

Schwitzgebel, R. L. A belt from big brother. *Psychology Today,* April 1969, 45–65.

Seiden, R. H. Campus tragedy: A study of student suicide. *J. Abnorm. Psychol.,* 1966, **71**, 389–399.

Selye, H. *The stress of life.* New York: McGraw-Hill, 1956.

Shaffer, L. F., & Shoben, E. J., Jr. *The psychology of adjustment.* Boston: Houghton Mifflin, 1956.

Sheldon, W. H. *The varieties of temperament.* New York: Harper & Row, 1942.

Singer, J. L., & Singer, D. Personality. *Annu. Rev. Psychol.,* 1972, **23**, 375–412.

Skinner, B. F. *Beyond freedom and dignity.* New York: Knopf, 1971.

Skinner, B. F. *Contingencies of reinforcement: A theoretical analysis.* New York: Appleton, 1969.

Sleight, R. B. The effect of instrument dial shape on legibility. *J. Appl. Psychol.,* 1948, **32**, 170–188.

Snyder, B. R., & Kahne, M. J. Stress in higher education and student use of university psychiatrists. *Amer. J. Orthopsychiat.,* 1969, **39**, 23–35.

Sobell, M. B., et al. Differences in baseline drinking behavior between alcoholics and normal drinkers. *Behavior Research and Therapy,* 1972, **10**, 257–267.

Sommer, R. *Personal space: The behavioral basis of design.* Englewood Cliffs, N.J.: Prentice-Hall, 1969.

Sommer, R. The ecology of privacy. *Library Quart.,* 1966, **36**, 234–248.

Spielberger, C. D., et al. Theory and measurement of anxiety states. In Cattell, R. B. (Ed.), *Handbook of modern personality theory.* Chicago: Aldine-Atherton, 1971.

Spielberger, C. D. (Ed.), *Anxiety and behavior.* New York: Academic, 1966.

Spielberger, C. D., & Weitz, H. Improving the academic performance of anxious college freshmen: A group counseling approach to the prevention of underachievement. *Psychol. Monogr.,* 1964, **78**(3), Whole No. 590.

Still, J. W. Man's potential and his performance. *The New York Times,* Nov. 24, 1957.

Super, D. E. *The psychology of careers.* New York: Harper & Row, 1963.

Thigpen, C. H. *The three faces of Eve.* New York: McGraw-Hill, 1957.

Tyler, L. E. Human abilities. *Annu. Rev. Psychol.,* 1972, **23**, 177–206.

Underwood, B. J. *Experimental psychology.* New York: Appleton Century Crofts, 1966.

Van Ormer, E. B. Retention during sleeping and waking. *Arch. Psychol.,* 1932, No. 137.

Voeks, V. *On becoming an educated person.* Philadelphia: Saunders, 1970.

Vroom, V. H. *Work and motivation.* New York: Wiley, 1964.

Vroom, V. H., & Deci, E. L. (Eds.), *Management and motivation.* Baltimore: Penguin, 1970.

Wallace, A. F. C. *Tornado in Worcester.* Washington: National Academy of Sciences, Disaster Study 3, No. 392, 1954.

Weiner, I. B. *Psychological disturbance in adolescence.* New York: Wiley, 1970.

White, R. W. (Ed.), *The study of lives.* Chicago: Aldine-Atherton, 1963.

White, R. W., & Watt, N. F. *The abnormal personality.* New York: Ronald, 1973.

Wilkinson, R. *The prevention of drinking problems: Alcohol control and cultural influences.* New York: Oxford University Press, 1970.

Wittreich, W. J. Visual perception and personality. *Scientific Amer.,* 1959, **200**, 58.

Wohlwill, J. F. Behavioral response and adaptation to environmental stimulation. In Damon, A. *Physiological Anthropology.* Cambridge, Mass.: Harvard University Press, 1971.

Wohlwill, J. F. The emerging discipline of environmental psychology. *Amer. Psychologist,* 1970, **25**, 303–312.

Wolpe, J. *The practice of behavior therapy.* New York: Pergamon, 1969.

Woodson, W. E., & Conover, D.W. *Human engineering guide for equipment designers.* Berkeley: University of California Press, 1964.

Wynne-Edwards, V. C. Self-regulating systems in populations of animals. *Science,* 1965, **147**, 1543–1548.

Yancey, W. L. Architecture, interaction, and social control: The case of a large-scale public housing project. *Environment and Behavior,* 1971, **3**, 3–21.

Yates, A. *Behavior therapy.* New York: Wiley, 1970.

Zimbardo, P. *The cognitive control of motivation.* Glenview, Ill.: Scott, Foresman, 1974.

GLOSSORIAL INDEX

A Glossary has been incorporated into this index. Glossary terms, in **boldface**, are followed by their definitions and any Subject Index page references, subentries, and/or cross-references.

GLOSSORIAL INDEX